DISCOVERING BUSINESS CONCEPTS

Compiled for

SIMON SMITH & TONY BITHELL

First published 2015 by
PALGRAVE MACMILLAN

Palgrave Macmillan in the UK is an imprint of Macmillan Publishers Limited,
registered in England, company number 785998, of Houndmills, Basingstoke,
Hampshire RG21 6XS.

Palgrave Macmillan in the US is a division of St Martin's Press LLC,
175 Fifth Avenue, New York, NY 10010.

Palgrave Macmillan is the global academic imprint of the above companies
and has companies and representatives throughout the world.

Palgrave® and Macmillan® are registered trademarks in the United States,
the United Kingdom, Europe and other countries.

ISBN 978–1–137–58143–3 paperback

This book is printed on paper suitable for recycling and made from fully
managed and sustained forest sources. Logging, pulping and manufacturing
processes are expected to conform to the environmental regulations of the
country of origin.

A catalogue record for this book is available from the British Library.

A catalog record for this book is available from the Library of Congress.

CONTENTS

List of Figures   vi

List of Tables   viii

Sources   ix

Introduction   x

1   **Introduction to the Business Enterprise**   1
Janet Morrison

2   **The Business Context and Products (Goods and Services)**   37
David Campbell, David Edgar & George Stonehouse

3   **Business Competences, Processes and Activities**   52
David Campbell, David Edgar & George Stonehouse

4   **International Trade and Global Competition**   67
Janet Morrison

5   **Strategies in a Globalized World**   104
Janet Morrison

6   **Competitive Advantage and Strategy**   142
David Campbell, David Edgar & George Stonehouse

7   **Change Management and Leadership**   160
David Campbell, David Edgar & George Stonehouse

8   **Quality**   178
David Campbell, David Edgar & George Stonehouse

9   **Ethics and CSR in International Business**   201
Janet Morrison

10   **Contextualizing Human Resource Management**   235
Robin Kramar & Jawad Syed

11   **Human Resource Management in Contemporary Transnational Companies**   257
Robin Kramar & Jawad Syed

12   **Marketing**   277
Janet Morrison

LIST OF FIGURES

1.1	Stakeholders, home and abroad	10
1.2	The multinational enterprise (MNE)	15
1.3	The singletier board of directors	18
1.4	Business functions in the organizational environment	22
1.5	The dimensions and layers of the international environment	26
2.1	The product life cycle	43
2.2	The Boston Consulting Group matrix	47
2.3	The GE matrix	49
2.4	Multinational market portfolio	50
3.1	The twin sources of core competences	54
3.2	Price and value added	60
3.3	A simplified schematic of the value-adding process	61
3.4	The value chain	62
4.1	Changes in world merchandise exports and GDP	71
4.2	Shares in world merchandise exports by region	71
4.3	The world's four leading trading countries in 2008	72
4.4	Porter's Diamond: the determinants of national advantage	75
4.5	The pros and cons of free trade	78
4.6	Subsidies to agricultural producers as a percentage of gross farm receipts in selected OECD countries, 2008	83
4.7	Merchandise trade flows between and within selected regions, 2008 (in $US billions)	84
4.8	Regional trade agreements notified through the GATT and WTO in the post-war era	91
4.9	G20 members	98
5.1	SWOT analysis	109
5.2	Porter's five forces model	110
5.3	The resource based view of the firm	112
5.4	Levels of strategy	116
5.5	Foreign integration in modes of internationalization	117
5.6	FDI options	122
5.7	General Electric (GE) businesses in 2009	124
5.8	Organization based on functional departments	129
5.9	The Multidivisional structure	130
5.10	The global matrix	131

5.11	Models of the international organization	132
6.1	The generic strategy framework	146
6.2	A simplified understanding of cost and differentiation strategies	149
6.3	Porter's global strategy framework	152
6.4	Configuration and coordination for international strategy	153
6.5	Hybrid strategy	154
7.1	Step and incremental change	163
8.1	Oakland's model of TQM	185
8.2	The EFQM excellence model	189
8.3	Types of benchmarking	194
9.1	Ethical choices start with the birth of the business	206
9.2	Encountering ethical challenges as the business grows	208
9.3	Carroll's pyramid of CSR	212
9.4	Corporations' influence on democratic processes in the US	218
9.5	Stakeholder management	219
9.6	The UN Global Compact	223
9.7	The right act and the good person	227
10.1	Key factors of the macroenvironment.	240
12.1	Levels of marketing	280
12.2	Generic marketing strategies	281
12.3	Global marketing strategy	283
12.4	Analysis of country markets	285
12.5	Market entry strategies	293
12.6	Market entry analysis	295
12.7	Rankings of global brands for 2007	299
12.8	Own-label share of consumer packaged goods spending	301
12.9	The marketing mix	304
12.10	Distribution channels	309
12.11	Overlapping spheres of ethical issues	312

LIST OF TABLES

1.1	Corporate governance principles recommended by the OECD	19
1.2	Transnationality index	24
1.3	PEST Analysis in the international business environment	27
1.4	Dimensions and layers of the international environment	29
3.1	A summary of the activities in the value chain	63
4.1	WEF global competitiveness rankings for 2010–2011	77
4.2	Regional trade groupings	92
6.1	Core competences, generic strategies and the value chain	157
7.1	Theories of leadership and key authors	166
7.2	Skills and traits critical to leaders	167
7.3	McGregor's theory X and theory Y manager	168
7.4	Transactional leadership and transformational leadership compared	172
8.1	Factors affecting customer-driven quality and the operating performance characteristics of an organization	179
8.2	Some definitions of quality	180
8.3	The quality gurus	181
8.4	Companies that have received the Baldrige Award	188
8.5	The DMAIC steps and tools used for Six Sigma	192
8.6	Garvin's eight dimensions of quality	193
10.1	An organization's macroenvironment	240
10.2	Hofstede's cultural dimensions	241

SOURCES

This custom publication has been compiled for us in the University of Chester. The Chapters included are reproduced from the following works:

Chapter 1 (pp. 3–36) from Janet Morrison: The Global Business Environment 3rd edition © Janet Morrison 2011

Chapter 2 (pp. 33–47) from David Campbell, David Edgar & George Stonehouse: Business Strategy 3rd edition © David Campbell, David Edgar & George Stonehouse 2011

Chapter 3 (pp. 48–61) from David Campbell, David Edgar & George Stonehouse: Business Strategy 3rd edition © David Campbell, David Edgar & George Stonehouse 2011

Chapter 4 (pp. 117–153) from Janet Morrison: The Global Business Environment 3rd edition © Janet Morrison 2011

Chapter 5 (pp. 154–192) from Janet Morrison: The Global Business Environment 3rd edition © Janet Morrison 2011

Chapter 6 (pp. 192–209) from David Campbell, David Edgar & George Stonehouse: Business Strategy 3rd edition © David Campbell, David Edgar & George Stonehouse 2011

Chapter 7 (pp. 258–274) from David Campbell, David Edgar & George Stonehouse: Business Strategy 3rd edition © David Campbell, David Edgar & George Stonehouse 2011

Chapter 8 (pp. 296–317) from David Campbell, David Edgar & George Stonehouse: Business Strategy 3rd edition © David Campbell, David Edgar & George Stonehouse 2011

Chapter 9 (pp. 215–248) from Janet Morrison: Business Ethics © Janet Morrison 2015

Chapter 10 (pp. 11–32) from Robin Kramar & Jawad Syed: Human Resource Management in a Global Context © Robin Kramar & Jawad Syed 2012

Chapter 11 (pp. 55–74) from Robin Kramar & Jawad Syed: Human Resource Management in a Global Context © Robin Kramar & Jawad Syed 2012

Chapter 12 (pp. 275–313) from Janet Morrison: International Business © Janet Morrison 2009

INTRODUCTION

Welcome to Chester Business School, University of Chester. In selecting this text, it is likely you are studying Business Studies or International Business in some capacity (whether 3 or 4 years of study, or combined honours). This book has been compiled to offer a cross-section of essential chapters that will help you throughout your studies. We are hoping the book provides great value for money as we have selected chapters for inclusion based on their direct relevance to core elements throughout your programme.

As you would expect, many of the chapters relate to general business topics, e.g. introduction to business enterprise and contexts, business competences, strategy, quality, and competitive advantage. International features are prevalent throughout and also include aspects of international trade and global competition. On top of this, we have built in some specialization in terms of human resource management, marketing and business ethics as these themes will run through your entire programme (definitely in year 1 and then depending on what you choose to specialize in the latter years).

Using the book will require a little guidance from the Programme Leaders as we have selected chapters independently. Thus, the text does not have the same flow as a regular textbook because it draws from 5 different books overall. Nevertheless, we have constructed the chapters in an order to ease usage as much as possible. If you have any questions, just email your programme leader.

Otherwise, we hope you find the text very useful and relevant to your studies – we are sure you will. We wish you the very best of luck on your studies.

Some useful contact details:

- Tony Bithell (Programme Leader for Business Studies) – t.bithell@chester.ac.uk
- Ian Shotton (Programme Leader of International Business as of September 2015) – i.shotton@chester.ac.uk
- Dr Simon M Smith (Programme Director and former International Business Programme Leader) – smith.simon@chester.ac.uk

INTRODUCTION TO THE BUSINESS ENTERPRISE

Outline of chapter

Introduction

What does the business enterprise exist to do?
Purpose and goals
Markets and consumers
Stakeholders and corporate social responsibility (CSR)

How does the enterprise carry out its goals?
Entrepreneurs
Companies
The multinational enterprise (MNE)
Who controls the organization?
Functions within the enterprise
The firm's view on the world

The enterprise in the international environment
Multiple dimensions
The multilayered environment

The enterprise in a dynamic environment

Conclusions

Learning objectives

1 To identify the range of purposes pursued by business enterprises in the changing environment, highlighting the role of diverse stakeholders

2 To appreciate the differing types of ownership and decision-making structures through which enterprises pursue their goals

3 To gain an overview of dimensions and layers of the international business environment, together with an ability to see how their interactions impact on firms

Critical themes in this chapter

- **Emerging economies – an introduction to the Brics**
- **CSR and sustainability – an introduction to these concepts, along with that of stakeholders**
- **International risks – the role of the entrepreneur**
- **Multilayered environment – an overview**
- **Multidimensional environment – an overview**

The world at his feet: starting a business is daunting but exciting for the young entrepreneur
Source: Istock

The rise of the social web sees Facebook soar in popularity

The founding father of the internet, Tim Berners-Lee, has said, 'the web does not just connect machines, it connects people' (Berners-Lee, 2008). The phenomenal rise of social networking in just a few years, allowing people to keep in touch and share information with friends, demonstrates the power of the internet as a social medium. In 2010, Facebook, founded in 2004 by a youthful Mark Zuckerberg in his Harvard student days, became the world's second most popular website, behind Google. Facebook is the world's largest online social network, with hundreds of millions of users, accessing it in 50 languages. Seventy per cent of these are outside the US. However, in the fast-moving world of social interaction, companies like Facebook can experience not just meteoric rise, but also precipitous falls. New competitors, such as Twitter, seem to spring up overnight, while MySpace, once considered the star of social networking, saw its popularity evaporate with the surge of Facebook. Is Facebook now threatened by Twitter? Facebook and Twitter are distinctive in their business models. Facebook allows people to keep in touch with their friends, and Twitter is a 'micro-blogging' site, allowing people to speak via 140-character tweets to anyone who cares to follow them. Twitter thus sees itself as more of an information company than a social networking one, according to its founder, Biz Stone (*The Economist*, 2010).

Facebook has become a global business. Its technological expertise and innovativeness, while not immediately obvious to users in the concrete way that an iPhone's attributes are visible to its customers, are nonetheless far-reaching. Its software engineers have been skilful at building systems that can handle increased volume quickly and efficiently, allowing the network to add millions of new users easily. Its innovations encourage greater sharing of data. Facebook Connect, launched in 2009, lets users take their identity and network of friends to other websites

and to other devices, such as game consoles. Facebook has also been skilful in tapping into the creative talent of independent developers of new applications, or 'apps'. The developers benefit from gaining access to a huge audience of users, and users enjoy a directory containing over 500,000 apps.

Although the cost of hardware for storing and processing data has fallen sharply, investment in new technologies is costly. Being relatively young companies started by enthusiasts, where are Facebook and other social networks finding the money needed to propel social networking to global

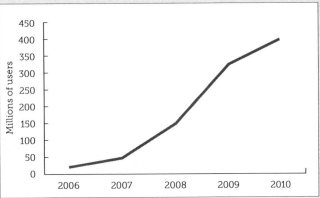

Facebook users worldwide

Source: Facebook website, at www.facebook.com

success? Developing a sustainable business model, which will provide services that users desire and generate profits in the long term, is the dream of every young business. A social networking platform such as Facebook, which holds huge amounts of personal data and is widely accessed globally, would seem to be in a commanding position to be a successful international business. But translating popularity among users into profits is a major challenge. Although Facebook had not yet made a profit, Microsoft invested $240 million in the company in 2007, and a Russian company, Digital Sky Technologies (DST), invested $200 million in 2009. DST thus acquired a 1.9% stake, which would imply

▶ More online ... For information about the company, go to Facebook's website at www.facebook.com and click on 'about'.

that Facebook is worth $10 billion. Facebook aimed to take in $500 million in revenues in 2009, but it was spending more than that on its technology (Gelles, 2009a). In contrast to Google, which has grown rich on selling the targeted advertising that appears alongside its search results, a site such as Facebook faces hurdles in attracting advertising. Because the content is user generated, and possibly in doubtful taste, many advertisers are reluctant to sign up to advertising on social networks. On the other hand, the Facebook audience is far bigger than that of any television network in the world, and, because of the enormous amount of personal data Facebook holds, advertisers can target particular groups of possible customers precisely. Moreover, users often recommend products to friends, and this can be a powerful marketing tool – which costs far less than a traditional marketing campaign.

Although the business prospects look bright from the owners' perspective, an international business strategy depends on numerous other factors – many external to the organization. As other software and internet companies have found, legal regulation must, sooner or later, be taken into account. Microsoft and Google were both founded by young, talented individuals with an ambitious focus on building a global force. Both have encountered regulatory hurdles and setbacks. Facebook has soared to fame, but faces down-to-earth regulatory hurdles, such as privacy laws which protect users' personal data. The company encountered resistance from users when it relaxed its privacy rules, allowing updates of personal data to be viewed publicly unless the user chose to restrict access. Mark Zuckerberg has said that privacy is no longer a 'social norm' (*The Telegraph*, 2010). However, the imposition of stricter privacy settings by regulators, including the European Commission, is a possibility. The world of social networking is helping to democratize the web, but it is also, perhaps paradoxically, concentrating power in the hands of new corporate actors, presenting challenges as well as opportunities for the 25-year-old head of Facebook and others following in his footsteps.

Sources: *The Economist* (2010) 'Profiting from friendship', 30 January; Gelles, D. (2009a) 'What friends are for', *Financial Times*, 3 July; Gelles, D. (2009b) 'Facebook draws criticism for privacy changes', *Financial Times*, 11 December; *The Telegraph* (2010) 'Facebook's Mark Zuckerberg says privacy is no longer a "social norm"', 11 January; Berners-Lee, T., speech before the Knight Foundation, Washington, DC, 14 September 2008, at www.webfoundation.org

Questions for discussion

◆ Why has Facebook grown so rapidly and become an international force so quickly?
◆ What are the risks to the continued success of Facebook?
◆ What are the impacts of social networking for international business?

Introduction

Business activities shape the daily lives and aspirations of people all over the world, from the farmer in rural Africa to the executive of a large American bank. Business enterprises present a rich variety of different organizations and goals, catering for customers ranging from the shopper purchasing a loaf of bread to the giant oil company agreeing to carry out exploration for a government. Business enterprises and their environments have become more complex in recent years, with expanding and deepening ties between societies and between the many organizations within those societies. Many organizations now see themselves as global players, in both their outlook and operations. Yet even the global company must adapt to differing environments and changing circumstances. These changes may be subtle adjustments or radical overhauls, altering the organization's goals, structure and ways of doing things. Understanding the dynamic interaction between the organization and the changing environment is key to business success in today's global competitive landscape. All business organizations, whatever their size and geographical scope, are faced with key questions to which they must respond, whether consciously or simply by carrying on.

We begin this chapter by identifying these key questions behind the business enterprise, which are, 'What do we exist to do?' and 'How should we be carrying out our goals?' We find that goals and means to accomplish them are intertwined, and that success for the enterprise depends on being able to deliver value to customers in a variety of different ways in differing environments. Increasingly, companies are looking at international expansion, to reach more customers and to deliver more efficient performance. We find that operating internationally does not mean simply copying a formula that has worked successfully in the home country. It promises great rewards, but presents new challenges, risks and organizational uncertainties.

Why do some firms falter internationally despite being successful in their home countries? Differences in culture influence how firms engage with organizations and communities in other countries. Similarly, responses to the changing environment differ from firm to firm. There is now a wider range of companies and countries engaged in global business, and changes, especially those involving technological advances, proceed at a rapid pace. We highlight two cross-cutting views of the international environment. The first is the differing dimensions of the environment, including economic, cultural, political, legal, financial, ecological and technological. The second is that of spheres, from the local, through to the national, regional and global. We thus provide a practical framework for understanding how enterprises interact through each dimension in multiple geographical environments.

What does the business enterprise exist to do?

business any type of economic activity in which goods or services (or a combination of the two) are supplied in exchange for some payment, usually money

international business business activities that straddle two or more countries

Business refers to any type of economic activity in which goods or services (or a combination of the two) are supplied in exchange for some payment, usually money. This definition describes the basic exchange transaction. The types of activity covered include trading goods, manufacturing products, extracting natural resources and farming. **International business** refers to business activities that straddle two or more countries. Businesses nowadays routinely look beyond the bounds of their home country for new opportunities. Moreover, although it used to be mainly firms in the more advanced regions of the world (such as North America, Europe and

Japan) which aspired to expand into other countries, now we see businesses from a much wider range of countries 'going global'. These include Chinese, Indian, African and Latin American firms. Consequently, in most countries, there are likely to be both domestic and foreign companies competing alongside each other.

Business has been around a very long time. Ancient societies grew prosperous largely because of thriving business activity, chiefly through trade with other countries, which brought economic power. The urge to do business seems to be universal, taking place in all societies, even under communism, which is avowedly against private enterprise. The small business that operates informally is very different from the ambitious company that seeks to compete in the cut and thrust of today's market economies. The basic questions and concepts that follow help to illuminate how businesses work in a variety of different contexts.

Purpose and goals

for-profit organizations businesses that aim to make money

not-for-profit organizations organizations such as charities, which exist for the purpose of promoting good causes, rather than to make a profit

social enterprise an enterprise that lies somewhere between the for-profit and not-for-profit organization, aiming to make money, but using it mainly for social causes

A business enterprise does not simply come into existence of its own accord. It is created by people, who may emerge in any society or geographic location, and who bring their own values and experience to bear on it. Businesses are founded in particular national environments, with their distinctive values and social frameworks. The founders could well envisage an overarching purpose or mission of contributing to society through employment and wealth creation. They will have some idea of what type of entity they wish to create in terms of organization. They will also focus on more immediate goals of providing specific goods or services to customers. These goals might change frequently, while broader goals are more enduring. Both the decision-makers and the circumstances will change, but the continuing question confronting them is 'What purpose are we fulfilling or should we be fulfilling?' Most of the world's businesses aim to make money, and are sometimes referred to as **for-profit organizations**, to distinguish them from **not-for-profit organizations**, such as charities. A third category exists, the **social enterprise**, which lies somewhere between the two: it aims to make money, but the money is mainly for social causes. (The social enterprise is discussed in Chapter 12.)

Although for-profit enterprises aim to make a financial gain, most founders would say that the profits are for some other purpose. Admittedly, in some businesses, the purpose might be crudely expressed as simply to enrich the owners. But most businesspeople would describe their goal as, for example, offering products which will satisfy customers. It need not be a wholly new product, but one that is more innovative technologically, a better design or cheaper than rivals'. It could be a 'greener' product than those of rivals, such as a more fuel-efficient car. No firm would realistically aim to outperform competitors on all criteria. Goals can be mutually exclusive: the low-cost product is unlikely to have the latest technology. These are issues of strategy, which are discussed more fully in Chapter 5. There is considerable variety in the way the company can position itself competitively, which tells us much about its expertise, culture and broader goals in society.

In today's global consumer markets we find competing companies from a variety of national backgrounds. One of the most rapidly growing products globally is the 'smartphone', which offers a variety of mobile internet services. The iPhone, made by US company Apple Computers, took the world by storm with its launch in 2007. But a number of competitors have entered the smartphone market, eyeing the good prospects for growth. They include Nokia, the Finnish company which has long dominated the mobile handset market (see the closing case study in Chapter 2); the

▸ More online ... For corporate information on Apple, go to www.apple.com/investors
Research in Motion's website is www.rim.net. Interesting headings are 'company' and 'investors'.
Asus's website is www.asus.com. Click on 'about asus' for corporate information.

Canadian firm Research in Motion, with its Blackberry products; and the Taiwanese firm Asus. These firms differ markedly in background and culture: their origins are in different continents (America, Europe and Asia), and their organizations have evolved in distinctive national cultures, while growing into global businesses. Apple, famous for its design and technology, has been guided by the vision of its charismatic founder, Steve Jobs, a veteran of tough competitive battles with larger rivals in North America. Nokia has built a position of dominance in global mobile phone markets, relying on a strong corporate culture rooted in its Scandinavian environment. By contrast, Research in Motion focuses on the Blackberry, which is a premium product favoured especially by business customers. Asus, with its rapidly growing strength in the computer market, is aiming to combine technological expertise with low-cost production in Asia to offer the consumer better value than global rivals.

Summary points **Business purpose and goals**

◆ The business enterprise has a broad purpose in society, as well as shorter term goals of providing products or services for customers.	◆ Over time, the business will need to rethink its goals as the competitive environment changes and the firm evolves.	◆ Firms stem from roots in national environments, which influence their culture even when they serve global markets.

Markets and consumers

market a location where exchange transactions take place, either with formal standing or informally

The **market** as a concept is an old one, referring to a location where exchange transactions take place, either with formal standing or informally. Today, the notion of a market is used in many contexts, and can cover a number of phenomena, although all stem from the core notion of exchange transactions. A market can be defined in four main ways:

* *A country, in terms of its consumers* – A country's consumers usually have similarities in product preferences, due to shared culture and history. National markets are the mainstay of the many companies which focus on their home markets.
* *A type of trading* – Trading can take place globally and not be confined to a specific place. Financial markets, for example, exist to carry out financial transactions, such as the stock market.

emerging economies/ markets fast-growing developing countries

Bric countries collective reference to Brazil, Russia, India and China, which are grouped together loosely as emerging economies

segment in marketing, a group of identifiable consumers, such as an age group, socio-economic group or culturally distinct group

* *A country in terms of its economy* – This rather recent use of the word usually occurs in the context of **emerging markets**, a term that has become widely used, but is rather loosely defined. It refers to fast-growing developing countries, the most notable of which are the **'Bric'** countries (Brazil, Russia, India and China). Their rapid economic rise has made them the centre of attention for many businesses, largely because of their growing ranks of middle-class consumers (see the case study on them which follows).
* *A group of consumers with similar characteristics and preferences* – In marketing, a group of identifiable consumers, such as people aged 18 to 30, is known as a **segment**.

The Brics take the stage

The 'Brics' is a term first used by economists at the US bank Goldman Sachs, who highlighted the large emerging markets for future growth (Goldman Sachs, 2003). Looking at trends extending until 2050, they concluded that the size and growth of the four economies – Brazil, Russia, India and China – were overshadowing today's developed nations, thus representing a shift in the balance of power in the world. The bank's economists did not see them necessarily forming a bloc which would become cohesive in itself, like the EU. In fact, apart from size and growing influence, they have little in common with each other, but in a twist of fiction becoming reality, the four have begun organizing their own summit meetings to discuss global issues. Do the Brics as a group represent a new force in the global economy, or is the term simply a way of drawing attention to four emerging markets?

The four are all large countries and economies. Together they occupy over 25% of the world's land area, and are home to 40% of the world's people. Their economies and political systems are very different. China and Russia are authoritarian states, while India and Brazil are turbulent democracies. All four countries have histories of closed economies and strong state guidance, and all have put in place reforms which have made them more market oriented and more welcoming to foreign investors, to varying degrees. However, in all, there are tensions between market reforms and the role of the state. Of the four, China is the most authoritarian, but its communist leaders have also been highly successful in guiding liberal market reforms. Its export-oriented economy has benefited from foreign investment and know-how. It is moving up the economic ladder, from the low-level, labour-intensive industries that are prevalent in developing countries, to higher technology industries. China's economy is by far the largest of the four, and its growth rate is the most impressive. Its ranks of growing middle-class consumers are now the fastest growing markets for consumer goods. Furthermore, the wealthy Chinese consumer is younger than in Japan or the US (see figure), splashing out on aspirational lifestyle purchases, such as luxury home furnishings and luxury

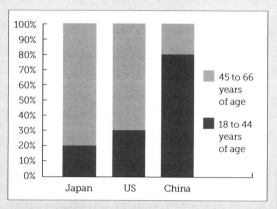

Wealthy consumers by age group
Annual household income of over $70,000, 250,000 renminbi, 8 million yen
Source: *Financial Times*, 10 October 2009

cars, in contrast to the more conservative spending habits of rich Japanese consumers.

India, with its billion-plus inhabitants, aspires to emulate China, but its still predominantly rural population, poor infrastructure and lumbering bureaucracy pose challenges for its democratically elected government to raise economic growth above 6–7% annually. Its exports pale beside China's, and it remains ambivalent about foreign investors in numerous sectors, such as retailing. Brazil, like India, is a democracy, characterized by social and cultural divisions, in addition to widespread poverty. Brazil's government has done much in recent years to improve the lives of its 200 million inhabitants. And Brazil has been active in international forums, voicing the concerns of developing nations and urging rich countries to bring down trade barriers which keep out imports from developing countries like itself.

Of the four countries, Russia is arguably the one which seems out of place. It is officially classified as an industrialized economy under the Kyoto climate change treaty, while the other three are developing economies. Historically, Russia was the superpower rival of the US during the cold-war era following the Second World War. Cold-war ideology has been buried, but the legacy of rivalry with the US lives on. Russia remains one of the world's heaviest military spenders, but behind China; and both are far behind

► More online ... The OECD's website is www.oecd.org, which offers a range of topics and country focus features.

the US, whose military spending is more than quadruple that of the other two combined. Russia's economy has slumped in recent years, and the state has taken greater control of key industries such as gas, which had been privatized in a wave of economic reforms. Despite hopes that a new democratic system would take firm root following the collapse of communism in 1989, the state has taken a stronger grip on political life. Russia possibly views inclusion among the Brics as an opportunity to revive its global political ambitions. Russia was happy to host the first summit meeting of the Brics in 2009.

Are the four countries likely to act as a coherent group? There are conflicts and rivalries among them. All four are cultivating trade and investment relations with countries in the developing world, particularly those rich in natural resources, such as African nations. Brazil and India aspire to become permanent members of the UN Security Council, but Russia and China, as existing members, have resisted. China and India fought a war in 1962 along their common border, which remains tense. Of the three, only Brazil is not a nuclear power, but it is moving in that direction. All four can be targeted for poor environmental records. China is the world's largest carbon emitter, but India and Russia are also among top emitters. Brazil is the leader in deforestation, although it is taking steps to regulate environmental degradation.

The Brics represent a shift in global economic power away from the developed world, in which the US was dominant. With the exception of Russia, their continued growth has stood out against recession in the rich world in 2008–9, helping to substantiate their claims for

Getting a buzz from shopping: These young Chinese shoppers carry the hopes of many of the world's leading brands. What other products are these shoppers likely to be buying?
Source: Istock

global recognition. Relations with the US and other developed nations are evolving as the Brics' political leaders forge new roles on the global political stage.

Sources: Barber, L., and Wheatley, J. (2009) 'Brazil keeps its economic excitement in check', *Financial Times*, 26 October; *The Economist* (2010) 'The trillion-dollar club', 17 April; Hille, K., Lau, J., and Waldmeir, P. (2009) 'Scramble to slake Chinese thirst for high-end brands', *Financial Times*, 10 October; Lamont, J. (2010) 'A good crisis brings greater influence', *Financial Times*, 29 January; Clover, C., and Belton, C. (2009) 'Crisis could be a catalyst for change', *Financial Times*, 13 October; Goldman Sachs (2003) 'Dreaming with BRICs: The Path to 2050', Global Economics Working Paper No. 99, at http://www2.goldmansachs.com

Questions for discussion

◆ Why are the Brics the new forces to be reckoned with in the world economy?
◆ In what ways are the Bric countries different from each other?
◆ In your view, are the Bric countries likely to co-ordinate their action on global policy issues?

An important market for many companies is urban, middle-class consumers, numbers of whom are growing fastest in the large emerging markets. There are probably one billion middle-class consumers globally, but there are over four billion other people further down the 'pyramid' whose needs also matter. Their importance has been highlighted in C.K. Prahalad's book, *The Fortune at the Bottom of the Pyramid* (2009). Increasingly, companies have broadened their focus to include products for this much broader spectrum of consumers, often living in poor countries where infrastructure is weak and levels of education are low. In these markets, price is crucial: a few cents more or less representing a major factor in the consumer's ability to buy a product. Why would a global company such as Procter & Gamble (P&G), whose beauty products cultivate a glamorous image, seek to sell basic soap in difficult conditions in Africa? Part of the answer lies in the dilemma faced by many large companies: weighing up the tremendous growth possibilities of new markets against the safety of existing mature markets where growth is minimal.

Summary points **Markets and consumers**

- A market can be a whole country, but it is usual, especially in a large emerging market such as China, to target particular products to identifiable groups of consumers, such as the urban middle class.

- Many large companies, finding expansion possibilities limited in the developed economies, are targeting consumers in developing countries. In these countries, economic growth and changing lifestyles create business opportunities for both domestic and foreign firms.

- A large company might design products to serve different markets, from basic goods in developing countries to premium branded products in developed countries.

Stakeholders and corporate social responsibility (CSR)

In answer to the question posed at the end of the last section – on why P&G would target African markets – we could simply cite the response suggested earlier: to make money. But this is only part of the story. The large company seeks success in a number of markets, both in terms of countries and types of consumer. It is driven by a desire to satisfy those consumers' needs, and also to provide worthwhile economic activity for its employees. These considerations are part of the answer to the question, 'What do we exist to do?' In recent years, companies have come to recognize that they are participants in society generally.

In the same vein, managers have become more aware of the interrelationships between the internal and external environment of the company. These perspectives bring the company into relationships with stakeholders. Figure 1.1 identifies a variety of stakeholders across home and foreign environments. A **stakeholder** may be anyone, including individuals, groups and even society generally, who exerts influence on the company or whom the company is in a position to influence (Freeman, 1984). The impacts may be direct or indirect, identifiable people or a more general notion of the community as something distinct from its current members. Stakeholders who have direct relations with the company include owners, employees, customers, suppliers and business partners. These might be located in any country where the firm does business. The government can be a direct stakeholder, especially if it has an ownership stake (discussed in the next section), or it can be an indirect stakeholder, framing the legal environment in which the firm operates.

stakeholder broad category including individuals, groups and even society generally, that exerts influence on the company or that the company is in a position to influence

► More online ... Nike's corporate website is www.nikebiz.com
Gap's corporate website is www.gapinc.com

Indirect stakeholders, while they affect and are affected by the company's operations, cover a range of broader societal interests which enjoy fewer direct channels of communication with managers. They include the local community, society generally and the ecological environment affected by the company's operations. On the other hand, the rapid rise of social IT has seen social networking, on websites such as Facebook and Twitter, expand into business activities and impact on companies. People anywhere can voice their views to a potentially large audience. Companies wishing to retain a tight control on stakeholder relations might see these developments as a threat, whereas more enlightened companies would see opportunities to gain valuable information on the views of customers and other stakeholders.

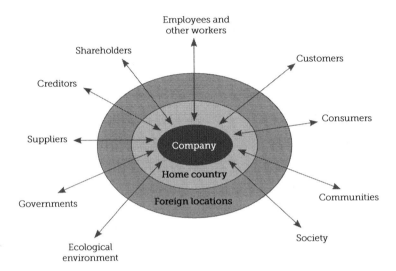

Figure 1.1 **Stakeholders, home and abroad**

In a company that operates mainly in its own domestic market, managers have a fairly clear idea of their main stakeholders. Their employees and customers are readily identifiable. In a company that operates internationally, identifying stakeholders is far more difficult – and more challenging. The company's branded products might be made by workers in far-flung locations, who are employed by a different company and have little contact with the company whose brand appears on the products. This type of operation, known as **outsourcing** or manufacturing under licence, has become common. It is exemplified by Nike, Gap and other familiar brands. Outsourcing, usually in order to manufacture products in a lower cost location than the firm's home country, is one of the major trends associated with globalization, which we discuss in the next chapter. The firm that decides to go down this route is impliedly making a statement about its view of its overall purpose and strategy.

In recent years, companies have increasingly tended to frame their purpose and goals in terms of stakeholders, a tendency that reflects a recognition of a broader role in society than the simple economic one. The approach to business activities that accords with this view rests on a belief in **corporate social responsibility (CSR)**. CSR as an approach recognizes that the business has wider responsibilities in society, extending to legal, moral, ethical and social roles. CSR, however, has become rather an umbrella term, covering a spectrum of approaches to business objectives, which are highlighted throughout this book and are brought together in a broad assessment in Chapter 12.

outsourcing the process by which an owner contracts out to another firm a business process, such as product manufacturing or a business service, usually under a licence agreement

corporate social responsibility (CSR) an approach to business which recognizes that the organization has responsibilities in society beyond the economic role, extending to legal, ethical, environmental and philanthropic roles

Whereas some companies prioritize CSR as their guiding strategy, others see CSR as voluntary activities separate from their mainstream businesses. The approach of many companies that fall between these two extremes is one of integrating business objectives with CSR goals. Known as an 'integrated strategy', it is the basis of the 'business case' for CSR (Husted and Salazar, 2006). This approach holds that, although a firm seeks profit maximization as a goal, purely economic motives are rather short term, and the firm would be smarter to look at long-term value creation, maintaining its capacity to generate profits in the future. This longer term perspective involves the

sustainability the principle that business should be carried out in ways which do not cause a detriment to the ability of future generations to fulfil their needs

sustainability of the firm's business, which is the notion that today's business should be carried out in ways which do not cause a detriment to the ability of future generations to fulfil their needs. Sustainability takes into account the firm's impacts on communities and the natural environment (see Chapter 11). In a sense, the principle of sustainability encourages a business to think of stakeholders in the future, not just the present. Most firms would probably say they uphold goals of stakeholder involvement, CSR and sustainability, but firms differ markedly in their commitment of resources to these goals.

Summary points Stakeholders

◆ Stakeholders interact with the firm at all levels, although companies differ in their responsiveness to stakeholder interests.

◆ CSR as an approach views economic goals as only one aspect of the firm's existence, and stresses social and ethical obligations which arise for the firm because it is part of society.

◆ In contrast to short-term economic goals, a longer term approach looks at the sustainability of the firm's business.

Critical thinking

What and who does the business exist for?

The preceding sections have focused on business goals, from basic ones such as making money and offering great products, to more idealistic ones such as serving society. In your view, which of these goals are the most important in today's world, and why? List them in order of priority.

How does the enterprise carry out its goals?

Although we speak of a *firm* forming goals and carrying them out, it is actually the *people* running the firm who take the key decisions. In this section, we look at the players and processes which make it function. We focus here initially on the forms, structures and processes which constitute a legal framework; this is a necessary consideration before the firm can get on with what it is 'really' about, such as manufacturing. Most businesses start in a small way, with founders who become the first owners. They bear considerable responsibility, especially in the early stages of the business. Having a great idea for a business is only the beginning, however. They must create a legal and organizational structure to carry it out, and decide on how it will be financed and managed. Each of these aspects of the business now has an international dimension for many enterprises, adding to the possible complications, but also offering tantalizing opportunities.

▶ More online ... The Global Entrepreneurship Monitor provides much comparative country data on entrepreneurs, at www.gemconsortium.com
McDonald's corporate website is www.aboutmcdonalds.com

Entrepreneurs

A person who starts up a business, usually with his or her own money, is known as an **entrepreneur**. The successful entrepreneur has a vision of the firm's goals, a great deal of energy and an appetite for a moderate amount of risk (Zimmerer et al., 2007). Not everyone would savour this prospect, often because cultural factors come into play, making some people more reluctant to take on personal risk than others. The founder of a business typically begins as a **sole trader**, also referred to as a self-employed person. The business of the sole trader has no independent existence from its owner. In practice, this means that if the business fails, the personal wealth of its owner can be used to cover the business's debts. In the worst scenario, the owner's resources could be wiped out in order to pay business debts. This risk is known as 'unlimited liability', and is one of the major drawbacks of being self-employed. The business at this stage might have only one or two employees, or even none, although it is common for family members to help out. It is a **small-to-medium size enterprise (SME)**. This category covers the vast majority of the world's business enterprises. It derives from the classification given below:

* Micro: 0–9 employees
* Small: 10–49 employees
* Medium: 50–249 employees
* Large: 250 or more employees

SMEs range from informal micro-enterprises to firms with up to 249 employees, making this a highly diverse category. These firms provide an important source of employment and economic activity in all countries. Although most are local firms such as family-owned restaurants, many SMEs have set their sights on becoming global in scope from the outset. These ambitious **born-global firms** tend to be in high-technology sectors. Whereas a firm traditionally grows gradually, expanding from local to a national and international business, the born-global firm's owners think from the outset in terms of international markets (Knight and Cavusgil, 2004: 124). Such firms tend to be the ones we think of when visualizing global business. Many well-known firms have grown from start-ups into global organizations.

McDonald's, founded as a single hamburger outlet in the 1950s, is an example, as is Microsoft (founded in 1975) and Google (founded in 1998). Of the three, it is striking that Google, the most recent, has grown the quickest, becoming the world's dominant internet search engine in just a few years. The fact that these firms are all American is indicative that the cultural environment, as well as the legal and financial institutions, is favourable to entrepreneurs.

For individual entrepreneurs, the franchise provides a less risky route to starting a business. The **franchise** agreement allows a businessperson to trade under the name of an established brand, backed by an established organization (the 'franchisor'), while retaining ownership of the business. Under the agreement, the business owner ('franchisee') pays fees to the franchisor organization for the right to sell its products or services. The franchisee does not have the freedom over the business that an independent owner would have, but stands a greater chance of success due to the strength of the established business 'formula' of the brand. Besides McDonald's, Burger King and other fast-food chains, there are numerous other goods and services providers, such as car rental companies, which have grown through the use of franchising.

---

entrepreneur a person who starts up a business and imbues it with the energy and drive necessary to compete in markets

sole trader the person who is in business on his or her own account, also referred to as a self-employed person

small-to-medium size enterprise (SME) business ranging from micro-enterprises of just one person to firms with up to 249 employees

born-global firm SME which aims to become global from the outset, often in a high-technology sector

franchising business agreement by which a business uses the brand, products and business format of another firm under licence

▸ More online ... Bosch's website is www.bosch.com, where much corporate information is available

Summary points **Entrepreneurs**

◆ For an entrepreneur who starts a business, the enterprise can be highly personal, involving commitment of energy, funds and some risk.

◆ The born-global firm, often in high-technology sectors, aspires to global markets from the outset.

◆ In a franchise arrangement, the business trades under the name of a well-known brand, so that the franchisee enjoys a greater chance of success.

◆ SMEs employ more people globally than larger firms. Although some are born-globals, with aspirations to global markets from the outset, most are local or national, making them important in national economies.

Companies

A business can carry on indefinitely as an unincorporated association or enterprise, that is, without formal corporate status. However, when it grows beyond a size that can be managed personally by the owner, it is usual for the owner to register it as a company, to give the business a separate legal identity and separate financial footing. The **company**, also called a 'corporation', is a legal entity separate from its owners. Registration with the correct authorities in each country (or individual state in the US) constitutes its creation, drawing a line between the company's finances and legal obligations and those of the owner(s). It is also possible to register as a European company within the EU, although for purposes such as taxation, the company is still considered a national entity. The company takes on a separate existence from its owners at the point when it is registered, by filing documents of its purpose and constitution with national authorities. This need not mean that the owner becomes distanced from the everyday running of the business, although some owners do decide to hire professional managers to take over the reins of the company, and confine themselves to making the bigger decisions on strategy.

Any registered company is legally owned by its **shareholders**, also known as stockholders. The whole of a company's shares are its share capital, also known as its **equity**. The shareholder is liable up to the amount invested, and therefore enjoys **limited liability**. Historically, shareholders faced more risk than they do now, as they could be liable for all the firm's debts. The introduction of limited liability made owning shares more attractive as an investment, and paved the way for widespread share ownership by the investing public.

Registered companies may be private or public companies. The **private limited company** resembles the family business in which the owner retains control. It has few shareholders, and these are 'insiders', often related. It is not allowed to sell its shares to the public. It faces fewer requirements for disclosure of its financial position than the public company. Although most are SMEs, many large international businesses are private companies. An example is Bosch, the German engineering company. Private companies are key economic players in Germany and many other countries.

The **public company** offers shares to the public, first in an **initial public offering (IPO)** on a stock exchange. It may call for further capital (in a **rights issue**) when it needs to grow its capital. Its shares are openly traded, and it faces considerable scrutiny of its accounts by national regulators in the country in which it is registered, and in which it lists on a stock exchange. The large, well-known companies that are

company a legal form of an organization which has a separate legal identity from its owner(s); also called a 'corporation'

shareholders legal owners of a company, known as 'members', who enjoy rights such as receiving dividends from company profits

equity in corporate finance, the share capital of a company

limited liability principle that the shareholder is liable up to the amount invested in the company

private limited company company whose shares are not publicly traded on a stock exchange

public company company which lists on a stock exchange and offers shares to the public

initial public offering (IPO) first offering by a company of its shares to the public on a stock exchange; also known as 'flotation'

rights issue for a company, a means of raising capital whereby existing investors are asked to increase their investment

▸ More online ... Corporate information about Google is found at http://investor.google.com

major global players are mainly listed public companies, such as Microsoft, Nestlé, BP and Toyota. We tend to think of the large public company as one run by professional managers, but even in these companies, founders' families or other investors can exert control through stakes in the company's equity and board membership, the latter of which is exemplified by Cemex, featured in the closing case study of this chapter. In general, the businessperson who wishes to maintain ownership and control will prefer the advantages of a private company, while one who wishes to attract a wide range of investors will probably convert the business into a public company after a few years as a private company. This was the pattern with Google, which listed after six years. However, Google adopted a dual share structure which kept control in the hands of the founders (see later discussion).

Summary points Companies

● Founders of businesses tend to register as limited companies, to gain the benefits of limited liability.

● Owners wishing to maintain ownership and control, without the requirements of extensive financial disclosure, choose to do business as private companies.

● Because of their publicly traded shares, public companies tend to have a higher profile.

Critical thinking

From entrepreneur to established company

The entrepreneur must think ahead in today's environment, envisaging the kind of company and people that will help the company to stay competitive. Becoming a public company is one of the big decisions, but not necessarily the right route for every company. How does the entrepreneur decide whether and when to go public?

The multinational enterprise (MNE)

Both private and public companies abound in the international environment. As they extend their operations outwards from their home countries, their organizations become more complex. A company can grow 'organically' by increasing its capacity and going into new markets without making major structural changes to the organization. When company executives become more ambitious internationally, they contemplate changes with deeper structural implications. A result has been a thriving global market in corporate ownership and control. As its strategy evolves, a company may buy other companies and sell those it no longer wishes to own. It may also buy stakes in other companies, often as a means of participating in a network of firms, rather than for purely ownership motives. This constant reconfiguration of companies and businesses has become a prominent feature of the international business environment. In these ways, companies can grow relatively quickly internationally and adapt their businesses organizationally as changes in the competitive environment occur. The main organizational arrangement through which these changes take place is the multinational enterprise.

multinational enterprise (MNE) an organization which acquires ownership or other contractual ties in other organizations (including companies and unincorporated businesses) outside its home country

The **multinational enterprise (MNE)** is a broad term signifying a lead company (the parent company) which has acquired ownership or other contractual ties in other organizations (including companies and unincorporated businesses) outside its home country. The parent company co-ordinates and controls (in varying

▶ More online ... ArcelorMittal's website is www.arcelormittal.com

transnational corporation (TNC) a company which owns and controls operations in one or more countries other than its home country

degrees) the international business activities carried out by all the organizations within the MNE's broad control. The term **transnational corporation (TNC)** is often used interchangeably with MNE, and has been used in previous editions of this book. The TNC is defined as a company which owns and controls operations in one or more countries other than its home country, including both companies and unincorporated enterprises (United Nations, 2008a). MNE has been the favoured term in this edition, as the notion of 'enterprise' is broader than 'corporation', recognizing the growing organizational diversity of international business.

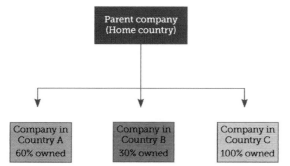

Figure 1.2 **The multinational enterprise (MNE)**

The MNE as an organizational form is not a strictly legal category, but it is recognized as central in international business organization and has been a key driver of globalization, discussed in the next chapter. The term covers businesses of all sizes, from SMEs to global companies with hundreds of thousands of employees. It covers private companies as well as public ones. Typically, the parent company located in the home country co-ordinates the activities of other companies in the group, known

affiliates organizations connected through ownership or other strategic ties to an MNE

subsidiary company a company owned wholly or substantially by another company, which is in a position to exert control

broadly as **affiliates**. The parent company can exert strong control, or it can operate on a loosely co-ordinated basis, delegating much decision-making to local managers. Its approach depends largely on the ownership structure of affiliates. A simple MNE is shown in Figure 1.2. In the figure, only the company in Country C is wholly owned and controlled. It is thus a **subsidiary company**. The parent has a 60% equity stake in the company in Country A, making it also a subsidiary, as this gives the parent a controlling stake. If a parent company holds a stake of at least 10% in another company, that other company is generally considered to be an affiliate. Thus, the 30% stake in the company in Country B makes this company an affiliate. MNEs can have quite complex webs of affiliates, and in some countries, especially in Japan and South Korea, affiliates own shares in each other, known as 'cross-shareholding', thereby giving the parent company effective control over an affiliate even though it might own only a small stake itself.

The MNE parent company is likely to be registered in its home country, and its subsidiaries registered in the countries where they carry out their activities. Hence, the subsidiary can be viewed as a 'local' company, even if controlled by a foreign parent. In some countries, foreign investors are not permitted by law to own 100% of a local company, but a sizeable stake can bring considerable power. In another twist, a private parent company can control subsidiaries which are publicly listed in their countries of operation (an example is the steel company ArcelorMittal). Managing subsidiaries in different country environments is one of the major challenges for today's international managers. The rise of MNEs from developing and emerging economies is one of the trends highlighted in this book, beginning with the closing case study of this chapter on Cemex of Mexico.

Next, we look at the roles and responsibilities within these different types of organization, which help us to understand the dynamic processes in play in these enterprises.

Summary points The MNE

◆ The MNE covers a range of organizational arrangements, but is usually organized as a parent company and subsidiaries.	◆ A subsidiary is a company which is at least 50% owned by a parent company.	◆ An affiliate company is one in which a parent company has a significant equity stake, but short of majority ownership.

Who controls the organization?

The sole trader or sole owner of a company may well take all the major decisions regarding the business, unfettered by the wishes of other owners and not accountable to anyone else within the business. Still, even a micro-enterprise has stakeholders, in that it exists in a community, has customers, makes an environmental impact and must comply with regulatory authorities. In the private company, there are typically only a few shareholders, often members of the same family. This does not necessarily make for smooth decision-making. Some of the fiercest corporate battles are between family members inside companies. In a public company, the public is invited to subscribe for shares. However, only a small proportion of the share capital need be offered to the public, and it is not uncommon for even a public company to be family dominated. This is often achieved by having a dual share structure whereby founders' shares carry more voting rights than ordinary shares (they are weighted ten to one in Google, for example). The shareholder who buys the company's shares is providing capital to enable it to function. The larger the stake (that is, holding of shares), the more influence the shareholder will expect to exert, although in practice, controlling interests may make this difficult. A share in a company carries certain rights, including the right to receive dividends and (normally) vote in annual general meetings. Importantly, the shareholder is a 'member' of the company, whereas the creditor of the company is not.

The shareholder can be an individual or an organization. A company can be a shareholder in another company, as is often the case with parent companies and subsidiaries. Financial institutions, such as pension funds, are some of the largest global shareholders, with huge sums to invest. A recent trend has been the increase in government ownership of companies, both directly and through investment companies formed for the purpose. In the recent past, it was relatively easy to distinguish between the state-owned enterprise and one in private hands. Nowadays, the boundaries have become blurred. We see state players acting through a range of companies, including public companies whose shares are traded on stock exchanges. The main ways in which governments own and control enterprises are:

- *Full ownership and control* – This is the traditional state-owned company, which acts like a limb of government and whose finances are managed by the government. These are sometimes referred to as nationalized industries. State-owned

► More online ... EDF's corporate website is www.edf.com/the-edf-group
The OECD's Principles of Corporate Governance can be found at www.oecd.org

companies have been major players in the economic development of many countries, including China and India. It should be remembered, however, that their political systems are very different: China is governed on authoritarian lines, and India is the world's largest democracy (see discussion in Chapter 7).

* *Partial ownership and degrees of control* – The government may choose to **privatize** a state-owned enterprise by registering it as a public company and selling off a proportion of shares to the public, while retaining a large stake and a controlling interest. This process creates a hybrid organization in culture and outlook, neither wholly public sector nor wholly commercial. An example is Electricité de France (EDF), which is now registered as a public company in which 13% of the shares are owned by private investors. Gazprom, the former Russian gas ministry, is another example. It is now majority-owned by the Russian government, and its free-floating shares are traded on the London Stock Exchange.

* *Creation of* **sovereign wealth funds** *and other investment vehicles* – Many governments operate through sovereign wealth funds to invest in a range of global companies, examined further in Chapter 9. Asian countries and oil-rich Middle Eastern countries are prominent among the states that have created these investment vehicles, which are active in global financial markets.

* *Government purchase of stakes in failing companies* – Some governments have become shareholders almost by default, through bailouts of troubled firms with public money. The US government felt compelled to pump taxpayers' money into some banks and car manufacturers during the financial crisis of 2008–9. In these cases, the government had no positive wish to run these enterprises, and would greatly have preferred that their managers could have found market solutions to their problems. The bailouts were a last resort, and these companies, including the carmaker General Motors (GM), are restructuring themselves as leaner, more competitive, companies. As the world's pre-eminent market economy, the US has had to rethink issues of market regulation and accountability of managers.

Accountability of managers in any company is ultimately to its owners, the shareholders. This underlying principle is the basis of the company's decision-making at the highest level, known as its **corporate governance**. Corporate governance differs from business to business, and is influenced by national economic, social, cultural and legal environments. It reflects broader perspectives on the company's role in society, which have come under the spotlight in the wider debate on corporate governance and CSR in recent years. A company's own heritage and corporate culture influence its corporate governance, both formally and informally. National governments are in a position to set legal requirements for corporate governance, as part of their company law and financial regulation frameworks. However, many would prefer to lay down broad principles rather than prescriptive frameworks, in the belief that a one-size-fits-all approach is not appropriate. The UK's Combined Code of Corporate Governance takes this approach. The **Organisation for Economic Co-operation and Development (OECD)**, which was established by representatives of the world's main developed economies in 1960, has been active in giving guidance on corporate governance. The OECD's overarching principles support market economies and democratic institutions. It has published Principles of Corporate Governance, which are intended to guide MNEs generally on best practice (OECD, 2004). These appear in Table 1.1.

privatization process of transforming a state-owned enterprise into a public company and selling off a proportion of shares to the public, usually while retaining a stake and a controlling interest by the government

sovereign wealth fund entity controlled by a government, which invests state funds and pursues an investment strategy; often active global financial markets

corporate governance a company's structures and processes for decision-making at the highest level

Organisation for Economic Co-operation and Development (OECD) organization of the world's main developed economies, which supports market economies and democratic institutions

Although the senior executives are probably the most influential people in the company, the highest legal authority is its board of directors. **Directors** bear ultimate responsibility for the company's activities. Collectively, they constitute the board of directors accountable to the company's shareholders. Structures differ from country to country. In Germany and other European countries, a two-tier board of directors is the norm. A supervisory board holds the ultimate authority for major decisions, while a management board is the 'engine of management' (Charkham, 1994). The single board is the norm in the Anglo-American type of structure. It is based on the belief that shareholders' interests are the primary focus of the company. The supervisory board in the two-tier system includes employee representation, reflecting the principle of **co-determination** The two-tier model is often said to represent a stakeholder approach to governance, in contrast to the focus on shareholder value which characterizes the single-tier model. However, co-determination in practice reflects the interests of groups of employees in the home country of the company (through their trade unions), rather than a broader stakeholder perspective.

directors people appointed by the company to bear ultimate responsibility for the company's activities

co-determination principle of stakeholder participation in corporate governance, usually involving a two-tier board, with employee representation on the supervisory board

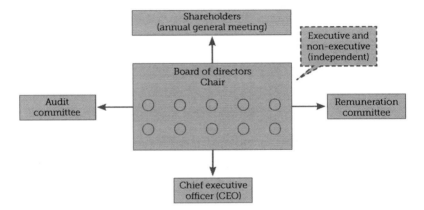

Figure 1.3 **The single-tier board of directors**

The directors who actively manage the company are its **executive directors**, headed by a **chief executive officer (CEO)**. The CEO occupies a pivotal role in decision-making and management of the company. The CEO must answer to the board, maintain the confidence of shareholders, inspire the company's workforce and deal with an array of stakeholders. Whenever the company's fortunes take a turn for the worse, the CEO is in the firing line. We highlight a wide variety of CEOs, in differing corporate and market environments, in the feature 'Meet the CEO' in each chapter of this book.

The boardroom is more relaxed for the **non-executive directors**, who are independent of the firm's management and owners. The non-executive director occupies a part-time role and, in theory, exerts more objective judgment on the company's activities than working managers do. On the other hand, knowledge about the business is now seen as necessary, following the 2008 financial crisis, in which directors' collective failure to curb excessive risk has been highlighted (Kirkpatrick, 2009). The onus is on non-executives to take their responsibilities seriously, and actively query the CEO over strategy. Nowadays, non-executives are keenly aware that, as board members, they are equally liable legally for corporate wrongdoing which they ought to have been aware of. There has been a tendency to appoint other CEOs and retired CEOs as non-executive directors. This approach is now changing as uncritical boards have been implicated in a number of situations where misguided strategies and

executive directors directors who actively manage the company

chief executive officer (CEO) the company's senior executive, who oversees its management and is accountable to the board of directors

non-executive directors part-time company directors who are independent of the firm's management and owners

excessive executive rewards were allowed to go unchecked. An example is Enron, the energy trading company which collapsed in 2001. Enron had a corporate governance system which looked admirable on paper. However, its senior executives were able to steer the company towards their own goals, and the bodies that should have provided a check on their actions (such as the board and its committees) failed to do so. Legislation in the US, in the form of the Sarbanes-Oxley Act of 2002, focused on liability and penalties for false financial reporting, but did not address structural issues of governance. More recently, excessive risk-taking is blamed in a series of bank failures in 2008, including Lehman Brothers of the US, once the country's fourth-largest investment bank, which collapsed under a mountain of $60 billion in bad debts (see Chapter 9 for a further discussion). Other banks, deemed to be too big to fail, such as Citigroup, were rescued by government bailouts, but public confidence in corporate governance had suffered, and regulatory reform was again perceived as necessary.

It is generally thought that a 'balanced' board, consisting of both executive and independent directors, representing both insider and outsider perspectives, constitutes best practice. A proportion of independent directors is usually recommended in national codes of corporate governance and in the OECD's Principles of Corporate Governance (see Table 1.1). It is usually thought to be good practice to separate the roles of chairman of the board and CEO, and to appoint a non-executive director as chairman. However, many companies, particularly American ones, combine the roles in a single person. An example is Cemex, featured in the closing case study, where the current chairman and CEO, who is the grandson of the founder, has held both offices since 1985.

Table 1.1 **Corporate governance principles recommended by the OECD**

Principle	The corporate governance framework should:
I	• Promote transparent and efficient markets • Be consistent with the rule of law • Identify responsibilities of different regulatory and supervisory authorities
II	• Protect and facilitate the exercise of shareholder rights
III	• Ensure the equitable treatment of all shareholders, including minority and foreign shareholders
IV	• Recognize the rights of stakeholders established by law or through mutual agreements • Encourage active co-operation between corporations and stakeholders in creating wealth, jobs, and the sustainability of financially sound enterprises
V	• Ensure that timely and accurate disclosure is made on all material matters regarding the corporation, including the financial situation, performance, ownership, and governance
VI	Board responsibilities: • Monitor management effectively • Align key executive and board remuneration with the longer term interests of the company and shareholders • Consider a sufficient number of non-executive board members capable of exercising independent judgment

Source: OECD (2004) OECD Principles of Corporate Governance, at www.oecd.org

Although shareholders as owners are, in theory, paramount in corporate decision-making, ordinary shareholders themselves have tended to have little direct influence in a number of important matters, such as executive remuneration and appointment

Guido Zegna CEO of Italian luxury group, Zegna

As the fourth-generation head of his family's luxury menswear group, Guido Zegna attributes the company's success to discipline and respect among the numerous family members who continue to run the company. Founded by his grandfather, the first Ermenegildo Zegna, in 1910, Zegna was originally a textile company and still has a weaving business. It expanded into the ready-to-wear sector in the 1960s, and now offers a number of different brands for differing consumer markets. Recent additions are sportier lines, Z Zegna and Zegna Sport, which are aimed at affluent under-30s in global markets. The company also offers womenswear and home furnishings. Eighty-eight per cent of the company's sales are exports. Zegna sells most of its products through its own retail outlets, which number over 500 worldwide. In recent years, established markets, such as the US and Japan, have seen sales slump, and sales in Russia have also been weak. On the bright side, sales in China grew 30% in 2008, and in the Middle East, 50%. Asia is now 40% of the company's global business, up from 25% in 2007. Zegna says: 'What we used to call the emerging markets have emerged' (Menkes, 2009).

Zegna views the presence of family members in key posts as responsible for the company's long success. He speculates that, were the company a public one, payouts might have been greater in the boom years of the early 2000s, but he says: 'Because we are all family we were very thrifty and kept the money for the business. We have a very long-term view' (Friedman, 2009). A cousin is the group chairman, and Guido's sister, Anna, is the company's image director. There are nearly a dozen younger family members eyeing jobs in the family business, but Guido Zegna says: 'We have adopted the corporate governance of a public company, and one of our rules is that before any member of the family can even begin at the family company they must have a college degree, they must speak one other language other than Italian – English – fluently, and they must have worked for eight years outside the family business' (Friedman).

The company has also adopted market research methods which are usually employed by public companies. This way, they can see customer preferences in different markets, and respond quickly. Guido Zegna says they find that menswear brands are more stable than womenswear brands, as customers are more loyal (Menkes). Listening to the customer is crucial to continued success. But, he says, 'our core values are our people. And we have to react quickly to change of lifestyle' (Menkes). Zegna celebrated its centenary in 2010, but the family remains focused on the future. Guido Zegna maintains that after the newer emerging markets such as Egypt, Morocco and India, 'luxury's new frontier is Africa' (Menkes).

Sources: Menkes, S. (2009) 'Zegna explores new markets in face of downturn', *New York Times*, 23 June; Friedman, V. (2009) 'Men's wear champion sets trend', *Financial Times*, 6 July; Zegna, A. (2010) 'Ethics and quality can go hand-in-hand', *Financial Times*, 20 February

Looking good, whatever the setting. As a family business, Zegna has prided itself on designs for changing lifestyles and new markets

Source: Istock

of directors. The CEO of Lehman Brothers, who received remuneration of $484.8 million between 2000 and 2008, when the company went bankrupt, faced stern questioning from US legislators in public hearings, mirroring widespread public disgust. European companies are required to hold a vote on executive remuneration, but this requirement is weak, as the vote is not binding. The practice of paying huge rewards to executives of poorly performing (or even failed) companies is now coming under the spotlight. The OECD is reviewing its Principles, last revised in 2004, strengthening those on accountability of directors and checks on executive pay (Kirkpatrick, 2009). The trend that has seen growing share ownership by governments, whether by design or default, is a factor in the corporate governance debate. A government is not an 'ordinary' shareholder, but is usually expected to uphold public interest. However, governments differ, just as countries and political systems differ, and these differences are reflected in how active a role they play and for what purposes.

Summary points Corporate decision-making

◆ Decision-makers in a company are its directors, who are accountable to the shareholders as owners.

◆ In practice, the CEO and other executive directors are the main decision-makers.

◆ Non-executive directors, in theory, play an important independent role in monitoring decision-makers. However, in practice, their willingness to stand up to executives can sometimes be questioned.

Critical thinking
Power and responsibility within the company
Boards of directors have been the targets of criticism in recent years, as having been 'asleep on the job' when managers were pursuing risky strategies which undermined shareholder value. What steps should companies take to give boards more effective oversight of corporate decision-making?

Functions within the enterprise

functions activities of a business which form part of the overall process of providing a product for a customer

Every business, whether large or small, involves a number of different types of activity, or **functions**, which form part of the overall process of providing a product for a customer. Physical resources, including plant, machinery and offices, must be organized and functions such as finance, purchasing and marketing must be co-ordinated, to enable the entire enterprise to function smoothly as a unit. Every business carries out basic functions, such as finance, even though in a small business, it is unlikely to hire specialists in each area, whereas a large organization has separate departments. The importance of particular functions depends in part on the type of business. Product design and production, along with research and development, feature mainly in manufacturing firms, whereas all firms have need of finance, HRM and marketing functions. They cover the entire life of a product, from the design stage to the delivery of a final product to the customer. They even extend beyond the sale, to include after-sales service and recycling. The main functions are set out in Figure 1.4.

In Figure 1.4, the headings in the rectangles represent the co-ordinating activities. The company's overall strategy determines what its goals are, and central managers must co-ordinate all the firm's activities to achieve those goals. We look at the part played by each of these functions in turn:

finance and accounting
business function
which concerns control
over the revenues
and outgoings of the
business, aiming to
balance the books and
to generate sufficient
profits for the future
health of the firm

operations the entire
process of producing
and delivering a product
to a consumer; covers
tangible goods and
services, and often a
combination of both

human resource
management (HRM)
all aspects of the
management of people
in the organization,
including recruitment,
training, and rewarding
the workforce

marketing satisfying the
needs and expectations
of customers; includes
a range of related
activities, such as product
offering, branding,
advertising, pricing, and
distribution of goods

- **Finance and accounting** – This function concerns control over the revenues and outgoings of the business, aiming to balance the books and to generate sufficient profits for the future health of the firm. This function is far more complex in large public companies than in SMEs. Trends towards more innovative finance and international operations have called for considerable professional expertise. At the same time, as discussed earlier, legal duties of financial reporting and disclosure are now increasingly under the spotlight. The company's chief financial officer (CFO) is a board member, and many go on to become CEO.

- **Operations** – Operations cover the entire process of producing and delivering a product to a consumer. It covers tangible goods and services, and often a combination of both. Production focuses on the operational processes by which products are manufactured. Production increasingly relies on sophisticated machinery and computerized systems. Quality, safety and efficiency are major concerns of production engineers and managers. A recent trend has been for manufacturing to take place in low-cost locations, often outsourced by a large MNE. The MNE, however, will still wish to maintain quality, even if a licensed manufacturer is making the product. Quality and safety have become more challenging as manufacturing has shifted to diverse locations (discussed in the next chapter).

- **Human resource management (HRM)** – Formerly known as 'personnel management', HRM focuses on all aspects of the management of people in the organization, including recruitment, training, and rewarding the workforce. In the large, hierarchical organization, these activities are formally structured, whereas in the small organization, they tend to be carried out informally, with less paperwork and less reliance on formal procedures. Organizations have become sensitive to the need to take into account the individual employee's own goals and development, as well as the needs of the company. An issue that arises in the MNE is how to adapt HR strategy and policies to differing countries where its subsidiary employees are located. Each country has its own set of employment laws, and in each country, social and cultural factors play important roles in work values and practices. International HR managers increasingly realize the fact that motivating staff in different locations requires differing approaches and reward systems.

- **Marketing** – Marketing focuses on satisfying the needs and expectations of customers. Marketing covers a range of related activities, including product offering,

Figure 1.4 **Business functions in the organizational environment**

branding, advertising, pricing, and distribution of goods. The large MNE might be assumed to devise a global marketing strategy for all markets, but, in fact, MNEs now tend to adapt products and marketing communications to differing country markets. Language, religion and values are all aspects of culture which affect consumer preferences in different markets (discussed further in Chapter 6). As MNEs turn their focus to the large emerging markets, especially China and India, they encounter considerable cultural diversity. These are some of the greatest challenges in international marketing, but their market potential makes them attractive opportunities.

- **Research and Development (R&D)** – R&D is the function of seeking new knowledge and applications which can lead to new and improved products or processes. R&D activities are part of the larger focus on innovation in the company. **Innovation** covers the full range of activities carried out by all within the organization to seek improvements and new ways of doing things, which can enhance competitiveness. (Innovation is discussed fully in Chapter 10.) R&D tends to focus on scientific and technical research, which is key to new product development. Pharmaceutical companies typically spend huge sums on R&D, as new medicines are their chief source of profits. For the media or internet company, innovation relies on creating new content (often adapted to new markets) and new ways of delivering content to the consumer.

Each of the business functions adapts and changes as a business expands internationally, as shown in the following examples:

- Financial reporting will involve different regulatory environments and accounting standards. Operations will be linked in global production networks.
- HRM will adapt to different cultures and laws.
- Marketing strategy will be designed for differing markets.
- R&D will be configured in different locations according to specialist skills in each.

For the international manager, understanding the differing cultural environments where the company operates, together with the various functional activities that take place in each unit, is crucial to the overall achievement of the company's goals. A company's approach to these challenges depends heavily on its own background and ways of engaging with other cultures, as we find in the next section.

research and development (R&D) seeking new knowledge and applications which can lead to new and improved products or processes

innovation activities which seek improvements and new ways of doing things

---

Summary points Business functions

- The main business functions are finance and accounting, operations, HRM, marketing and R&D.
- In a small firm, functions are typically carried out by staff who are mainly generalists, but the large organization has specialist departments.
- Functional strategies and policies in the MNE tend to be determined by the head office, but in the decentralized organization, there is much autonomy at local level.
- Some functions, such as R&D, are now seen as best located in the environment where the research skills are located.

The firm's view on the world

A company might aspire to be a global leader in its field, and might have technologically superior products, but it must still organize global production efficiently and offer attractive products to consumers at keen prices in a wide variety of different national markets. Some companies have proved themselves to be adept in meeting these challenges, while others struggle. The company tends to see the world at least

▶ More online ... The transnationality index can be found at the website of the
UN Conference on Trade and Development (UNCTAD) at www.unctad.org

partly through the eyes of its own country's national culture. How does this affect its success internationally?

Perspectives on other cultures, held by both individuals and organizations, vary from the ethnocentric at one extreme to the polycentric at the other. The **ethnocentric** organization has an unquestioning belief that its own national culture and ways of doings things are the best. A strong sense of national power can be a source of this outlook, along with a view that the country's culture and history have helped to make it a world leader. Companies based in the US and Japan are usually cited as ethnocentric. The ethnocentric company tends to be dominated by the head office in its home country, which takes the major strategic decisions. Japanese companies have been noted for modelling all their foreign operations on those in their home country, overseen by experienced managers sent from Japan. However, these companies have adapted their manufacturing methods to differing cultures as their operations have become internationalized. This apparent shift might reflect the focus in Japanese management practices on harmony and employee involvement.

ethnocentric an unquestioning belief that one's own national culture and ways of doings things are the best

polycentric openness to other cultures and ways of doing things

The **polycentric** organization is one which is open to other cultures and ways of doing things. It accepts that its own cultural assumptions are a part of its background, but strives to understand and work with those in other countries as it becomes international in scope. The polycentric company appreciates the need for cross-cultural skills in international business (discussed in Chapter 6). Small, open countries are often cited as those which tend to have more polycentric organizations. A transnationality index has been compiled by the UN Conference on Trade and Development (UNCTAD) every year since 1995. It surveys the relative importance of foreign assets, employees and revenues for individual companies. Those ranked the highest have the highest proportions of foreign over home weightings in each category. The top ten companies are shown in Table 1.2, with the addition of a few other notable companies in the rankings.

Table 1.2 **Transnationality index**

Transnationality ranking	Company	Home country	Industry	Transnationality index (%)
1	Barrick Gold Mining	Canada	Mining	94
2	Xtrata	UK	Mining	92
3	Linde	Germany	Industrial and construction	89
4	Pernod Ricard	France	Beverages	87
5	WPP	UK	Business services	87
6	Liberty Global	US	Telecommunications	85
7	Vodafone	UK	Telecommunications	85
8	Philips Electronics	Netherlands	Electricals and electronics	85
9	Nestlé	Switzerland	Food and beverages	83
10	Hutchinson Whampoa	Hong Kong (China)	Telecommunications	83
Selected others				
11	Honda	Japan	Motor vehicles	82
71	General Electric	US	Electricals and electronics	53
87	Toyota	Japan	Motor vehicles	45
92	Walmart	US	Retailing	41

Source: UN (2008) *World Investment Report 2008* (Geneva: UN)

As can be seen, only one US company is in the top ten, and no Japanese companies, although Honda, the Japanese carmaker, is ranked eleven. Honda has been highly successful internationally. It is generally felt that the polycentric firm is better able to succeed in international business than the ethnocentric one, as its managers are better able to adapt to local conditions. These firms, however, tend to be more decentralized, giving latitude to local managers, which can make it more difficult for them to pursue global strategic goals. In this respect, therefore, the ethnocentric firm might have an edge, as it imposes its own systems on all subsidiaries, and maintains a strong corporate culture, which tends to override the national cultures of local subsidiaries.

geocentric organization which aims to focus on global corporate goals, but allowing for local responses and adaptation

A third category is the geocentric organization, which lies between the ethnocentric and polycentric approaches. The **geocentric** organization aims to focus on global corporate goals, but allowing for local responses and adaptation (Perlmutter, 1969). The geocentric approach sees the differing local environments as a potential source of value, rather than as an obstacle to be overcome, and aims to recognize local inputs within a global perspective.

Summary points **The firm's view on the world**

◆ The ethnocentric firm views the world through the values and norms of its own national culture, tending to impose these ways of thinking on foreign operations and markets.

◆ The polycentric firm is open to different cultures, seeking to understand foreign operations and markets in terms of their distinctive cultural environments.

◆ The geocentric firm aims to balance central control with adaptation to cultural differences in diverse locations.

Critical thinking

The company's world vision

Think of some companies you are familiar with, for example as a frequent customer. Which ones are ethnocentric, and which are polycentric? Which of these companies are more successful in the current competitive environment?

The enterprise in the international environment

The opening case study of this chapter featured a number of aspects of the environment which impact on companies and pose challenges for managers. Among these were the cultural and political environments. These dimensions of the environment stem largely from the characteristics which go to make up societies: every society has a cultural heritage, a social makeup, distinctive economic activities, political arrangements, one or more legal frameworks and technological capacities. A description of each of these aspects of a society gives a picture of the society as a whole. However, these dimensions do not stop at national borders. Any dimension will have a layered perspective in terms of geography. For example, the political environment is made up of local community, national government and international relations. These are shown in Figure 1.5. For enterprises, it is necessary to see both the small picture, such as local politics, as well as the big picture, which might be the country's position in relation to trading partners. In fact, understanding the big picture sometimes helps in understanding local currents, and vice versa. Thus, local political leaders could well be influential in attracting a foreign investor wishing to build a factory, from a country with which the national government has concluded a trade and investment agreement. We first identify the dimensions and layers.

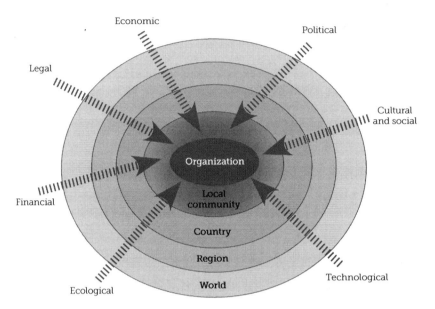

Figure 1.5 **The dimensions and layers of the international environment**

Multiple dimensions

PEST analysis of a national environment which stands for political, economic, social and technological dimensions

Dimensions of the environment are shown in Figure 1.5. These key dimensions can be grouped in a **PEST** analysis, which stands for political, economic, social and technological dimensions. Detailed elements of the PEST framework are shown in Table 1.3.

To make the PEST analysis more complete, the legal environment is considered with the political, and the cultural environment is taken with the social, making it the sociocultural environment. This book recognizes the usefulness of the latter combination, as reflected in Chapter 6. However, we focus on the political and legal environments separately (in Chapters 7 and 8), highlighting the interconnections between the two dimensions. We also add the financial environment and ecological environment, in Chapters 9 and 11. They occur in Part 4, on global issues, as these are areas which have grown in global significance. The technological environment, also highly globalized, falls in Part 4 for the same reason. All these dimensions interact to some extent. The PEST analysis, therefore, is a blunt tool for understanding societies. It also tends to take a rather static view, not capturing changes over time. In this book, we aim to do both: to look at background forces and changes taking place. In many instances, there is tension between established norms and institutions, on the one hand, and, on the other, newer forces seeking to bring about changes – often changes emanating from outside the country. Bearing these dynamics in mind, we describe each of these dimensions below:

- *Cultural and social environment* – covers values, attitudes, norms of behaviour and social relations among people who can be identified as a coherent group. Cultures are usually grouped as national cultures, which are held together by language, a historical sense of belonging and a loyalty to a national homeland. As

Table 1.3 **PEST Analysis in the international business environment**

Political and legal
• Political stability • Form of government, for example democratic, authoritarian • Level of freedoms, for example freedom of expression and association • Incentives to foreign investors • Competition law and policy • Employment law
Economic
• Level of economic development • Trends in GDP • Rate of inflation • Wage levels and level of unemployment • Strength of currency and convertibility • Rates of taxation
Sociocultural
• Growth rate of population, and age distribution of population • Language(s) • Main religious and cultural groupings • Educational attainment levels • Level of social cohesion • Role of women
Technological
• Government spending on R&D • Legal regime for patent protection • Energy availability and costs • Transport infrastructure and costs • Innovation system, including availability of skilled workforce • Level of technology transfer

indicated above, however, national cultures are only part of a person's identity. Religions, which have adherents worldwide, may play an important part. Lifestyle, such as modern consumer lifestyle is also relevant to people, and lifestyle reflects many aspects of a person's life apart from national culture, such as age, education, and whether he or she lives in an urban or rural setting.

- *Economic environment* – covers the kind of economic activities that make up people's livelihoods, the country's sources of wealth and the extent of the country's industrialization. The economy's growth rate is an indicator of the economy's overall health, as is its ability to provide new jobs for those coming into the labour market each year. Key to creating jobs is whether the country is attracting foreign companies wishing to set up business. This foreign direct investment (discussed in the next chapter) has been a major driver of globalization, which has brought economic growth to many developing economies.

- *Political environment* – covers the country's system of government and the powerful groups and individuals who shape the way it operates in practice. All businesses, domestic and foreign, seek a stable political environment, preferably one which encourages enterprise activities. In some countries, political power is concentrated, and in others, democratic processes are more influential in determining who wields political power. The existence of freedom of expression for individuals and media is also an indication of the type of political environment in a country.

- *Legal environment* – covers the system of laws within a country, backed up by the authority of the state. It covers how laws are made and how they are enforced in practice. In any country, businesses look for clarity and predictability in the laws that pertain to them, with fair, impartial implementation and enforcement. These characteristics indicate the existence of the rule of law in a country. Where a country is fragmented, with differing law-making authorities in separate regions, instability can result, making it more difficult to do business in the country, especially for foreign firms unfamiliar with the differing authorities.

- *Technological environment* – covers the nature and extent of applied scientific knowledge, which is used for practical purposes. The depth of a country's scientific education and training, and the extent of government funding for R&D are indicators of the country's technological environment. It is important for businesses that new products and inventions are protected in law. These assets are referred to as **intangible assets**, as they represent rights over products, which can be exploited. They can be contrasted with **tangible assets**, which are physical assets such as machinery and stock. Intangible assets are protected by laws relating to **intellectual property (IP)**. They include patents for the firm's inventions, copyright for written works, music, film and software, and trademarks, such as company logos. As countries climb the technological ladder, the protection and enforcement of IP rights are demanded by businesses (discussed in Chapter 10).

- *Financial environment* – covers banking and other financial services which serve other businesses as well as consumers. National financial systems differ in their openness to outsiders, their transparency and their levels of regulation. Most countries' financial systems have become more open in recent years to outside investors such as foreign banks wishing to set up operations in the country or invest in domestic companies. However, financial markets are prone to volatility, and investors look to well-capitalized banks and sound regulatory systems to maintain confidence and stability. When confidence wanes in one part of the world, it can quickly spread across financial institutions in other parts of the world, as the crisis of 2008 demonstrated.

- *Ecological environment* – covers all living things and relationships between them in their natural habitats. Environmental degradation in today's world has been caused substantially by human activity, especially through industrialization, urbanization and modern large-scale agriculture. Businesses are gaining greater knowledge and awareness of the environmental impacts of their operations in differing locations, as well as their impacts on global phenomena such as climate change.

intangible assets rights over products, such as trademarks and patents, which can be exploited commercially; they can be contrasted with tangible assets

tangible assets physical assets such as machinery and stock

intellectual property (IP) property in intangible assets, such as patents, copyrights and trademarks, which can be legally protected from use by others unless permission is obtained from the owner

Summary points **Multiple dimensions**

- ◆ The PEST analysis takes in four essential aspects of the environment, which can be supplemented by additional elements, including the legal environment as a separate dimension, the financial

environment and the ecological environment.
- ◆ Each of the dimensions of the environment covers a range of phenomena, including institutions, processes and historical legacies.

- ◆ The PEST analysis is a rather blunt instrument in that it underestimates changes over time and interactions with other dimensions.

The multilayered environment

It is common to speak of *global* firms facing competition in the *global* environment, but in fact, global competition is frequently played out in local environments. Local companies, with their intimate knowledge of local markets, can be some of the toughest competitors which global companies encounter. The international environment can be conceived as layered spatial areas, visualized as concentric circles, beginning with the smallest unit, the local community. Local communities exist in the larger unit of the country, which is itself part of a geographic region, and beyond that, the world. These layers are shown in Table 1.4. The table gives examples of key phenomena as well as relevant institutions and organizations in each sphere. There is considerable interaction and interdependence between these different spheres as countries and regions become more interconnected. Growing connectedness

Table 1.4 **Dimensions and layers of the international environment**

Layers and dimensions	Local community	Country	Region	World
Cultural and social	Families; local customs; schools; urban or rural	National culture; language; sense of shared history	Cultural affinity across the region; movement of people between countries	Human rights; world religions; consumer culture
Economic	Local businesses; predominant industries	National industries; industrial structure; national income and economic growth	Degree of economic integration; regional trade relations	Global economic integration; WTO and multilateral trade agreements; global companies and industries
Political	Local government and politics	Political system; degree of civil and political freedoms	Degree of political co-operation; shared institutions (for example the EU)	International governmental co-operation (for example the UN)
Legal	Delegated law-making; planning; health and safety	Rule of law; independent judiciary and court system; national legislation	Legal harmonization; mutual recognition of court judgments	International law and the International Court of Justice (ICJ)
Technological	Schools and colleges; research centres	National school system; universities; government funding for R&D	Cross-border research ties; co-operation among universities	Global spread of breakthrough technology; global R&D networks
Financial	Penetration of banks and financial services	National financial system; regulatory system	Cross-border financial flows; regional regulation (for example the European Central Bank)	Global financial flows; international institutions (for example the IMF and World Bank)
Ecological	Ecosystems; pollution levels; air quality	Areas of environmental stress; environmental protection laws	Regional institutions; co-operation over regional resources (for example rivers)	Climate change; international co-operation on emissions reduction

between people and organizations is a quintessential aspect of globalization, discussed in the next chapter. It is tempting to fall for the view that all aspects of the business environment are inevitably moving towards the global, but this would be a mistake. Some aspects of the international environment seem to be moving towards global governance, such as financial regulation, but each layer of the environment has its own characteristics and players. Although they are becoming interconnected, they are not melding together into a whole, but retain distinctiveness, which business strategists ignore at their peril.

We look at each of these layers from the perspective of the business:

* *Local community* – Wherever the MNE operates, there will be a local community in which its impacts are immediate. A factory or other industrial process impacts on local people and the natural environment in the area. As an employer, it can bring jobs and wealth, but its impact on the environment is potentially damaging. These are stakeholder issues which involve dialogue within local communities.

* *Country* – The national environment is probably the most influential for a business. National laws cover company regulation, employment conditions and the environment. A country's national culture is influential in strategic decisions about potential markets and location of operations. A country's political system and leadership decide the policies which determine how stable it will be for foreign business investors.

* *Region* – Every country is located in a region and is drawn into relations with neighbouring countries. These relations can give rise to conflicts – regional wars are sadly not uncommon. But relations are more often beneficial. Regional trade agreements have flourished in recent years, allowing for free movement of goods between countries in the region. The European Union (EU) is the most highly developed regional grouping (discussed in Chapter 3). Regions can pool resources to deal with common threats such as climate change.

* *World* – There is increasing awareness of global phenomena, such as climate change, which require co-operation among all players, both businesses and governments, at all levels. To co-ordinate this co-operation, global regulatory frameworks are emerging. This is happening in respect of climate change. It is also happening in the area of human rights and financial regulation. Although national structures have been dominant in these areas, international frameworks are gaining authority. The international organizations highlighted in Table 1.4 are introduced in the next chapter. Business strategists are now looking beyond national regulation to rule-making at international level.

Summary points   Multiple layers

◆ The international enterprise encounters a range of distinctive geographical environments, beginning with the community and moving outward to the country, region and global environments.

◆ There is interaction and interdependence between these layers.
◆ Each environmental dimension, such as the political environment, is observable in each of these layers.

◆ In some areas, such as financial regulation, international rule-making is becoming more important, but national and regional institutions remain pivotal, often acting in conjunction with international organizations.

Critical thinking

The multilayered environment

The MNE must be attuned to the changing environment at local, national, regional and global levels. In many areas, such as climate change, there is potentially conflict between the signals coming from these differing sources. Which should have priority for the MNE, or can it balance all of them?

The enterprise in a dynamic environment

Decisions about what the firm ought to be doing, and how, were discussed in the early sections of this chapter. Here we revisit that process, focusing on the environmental context. The firm's purpose is derived largely from its expertise and experience, usually beginning in its home market. The experience it gains from international expansion can contribute to a redefining of its aims as it grows. This evolution depends, too, on its activities in foreign countries, and the extent to which foreign partners play a part in strategy formation. As we have seen, the polycentric company is likely to be more outward looking and decentralized than the ethnocentric company. On the other hand, ethnocentric companies number among the world's largest and most famous brands. Coca-Cola and McDonald's are two, both of which are in food and beverages, sectors which are noted for differing national preferences. These companies, both US American, grew internationally as their products typified American lifestyle, which has been influential in the growth of consumer societies across the world. They have adapted to local differences in different countries, while maintaining a focus on their global brands. These companies are now pursuing growth strategies in the large emerging markets of China and India. In their home market, where growth has slowed, they are seeking innovations in healthier alternatives to their traditional products, the Big Mac and Classic Coke. As these changes show, strategy is closely linked to the changing environment. When established markets slow, companies aim to pursue new opportunities worldwide.

Large firms have become adept at designing global strategy which takes account of local differences. Indeed, local differences can be turned into a source of competitive advantage for the MNE. We see this thinking behind the decisions of large MNEs to outsource manufacturing in low-cost countries. This trend, discussed further in the next chapter, has had significant impacts in both home and host countries. Consumers in developed countries have benefited from a huge range of products at lower prices than those manufactured in their own countries. Host economies have benefited from the investment of foreign companies, the employment created, and the opportunities to gain valuable technological expertise. The greatest beneficiaries have been the large emerging economies, China in particular.

The geographical scanning of MNEs has had consequences in the ways companies perceive the international environment. Developing countries that host outsourced manufacturing are no longer perceived as remote by brand owners and consumers. Workers in outsourced factories are stakeholders of the MNE, even though not employed by it. The host country's government, too, is a stakeholder, whose law and policies are influential for the MNE. In addition, growing concern at international level regarding human rights has heightened awareness of this issue among the company's most valued stakeholders – its shareholders. For the student of international business, the coming together of global and local forces is one of the aspects of the business environment which is becoming most challenging. International markets offer opportunities for the MNE, but they also pose risks. When rethinking long-term strategy, especially in times of economic downturn, some MNEs find it prudent to curb international expansion and focus on familiar markets close to home. For others, the lure of international expansion, especially in emerging markets, is perceived as a golden opportunity when home markets are becalmed. These divergent approaches are explored in the next chapter.

Summary points   **The business in its environment**

- The company evolves as it branches out into new environments. This is true even of ethnocentric companies.

- Global corporate strategies take account of local conditions and preferences.

- Manufacturing in low-cost countries has boosted economic growth in the large developing countries, and has led to abundant low-cost consumer goods in developed countries.

A symbol of modern consumer society: the glistening new shopping mall is a magnet for shoppers, and can now be found in many different countries, especially the large emerging markets

Source: Istock

Conclusions

1 The business enterprise exists to provide goods or services of value to its customers. It interacts with a range of stakeholders, including employees, consumers, the community and society in general.

2 A business typically starts life as the project of an entrepreneur, who invests energy, creativity and resources into the new enterprise.

3 Owners of businesses register them as companies to obtain the advantages of limited liability. Many remain private companies, especially family firms, but many go on to become public companies, attracting outside investors.

4 The multinational enterprise (MNE), consisting of a parent company and subsidiaries, has become a favoured organizational model for international expansion.

5 The company's chief executive officer (CEO) is accountable to the board of directors, which in turn is accountable to the company's shareholders for how the business is run.

6 Accountability mechanisms within companies are the focus of current debate, prompted by public concerns on issues such as risk strategy and executive pay.

7 The key business functions are carried out by all businesses, but in large companies they take the form of specialist departments. As businesses grow and expand internationally, possibilities emerge for changing location and policies in each functional area.

8 Companies differ in their perspectives on the world. The ethnocentric firm sees the world in terms of its own values, while the polycentric firm is more open to ideas from other cultures. The geocentric firm focuses on both corporate goals and local responses.

9 Multiple dimensions of a national environment can be expressed in terms of the PEST analysis: political, economic, sociocultural and technological environments. However, other important dimensions would include financial, legal and ecological.

10 The firm's external environment can also be visualized in layers: local, national, regional and global. Environmental dimensions, such as the political environment, manifest themselves at each of these levels.

Review questions

1 How does a business decide what its goals will be, and in what markets?

2 Define stakeholders and explain the stakeholder approach to corporate strategy.

3 What is CSR, and why is it becoming more important in the formation of corporate goals?

4 What are the advantages and disadvantages of being a sole trader?

5 What are the aspects of the limited company which distinguish it from other types of business ownership?

6 What is distinctive about the entrepreneurial enterprise?

7 What is distinctive about the MNE as a type of organization?

8 Explain the reasons behind the adoption of multidivisional structure for large companies.

9 How does corporate governance differ from the day-to-day management of a company?

10 Why are independent (non-executive) directors considered essential in corporate governance?

11 Explain the shareholder and stakeholder perspectives on corporate governance.

12 Describe each of the main functions within the business enterprise.

13 The polycentric organization might be thought to be advantageous in international operations, but many successful MNEs have been ethnocentric. Why might this be the case?

14 What are the advantages and limitations of a PEST analysis?

Key revision concepts

Company, p. 13; Corporate governance, p. 17; Corporate social responsibility (CSR), p. 10; Emerging economy/market, p. 6; Entrepreneur, p. 12; Ethnocentric/polycentric organization, p. 24; Intellectual property, p. 28; Market, p. 6; Multinational enterprise, p. 14; PEST analysis, p. 26; Privatization, p. 17; Public company, p. 13; Shareholder, p. 13; Stakeholder, p. 9

Assignments

◆ Offer advice to the following CEO: Tom is the CEO of a large retailing company whose recent financial performance, especially in its established western markets, has been lacklustre. Competitors are gaining ground in large emerging economies, but these can be costly to enter. Tom's board of directors is dominated by members of the founding family who are very risk-averse.

◆ The PEST analysis was designed to illuminate specific dimensions of a national environment. How can it be adapted to take into account other dimensions and broader scope, bringing in regional and global impacts?

Further reading

Bartlett, C. and Ghoshal, S. (2002) *Managing Across Borders: The Transnational Solution*, 2nd edn (Boston: Harvard Business School Press).

Brown, A. (1998) *Organisational Culture*, 2nd edn (London: Pitman).

Johnson, G., Scholes, K. and Whittington, R. (2004) *Exploring Corporate Strategy*, 7th edn (London: Pearson).

Kay, J. (2000) *Foundations of Corporate Success* (Oxford: Oxford University Press).

Mintzberg, H. (2000) *The Rise and Fall of Strategic Planning* (London: Financial Times Prentice Hall).

Monks, R. and Minow, N. (2003) *Corporate Governance* (Oxford: Blackwell).

Mullins, L. (2004) *Management and Organizational Behaviour*, 7th edn (London: Financial Times Prentice Hall).

Prahalad, C.K. (2009) *The Fortune at the Bottom of the Pyramid* (Philadelphia: Wharton School Publishing).

Pugh, D.S. (ed.) (1995) *Organization Theory: Selected Readings*, 4th edn (London: Penguin Books).

Quinn, J., Mintzberg, H., James, R., Lampel, J. and Ghoshal, S. (eds) (2003) *The Strategy Process* (London: Financial Times Prentice Hall).

Wheelen, T. and Hunger, J. (2009) *Strategic Management and Business Policy*, 12th edn (New Jersey: Addison Wesley).

Cemex constructing a brighter future

The opening case study featured a youthful entrepreneurial company, Facebook, which, based in the US, has shot to fame in the fast-moving internet world. Here we turn to an established company, over a hundred years old, based in a poor country, Mexico, in a sector perceived as unglamorous: construction and cement. Perspectives on the sector differ, however. Whereas the rich world views cement as a commodity, and a highly pollutant one at that, in the developing world cement is more valued as a branded product, resonating with people aspiring for improved housing and more comfortable lives. Cemex has long focused on low-cost housing in its home market, alongside financing schemes to bring better housing within the reach of the poor. But it attracts attention mainly for its ambitious global expansion.

Although Cemex's predecessor company was formed in 1906, the formation of Cementos Mexicanos, later changed to Cemex for short, dates from the 1931 merger of two companies under the leadership of Lorenzo Zambrano. The company remained national in scope and relatively unambitious for 35 years, enjoying a privileged position in the rather closed Mexican market for cement and construction materials. But when the Mexican economy gradually opened up in the 1970s, creating more competitive markets, Cemex decided the time was right to embark on expansion by acquisition, both in Mexico and internationally. It listed as a public company on the Mexican stock exchange in 1976. Domestic acquisitions in Mexico propelled it to domination of the Mexican cement market by 1990. But the Zambrano family, which still runs the company, had far greater ambitions in mind. Lorenzo Zambrano, the founder's grandson, took over as chairman and CEO in 1985, posts he still held in 2010.

Cemex is now the world's third largest cement company, after Lafarge of France and Holcim of Switzerland. Cement as a sector relies on building activity to flourish, and its fortunes, along with those of its rivals, can dive when economies slow down and construction declines, as happened in the rich world in the recent recession. As an emerging-market multinational, Cemex has benefited from its experience in a poor developing country to gain advantages in other developing countries.

It has acquired businesses in Spain, throughout Latin America and in Asia, but its most ambitious acquisitions have been in the US and UK (see figure). It has long targeted the US market, where its advantages of an efficient, low-cost approach help to build market share. It purchased Southdown, a Texas company, in 2001, which it combined with existing American operations, making it the largest cement maker in the US. Cemex went on to buy RMC of the UK in 2005. The purchase of Rinker Group of Australia in 2007 was a turning point for Cemex. Cemex had to borrow in the region of $14 billion from banks to finance the purchase, which Zambrano felt was worth it because of Rinker's strong presence in the US. This was despite the fact that the US Justice Department required Cemex to shed 39 ready-mix concrete facilities in the US because of its potentially dominant market position in some localities. The takeover of Rinker was a huge gamble, and the aftermath proved to be a difficult period for the company, as the US housing slump soon followed. Cemex's share price, by now quoted on the New York Stock Exchange, plunged from $37

A business empire built on cement: Cemex has pursued its global ambitions from its solid foundation in Mexico

Source: Cemex

in 2007 to just $4 in 2009. Cemex had to sell Rinker's Australian operations to Holcim in 2009, to help pay down the debt.

A setback occurred in 2008 when Venezuela nationalized Cemex's operations in the country. Other cement makers settled compensation terms with the Venezuelan government, but Cemex held out for a better deal. Despite the setbacks, in 2010, Zambrano was upbeat about the company's ability to manage the debt and revitalize the business. He has contemplated selling minority stakes in some of the company's many wholly owned subsidiaries around the world. One of Cemex's chief advantages in global markets has been its skill in utilizing information technology (IT), bringing efficiency to all its operations, which competitors find hard to match. Cemex has been conscious of the challenges posed by climate change, and has made strides in reducing emissions and incorporating sustainability goals into its strategy.

Although a public company, Cemex remains in the control of the founding family. Family members do not hold the bulk of the company's shares, but they dominate its corporate governance. Only one of the thirteen members of the board of directors is independent; six are members of the Zambrano family. One might question whether the company's governance structure is able to provide the independent oversight needed for running a public company. In particular, risky acquisitions and excessive

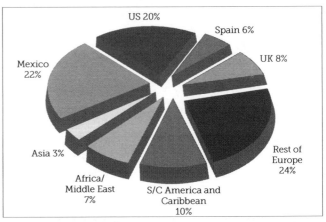

Breakdown of Cemex sales

Source: Cemex Annual Report, 2009, at www.cemex.com

debt have arguably been problematic from a strategy perspective, but the insider-controlled board was not in a position to question the running of the company. Cemex is now eyeing new acquisitions in the large emerging markets, where it feels its competitive advantages can be exploited. Lessons of the recession for many MNEs have been to strengthen independent corporate governance structures and to pay greater heed to the interests of stakeholders. For now, Cemex is not going down this road of corporate reform.

Sources: Cemex Annual Report, 2009, at www.cemex.com; Thomson, A. (2010) 'Cemex to cut debt in stakes sale', *Financial Times*, 26 April; Patalon, W. (2007) 'Global Cement Giant Cemex looks to cut costs, debt after Riker Buyout', *Money Morning*, 14 December, at http://moneymorning.com; Lapper, R. and Wheatley, J. (2008) 'Higher ground', *Financial Times*, 11 March

Questions for discussion

- How did Cemex build its dominance in Mexico?
- How was Cemex able to expand so rapidly in global markets? Are its prospects bright for future expansion?
- What are the shortcomings of Cemex's corporate governance?

Chapter 2

The business context and products (goods and services)

Introduction and chapter overview

The purpose of the organization drives its strategic development and the way in which it views its place in society. This purpose is often articulated through the vision and mission statements and enacted through products and strategy. The combination of business context, products and strategy gives rise to a range of business models that are employed as important aspects of competitive strategy.

In this chapter, we discuss the purpose of the organization and profile the different types of business models before examining what we mean by products and the need for a balanced product portfolio. The chapter provides the first stage or foundations for understanding what organizations are all about, and sets the context within which the internal environmental analysis can be undertaken.

Learning objectives

After studying this chapter, you should be able to:

- explain how to determine the purpose of an organization
- identify different types of business models
- define what is meant by a product and describe Kotler's five levels of product benefit
- describe and criticize Copeland's product typology
- understand the stages in, and uses of, the product life cycle
- explain the concept of 'portfolio'
- describe the composition and limitations of the BCG matrix and the GE matrix

2.1 Business purpose, context and models

The purpose of a business or organization is reflected in the vision and mission statements. These are then translated into strategic intent, strategic aims, objectives and, ultimately, action and direction. As such, the purpose of the organization is central to its strategic development.

The **vision** is an attempt to articulate what the organization should be like in the future. It is what the organization is seeking to become.

The **vision** tends to be long term in nature and defines the desired future state of the organization in terms of its contributions to stakeholders, society and its strategic direction. Examples of vision statements include PepsiCo, which claims

37

The **mission statement** provides direction for the organization by defining what the organization is and its reason for existing. As such, the mission statement often encapsulates the vision and values.

'Our vision is put into action through programs and a focus on environmental stewardship, activities to benefit society, and a commitment to build shareholder value by making PepsiCo a truly sustainable company', and Oxfam, which claims 'that diverse communities of women and men living in poverty will exercise their rights to a decent and secure standard of living in a rich industrialized society'.

The **mission statement** is a short, succinct statement of the purpose or reason for existence of the organization. Google's mission is to 'organize the world's information and make it universally accessible and useful', while Nike claims 'To bring inspiration and innovation to every athlete in the world. If you have a body, you are an athlete.'

This purpose is also influenced by the business context within which the organisation operates. Commonly, business context can be divided into for-profit organizations, non-profit organizations (commonly public sector) and not-for-profit organizations (voluntary or charity sector). It is the context that will influence what the organization seeks to achieve and how it measures success. The context will also influence the business model.

What is a business model? According to Slywotzky (1996, p. 52), a business model is:

> the totality of how a company selects its customers, defines and differentiates its offerings, defines the tasks it will perform itself and those it will outsource, configures its resource, goes to market, creates utility for customers, and captures profits. It is the entire system for delivering utility to customers and earning a profit from that activity.

So business models are fundamental to the design of the organization. Business models also reflect the technological and other environmental changes that occur at the time the business is operating or is formed or evolved.

Business models can be built around:

- *an advertising model*, where revenues (or rents) are earned by adverts, promotions or, in the case of websites, redirecting consumers
- *a brokerage model*, where the business acts as an agent. This includes market exchanges, auctions or classifieds
- *a utility model*, which represents a charge for using the product or service
- *a subscription model*, where revenues come from membership of some 'protected' user group or market
- *a community model*, clearly evident in the use of Web 2.0 technologies and social networking, such as Bebo, Friends Reunited and so on
- *an affiliate model*, where organizations work together to increase market scope or share
- *a manufacturer model*, which represents the classic economic conversion of raw materials into higher value products (goods or services)
- *a merchant model*, either in virtual form, mail order or physical presence
- *an infomediary model*, where information is provided as the core product offering, often combined with other business models.

So there are many different and interrelated or overlapping business models. For the purpose of business strategy, it is useful for us to understand 'what business the organization is in' and what form of business model it is using. We can then better appreciate and understand what the organization is doing, will do, and why.

CASE STUDY   Gate Security Systems Ltd

For the past seven years, Gate Security Systems Ltd (GSS) had provided the technology and staffing for all of the security check-in activities demanded by busy airports in the UK and elsewhere. By 2009, GSS was providing and delivering these services at six airports in Europe as well as three in the UK.

This work is extremely lucrative. All airports have to have state-of-the-art security, so as to be able to pick up any wrongdoing on the part of members of the travelling public. As well as the high-profile attention to 'the terrorist threat', airport security has to be able to detect the smuggling of drugs, firearms and illicit jewellery, gold and silver. Airport security also has to be able to try and relate mismatches and lack of fit in passports, travel documentation and other identity. Airport security has also to be able, when necessary or required, to provide instant tracking for financial transactions and credit card fraud. Airport security systems and technology have to be capable of scanning all kinds of luggage and detecting any explosives, contraband or firearms without any failure or lapse at all.

The airports themselves have to be secure from incursions of any sort. This means that there has to be a system for the checking of vehicle access and egress when people are being set down and picked up, and when they are being ferried to and from the car parks and hotels, which in many cases are many hundred metres from the terminals and points of arrival and departure. This also applies to all deliveries of everything, both to the public and also the secure areas.

GSS undertook to provide all these services, and the company gave guarantees over the absolute integrity of its staff and systems. However, because of the combination of political, media and public pressure for total security in all aspects of air travel and transport operations, a series of hasty, costly and ineffective decisions were taken.

Like many others providing these services around the world, GSS fell foul of what was called 'the rush for technology', which would make all air travel and transport totally secure in the wake of the 9/11 attacks in New York and the 7/7 attacks in London. Again like many others, GSS upgraded its scanning and information processing technology very quickly, only to find that in common with over 150 airports around the world, the equipment could not distinguish fully between solid objects and liquids, if these were in packaging. To be fully effective, therefore, meant that, in practice, every item of hand baggage and checked-in luggage had to be opened and searched. The technology also had difficulty with accurately identifying other substances and items, including clothing made out of nylon or terylene.

Accordingly, this technology had to be discarded shortly after its installation, and then replaced with something that had been better designed and more state of the art. This cost GSS £700m. However, the new technology was also found to be lacking; in particular, some of the most common and notorious faults were:

- it could not distinguish between substances of a similar consistency; in particular, it could not distinguish between semtex explosives and toothpaste
- it could not distinguish between different liquids; although it could identify liquids as being liquids, it could not, for example, distinguish between coffee and paraffin.

These and other faults and shortcomings led to global, international and regional directives on what could and could not be carried in hand luggage and what had to be checked in and placed in the luggage holds of airlines.

There were then additional problems with the security of the airport facilities themselves. Following a small and isolated (but nevertheless very serious) terrorist attack on one of the airports supposedly protected by GSS, a full strategic review was ordered by BAA, the owner and operator of three airports for which GSS provided the security service and technology. The review was scheduled for the first week in September 2009, and it was to take place at Stansted, one of London's airports.

On the day the review was supposed to start, the airport had to be closed because environmental protesters breached the perimeter fence and then staged a sit-in on the main runway. When the review did finally get underway, the following quickly became clear:

- the company had failed to invest in technology upgrades and staff training. Following the £700m loss, it bought the cheapest options that it could find, rather than either searching for the best, or commissioning its own technology
- the need to upgrade security checks and tighten the ability to spot suspicious objects and people as they passed through the airport was undermined by the lack of adequate staffing levels or staff training
- the speed at which people moved through the security check-in processes, especially at busy times, was unacceptable, and following a series of media exposés, the government ordered BAA to improve throughput speeds at all times. When BAA tried to shift the blame on to GSS, the government ignored this, stating that it was up to BAA to sort the matter out immediately.

Because of the environmental protest and demonstration, it had become absolutely clear to the review body that there was a priority need to check the security of airport premises.

Case study questions

1   What is the context in which GSS is carrying out its activities?
2   What is the key business model present, and where

do the fundamental strengths and weaknesses of the approach lie?
3   What is the product/service portfolio on offer here, and to whom? What are the product life cycle problems that have to be addressed in industries, sectors and circumstances such as these?
4   What options are open to the various parties as the result of the review findings indicated above?

2.2   Defining product and services

A **product** is anything that is offered for sale.

A **good** is tangible and is something that can be owned.

A **service** is something that is done on the buyer's behalf and is intangible in nature.

Most organizations will offer their main purpose or 'value proposition' as a product. We can define a **product** as anything that is offered for sale. Hence, a product might be a physical good, such as a car, a service, such as a lawyer, or a mixture of both, such as a restaurant. A **good** is tangible and is something that can be owned. A **service** is something that is done on the buyer's behalf and is intangible in nature. Some products contain both a good and a service element, such as when we purchase hairdressing services from a barber or hairdresser (the service) who then also washes and blow-dries the hair using hair care products (such as shampoo – goods). The totality of the hairdressing product contains both goods and services.

In product strategy, it is useful to think how value might be added to the product from the customer's point of view. To do this, it can be helpful to consider the product's features and benefits in a number of levels. Different approaches can give different numbers of levels. Here we consider Kotler's five-benefit model (1997):

1   *The core benefit* provided by the product. In a car, for example, this would be the ability to transport. Since all the products on the market will provide this benefit, this will rarely be the level on which companies compete.
2   *The generic product*, which includes everything that would be necessary to make the product function. For the car, this might include the seats, appropriate controls and legal safety equipment.
3   *The expected product*, which is all that the customer has come to expect in a product. In our example of a car, this might include a radio, comprehensive guarantee and certain levels of performance.
4   *The augmented product* goes beyond the customer's expectations to provide something extra and desirable, for example air conditioning and on-board satellite navigation in a car.
5   *The potential product* is the product level that encompasses all that the product might ultimately become, but currently does not incorporate. The ownership of a certain car, for example, may confer on the owner a certain status in society, provide them with opportunities that would otherwise not present themselves or even assist in the attraction of a sexual partner.

In mature markets, competition is normally at the augmented product level or above, and the basic product is taken for granted. What is in the expected product in one market may be in the augmented product in another. Air conditioning in a car might be a bonus in a temperate climate, but a necessity in a tropical one. Thus, a car company that had gained a competitive advantage by superior reliability would lose that advantage once all cars had become reliable. It then has to be able to offer something else or face a lack of competitiveness. Over time, the augmented product becomes the expected product, so there has to be a continuous search for something extra to offer.

Augmentation adds to costs, and the company has to consider whether the customer will be willing to pay for the extra costs in the final price. Sometimes, after a period of rivalry, where competitors try to compete by adding more and more features and cost, a market segment emerges for a basic stripped-down, low-cost version that just supplies the expected benefits.

GURU GUIDE

Philip Kotler was born in 1931 in Chicago and received his MA from the University of Chicago and his PhD from MIT. His initial study was in economics and his postdoctoral work was in mathematics at Harvard University and behavioural sciences at University of Chicago. He is currently the SC Johnson & Son Professor of International Marketing at Kellogg School of Management, Northwestern University.

Professor Kotler has extensive consulting experience and has been a member of several boards, including the advisory board of the Drucker Foundation, and he was also the chairman of the College of Marketing of the Institute of Management Sciences. He has several honorary doctorates, most notable among them Stockholm University, the University of Zurich and the University of Economics and Business Administration in Vienna. Professor Kotler has received several best article awards, and other prestigious awards, including the American Marketing Association's Distinguished Marketing Educator Award and the European Association of Marketing Consultants Marketing Excellence Award.

Professor Kotler is a distinguished figure in marketing management. His work has been influential in understanding theories and concepts related to marketing and his work is often considered as seminal in marketing management. He has published extensively in a range of areas of marketing and continues to push forward thinking in the field. Most recently, his work has contributed to debates around social marketing, ethics and 'negative' image.

Copeland's product typology and strategy

There is a commonly held view that different types of products need to be managed and brought to market in different ways. Services, for example, cannot be stored, must be consumed at the point of production, are intangible, and it is difficult to judge quality in advance. As a result of these factors, we might anticipate off-peak pricing offers, the need for supplier credibility, and difficulties in advertising not experienced by physical products. Industrial products are less likely to be sold direct to the end user than consumer products, with advertising being relatively more important for consumer products and high-quality personal contact being relatively more important for industrial products, hence the use of sales representatives to speak directly to industrial buyers.

There have been a number of attempts to build on product characteristics to produce classification systems for products that will serve as a comprehensive guide. A system based on dividing consumer products into convenience, shopping and specialty goods (Copeland, 1923) has endured and is one of the most popular product classification systems used at the present time:

Convenience goods are products where purchase is relatively frequent, at low prices, and the customer sees little interest or risk in the purchase.

- *Convenience goods:* Convenience goods are products where purchase is relatively frequent, at low prices, and the customer sees little interest or risk in the purchase. Examples would include low-price confectionery, batteries and carbonated drinks. As a consequence, the customer will typically buy the product available in the most convenient outlet, and the supplier will have to make the product available in as many outlets as possible. Point of sale display and simple reminder advertising with little information content are likely to be important.

Shopping goods are those that are typically more expensive, of more interest to the purchaser, and some risk is seen in the purchase.

- *Shopping goods:* Shopping goods are those that are typically more expensive, of more interest to the purchaser, and some risk is seen in the purchase. Examples would include cars, PCs and cameras. The customer will typically 'shop around' to make comparisons and gather information. These goods do not, therefore, have to be available in all possible outlets, and promotional material will usually have a high information content. In some categories of shopping goods, such as PCs, customers can demonstrate a high level of technical knowledge that assists them in their purchase and producers must usually satisfy customers on a technical level before a sale is made.

Specialty goods are seen as products that are so differentiated from others, often carrying considerable prestige, that customers may insist on only one brand.

- *Specialty goods:* Specialty goods are seen as products that are so differentiated from others, often carrying considerable prestige, that customers may insist on only one brand. High prices, high levels of service and restricted distribution would be appropriate. An example would be that of Hasselblad cameras, which dominate certain parts of the professional photography market. There is no need or benefit for the products to be available in every camera shop, but they would tend to appear in shops where customers would expect a high level of service and expertise.

Specialty goods: Belgian chocolates

Limitations of Copeland's framework

The use of classification systems is widely accepted by managers and academic researchers. It is easy to show how they work in practice, and many examples can be produced to show how appropriate they are. A strong argument against their slavish adoption is that they can exhibit circular logic. In other words, we examine how a product is marketed, and on this basis assign it to a particular classification. We then use that to say how it *should* be marketed. This is a recipe for maintaining the status quo, and companies adopting this practice, even if implicitly, will never lead with new product strategies. Over time, many products will gradually change from shopping goods to convenience goods. Thus, some watches will be speciality goods, some will be shopping goods, and now the lowest priced watches on the market will effectively be convenience goods.

Changes in technology and customer taste or fashion may also create opportunities for things to be done differently, and there will always be part of a market that will respond to an approach that is different from the norm. Some organizations recognized that technology, in reducing transaction cost, could make telephone banking viable. Avon was built on the basis that some customers would be prepared to buy cosmetics from people selling them on their doorsteps as opposed to buying in conventional retail outlets.

Product type may be a useful starting point to guide management thinking, but it is not a substitute for creativity and analysis.

2.3 The product life cycle

The **product life cycle** is the complete 'life' of a product or service from its inception and growth, through shake-out and maturity, to its eventual decline and death.

The product life cycle concept is based on the analogy with living things, in that they all have a finite life. All products would be expected to have a finite life, whether it be long or short. The life cycle can operate at an individual product level, a product type or a product class level, where arguably a market life cycle would be a more appropriate title. At the individual product level, the product life cycle is a useful tool in product planning, so that a balance of products is kept in various stages of the life cycle.

At the product class level, we can use the product life cycle concept to analyse and predict competitive conditions and identify key issues for management. It is conventionally broken into a number of stages, as shown in Figure 2.1. We shall explore the key issues posed by the different stages.

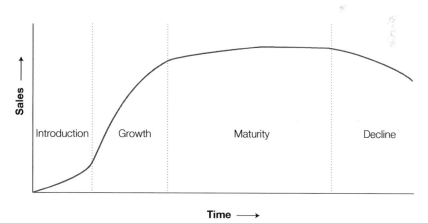

Figure 2.1 The product life cycle

The introduction stage

The introduction stage follows the product's development. It is new to the market and will be bought by 'innovators', a term used to describe a small proportion of the eventual market. The innovators may not be easy to identify in advance and there are likely to be high launch and marketing costs. Because production volumes are likely to be low (because it is still at a 'pilot' stage), the production cost per unit will be high.

The 'price elasticity of demand' will strongly influence whether the product is introduced at a high 'skimming' price, or a low 'penetration' price. Price skimming is appropriate when the product is known to have a price inelastic demand, such as new pharmaceuticals or defence equipment. Penetration is appropriate for products with price elastic demand and when gaining market share is more important than making a fast recovery of development costs.

Pioneer companies – those that are first to the market with a particular product – are usually forced to sell the product idea in addition to an existing brand, and the early promotion may help competitors who enter the market later with 'me too' versions of the product idea.

> **Pioneer companies** are those that are first to market with a particular product.

Entering the market at an early stage is usually risky. Not only will the company be incurring a negative cash flow for a period, but many products fail at this stage. Against this risk is the prospect of increasing market share in the new product area faster than the 'me toos', such that the first product may become the industry standard in future years.

The growth stage

During the growth stage, sales for the market as a whole increase and new competitors typically enter to challenge the pioneer for some of the market share. The competitors may develop new market segments in an attempt to avoid direct competition with the established pioneering market leader.

The market becomes profitable and funds can be used to offset the development and launch costs. This is an important time to win market share, since it is easier to win a disproportionate share of new customers than to get customers to switch brands later on. As new market segments emerge, key decisions will need to be made as to whether to follow them or stay with the original. It has been shown that in the electronic calculator market, for example, demand was initially concentrated among scientists and engineers (Brown, 1991). Then businesses starting using them, then university students and finally the market reached its height when demand was found among schoolchildren. A pioneer wishing to stay in all these markets would have to make the brave decision to move out of organization-to-organization business into a mass consumer market.

The maturity stage

Maturity is reached when a high proportion of people who will eventually purchase a product have already purchased it once. It is likely to be the longest stage, but depending on the market, this could range from days or weeks to many decades. It is important at this stage either to have achieved a high market share, or to dominate a special niche in the market. It can be expensive and risky to achieve large market share changes at this time, so that some companies prefer to concentrate their competitive efforts on retaining existing customers, and competing hard for the small number of new customers appearing.

It has been pointed out that market share among leading competitors is often stable over extremely long periods of time (Mercer, 1993), and this may be used as a criticism of the product life cycle concept. However, over the time of maturity in the market, companies have to be vigilant in detecting change in the market, and be ready to modify or improve products and to undertake product repositioning if necessary.

The decline stage

It is part of product life cycle theory that all markets will eventually decline, and therefore companies have to be ready to move to new markets when decline seems to be inevitable, or to be ready with strategies to extend the life cycle if this is felt to be feasible. Appropriate extension strategies could include developing new uses for the product, finding new users, and repositioning the product to gain a presence in the parts of the market that will remain after the rest of the market has gone. Even where markets have reached an advanced stage of decline, particular segments may remain that can be profitable for organizations able to anticipate their existence and dominate them.

Companies that succeed in declining markets usually adopt a 'milking' strategy, wherein investment is kept to a minimum, and take up any market share that may be left by competitors that have left the market because of the decline. There is a certain recognition that death will come eventually and thus any revenues that can be made in the interim are something of a bonus.

Example   **The human life cycle metaphor**

The concept of life cycle does not just apply to products, it also applies to humans. Human beings undergo a life cycle that has a huge bearing, not just on our biological changes, but also on behaviour.

We undergo introduction when we are conceived and grow inside our mother. After birth, we begin to grow – a process that continues until, after puberty, we reach our full height and weight. Our maturity phase is the longest. For most people, it will last from our mid-teens until the time when our faculties begin to fail us – perhaps in our sixties or seventies. When we reach old age, we begin to decline. Our eyesight may begin to deteriorate, we slow down and we may lose some of our intellectual sharpness. Finally, when decline has run its course, life is no longer viable, and we die.

Criticisms of the product life cycle

The product life cycle appears to be widely understood and used as a tool for strategic analysis and decision-making (Greenley and Bayus, 1993). Despite this, some important criticisms have been made. While it is easy to go back into history and demonstrate all the features of the concept, it is hard to forecast the future and, in particular, it is hard to forecast turning points. Not to try to do so at all, however, would seem to avoid confronting hard strategic issues.

Another criticism is that life cycles may sometimes not be inevitable as dictated by the market, but created by the ineptitude of management. If management assume that decline will come, they will take the decision to reduce investment and advertising in anticipation of the decline. Not surprisingly, decline does come, but sooner that it otherwise would have done had the investment not been withdrawn.

In a large-scale survey of UK companies, Hooley (1995) confirmed the existence of the familiar bell-shaped pattern of sales in many markets. The study challenged the widely held view that profits would be low or negative in the early stages of the life cycle, and found that the market position of organizations could quickly move to profit in the growth stage of the life cycle. This trend has been observed many times in industries such as creative technology, games and fashion. In essence, life cycles are shorter and need to provide returns quicker.

2.4   Product portfolio theory

Given that products represent the main output of an organization, it is essential to ensure that what is offered to the market allows for a sufficient range of products as well as products at different stages of development or maturity. The range of products offered is termed the **product portfolio**. The challenge for organizations is to balance the portfolio to provide a degree of sustainability and return for **stakeholders**.

The **product portfolio** is the range of products offered.

Stakeholders are the people who can influence or are influenced by the organization. They can be primary (active) stakeholders, such as customers, suppliers, labour, financial institutions, or secondary (passive) such as government, local community, lobby groups.

The notion of portfolio exists in many areas of life, not just for products. Underpinning the concept is the need for a business to spread its opportunity and risk. A broad portfolio signifies that a business has a presence in a wide range of product and market sectors. Conversely, a narrow portfolio implies that the organization only operates in a few (or even one) product or market sectors.

A broad portfolio offers the advantage of robustness in that a downturn in one market will not threaten the whole company. Against this advantage is the problem of managing business interests that may be very different in nature – the company may be said to lack strategic focus. An organization operating with a narrow portfolio (perhaps just one sector) can often concentrate solely on its sector but it can become vulnerable if there is a downturn in demand in the one sector it serves.

The BCG matrix

The Boston Consulting Group matrix offers a way of examining and making sense of a company's portfolio of product and market interests. It is a way of viewing the entire product range to see a company's products as a collection of items in a similar way that a holder of shares in several companies might consider the decisions on what to do with the shares.

GURU GUIDE

The **Boston Consulting Group** (BCG) was founded in 1963 by Bruce D. Henderson as the management and consulting division of the Boston Safe Deposit and Trust Company, itself a subsidiary of the Boston Company.

Henderson, a former Bible salesman, had gained an engineering degree from Vanderbilt University before attending Harvard Business School (HBS). He left HBS 90 days before graduation to work for Westinghouse Corporation, where he became one of the youngest vice presidents in the company's history. He left Westinghouse to head Arthur D. Little's management services unit before accepting an improbable challenge from the CEO of the Boston Safe Deposit and Trust Company to start a consulting arm for the bank.

Source: Adapted from the BCG website. See http://www.bcg.com for full details.

One way of looking at the products in a portfolio is to consider each product in its position in the product life cycle and aim to have a balance of products in each stage. A more sophisticated approach is based on the idea that market share in mature markets is highly correlated with profitability, and that it is relatively less expensive and less risky to attempt to win share in the growth stage of the market, when there will be many new customers making a first purchase. This is the approach taken by the BCG matrix. It is used to analyse the product range with a view to aiding decisions on how the products should be treated in an internal strategic analysis. Figure 2.2 shows the essential features of the Boston matrix.

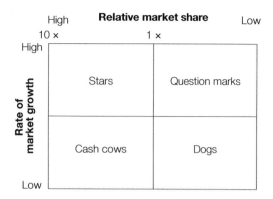

Figure 2.2 The Boston Consulting Group matrix

Source: Product Portfolio Matrix, © 1970, The Boston Consulting Group

The two axes of the matrix are:

- *The market share measure:* The horizontal axis is based on a particular measure of market share – share relative to the largest competitor. A product with a share of 20% of the market, where the next biggest competitor had a share of 10%, would have a relative share of 2, whereas a product with a market share of 20%, and the biggest competitor also had 20%, would have a relative share of 1. The cutoff point between high and low share is 1, so high market share products in this analysis are market leaders. This arrangement of scale is sometimes described as being 'logarithmic' in nature.
- *The market growth measure:* The vertical axis is the rate of market growth, with the most relevant definition of the market being served. A popular point used to divide high and low growth in the market is 10% year-on-year growth, but the authors have found it useful in practical situations to use growth that is faster than the rate of growth in the economy as a whole, which, after inflation, is usually between 1% and 2.5% a year.

The following is a description of the matrix:

- *Cash cows:* A product with a high market share in a low growth market is normally both profitable and a generator of cash. Profits from this product can be used to support other products that are in their development phase. Standard strategy would be to manage conservatively, but to defend strongly against competitors. This product is called a 'cash cow' because profits from the product can be 'milked' on an ongoing basis. This should not be used as a justification for neglect.

- *Dogs:* A product that has a low market share in a low growth market is termed a 'dog', in that it is typically not very profitable. To cultivate the product to increase its market share would incur cost and risk, not least because the market it is in has a low rate of growth. Accordingly, once a dog has been identified as part of a portfolio, it is often discontinued or disposed of. More creatively, opportunities might be found to differentiate the dog and obtain a strong position for it in a niche market. A small share product can be used to price aggressively against a large competitor as it is expensive for the large competitor to follow suit.

- *Stars:* Stars have a high share of a rapidly growing market, and therefore rapidly growing sales. They may be the sales manager's dream, but they could be the accountant's nightmare, since they are likely to absorb large amounts of cash, even if they are highly profitable. It is often necessary to spend heavily on advertising and product improvements, so that when the market slows, these products become cash cows. If market share is lost, the product will eventually become a dog when the market stops growing.

- *Question marks:* Question marks (sometimes termed 'problem children') are aptly named as they create a dilemma. They already have a foothold in a growing market, but if market share cannot be improved, they will become dogs. Resources need to be devoted to winning market share, which requires bravery for a product that may not yet have large sales, or the product may be sold to an organization in a better position to exploit the market.

The matrix does not have an intermediate market share category, but there are large numbers of products that have large market share, but are not market leaders. They may be the biggest profit earners for the companies that own them. They usually compete against the market leader at a disadvantage that is slight, but real. Management need to make efficient use of marketing expenditure for such products and try to differentiate them from the leader. They should not normally compete head on, especially on price, but attempt to make gains if the market changes in a way that the leader is slow to exploit.

Accurate measurement and careful definition of the market are essential to avoid misdiagnosis when using the matrix. Critics, perhaps unfairly, point out that there are many relevant aspects relating to products that are not taken into account, but it was never claimed by The Boston Consulting Group that the process was a panacea and covered all aspects of strategy. Above all, the matrix helps to identify which products to push or drop, and when. It helps in the recognition of windows of opportunity, and is strong evidence against simple rules of thumb for allocating resources to products.

A composite portfolio model: the GE matrix

The limitations of the BCG matrix have given rise to a number of other models that are intended to take a greater number of factors into account, and to be more flexible in use. A leading example is the General Electric (GE) matrix, developed by McKinsey & Company in conjunction with the General Electric company in the USA. It is mainly applied to strategic business units (SBUs) such as the subsidiaries of a holding company. The model rates market attractiveness as high, medium or low, and competitive strength as strong, medium or weak. SBUs are placed in the appropriate category, and although there is no automatic strategic prescription, the position is used to help devise an appropriate strategy.

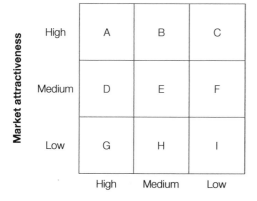

Figure 2.3 The GE matrix

Source: C.W. Hofer and D. Schendal, *Strategy Formulation: Analytical Concepts*, copyright 1978 West Publishing

Market attractiveness criteria will be set by the user, and could include factors such as market growth, profitability, strength of competition, entry/exit barriers, legal regulation and so on. Competitive strength could include technological capability, brand image, distribution channel links, production capability and financial strength. The flexibility to include as many variables as required is useful, but could lead to oversubjectivity. Most users of the model recommend that the variables be given a weighting to establish their relative importance, which will, in turn, reduce the potential for bias. In practice, managers tend to be aware that the tool is likely to be used as a basis for resource allocation and, consequently, they may attempt to influence the analysis in the favour of their own product or SBU. The analysis gives rise to a three-by-three matrix (Figure 2.3).

The GE matrix can be described as follows:

- For products in cell A, the company would invest strongly, as this is potentially an attractive strategic position, where distinctive competences can be harnessed to good opportunities.
- In B, the company could be aggressive and attempt to build strength in order to challenge, or it could build selectively.
- In C, there are real dilemmas, in that there is the difficulty of competing well against stronger competitors – most plausible options would be to divest, as the opportunity might be attractive to others, or to specialize around niches where some strength could be built.
- D would indicate investment and maintenance of competitive ability.
- E and F would indicate risk minimization and prudent choices for expansion.
- G and H would indicate management for earnings.
- I would require divestment or minimizing investment.

Extreme care is required in the judgements that would place products or SBUs into any one category, and the model does not directly take into account synergies between different products or business. The astute reader will recognize that the model represents a means of relating competences to the external environment, and that it is also a means of taking SWOT a stage further.

Multinational market portfolio analysis

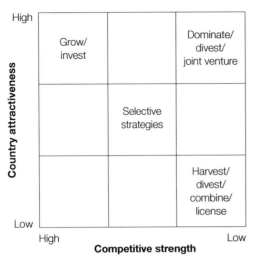

Other portfolio models can be used to help inform strategic decisions and understand both current balance of activity and potential futures.

The multinational market portfolio relates country attractiveness to the competitive strengths of the organization. The grid represents nine potential positions by which geographic regions can be analysed and categorized. Figure 2.4 indicates the options arising from the grid. Clearly, when countries or regions are mapped, it would indicate that high strength and high attractiveness could be areas for investment and growth, while countries appearing in the low strength/low attractiveness zone should be harvested, divested, combined or licensed. The remaining boxes indicate the potential strategies should the region be plotted in them.

Figure 2.4 Multinational market portfolio
Source: Adapted from Harrell and Kiefer, 1993

This is a helpful chapter to read before starting your report using the **Strategic Planning Software** (www.planning-strategy.com).

For test questions, extra case studies, audio case studies, weblinks, videolinks and more to help you understand the topics covered in this chapter, visit our companion website at www.palgrave.com/business/campbell.

VOCAB CHECKLIST FOR ESL STUDENTS

Affiliate	Illicit	Repositioning
Analogy	Incursion	'Rule of thumb'
Astute	Ineptitude	Seminal
Auction	Innovators	'Sit-in'
Augment	Logarithmic (see 'logarithm')	Slavish
Brokerage	Lucrative	Smuggling
Classifieds	Merchant	State of the art
Confectionary	Misdiagnosis	Stewardship
Contraband	Mission statement	Subsidiary
Distribution channel	Panacea	Temperate climate (see
Divestment	Perimeter	'temperate')
Egress	Pharmaceuticals	Typology

Definitions for these terms can be found in the 'Vocab Zone' of the companion website, which provides free access to the Macmillan English Dictionary online at www.palgrave.com/business/campbell.

REVIEW QUESTIONS

1   Explain how the purpose of the organization can impact on its strategic priorities.
2   Define what is meant by a business model and give examples of different types of business models in the retail sector.
3   Explain what is meant by the term 'product' and how products provide benefit to users.
4   Using theory related to the concept of 'portfolio', explain why it is important for an organization to have a balanced portfolio.

DISCUSSION TOPIC

All organizations, private, public or voluntary, need an effective business model. Discuss.

HOT TOPICS – Research project areas to investigate

If you have a project to do, why not investigate ...

- ... the critical success factors of business models for delivering online trading of sports goods.
- ... the effectiveness of the BCG matrix as a framework for portfolio management in creative industries such as computer gaming.
- ... how perceptions of managers change towards customer values, as organizations move through the product life cycle.

Recommended reading

Aaker, D.A. (1995) *Strategic Market Management* (4th edn), New York: John Wiley & Sons.

Coates, N. and Robinson, H. (1995) 'Making industrial new product development market led', *Marketing Intelligence and Planning*, **13**(6): 12–15.

Doyle, P. (1994) *Marketing Management and Strategy*, Englewoods Cliffs, NJ: Prentice Hall.

Jobber, D. (1995) *Principles and Practice of Marketing*, New York: McGraw-Hill.

Lancaster, G. and Massingham, L. (1993) *Marketing Management*, London: McGraw-Hill.

Sowrey, T. (1990) 'Idea generation: identifying the most useful techniques', *European Journal of Marketing*, **42**(5): 20–9.

Von Hippel, E. (1978) 'Successful industrial products from customer ideas', *Journal of Marketing*, **42**(1): 39–49.

Chapter references

Brown, R. (1991) 'The S-curves of innovation', *Journal of Marketing Management*, **7**(2): 189–202.

Copeland, M.T. (1923) 'Relation of consumers' buying habits to marketing methods', *Harvard Business Review*, 1: 282–9.

Greenley, G.E. and Bayus, B.L. (1993) 'Marketing planning decision making in UK and US companies: an empirical comparative study', *Journal of Marketing Management*, 9: 155–72.

Harrell, G.D. and Kiefer, R.O. (1993) 'Multinational market portfolios in global strategy development', *International Marketing Review*, **10**(1): 60–72.

Hooley, G.J. (1995) 'The lifecycle concept revisited: aid or albatross?, *Journal of Strategic Marketing*, 3: 23–39.

Kotler, P. (1997) *Marketing Management Analysis, Planning, Implementation, and Control* (9th edn), Englewood Cliffs, NJ: Prentice Hall International.

Mercer, D. (1993) 'Death of the product life cycle', *Adman*, September: 15–19.

Slywotzky, A. (1996) *Value Migration: How to Think Several Moves Ahead of the Competition*, Boston, MA: Harvard Business School Press.

Chapter 3

Business competences, processes and activities

Introduction and chapter overview

In Chapter 1 we considered the different schools of strategic thought and established that there has been, and continues to be, considerable debate in the academic literature as to the sources of competitive advantage. We recognized that the debate centres around the question 'how do organizations achieve superior performance?' and that two positions have emerged as the most prominent potential answer to this question.

The competitive positioning school of thought, based primarily on the work of Michael Porter (1980, 1985), stresses the importance of how the organization is positioned in respect to its competitive environment or industry, and the resource-based or competence school (Prahalad and Hamel, 1990; Heene and Sanchez, 1997) argues that it is the competences (abilities) of the business and the distinctive way that it organizes its activities which determine the ability to outperform competitors. As with most controversies, we suggest that both schools of thought have their merits – both are partial explanations of the source of competitive advantage.

This chapter concentrates on a key element of the internal analysis, the organization's competences or strategic capabilities. To do this, we develop an understanding of the dynamics of the organization and in particular the concepts of competences, processes and 'value-adding' activities.

Learning objectives

After studying this chapter, you should be able to:

- explain the concepts of core competences, competences, resources and the relationships between them
- determine the relationship between core competences and core activities
- explain how the configuration of value-adding activities can improve business performance
- explain the concept of the value chain and the value chain framework
- explain how the value chain framework 'works'

3.1   Identifying business processes

A key part of the internal analysis of an organization is an understanding of how the business does things, in other words, how the organization manages, deploys and aligns its resources and capabilities in order to deliver its products and supporting activities.

The concept of business processes is not new, indeed Adam Smith (1776) referred to them in an attempt to explain the stages of production for making a pin. What is significant is that business processes lie at the heart of what a business does and how it does it. The result is that processes can be directly related to the production process or may be used to support it, they may be what is termed 'upstream', that is, at the early stages of the construction of the product, or 'downstream', that is, at the end stages of the product, and they may be supported in a physical way or an intangible way. The nature of business processes has made them the subject of many studies, mainly in attempts to improve efficiency (lean production, business process redesign) or effectiveness (customer-centric approaches, value-based processes).

KEY CONCEPT

Lean production (or lean manufacturing) is often known simply as lean. The approach works from the perspective of value creation and the consumer, or user of the system. Value is any process or activity that the consumer will pay for and, as such, all other elements are deemed wasteful, and thus targeted for elimination.

What is clear is that the form, sustainability and effectiveness of an organization's business processes rely on the organization's available resources, competences and configuration of activities. We shall explore each of these in turn.

3.2   Resources, competences and core competences

The terms 'competence' and 'capability', 'core competence' and 'distinctive capability' are often used interchangeably in textbooks on business strategy. Although some writers (Stalk et al., 1992) argue that there are significant differences between the terms 'competence' and 'capability', we will use the terms to mean broadly the same things based on the following definitions:

> A **competence** is an attribute or collection of attributes possessed by all or most of the companies in an industry.

- A competence is an attribute or collection of attributes possessed by all or most of the companies in an industry. Such attributes are commonly termed 'threshold competences'. Without such attributes, a business cannot enter or survive in the industry. Competences develop from resources and embody skills, technology or know-how. For example, in order to operate in the pharmaceuticals industry, it is necessary to possess the ability to manufacture medicines (by using specially designed factory equipment) and, importantly, a detailed understanding of how medicines work on the human body. Every successful survivor in the industry possesses both areas of competence.

> A **core competence** is an attribute, or collection of attributes, specific to a particular organization that enables it to produce above-average performance.

- A core competence or *distinctive capability* is an attribute, or collection of attributes, specific to a particular organization that enables it to produce above-average performance. It arises from the way in which the organization has employed its competences and resources more effectively than its competitors. The result of a distinctive capability is an output that customers value higher than that of competitors. It is based on one or more factors – superior organizational knowledge, information, skills, technology, structure, relationships, networks and reputation.

- A *resource* is an input employed in the activities of the business. Success rests in large part on the efficiency by which the business converts its resources into outputs. Resources fall into four broad categories – human, financial, physical (buildings, equipment or stock) and intangible (know-how, patents, legal rights, brand names or registered designs).

KEY CONCEPT

Competitive advantage is often seen as the overall purpose of business strategy. Some texts use the phrase 'superior performance' to mean the same thing. Essentially, a business can be said to possess competitive advantage if it is able to return higher profits than its competitors. The higher profits mean that it will be able to commit more retained profit to reinvest in its strategy, thus maintaining its lead over its competitors in an industry. When this superiority is maintained successfully over time, we refer to it as a 'sustainable' competitive advantage. Competitive advantage can be lost when management fail to reinvest the superior profits in such a way that the advantage is not maintained.

Core competences tend to be both complex and intangible, so it is necessary to explore the nature of the resources and competences that underpin them before exploring the concept further. The purpose of such analysis is to allow managers to identify which resources and competences act as the foundation of existing or potential core competences (Figure 3.1). It is extremely important to note that not all the competitors in an industry will possess core competences or distinctive capabilities (Kay, 1995). It is only those players who are producing above-average performance who can be considered as possessing core competences. Those with only average or below-average performance possess competences and resources, without which they could not compete in the industry at all, but not core competences. This can be expressed as follows:

Core competence (distinctive capability) = superior acquisition and employment of resources + superior development of 'general' competences.

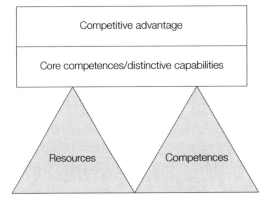

Figure 3.1 The twin sources of core competences

GURU GUIDE

John Kay was born in 1948 in Edinburgh. He was educated at Edinburgh University and Nuffield College, Oxford University. In 1971, he became one of the youngest lecturers to teach economics at Oxford University. In 1979, he become the first research director of the Institute of Fiscal Studies, and was soon its director. In 1986, he accepted a chair at the London Business School, and founded the renowned consultancy firm London Economics. In 1991 he became a visiting professor at London Business School, and in 1996, he took a directorship at the newly created Said Business School in Oxford.

Professor Kay has been a director with Halifax plc. He was also a member of the task force set up to revive Lloyds insurance market and a member of the steering group for the government's review of company law. He is an elected fellow of the Academy of Management. Since 2007 he has been a member of the Scottish government's Council of Economic Advisers.

He is renowned economist, and has written several influential texts on economics, and has written a column in the *Financial Times* since 1995. Kay's work embraces the concept of adding value and allows us to better understand how business strategy can add value. Much of his work opened up issues that are currently being grappled with. These include sustainability, innovation and distinctive competence.

3.3 Resource analysis

Tangible assets include stocks, materials, machinery, buildings, human resources, finance and so on.

Intangible assets include skills, knowledge, brand names, goodwill and patent rights.

Resources can be both 'tangible' and 'intangible'. They are the inputs that enable an organization to carry out its activities. Tangible assets include stocks, materials, machinery, buildings, human resources, finance and so on. Intangible assets include skills, knowledge, brand names, goodwill and patent rights (see Coyne, 1986; Hall, 1992). Intangible resources are often produced within the organization but tangibles are obtained from outside organizations. Such resources are obtained in resource markets in competition with businesses from within and outside the industry. Relationships with the suppliers of resources can form an important part of the organization's core competence, for example its ability to attract the most appropriately skilled human resources in the job market.

When we analyse a company's resources as part of an internal analysis, three frameworks can be employed to provide a comprehensive review:

1. We might consider them by *category* – human, financial, production technology, information and communications technology, and materials. These resources are then evaluated quantitatively (how much or how many) and qualitatively (how effectively they are being employed). Physical resources like buildings and machinery will typically be audited for capacity, utilization, age, condition, contribution to output and so on. Materials and stocks can be assessed on the basis of quality, reliability, availability, number of suppliers, delivery times and unit costs. Human resources are considered in terms of numbers, education, skills, training, experience, age, motivation, wage costs and productivity in relation to the needs of the organization.

2. We can analyse resources according to their *specificity*. Resources can be specific or non-specific. For example, skilled workers tend to have specialized and industry-specific knowledge and skills. Some technology, for example computer software, is for general (non-industry-specific) business use, like word-processing, database and spreadsheet software. Other computer

software applications, like airline computer reservation systems, are written for highly specialized uses. Whereas non-specific resources tend to be more flexible and form the basis of competences, industry-specific resources are more likely to act as the foundations of core competences, for example the specialized knowledge of scientists in the chemical industry.

3   Resources can be evaluated on the basis of how they contribute to internal and external *measures of performance*. Internal measures include their contribution to:

- business objectives and targets – financial, performance and output measures
- historical comparisons – measures of performance over time (such as against previous years)
- business unit or divisional comparisons.

External measures can include:

- comparisons with competitors, particularly those who are industry leaders and those who are the closest competitors and are in its strategic grouping
- comparisons with companies in other industries.

By employing these techniques of analysis, an organization is able to internally and externally benchmark its performance as a stimulus to improving performance in the future. Performance, however, is based on more than resources and competences.

3.4   Core competences

Core competences are distinguished from competences in several ways:

- they are only possessed by those companies whose performance is superior to the industry average
- they are unique to the company
- they are more complex
- they are difficult to emulate (copy)
- they relate to fulfilling customer needs
- they add greater value than 'general' competences
- they are often based on distinctive relationships with customers, distributors and suppliers
- they are based on superior organizational skills and knowledge.

In the motor industry, for example, all manufacturers have the competences and resources required to build motor vehicles, but a company like BMW has core competences in design, engine technology and marketing that are the basis of its reputation for high-quality, high performance cars. These core competences make it possible for BMW to charge premium prices for its products. In this way, core competences are the basis of an organization's competitive advantage.

Kay (1993) presents a slightly different explanation, arguing that competitive advantage is based on what he terms 'distinctive capability'. **Distinctive capability can develop from reputation, architecture (internal and external relationships), innovation and strategic assets.** Marks & Spencer's competitive advantage can be explained in terms of its reputation for quality, its special relationships with its suppliers and its customers. Marks & Spencer has exacting but mutually

Distinctive capability can develop from reputation, architecture (internal and external relationships), innovation and strategic assets.

profitable relationships with the businesses that supply its products. It demands high quality at reasonable cost, and flexibility in return for large volumes of business. Its relationship with customers is based on its reputation for good service, refunds and exchanges of goods, and high-quality products. The end result is that it has a performance that is superior to most of its high-street competitors.

Core competence arises from the unique and distinctive way that the organization builds, develops, integrates and deploys its resources and competences. An existing core competence can be evaluated for:

- *customer focus:* does it adequately focus on customer needs?
- *uniqueness:* can it be imitated by competitors, and if so, how easily?
- *flexibility:* can it be easily adapted if market or industry conditions change?
- *contribution to value:* to what extent does it add value to the product or service?
- *sustainability:* how long can its superiority be sustained over time?

Competences can also be judged against these criteria in order to evaluate their potential to form the basis on which new core competences can be built.

Core competences can never be regarded as being permanent. The pace of change of technology and society are such that core competences must be constantly adapted and new ones cultivated. A good example of the need to adapt comes from an examination of IBM. In the 1980s, IBM had core competences in the design, production, marketing and sales of PCs. The value that customers attached to these competences was lost in the late 1980s and early 1990s because competitors were able to match IBM's competences in design and production of PCs and at a lower price. IBM had failed to adapt its core competences so that they became merely industry-wide competences. Its superiority was eroded because it failed to sustain its advantage.

The aim of an analysis of resources, competences and core competences is, therefore, to:

- understand the nature and sources of particular core competences
- identify the need for and methods of adaptation of existing core competences
- identify the need for new core competence building
- identify potential sources of core competence based on resources and competences
- ensure that core competences remain focused on customer needs.

Resources, competences and core competences are obviously closely related to the ways that a business organizes and performs its value-adding activities. In the resource-based view of strategy, the concept of 'dynamic capabilities' has emerged as a term to encapsulate these areas.

Dynamic capabilities represent the ability of organizations to innovate, adapt and adopt in terms of their tangible and intangible resources, and are the foundation of many forms of competition in today's business environment. It is therefore necessary to analyse the way in which value-adding activities are configured and coordinated (Teece, 2007).

Dynamic capabilities represent the ability of organizations to innovate, adapt and adopt in terms of their tangible and intangible resources.

David J. Teece has a PhD in economics from the University of Pennsylvania, and has held teaching and research positions at Stanford University and Oxford University. He has previously held the position as Mitsubishi Bank chair, and has been director of the Institute for Management, Innovation, and Organization at the University of California at Berkeley. He has received four honorary doctorates. He is Thomas W. Tusher Professor in Global Business and director of the Institute of Management, Innovation, and Organization at the Haas School of Business, University of California, Berkeley. Dr Teece was a co-founder and chairman of the Law and Economics Consulting Group, and co-founded the Berkeley Research Group in 2010.

Dr Teece has over 30 years' experience as an active consultant, engaged in economic, business, and financial consulting services to businesses and governments around the world. He has worked on matters in industries ranging from music recording to DRAMS, software, lumber and petroleum, and has testified in both federal and state courts, before Congress, and before the Federal Trade Commission, as well as in several international jurisdictions.

He is the author of more than 200 books and articles. According to *Science Watch* (November/ December 2005), he is the lead author of the most cited article in economics and business worldwide, 1995–2005. He is also one of the top 10 cited scholars for the decade, and has been recognized by Accenture as one of the world's top 50 business intellectuals.

KEY CONCEPTS

Competence leveraging refers to the ability of a business to exploit its core competences in new markets, thus meeting new customer needs. It can also refer to the ability of the business to modify and improve existing core competences.

Competence building takes place when the business builds new core competences, based on its resources and competences. It is often necessary to build new competences alongside existing ones when entering new markets, as it is unlikely that existing competences will fully meet new customer needs.

3.5   Analysis of value-adding activities

Value chain analysis seeks to provide an understanding of how much value an organization's activities add to its products (goods and services) for its consumers compared to the costs of the resources used in their production (the value margin).

Value chain analysis (Porter, 1985) seeks to provide an understanding of how much value an organization's activities add to its products (goods and services) for its consumers compared to the costs of the resources used in their production (the value margin). A given product can be produced by organizing activities in a number of different ways. Value chain analysis helps managers to understand how effectively and efficiently the activities of their organization are configured and coordinated. The acid test is how much value is added in the process of turning inputs into final products. Value is measured in terms of the price (or emotional commitment) that customers are willing to pay for the product (Figure 3.2).

From Figure 3.2, it can be seen that when the market price (MP) has been set, it still results in a section of consumers who have a reserved price (RP) in excess of the MP. In other words, they are prepared and able to pay more than the MP for the product. The implication of this (beyond market segmentation and fencing) is that they may be made to part with higher than MP if additional value or urgency can be portrayed (real or perceived).

CASE STUDY Northern Rock

On the morning of 6 September 2007, people in the UK switching on their televisions to see the early news bulletins were astounded to see pictures of hundreds of Northern Rock bank customers queuing hours before the bank opened to get their money out.

This was because Northern Rock had had to declare a cash flow crisis, and a loss of institutional, customer and consumer confidence. A chapter of accidents, a lack of key resources, and an attitude of collective and individual vanity that caused a small provincial UK bank to consider itself a truly global player in its industry had brought this about.

Northern Rock was (and remains) a small regional UK bank, specializing in lending mortgage money to people in mid to low income brackets who wished to buy their own homes. The company had found itself under great pressure to increase its lending volumes and enhance its customer base, using finance available on the global financial markets to underwrite these activities. Now it was faced with ruin.

The problems of Northern Rock (and indeed many of the UK retail banks and mortgage lenders) had roots set deeply in the past. All the UK retail banks had found themselves under great pressure to expand the volumes of credit available, the bases on which this credit would be made available, and the range of people to whom credit would be made available. Taking people's homes as the security against which loans and mortgages were made available, the availability of, and volumes of, credit were greatly increased. The results were a property boom, in which houses were bought and sold for ever increasing prices, and a consumer credit boom, in which the money released from the housing market was used to purchase home improvements, holidays, cars and other retail items.

Over the past 15 years, the UK property market had therefore grown greatly in all parts. House sales and values were at record highs. All parts of the retail sector had also grown over the same period, especially the home furnishings, home improvements and garden sectors. However, it became apparent that this could not be sustained over the long term, and in 2003, the British Retail Consortium first drew attention to some of the problems and issues that might come up, declaring that the UK 'do it yourself' (DIY) sector was overprovided by 25%, that is, that one of the four main providers in this sector would either be taken over by one of the others, or else one of them would go bankrupt.

Nevertheless, property values continued to rise. There then was a boom in off-balance, self-certificated and subprime lending in the UK, in which homeowners on otherwise modest incomes, that is, the core customer base of Northern Rock, could remortgage their properties to a stated, notional or alleged value, and draw out the residue as cash. This cash would then be used on consumer goods and other purchases, as above. Some of the finance houses started to lend not just to the full value of the property, but to a maximum of 125% of the stated value.

Over the 15-year period, the banking sector had been able to source short- and medium-term funds from anywhere in the world. The banking sector had also, in common with many others, been able to buy and sell credit and debts as assets. These assets became a commodity themselves, to be traded between banks, finance houses and other cash and credit providers located anywhere in the world. Northern Rock had become an enthusiastic player in this practice, and for a short time had been able to raise as much money as it wanted through the purchasing and sale of what came to be known as 'bundles of assets'.

The bundles were being traded on the basis of less than full information, and in many cases banks were buying and selling to each other on the basis of valuations that were dreamed up on the spot, purely in order to meet the present obligations.

The Frankfurt brokers drew the attention of the financial institutions to this, and the national banks and financial regulatory bodies in the UK, the USA, Japan and the EU conducted their own investigations. They too became worried, and now faced the problem of having to do something about this without completely destabilizing the property and financial markets. The extent of the problem initially emerged very slowly. However, it became clear that this was indeed a major problem for the international banking sector, which resulted in a widespread loss of confidence and certainty across the world.

The results were cataclysmic for the whole sector, and many banks in the USA, the UK and elsewhere were forced to close or else merge with others. For Northern Rock, the outcome was ruin by any other name, although it was saved from bankruptcy by being taken into government ownership.

Case study questions

1 What resources did Northern Rock need in order to develop its strategy to be a global organization in its sector? What resources did the company lack?

2 How should the problems of 'bundling of assets' have been addressed?

3 What further lessons are there for managers who seek a resource-based strategy for their organizations?

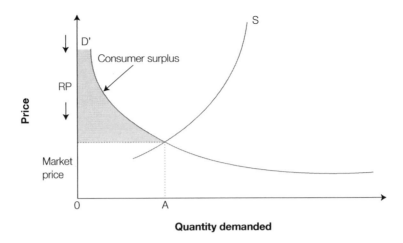

Figure 3.2 Price and value added

There are six common types of value (real or perceived) that can be created for the consumer and used as tools for differentiating a 'product'. These are:

- *Economic value:* best expressed in terms of wealth, resources or the economic conversion process
- *Physical value:* associated with a person's wellbeing, health, comfort or rest
- *Emotional value:* linked to a person's emotions and includes fear, joy, contentment or excitement
- *Social value:* reflecting the interpersonal and relationship dimension of society
- *Cognitive value:* in relation to the quest for knowledge and, ultimately, wisdom
- *Political value:* relates to influence, control and power.

Physical value: first class

Value can be increased by:

1 Changing customer perceptions of the product so that they are willing to pay a higher price for a product than for similar products produced by other businesses

2 Reducing production costs below those of competitors.

These two ways of increasing value relate to the concepts of efficiency and effectiveness:

- **Efficiency** is the ability to accomplish a task with minimum, time, effort or use of resources
- **Effectiveness** is the ability to deliver the expected result or value for the user or consumer.

Efficiency is the ability to accomplish a task with minimum, time, effort or use of resources.

Effectiveness is the ability to deliver the expected result or value for the user or consumer.

KEY CONCEPT

The **value added** to a good or service is the difference in the financial value of the finished product compared to the financial value of the inputs. As a sheet of metal passes through the various stages in car production, value is added so that a tonne of metal worth a few hundred pounds becomes a car worth several thousand pounds. The rate at which value is added depends on how well the operations process is managed. If the car manufacturer suffers a cost disadvantage by, say, holding a high level of stock or working with out of date machinery, then the value added over the process will be lower.

There are clear linkages between value-adding activities, core competences, competences and resources. Resources form the inputs to the organization's value-adding activities, while competences and core competences provide the skills and knowledge required to carry them out. The more that core competences can be integrated into value-adding activities, the greater will be the value added.

These forms of value adding tend to represent the basis of competitive advantage, that is, lower cost or differentiation.

The value-adding process

Businesses can be regarded as systems that transform inputs (resources, materials and so on) into outputs (goods and services). This is illustrated in Figure 3.3.

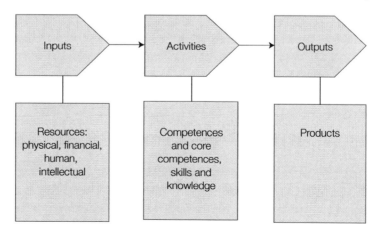

Figure 3.3 **A simplified schematic of the value-adding process**

The activities inside the organization add value to the inputs. The value of the finished goods is equivalent to the price that a customer is willing to pay for the goods. The difference between the end value and the total costs is the 'margin' – the quantity that accountants would refer to as the 'profit margin', before interest, taxation and extraordinary items.

The value chain can be used to analyse the value created by the economic conversion of the raw materials into products (primary activities) or by additional value created by factors that can impact on such a process (secondary activities).

The value chain

The activities of the organization can be broken down into a sequence of activities known as the 'value chain', as described by Porter in 1985 (see Figure 3.4).

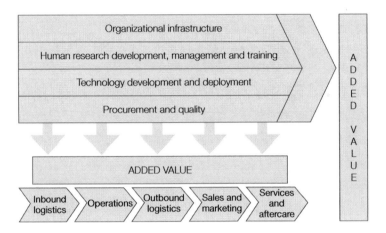

Figure 3.4 The value chain
Source: Adapted from Porter, 1985

The activities within the chain may be classified as primary activities and support activities:

- *Primary activities* are those which directly add value to the final product.
- *Support activities* do not directly add value themselves but indirectly add value by supporting the effective execution of primary activities.

Table 3.1 describes the primary and secondary activities.

Analysis of the value chain

An organization's value chain links into the value chains of other organizations, particularly those of suppliers and distributors. This 'chain' of value chains is sometimes called the 'value system' or 'total supply chain'. Linkages with suppliers are known as 'upstream' linkages, while those with distributors and customers are 'downstream' linkages.

Different types of organization will have different value chains. For example, the value chain of Dixons, the electrical goods retailer, does not include the design and manufacture of the products it sells. Marks & Spencer's value chain does include some design but does not include manufacturing.

Table 3.1 A summary of the activities in the value chain

Primary activities	Inbound logistics	Receipt and storage of materials (inputs) Stock control and distribution of inputs
	Operations	Transformation of inputs into final product
	Outbound logistics	Storage and distribution of finished goods
	Sales and marketing	Making the product available to the market and persuading people to buy
	Service	Installation and after-sales support
Support activities	Procurement	Purchasing of resources
	Technology development	Product, process and resource development
	Infrastructure	Planning, finance, information systems, management
	Human resource management	Recruitment, selection, training, reward and motivation

Similarly, not all of an organization's activities are of equal importance in adding value to its products. Those which are of greatest importance can be considered as 'core activities' and are often closely associated to core competences. Thus in a fashion house like Calvin Klein, design activities are of the greatest importance in adding value and the organization's core competences are concentrated in this area.

Analysis of value-adding activities helps to identify where the most value is added and where there is potential to add greater value by changing the way in which activities are configured and by improving the way in which they are coordinated. It is important to note that an organization's value chain is not analysed in isolation but that it is considered in conjunction with its external linkages to suppliers, distributors and customers.

A value chain analysis would be expected to include:

- a breakdown of all the activities of the organization
- identification of core activities and their relationships to core competences and current organizational strategies
- identification of the effectiveness and efficiency of the individual activities
- examination of linkages between activities for additional added value
- identification of blockages that reduce the organization's competitive advantage.

A useful technique in value chain analysis involves comparison with the value chains of competitors to identify the benefits and drawbacks of alternative configurations.

The aim of value chain analysis is to identify ways in which the performance of the individual activities and the linkages between them can be improved. This may involve identification of improved configurations for activities or improved coordination of them. It is particularly important to consider the extent to which value chain activities support the current strategy of the organization. For example, if the current strategy is based on high quality, then the activities must be configured so as to ensure high-quality products. On the other hand, if the organization competes largely on the basis of price, then activities must be organized so as to minimize costs.

The onset of the internet and the emergence of a range of e-businesses have resulted in a new version of the value chain, basically depicting the different form of business processes and the virtual nature of many businesses. In this respect, the traditional primary activities of inbound logistics, operations, outbound logistics, sales and marketing, and after-sales support are replaced with attracting customers, selecting services, organizing information, distributing and supporting. While new technology has impacted and will continue to impact on the business landscape, the value chain is still a useful model to use to understand what a business does and how it does it. However, this does not imply that a business must itself undertake all the activities they require, as they can outsourced to other organizations for whom the activity is core.

STRATEGIC
PLANNING SOFTWARE

This is a helpful chapter to refer to when completing 1.2.2 Value Chain within the Internal Analysis section in Phase 1 of the **Strategic Planning Software** (www.planning-strategy.com). For more information on the value chain, also see Chapter 6.

www.palgrave.com
Companion Website

For test questions, extra case studies, audio case studies, weblinks, videolinks and more to help you understand the topics covered in this chapter, visit our companion website at www.palgrave.com/business/campbell.

VOCAB CHECKLIST FOR ESL STUDENTS

Astounded	Eroded	Specificity
Benchmark	Fencing	Steering group (see 'steering
Cataclysmic	Infrastructure	committee')
Configuration	Installation	Subprime lending (see
Cultivated	Leveraging	'subprime')
Deploy	Networks	Sustainability
E-businesses	Outperform	Threshold
Elimination	Qualitatively	
Emulate	Quantitatively	

Definitions for these terms can be found in the 'Vocab Zone' of the companion website, which provides free access to the Macmillan English Dictionary online at www.palgrave.com/business/campbell.

REVIEW QUESTIONS

1   Explain the difference between competence and core competence.
2   Explain each element of the value chain and how organizations can create value through efficient and effective activities.
3   Evaluate how value-adding activities can be configured to improve business performance in the banking sector.

DISCUSSION TOPIC

It is important to create value for consumers. This value needs to be real and tangible in order to be attractive. Discuss.

HOT TOPICS – Research project areas to investigate

If you have a project to do, why not investigate ...

- ... the appropriateness of the value chain as a tool for a not-for-profit organization.
- ... how organizations decide to configure their resources during times of financial crisis.
- ... perceptions of managers as to whether outsourcing is the best way to gain competences quickly.

Recommended reading

Barney, J.B. and Clark, D.H. (2007) *Resource-based Theory: Creating and Sustaining Competitive Advantage*, Oxford: Oxford University Press.

Jarillo, J.C. (1993) *Strategic Networks: Creating the Borderless Organization*, Oxford: Butterworth-Heinemann, Chapters 3–5.

Petts, N. (1997) 'Building growth on core competences: a practical approach', *Long Range Planning*, **30**(4): 551–61.

Porter, M.E. (1985) *Competitive Advantage*, New York: Free Press.

Chapter references

Coyne, K.P. (1986) 'Sustainable competitive advantage: what it is, what it isn't', *Business Horizons*, **29**(1): 54–61.

Hall, R. (1992) 'The strategic analysis of intangible resources', *Strategic Management Journal*, **13**(2): 135–44.

Heene, A. and Sanchez, R. (1997) *Competence-based Strategic Management*, London: John Wiley.

Kay, J. (1993) *Foundations of Corporate Success*, Oxford: Oxford University Press.

Kay, J. (1995) 'Learning to define the core business', *Financial Times*, December 1.

Porter, M.E. (1980) *Competitive Strategy: Techniques for Analysing Industries and Competitors*, New York: Free Press.

Porter, M.E. (1985) *Competitive Advantage*, New York: Free Press.

Prahalad, C.K. and Hamel, G. (1990) 'The core competence of the corporation', *Harvard Business Review*, **68**(3): 79–81.

Smith, A. (1776) *An Enquiry into the Nature and Causes of the Wealth of Nations*, London: Strachan and Cadell.

Stalk, G., Evans, P. and Shulmann, L.E. (1992) 'Competing on capabilities: the new rules of corporate strategy', *Harvard Business Review*, **70**(3): 57–69.

Teece, D.J. (2007) 'Explicating dynamic capabilities: the nature and micro foundations of (sustainable) enterprise performance', *Strategic Management Journal*, **28**(13): 1319–50.

CHAPTER 4

INTERNATIONAL TRADE AND GLOBAL COMPETITION

Outline of chapter

Introduction

Trade and economic growth

Theories of international trade
The theory of comparative advantage
Product life cycle theory from the trade perspective
Newer trade theories
Porter's theory of competitive advantage

National trade policies
Government perspectives on trade
Tools of governmental trade policy

Global and regional trade patterns

International regulation of trade
GATT principles
WTO and the regulation of world trade
Multilateral trade agreements and the WTO

Regional and bilateral trade agreements
Categories of regional trade agreements
Focus on regions – Europe, The Americas, Asia, Africa

Multilateralism at the crossroads

Globalization and world trade

Conclusions

Learning objectives

1 To appreciate the contributions of theories of international trade to an understanding of the ways in which companies, industries and nations compete in the global environment
2 To understand the rationale and mechanisms of national trade policies
3 To understand the evolution of the multilateral trading system, in terms of its structures, processes, and issues to be resolved
4 To assess the impact of regional integration on the business environment

Critical themes in this chapter

- **Multilayered environment – national trade policies; bilateral, regional and multilateral trade agreements**
- **Emerging economies – growing influence in international trade**
- **The role of the state – national trade policies and tools; protectionism**

The growth in container shipping reflects the importance of trade in the global economy

Source: Istock

BHP Billiton digs deep in global markets

BHP Billiton is the world's largest diversified natural resources company. Mining is its core activity, with divisions in minerals, coal and iron ore, but it is also a significant oil and gas producer. This diversity has helped the company to withstand the instability of commodities markets. Although its profits for many metals fell steeply in 2009, its iron ore and petroleum divisions performed well. Its other great advantage has been its sheer size, which gives it a strong market position, especially in iron ore, which is our focus here. Iron ore is the main ingredient in steel and one of the key commodities associated with industrialization, whether in manufacturing cars or building skyscrapers. Demand for iron ore has surged ahead from the fast-growing emerging economies, such as China, Brazil and India. All are big producers of iron ore, although China is by far the largest, producing 770 million tonnes in 2008, nearly double the amount produced in Brazil. But China's domestic demand exceeds its own production, forcing it to import from abroad (see figure). In addition, China's low-grade iron ore and dwindling production have been other factors leading it to shift to importing, in both its large state-run steel producers and smaller private firms. This is good news for the seaborne iron ore sector, in which BHP Billiton ranks third in the world, behind Vale of Brazil (first) and Rio Tinto of the UK (second). China imported only 20% of its iron ore in 2000, but by 2009, the proportion had jumped to 70%, much of it from Australian mines controlled by Rio and BHP Billiton.

BHP Billiton was formed from a merger in 2001 of BHP (formerly Broken Hill Proprietary Co.) of Australia and Billiton, a UK company, both companies dating back to the nineteenth century in their origins. The merged company is listed in both the UK and Australia, where there are separate groups of shareholders. In theory, there are separate boards, but they consist of the same people. The management is also unified, and the company's headquarters are in Melbourne. The merged company has become a powerful force, accounting for 18% of Australia's GDP. China is now Australia's largest export market, and mining exports account for 37.9% of its total exports.

Ambitious expansion strategies have led BHP Billiton to make acquisitions around the globe. It now has 100 sites in 25 countries. But its most audacious move was a bid for its rival, Rio Tinto, in 2007. Had the merger gone ahead, the combined company would have controlled about 75% of the seaborne iron ore market, effectively creating a duopoly. Although competition authorities in the US and Australia approved the deal, the EU took a critical view, largely due to the potential to control prices. The European

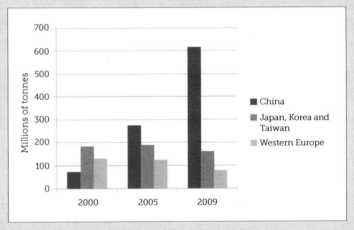

Seaborne iron ore imports
Source: *Financial Times*, 31 March 2010

Commission set a condition for approval which required BHP Billiton to dispose of other assets. Discouraged from going ahead, it dropped the bid. However, in 2009, BHP executives came forward with another proposal, this time to create a 50–50 joint venture with Rio Tinto, which would operate the rich Western Australia iron ore field. It would be a 'hands-off', independent company, with its own management. The parent companies argued that this would be a 'production-only' deal, combining infrastructure, but not pricing power (*Financial Times*,

▶ More online ... BHP Billliton's website is at www.bhpbilliton.com

1 April 2010). This proposal, too, attracted the attention of competition authorities, including those in Australia, Japan and the EU. Few believe that the joint venture would be autonomous in practice, given its powerful owners. Pricing was again a key issue. The two companies gave up plans for the joint venture late in 2010.

For 40 years, global iron ore pricing has been based on a system of annual contract negotiations which set 'benchmark' prices. But with rising demand, these prices have lagged behind 'spot' prices which obtain in commodity markets. The mining companies have argued, therefore, that they have lost money, as their prices were effectively capped when dealing with major customers. They have proposed a new system based on quarterly spot market prices, and they have persuaded steel customers in China and Japan to change to the new system. The result is likely to be steep price rises in iron ore globally. Although for Asian economies, with their healthy industries, these rises could possibly be absorbed, for European manufacturing, with its fragile steel industry, the price rises would be damaging. The European steel industry complained in 2010 to the EU Commission about possible 'illicit co-ordination of price increases' by the big mining companies (*Financial Times*, 1 April 2010). The Chinese government has also announced an investigation into iron ore pricing.

BHP Billiton has said in the past that it wished to see a system of market-based pricing in iron ore, as for oil or coal (MacNamara, 2009). However, these other global industries are not as concentrated in the hands of a few players. In 2010, Australia's Labour government announced the impending imposition of a 40% mining supertax, which would fall heavily on BHP Billiton. Although rebates and a lower corporation tax would help to soften the blow, the company still felt the tax would be unfair. It waged a public media campaign against the measure, which was perceived as largely to blame for the toppling of the government. The prime minister, Kevin Rudd, was replaced by Julia Gillard, who was more sympathetic to BHP's arguments; a temporary deal for a lower rate of tax, at about 30%, was reached. However, Labour did not achieve an outright majority in the elections that followed, leaving the issue of the mining tax still in doubt. BHP Billiton has prided itself on its corporate citizenship, but paying a windfall tax was probably not one of the elements it had in mind.

Sources: *Financial Times* (2010) 'Iron ore deal sparks European steel fury', 1 April; MacNamara, W. and Waldmeir, P. (2010) 'Ore struck', *Financial Times*, 6 April; MacNamara, W. (2009) 'BHP in plea over iron ore pricing', 13 August; Wachman, R. (2010) 'BHP and Rio Tinto hit by Australian supertax', *The Guardian*, 4 May; Blas, J. (2010) 'Annual contract system collapses', *Financial Times*, 31 March; Jolly, D. (2010) 'EU opens antitrust investigation into mining deal', *New York Times*, 25 January; BHP Billiton Annual Report, 2009, at www.bhpbilliton.com

Questions for discussion

◆ Why is the iron ore market a crucial one in today's global economy?
◆ What impacts to the iron ore market would have resulted from a successful takeover of Rio Tinto by BHP Billiton?
◆ Would it be preferable for iron ore to be priced on the old benchmark system, or on the new spot-price model, and why?

Introduction

Businesses seeking markets have across the ages looked to trade beyond their home country. Growth in international trade has been a major contributor to the rise of the industrialized countries, stretching back to the Industrial Revolution. Indeed, when we look at the flourishing trade between Asia and Europe as far back as the medieval era, we are tempted to think that globalization has been happening a long time. However, both the volume of trade and the patterns of trade between nations have changed greatly over the years. In the decades following the Second World War, the dominant trading powers were the US, Japan and Europe. From the 1990s and into the twenty-first century, there has been a shift towards Asia, in which the large emerging economies have become leading traders. Two major factors can be highlighted in this shift towards Asia: globalization of production by MNEs and the opening up of national economies. Understanding the impacts of these factors on the global trading system, including particular regions and national economies, is key to formulating business strategies in the changing environment.

We begin this chapter with an overview of international trade, highlighting shifts in trading relations now taking place. We look at the major theories that help to explain changing patterns of world trade. We then analyse divergent views on the issues of free trade and protectionism, which have shaped national perspectives. Belief in the benefits of free trade has underpinned co-operative agreements to open markets, guided particularly by the World Trade Organization (WTO). We examine the role of the WTO as trade envelops more developing and emerging economies. Multilateralism is coming under threat from the growth in regional and bilateral trade agreements. These developments have taken place in a context of globalization, highlighting the interdependence of national economies. Nonetheless, governments continue to focus on national perspectives, leading to fears that protectionist pressures are gaining ground.

Trade and economic growth

Since the end of the Second World War, trade has grown at a remarkable rate: from 1950 to 2002 the volume of world exports tripled, and production doubled. In the 1990s, trade grew on average 6.5% annually, while output grew at 2.5% annually. The following decade showed similar growth, but sharp declines occurred towards the end, as the global credit crunch and recession affected trade and economic activity generally (see Figure 4.1). Extended supply chains across national borders should be taken into account when looking at trade data in relation to GDP. Over 40% of world trade is accounted for by **intermediate goods**, components and parts which might cross national borders more than once before being made into final products. These goods are counted each time they cross national borders. Trade in intermediate goods is particularly relevant for Asian countries, where the proportion can be over half. China's imports are 57% made up of intermediate goods which are destined for factories, to be made into final products for export to other countries. Similarly, about 42% of its exports are made up of intermediate goods. It is because of this double counting that swings in trade growth appear to be greater than changes in GDP growth.

intermediate goods components and parts which cross national borders before being made into final products

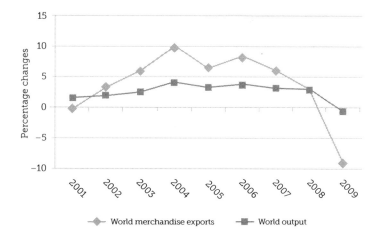

Figure 4.1 **Changes in world merchandise exports and GDP**

Source: IMF, Data and statistics, at www.imf.org

Three major trading regions, Europe, North America and Asia, account for over 80 per cent of global trade. From Figure 4.2, it can be seen that in the post-war period, Asia's share in global merchandise exports has grown and North America's share has decreased. Europe remains the best-performing region, but its share has declined from over 50% in 1973 to 41% in 2008, largely due to the gains by Asian exporters.

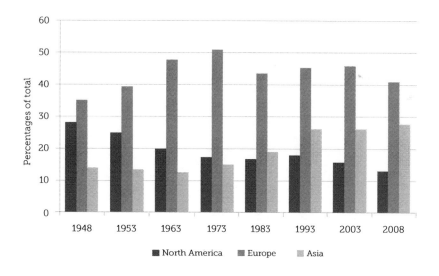

Figure 4.2 **Shares in world merchandise exports by region**

Source: WTO, International trade statistics 2009, at www.wto.org

China is now challenging Germany as the world's largest exporter of merchandise, as Figure 4.3 shows. In exports of manufactured goods, China became the global leader in 2008. China's exports of manufactured goods grew at a rate of over 25% a year from 2000 to 2008 (WTO, 2009). Of the four leading traders, the US stands out as being the largest importer by far, but it shows the greatest imbalance between exports and imports. The trade deficit of the US is mirrored by the trade surplus of China. The US had a trade deficit with China of $268 billion in 2008 (US Trade Representative's Office, 2009).

▸ More online ... The WTO's trade statistics are at www.wto.org
The US Trade Representative's Office provides trade data for the US, at www.ustr.gov

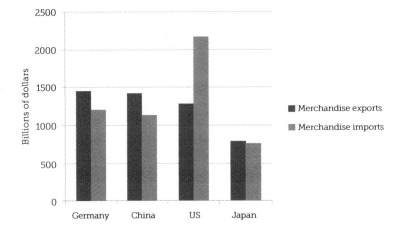

Figure 4.3 **The world's four leading trading countries in 2008**

Source: WTO, International trade statistics 2009, at www.wto.org

China's development model has been based on manufacturing for export. Favourable tax treatment of foreign investors, including tax-free export zones, has helped to turn the country into a powerhouse for exports of consumer goods globally. In the early stages of development, basic advantages such as low labour costs help to ensure this success. These advantages are particularly evident in low-technology sectors in which labour is a major component. The bulk of China's trade surplus has been derived from sectors such as toys, textiles and footwear. As we have seen, globalization has been characterized by the shift of much manufacturing to low-cost environments. As an economy matures, its advantages tend to slip away to developing countries which can undercut it in costs. For this reason, countries whose advantages are mainly based on low-cost labour seek to move up the value chain. South Korea and Taiwan, which industrialized prior to China, have moved up to higher value-added goods such as high-technology products. China's growth in the export of higher technology products, such as electronics, has been linked to the growth in imports of components, many from Taiwan and South Korea. For China, building its own technological and innovative capacity will propel it up the value chain.

Summary points Trade and economic growth

◆ Trade has grown faster than GDP in the post-war period, although both declined in 2008–9 as economic downturn affected global markets.

◆ China has become the world's largest exporter of manufactured goods, and the second largest exporter of merchandise generally.

◆ Crucially for developing countries, trade aids economic

growth. Initially, developing countries benefit from a low-cost manufacturing environment. Rising up the value chain in terms of technology contributes to economic development.

Critical thinking

Trade and economic growth

Although trade is boosting growth in developing countries, often in conjunction with FDI, these economies can become entrenched in low-cost manufacturing activities, which can damage growth prospects in the long term. How does this happen, and what can be done about it?

Theories of international trade

import the purchase of
goods or services from a
buyer in another country

In Chapter 2, we found that exporting, the selling of goods abroad, is a favoured internationalization strategy of many firms. **Imports** are goods bought from abroad, and, as we saw, growth in imports is associated with globalization. The first major theorist of international trade, Adam Smith, believed that all countries benefit from unrestricted trade. Free trade is said to exist where citizens can export and import without restrictions or barriers imposed by governments of either the exporting or the importing country. In his book, *The Wealth of Nations* (published in 1776), Smith argued in favour of the 'the invisible hand' of market forces, as opposed to government intervention (discussed in the last chapter). When countries produce the products in which they are the most efficient producers, they are said to have an **absolute advantage** in these products. A country may then sell these goods overseas, and purchase from overseas goods that are produced more efficiently elsewhere. Thus, both countries benefit from trade.

absolute advantage
enjoyed by a country
which is more efficient
at producing a
particular product than
any other country

The theory of comparative advantage

comparative advantage
enjoyed by a country
where production of
a particular product
involves greater relative
advantage than would be
possible anywhere else

Starting from the principle of absolute advantage, David Ricardo ([1817]1973), writing some 40 years after Adam Smith, developed his theory of **comparative advantage.** His theory contends that, if Country A is an efficient producer of wheat and Country B an efficient producer of clocks, it pays A to purchase clocks from B, even if it could itself produce clocks more efficiently than B. According to Ricardo, if countries specialize in the industries in which they have comparative advantage, all will benefit from trade with each other; consumers in both countries enjoying more wheat and more clocks than they would without trade. According to Ricardo's theory, therefore, trade is not a 'zero-sum' game, that is, where one side's gain is the other's loss, but a 'positive-sum' game, that is, one in which all parties benefit.

In reality, most countries do not specialize in ways envisaged by Ricardo's theory. Further, the model does not allow for dynamic changes that trade brings about. Economists base the benefits of free trade on 'dynamic gains' that contribute to economic growth. Free trade leads to an increase in a country's stock of resources, in terms of both increased capital from abroad and greater supplies of labour. In addition, efficiency may improve with large-scale production and improved technology. Opening up markets and creating more competition can provide an impetus for domestic companies to become more efficient. Trading patterns are also influenced by historical accident, government policies, and the importance of MNEs in the global economy – all of which have been incorporated into newer trade theories.

Summary points Theory of comparative advantage

● Ricardo's theory of comparative advantage holds that countries will ultimately benefit by concentrating on the industries in which they hold efficiency advantages over other countries.
● The theory presents a static view of trade, and Ricardo could not have envisaged the role of the modern MNE in international trade.

Product life cycle theory from the trade perspective

Raymond Vernon's theory of the international product life cycle was introduced in Chapter 2, for its early contribution to our understanding of FDI and the location of production. The theory also helps to explain trade from the perspective of the firm (Wells, 1972). It traces the product's life from its launch in the home market, through to export to other markets, and, finally, its manufacture in cheaper locations for import into its original home market. The theory observes that, over the cycle, production has moved from the US to other advanced countries, and finally to developing countries, where costs are lower.

This simple outline of the product life cycle rests on a view of manufacturing which has been rather overtaken by globalization. In modern supply chains, a firm may use components from various locations, and choose yet another for assembling the final product. Because of the rapid pace of technological innovation and shortened product life cycles, a company in industries such as consumer electronics may well introduce a new product simultaneously in a number of markets, wiping out the leads and lags between markets. The model is useful in explaining production patterns for some types of products, such as standardized consumer goods, but is less useful in predicting future patterns, especially in industries dominated by a few global players. Moreover, the theory takes little account of trade barriers and government trade policies. Trade barriers of various kinds (discussed later in this chapter), are typically imposed to block imports or protect local industries.

Summary points **Product life cycle theory**

◆ This theory envisages a new product as passing through four phases from launch to maturity. Initially, it is exported abroad, but as it ages, it becomes more standardized and less costly to produce, eventually leading to production in low-cost locations around the globe.

◆ Vernon's theory can be helpful in analysing how trade has evolved in conjunction with production in low-cost economies.

Newer trade theories

More recently, theorists have turned their attention to the growing importance of MNEs in international trade, taking into account the globalization of production and trade between affiliated companies (see Chapter 2). Krugman, in his book, *Rethinking International Trade* (1994), emphasized features of the international economy such as increasing returns and imperfect competition. More precisely, he said, 'conventional trade theory views world trade as taking place entirely in goods like wheat; new trade theory sees it as being largely in goods like aircraft' (Krugman, 1994: 1). For companies, innovation and economies of scale give what are called **first-mover advantages** to early entrants in a market. This lead increases over time, making it impossible for others to catch up. For firms able to benefit in this way, the increased share in global markets has led to oligopolistic behaviour in some industries, such as the aircraft industry. For countries, there are advantages to be gained from encouraging national firms which enjoy first-mover advantages. There are clear implications here that government intervention can play a role in promoting innovation and entrepreneurship, thereby boosting competitive advantage of nations.

first-mover advantages precept that countries or firms which are first to produce a new product gain an advantage in markets that makes it virtually impossible for others to catch up

Summary points **Newer trade theories**

◆ Newer theories take account of globalization of production and the manufacture of complex products.

◆ First-mover advantages contribute to gains in industries where innovation and economies of scale are important, making it impossible for later entrants to catch up.

Porter's theory of competitive advantage

In his book, *The Competitive Advantage of Nations*, published originally in 1990, Michael Porter developed a theory of national **competitive advantage**. His considerable research, which is set out in the book, attempts to find out why some countries are more successful than others. Each nation, he says, has four broad attributes that shape its national competitive environment (Porter, 1998a: 71):

competitive advantage theory (devised by Porter) that international competitiveness depends on four major factors: demand conditions, factor conditions, firm strategy and supporting industries

* *Factor conditions* – The nation's position in factors of production, such as skilled labour or infrastructure and natural resources necessary to compete in a given industry.
* *Demand conditions* – The nature and depth of home demand for the industry's product or service.
* *Related and supporting industries* – The presence or absence in the nation of supplier industries and related industries that are internationally competitive.
* *Firm strategy, structure, and rivalry* – The conditions in the nation governing how companies are created, organized, and managed; and the nature of domestic rivalry.

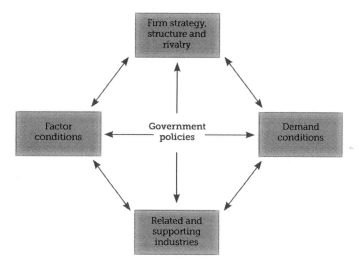

Figure 4.4 **Porter's Diamond: the determinants of national advantage**

Source: Adapted from Porter, M., *The Competitive Advantage of Nations* (Basingstoke: Macmillan Press, 1998), p. 72

The four attributes, or determinants, form a diamond shape, as shown in Figure 4.4. The first two determinants, factor conditions and demand conditions, relate to the national environment, which, for Porter, includes social and cultural environment as well as natural resources and labour market attributes. The third and fourth determinants relate to the nation's firms and industries. Porter stresses that the four determinants are interdependent. Favourable demand conditions, for example, will contribute to competitive advantage only in an environment in which firms are able and willing to respond. Advantage based on only one or two determinants may suffice in natural resource-dependent industries, or those with lower technological input, but to sustain advantage in the modern knowledge-intensive industries, advantages throughout the diamond are necessary.

Porter adds that there are two additional variables in his theory. They are chance and government. Chance can open up unexpected opportunities in a variety of ways: new inventions, external political developments, and shifts in foreign market demand. He cites the fall of communism, which resulted in the opening of Central and Eastern

Europe, as an example. His categorization of these occurrences as happening as if by chance is perhaps unfortunate, and it would be preferable to see them from the business perspective as simply opportunities. On the other hand, government policies can be highly influential, and these are therefore shown in the centre of Figure 4.4. Government policies highlighted by Porter include a strong antitrust policy, which encourages domestic rivalry, and investment in education, which generates knowledge resources. Government policies can play a crucial role in building national competitive advantage. Porter stresses that this role, however, is indirect rather than direct (Porter, 1998b: 184–6). Government remains an 'influence' rather than a 'determinant' in his model. However, government probably plays a larger direct role than his model suggests. Governments in market economies are taking on a more directly interventionist role, including ownership stakes in companies, in addition to a regulatory role. In countries climbing the economic ladder, the role of government has been a key to international success. Both these dimensions of government action are indicative of an enhanced role of the state, which is a critical theme in this book. Government guidance was crucial in Japan (see Chapter 3). In the more recent case of China, economic development has been directed by government. An important policy has been to attract FDI with business-friendly taxation regimes and the setting up of special economic zones. In addition, state-owned organizations have been instrumental in natural resources, energy, banking and the development of infrastructure. China and India provide contrasting examples. Transport and other infrastructure have developed rapidly in China, but have progressed slowly in India, largely because of lack of government impetus and complex rights over land (see closing case study in Chapter 3). On the other hand, the Indian government has prioritized investment in high-technology education, in order to attract computing and IT services industries, which have driven the country's economic growth.

Porter emphasizes that the diamond is a tool not just for explaining past competitive advantage, but also for predicting how industries will evolve in the future. The theory is useful in demonstrating the interaction between different determinants of national competitive advantage, but it probably underemphasizes world economic integration. For example, both capital and managers are now likely to be mobile. Similarly, related and supporting industries are increasingly internationalized, thanks largely to cheaper transport, reductions in import duties, and the advances in communications technology. By the 1990s, an estimated one-third of all manufactures trade involved intermediate goods (World Bank, 2000), and this proportion has now risen to 40% (UNCTAD, 2009). Intra-firm trade between MNEs and affiliates accounts for a high proportion of world exports. Intra-firm exports make up 60% of the total exports from firms under control in the US, 70% in Sweden and 20% in Japan (Onodera, 2008). It should be noted, however, that the low proportion for Japanese MNEs is probably due to the fact that Japanese firms trade heavily in *inter*-firm networks, where firms are legally distinct. Internet growth has contributed to both the growth in global sourcing of components and the growth in international trade in services.

There is an essential difference between comparative advantage, which pertains to the national *economy*, and competitive advantage, which pertains to the *companies* that make it up (Hirst and Thompson, 1999). Competitive advantage in areas such as manufacturing and services can be deliberately created and maintained (through government policy and corporate strategy), whereas comparative advantage obtains where natural factor endowments are paramount, as in agricultural and extractive industries (Hirst and Thompson, 1999; Gilpin, 2000). Hirst and Thompson

▸ More online ... Highlights of the WEF competitiveness league table may be found at http://www.weforum.org/

go on to suggest that, on the whole, it makes more sense to speak of companies, rather than countries, competing with each other. Countries do compete in, for example, attracting FDI, but here, location advantages often focus on particular regions and cities, rather than on whole countries. And competition is based on many aspects of the business environment, such as social and cultural values, which are not measurable in the same ways that relative cost structure, productivity and exchange rates are measurable (Hirst and Thompson, 1999: 122). Nonetheless, international competitiveness 'league tables', which have been compiled annually for a number of years, assess countries in terms of competitiveness. Table 4.1 shows rankings compiled by the World Economic Forum (WEF), along with the criteria used.

Table 4.1 **WEF global competitiveness rankings for 2010–2011**

The WEF criteria	WEF competitiveness ranking 2010–2011	
12 pillars	**Top 15**	**The Brics**
1 Institutions	1 Switzerland	27 China
2 Infrastructure	2 Sweden	51 India
3 Microeconomic stability	3 Singapore	58 Brazil
4 Health and primary education	4 US	63 Russia
5 Higher education and training	5 Germany	
6 Goods market efficiency	6 Japan	
7 Labour market efficiency	7 Finland	
8 Financial market sophistication	8 Netherlands	
9 Technological readiness	9 Denmark	
10 Market size	10 Canada	
11 Business sophistication	11 Hong Kong	
12 Innovation	12 UK	
	13 Taiwan	
	14 Norway	
	15 France	

Source: World Economic Forum (2010) Global Competitiveness Index 2010–2011 (Geneva: WEF)

The WEF ranked a total of 139 countries in its 2010 survey. It defines competitiveness in terms of institutions, policies, and other factors (World Economic Forum, 2009b: 4). The criteria contained in the twelve pillars focus on various indicators of a country's level of development; economic indicators are only part of the picture. An established institutional framework, high levels of education at all levels, a sound financial system and technological strengths are all attributes which propel a country up the rankings. These are more likely to be found in the advanced economies than in the developing ones. For this reason, the Brics' rankings are relatively low. It is notable that seven EU member states are in the top 15, whereas Greece (83) and Bulgaria (71) fall well below them in these rankings, highlighting variations within the EU (see Chapter 3). The US slipped from second in 2009 to fourth in 2010, reflecting institutional weaknesses.

Summary points **The theory of competitive advantage of nations**

◆ Porter's theory of competitive advantage is based on four sets of attributes: factor conditions, demand conditions, structure of domestic industries, and related industries.

◆ Other factors highlighted by Porter are chance and government policies. Together with the four sets of attributes, they form a diamond shape, which is a tool for analysing a nation's competitive advantage.

> **Critical thinking**
> Porter's theory of competitive advantage
> Porter's theory has been criticized for underestimating the role of government policies. How can the rise of China be explained in terms of Porter's diamond of competitive advantage of nations? What weaknesses in the theory have become evident?

National trade policies

National economic prosperity for almost all countries is more than ever tied in with international trade. However, benefits are not spread evenly, either between countries or between groups within individual countries. Richer countries are in a stronger position than poorer countries to use trade to foster national goals, such as food security, or benefit particular industries, such as the car industry (see case study on food security in Chapter 12). Governments face innumerable political and social, as well as economic, pressures to intervene in trade. **Protectionism** is the deliberate policy of favouring home producers, for example by subsidizing home producers or imposing import tariffs. Figure 4.5 summarizes the pros and cons of free trade which are discussed in this section. The term 'free trade' is misleading. There has never been 'free' trade in the sense of no cross-border barriers at all. 'Trade liberalization' is therefore more accurate, to indicate measures *towards* free trade, which involve reducing border controls and reducing governments' scope for curtailing imports. In this section, we look first at national priorities and then at policy tools for promoting them.

protectionism government trade policy of favouring home producers and discouraging imports

The free trade debate

In favour of free trade:

- Free trade benefits all countries
- A country risks falling behind if it is isolated from global markets
- Costs of protecting industries can be high, and tend to go to uncompetitive industries

In favour of protectionism:

- Protection of national industries promotes independence and security
- It protects domestic employment
- It supports national industries, allowing them to compete globally, and adding to national wealth

Figure 4.5 **The pros and cons of free trade**

Government perspectives on trade

Governments are perceived as ultimately responsible for the safety and well-being of those within their borders, including individual citizens, groups of people, industries and companies. We highlight below four major policy areas in which trade policy is shaped by national interests.

Promoting industrialization

Industrialization may be promoted by restricting the flow of imported products, thereby encouraging domestic manufacturing. We have seen in Chapter 3 that industrialization in many countries, such as Japan and the newly industrialized countries of South East Asia, has been guided by government, through industrial policy. These countries have made rapid transitions from mainly agricultural to industrial economies. The 'infant industries' argument holds that developing countries should protect infant industries in which they have potential comparative advantage until they are strong enough to survive when protections are removed. Japan is an example of both successful infant industry support and industrial policy (Gilpin, 2000). For Singapore and other tiger economies, foreign direct investors provided the impetus for development. Industrialization may focus on **import substitution,** that is, producing goods for domestic consumption which otherwise would have been imported. India is an example, featured in the closing case study of Chapter 3. Domestic industries nurtured through protective measures in this way do not always become competitive in world markets. Export-led development, by contrast, focuses on growth in export-oriented goods. Industrialization in China has taken this route.

import substitution approach to economic development which favours producing goods for domestic consumption that otherwise would have been imported

Protecting employment

By restricting imports, governments aim to safeguard domestic jobs. However, the situation is seldom as simple as this. A common fear of US workers in manufacturing industries is that their jobs have gone to lower-paid overseas workers. Work in lower-skilled jobs, as in the textile industry, is particularly vulnerable to being lost to low-cost imports. Proponents of trade liberalization would argue that protectionist measures are damaging to the economy in the long term. They assert that restricting imports may lead to retaliation, so that a country's exporters in profitable sectors may suffer, causing job losses in those sectors. Import restrictions may also have a dampening effect on *foreign* workers' incomes, which translates into a decrease in jobs in domestic export industries. Workers in industrialized countries who are displaced by global competitive forces are usually those without the skills to benefit from the newer job opportunities. Whole regions can suffer as a result. In the long term, it could be argued, governments need to look at education and training needs of the economy to enhance competitive advantage. Nonetheless, protectionist pressures are very strong; special interests' regional strongholds are often effective in mobilizing political support.

Protecting consumers

Conventional wisdom holds that consumers benefit from free trade in that competition in markets brings down prices and increases choice among all products, from agricultural produce to televisions. Both agriculture and consumer electronics have become global industries. The industrialization and globalization of the food chain have resulted in agricultural produce and livestock being transported hundreds – even thousands – of miles to markets. An outcome is that any health and safety concerns, such as contamination from BSE in beef, can have wide ramifications.

Governments have at their disposal a variety of regulatory measures in respect of consumer products such as food and medicines, whether produced at home or abroad. However, levels of regulation and quality controls differ from country to country. With the rise in world trade, it becomes difficult in practice for governments and port authorities to keep out dangerous imported toys or contaminated food.

Promoting strategic interests

Strategic interests cover a number of considerations. It is often thought that the strategic sensitivity of defence industries dictates that domestic suppliers are preferable to foreign ones, and thus should be protected. The strategic necessity argument can

MEET THE CEO

▶ More online ... P&G's website is www.pg.com

Robert McDonald CEO of Procter & Gamble (P&G)

If P&G wished to signal to the world that it is shifting its focus to emerging markets, it could have found no better way than to appoint Robert McDonald as CEO in 2009. Taking over from A.G. Lafley, who had continued a long-term restructuring of the company, as well as presiding over notable acquisitions such as Clairol beauty products, McDonald represents a shift in focus more towards emerging markets and lower-end products. McDonald describes his appointment as 'continuity with change' (Birchall, 'Analysis ...'). P&G has always appointed new CEOs from within, and McDonald is no exception, having been with the company 29 years. Before joining the company, he was in the US Army, specializing in managing in rough terrains. A decade-long stay in Asian markets (the Philippines and Japan) led him to see the scope for designing products for lower-income customers, especially in the developing world. He allegedly travelled by canoe to outlying Philippine islands to ask villagers what detergent and soap they were using. He says of the private label competition, 'There is no reason for anyone to have to use a private label. We should be able to innovate at multiple price points' (Birchall, 'Analysis ...'). In 2009, only about half of P&G's product lines had a lower-priced version, and he wishes to see this proportion rise to 75%. His refocusing is not just on developing countries. He points out that minority communities of Hispanics and African Americans in the US are likely to become the majority before 2045. Designing products and packaging to suit recent Mexican immigrants, with lower prices than the company's mainstream products, is a way of attracting Hispanic consumers.

McDonald argues that a free trade environment is most conducive to global growth and prosperity. It has also facilitated the company's expansion of its international business: 20% of P&G jobs in the US depend on the company's international business, which represents 60% of its annual sales revenues of $79 billion in total. He is concerned that the US government is becoming more protectionist, saying, 'It is short-sighted for the US government to think they can create jobs at home by hurting our ability to

P&G has become adept at designing products and packaging, such as laundry detergent, for poorer consumers

Source: Istock

compete internationally' (Birchall, 'P&G warns ...'). He points to the situation in India and China, where half a billion people have come out of poverty. The impressive growth figures of their economies have rested, he says, on free trade. And he urges that P&G's strategy must focus on these markets because this is where future growth will lie.

Sources: Birchall, J. (2009) 'Analysis: tumble cycle', *Financial Times*, 18 December; Birchall, J. (2009) 'P&G warns over growth of global protectionism', *Financial Times*, 18 December; Birchall, J. (2009) 'P&G sales drive targets Hispanics', *Financial Times*, 28 December; Wolf, C. (2009) '"Very Procter" McDonald reached top job with canoe and parachute', Bloomberg news, 11 June, at www.bloomberg.com

▶ More online ... The Airbus website is www.airbus.com

be extended to a great number of products. It was used to provide federal funding for the semiconductor industry in the US in the 1990s, as semiconductors are crucial to defence systems. Food production is one of the most heavily protected industries, because of the strategic importance of safeguarding food supply and also agricultural employment. On this reasoning, subsidies and import restrictions have long bene-fited Japanese farmers, while Japanese consumers have paid well above world prices for their food. These barriers are only slowly coming down. In 2008, after 20 years of price stability, sharp rises in global prices of basic commodities, including wheat and rice, caused shortages around the world, leading to food riots in some countries. As a result, food security has risen up the agenda, and a number of countries, including China and Saudi Arabia, are acquiring farmland in poor developing countries, mainly in Africa, where food is being grown to feed their home populations. This practice is being monitored by the UN's Food and Agricultural Organization, for its long-term implications, especially in the developing countries which are giving over land for this purpose (see case study in Chapter 12). These countries themselves have a growing problem of food security.

Strategic industries are also a target of policymakers. Strategic trade policy holds that governments can assist their own firms in particular industries to gain competi-tive advantage. This theory mainly applies to oligopolistic industries such as the aerospace industry, in which the US helped Boeing by providing it with lucrative defence contracts, while European governments helped Airbus through subsidies. Both sides have accused each other of breaching WTO rules restricting state aid, resulting in a long-running legal action under the WTO's dispute procedure.

Trade policies may be linked to foreign policy objectives, as was clearly demon-strated during the cold war, when trade followed political and military alliances. Government overseas aid packages to developing countries may be tied to trade. Trade policies are often based on historical relationships between countries, for example those between the former colonial powers of Europe and their former colonies. This resulted in another long-running dispute between the EU and US. The so-called 'banana dispute' had its roots in the preferential treatment that former colonies in the Caribbean have continued to receive, which were found to contravene WTO rules.

Protecting national culture

For governments, maintaining national culture and identity is an important aspect of social stability. This covers literature, film, music and other cultural products. The growth of the internet and global media has led to fears of cultural globalization, prompting some national authorities to limit foreign content and foreign ownership in these sectors. Internet censorship, which has become highly elaborate in some countries, is based in some measure on the perception by the government that the free flow of content from abroad can undermine national cultural and social values (see case study in Chapter 8).

Summary points Why governments intervene in trade

◆ Governments have differing priorities within their domestic economies. For developing countries, industrialization can be promoted through export-led FDI.

◆ Protecting domestic employment is a concern of all governments, as it is closely linked to social stability.

◆ Governments see trade as strategically important, and aim to safeguard strategic industries, both for domestic security and to create globally competitive industries.

▶ More online ... Japanese carmakers have a US association, the Japan Automobile Manufacturers Association, at www.jama.org, where there is information on their role in the US car industry.

Critical thinking

Government intervention in trade

Although governments pay lip service to free trade, protectionist pressures abound. Weigh up the possible benefits to the national economy against the risks when governments intervene in trade to foster national strategic objectives. Give examples.

Tools of governmental trade policy

Government policies affect trade in numerous ways, both directly and indirectly. Of direct impact is the manipulation of exchange rates. Devaluing a country's currency will have the immediate effect of making exports cheaper and imports more expensive (see Chapter 9). However, governments now have less scope for manipulating exchange rates in increasingly interlinked currency markets. Similarly, most governments are now party to multilateral and regional trading arrangements which curtail their ability to control trade. We will therefore look at government policy options in the context of changing global and regional contexts. The traditional tools for controlling trade are tariffs, quotas, subsidies, and other non-tariff barriers to trade.

tariff tax imposed by governments on traded goods and services, usually imports but can also be on exports

The classic tool of trade policy is the **tariff**, or duty payable on goods traded. Tariffs are usually imposed on imported goods, but they can also be imposed on exports. When we think of protectionism, we think naturally of tariff barriers. The tariff raises the price of an imported product, thereby benefiting domestic producers of the same product. Japanese whisky producers have been protected in this way by huge import duties levied on foreign whisky. The sums collected also swell government coffers. The main losers are the consumers, who pay higher prices for the imported product. While tariffs on manufactured goods have diminished dramatically, thanks to the multilateral GATT (discussed later), tariffs on agricultural products are still common.

import quota a barrier to trade which consists of limiting the quantity of an imported product that can legally enter a country

The **import quota** limits the quantity of an imported product that can legally enter a country. Licences may be issued annually to a limited number of firms, each of which must stay within the amounts specified in its import licence. Limits are set so as to allow only a portion of the market to foreign goods, thus protecting the market share of domestic producers. Restricting supply in this way is likely to result in higher prices for consumers. Import quotas are sometimes evaded by companies shipping goods via other countries with quota to spare when their home country's quota is used up. An exporting firm may ultimately set up production in a country to avoid the imposition of quotas.

voluntary export restraint (VER) tool of government trade policy by which trading partners wishing to export into a country are encouraged to limit their exports, or else incur the imposition of tariffs or import quotas

An alternative to the import quota is the **voluntary export restraint (VER)**, which shifts the onus on the exporting country to limit its exports, or possibly risk the imposition of quotas or tariffs. A leading example of the VER has been Japanese car exports to the US. In the 1980s, when the Japanese motor industry was growing apace and making rapid inroads in the American market, the US government persuaded Japan to agree to a VER. A way around these restrictions is to set up local production, which Japanese manufacturers have done in the US and other markets. The protectionist urge, however, is still strong, as governments have imposed **local content requirements**, to insure that local component suppliers gain. Japanese motor manufacturers have responded by locating associated Japanese component manufacturers near to assembly plants in the overseas location, thus facilitating just-in-time operations and maintaining high levels of local content.

local content requirements trade policy which requires foreign investors to use local component suppliers in, for example, manufacturing

subsidies payments from public funds to support domestic industries; can also be export subsidies to home producers to bolster a country's exports

Government **subsidies** are payments from public funds to support domestic producers. Some subsidies to domestic producers are justified by governments as a strategic need. For example, they maintain the livelihoods of farmers who provide basic domestic food supplies. This justification can be distinguished from the argument used to justify programmes to boost farmers' incomes for the purpose of enabling them to export cheaply. The latter line of reasoning is that the extra funds, which are export subsidies, will boost the local producers' competitive position in global markets, and can be helpful across many sectors, including agricultural products and cars. Export subsidies run counter to WTO rules as they distort markets. Some types of state funding fall into a more nebulous, 'grey' area. For example, R&D grants can help local producers indirectly, and funds to promote green technology are viewed as legitimate. There are other types of state aid, including loans at preferential rates and tax concessions. Although countries within a 'strong state' tradition, such as France, are more likely to favour state aid than the US and UK, which are in the liberal market tradition, all three – and many others, including the Brics – have pumped public funds into domestic industries.

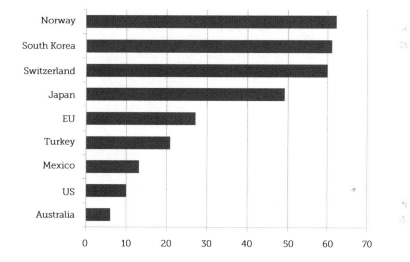

Figure 4.6 **Subsidies to agricultural producers as a percentage of gross farm receipts in selected OECD countries, 2008**

Source: OECD (2009)
Agricultural Policies in OECD Countries: Monitoring and Evaluation (Paris: OECD)

Advocates of trade liberalization criticize subsidies on several grounds. Subsidies work against a 'level playing field' for trade, as unsubsidized foreign firms claim that they face unfair competition. And, although subsidies aim to increase the competitiveness of domestic firms, they do not encourage local firms to be more efficient. Often, they protect inefficient producers (and jobs), creating a culture of dependence on subsidies. Agriculture is a traditionally heavily subsidized sector (see Figure 4.6). The EU, through the Common Agricultural Policy, has provided substantial subsidies for farmers since 1962, creating considerable trade friction with other nations. The extent of EU support diminished in the 1990s, but agriculture continues to be a highly politically sensitive sector. Across the OECD, the level of support was 21% in 2008, the lowest level it has been since the 1980s (OECD, 2009a). The reason, however, is not a general shift of government policy away from subsidies, but the fact that world prices for agricultural commodities rose sharply in 2008, following two decades of relative stability.

As trade in the post-war period has expanded, tariff barriers have generally come down, largely as a result of multilateral initiatives (discussed below). On the other hand, many non-tariff barriers have proliferated, in both developed and developing countries. Countries have increasingly used the WTO's anti-dumping rules to block imports. These are discussed in the next section.

Summary points **Tools of government trade policy**

- Government trade policies can be aimed at protecting the country's producers, through programmes such as state

subsidies, or discouraging foreign producers, through import duties and import quotas.

- Although formal tariff barriers have tended to come down, non-tariff barriers still proliferate, indicating the strength of protectionist pressures.

Global and regional trade patterns

Figure 4.7 shows merchandise trade flows within and between regions. Europe is the largest of these regions, accounting for 41% of world merchandise exports. It is a significant exporter to the other three regions, as the figure shows, but the bulk of European countries' trade (69.7%) is with other European countries. Europe is Asia's largest export market, but Asian countries' main markets are other Asian countries: 55.9% of Asia's trade is intra-regional. North America is another important destination for Asian exports, amounting to $775.02 billion in 2008. Goods from Asia account for 28.6% of North America's imports, whereas goods from North America account for only 9.6% of Asia's imports. North America's intra-regional trade flows amount to only 37.5% of the region's trade. Of the three countries in North America, both Canada and Mexico are dependent on exporting to the US, whereas most of the exports from the US go to destinations outside the region.

African countries are less economically integrated than other regions: only 11.7% of their trade flows are within the region. As we discuss later in this chapter, efforts towards regional integration are helping to increase cross-border trade within Africa. Africa's largest export market is Europe, while European countries supply the largest portion of Africa's imports (40.5%). Asian exports to Africa, however, are on the increase. China's exports to Africa rose from $26.19 billion in 2006 to $50.16 billion in 2008, nearly doubling in two years.

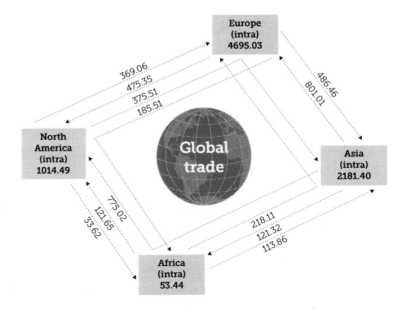

Figure 4.7 **Merchandise trade flows between and within selected regions, 2008** (in $US billions)

Source: WTO, International trade statistics 2009, at www.wto.org

Africa's natural resources: the example of Ghana

Ghana has long been blessed with gold reserves, valuable and relatively easy to mine in comparison with the metal found in other gold-rich African countries, such as South Africa. And Ghana has been fortunate: although mines in other countries have become dangerous or unproductive, it registered a 10% increase in production in 2008. The price of gold surged following the financial crisis of 2008, as investors sought safe havens. Ghana's mining companies have benefited, and so has the country, but the government is now looking at whether the country is getting a fair return. President John Atta Mills was elected in 2008, marking the second peaceful transfer of power in the country, an example that stands out in Africa's turbulent political scene. The new government is now looking at how best to exploit further gains for the country while continuing to encourage foreign investors.

Ghana introduced incentives to attract foreign mining companies to invest in 1986. Mining companies have invested $6.7 billion in the country since 1994. Seven companies altogether made $2.1 billion in revenues, $146 million of which (about 7%) went to the Ghanaian state, mainly through royalties and taxes. Mining multinationals, Newmont of the US and South Africa's AngloGold Ashanti, have led the investment in Ghana's goldmines, but both have been implicated in cyanide spills and human rights violations.

Ghana remains a very poor country. Although the numbers living in poverty have diminished to just under a third of the population, progress in poverty reduction has been disappointingly slow in rural areas (IMF, 2009). Ghana ranks a lowly 152 out of 182 countries in the UN's human development index (UNDP, 2009). With gold prices now rising, the Ghanaian parliament voted to raise the royalties from 3% to 5% in 2010. However, the companies have resisted stoutly. They argued that their agreements were sacrosanct, incapable of being overridden by new law (Burgis, 2010). They also said that planned future investments would be jeopardized if the government altered their terms. Ghana's government is well aware that its reputation with

foreign investors could be dented if it imposed more onerous terms, and the country depends on gold for 40% of its exports. But it is also aware that environmental damage, particularly from cyanide spills, has been an issue for communities, leaving the perception that mining companies take the profits with minimal accountability to communities. In a report of 2009, the IMF found Ghana to have 'weak institutional capacities for environmental management' (IMF, 2009).

The government's resolve is facing another challenge in that oil discoveries off its coast in 2007 look set to usher in an oil boom. The Jubilee field is forecast to pump 120,000 barrels of oil per day from 2010 onwards. Oil earnings could eclipse those of gold and cocoa, its other primary natural resource. The government is firm that the oil investments must take into account benefits to all sectors of the economy. The world's large oil companies have eyed the prospects in Ghana, which look inviting in comparison to the resource nationalism evident in countries such as Russia and Venezuela. Tullow Oil of the UK, which acquired three exploration licences from the government, has been successful in its oil explorations in a number of offshore sites. It has worked with other specialist foreign companies in the field, including Kosmos Energy of Texas. ExxonMobil came forward in late 2009, agreeing to buy the stake held by Kosmos in Ghana's oil fields. However, Ghana's government initially blocked the bid by ExxonMobil, and was said to favour a deal with CNOOC, the Chinese state-owned oil company.

US President Barack Obama, on a visit to Ghana in 2009, praised the country for its governance, but warned that the oil issue could detract from its success (Hoyos, 2009). Ghana's oil seemed to be a prize dangling between an established superpower and an aspiring one: the strategic interests of both were at stake. Ghana's government had many factors to consider. Which potential investors had the technology and development expertise needed over the long term? How can the benefits for Ghana as a country be maximized? Ghana's president said, 'We must make sure oil and gas become a blessing. We must get

▶ More online ... Newmont Mining is at www.newmont.com
ExxonMobil is at www.exxonmobil.com
Tullow Oil is at www.tullowoil.com

Turning the prospect of oil riches into reality: Tullow's employees are shown at work in Ghana's Jubilee oil field

Source: Tullow Oil

competent people to manage the resources, to account for the resources and we must use them to build a stronger economy and invest in our people' (Wallis, 2009). Ghana's president remained reluctant to allow the deal with ExxonMobil to go through. In August 2010, the agreement Kosmos had signed with ExxonMobil was ended.

Sources: Burgis, T. (2009) 'Gold-diggers boost production to help meet world demand', *Financial Times*, 4 December; Hoyos, C. (2009) 'Ghana moves to block Exxon bid for stake in Jubilee field', *Financial Times*, 13 October; Burgis, T. (2010) 'Mining money fails to usher in golden era for Ghana', *Financial Times*, 23 March; Wallis, W. (2009) 'Finds put Ghanaians on a roller coaster of expectations', *Financial Times*, 4 December; *The Economist* (2010) 'Carats and sticks', 3 April; IMF (2009) *Ghana: Poverty Reduction Strategy Report* (Washington, DC: IMF); UNDP (2009) Human Development Index, as www.undp.org

Questions for discussion

◆ Why are natural resources in Ghana, as in other African countries, considered a curse as well as a blessing?
◆ What is the role of foreign oil companies in exploiting Africa's resources, and how is it changing?
◆ What advice would you give to Ghana's government in deciding which foreign investors to welcome and on what terms?

► More online ... The WTO website is http://www.wto.org
The International Monetary Fund (IMF) website is http://www.imf.org
The World Bank's website is http://www.worldbank.org

Summary points   Global trade patterns

◆ Intra-regional trade is more significant in Europe and Asia than in the other continents.

◆ Asian countries export largely to the EU and North America, but the US has a large trade deficit with Asian countries, as its imports far exceed its exports.

◆ Africa is becoming integrated in world trade, its major trading partners being in Europe. However, trade relations with Asia, especially China, are increasing.

Critical thinking

Neighbours first?

Which regions have the greatest disparity between intra-regional trade and trade with the rest of the world? In your view, would countries be best advised to foster greater regional ties or to trade more with other world regions, and why?

International regulation of trade

Bretton Woods agreement agreement between Allied nations in the aftermath of the Second World War, which was intended to bring about exchange rate stability; established the IMF and World Bank

multilateral agreement international agreement signed by many countries, usually in the form of a treaty which creates legal obligations

Institutional arrangements put in place in the immediate aftermath of the Second World War have played a major role in establishing a global trading order. The preceding era, scarred by the Great Depression of the 1930s, had seen protectionism and a decline in world trade. Under the **Bretton Woods agreement**, reached at a conference of the allied nations in 1944, exchange rate stability would be achieved by pegging every currency to gold or the US dollar (see Chapter 9). Negotiators envisaged the **multilateral agreement** involving many countries as a means of dismantling barriers to trade. They also laid plans for an international trade organization (ITO) to bring down tariff barriers, but the charter eventually drawn up in 1948 met with little enthusiasm from nations, still reluctant to endorse free trade. Instead, a more modest set of proposals for a weaker institutional framework was formulated, in the General Agreement on Tariffs and Trade (GATT), which we introduced in Chapter 2. Under the GATT, successive rounds of negotiations have brought about global trade liberalization, leading to the establishment in 1995 of the WTO, reminiscent of the stronger body envisaged in early days after the war. The WTO now has 153 member states. Two other institutions set up as a result of post-war initiatives were the International Monetary Fund (IMF) and the International Bank for Reconstruction and Development (the World Bank), both of which are discussed in Chapter 9. The Bretton Woods system disintegrated in the early 1970s, bringing about a resurgence of protectionism. The period 1945–70 has been called the 'golden age of capitalism' (Michie and Kitson, 1995). In this section, we examine how the WTO's regulatory framework has evolved.

GATT principles

most-favoured-nation principle (MFN) GATT principle by which the most favourable tariff treatment negotiated with one country is extended to similar goods from all countries

The GATT provided the principles and foundation for the development of a global trading system, which were carried forward into the WTO. Perhaps the most important of these is non-discrimination, or the **most-favoured-nation principle (MFN)**. There are two aspects to this principle:

1   Favourable tariff treatment negotiated with one country will be extended to similar goods from all countries.

▸ More online ... The WTO has a gateway on anti-dumping issues, at www.wto.org/english/tratop_e/adp_e/adp_e.htm

2 Under the principle of 'national treatment', imported goods are treated for all purposes in the same way as domestic goods of the same type.

MFN status is negotiated between countries, and while it is the norm among trading partners, there are exceptions. US legislation has linked MFN treatment with human rights record. Because of its poor human rights record, China was granted only temporary MFN status from 1980 onwards, which was renewed annually. Unconditional MFN status came in 2000, paving the way for China's WTO membership. Russia is the one Bric country which is not a WTO member.

Other GATT principles include reciprocity, requiring tariff reductions by one country to be matched by its trading partners; and transparency, ensuring that the underlying aims of all trade measures are clear. The principle of fairness allows a country that has suffered from unfair trading practices by a trading partner to take protectionist measures against that country. Defining fair practice is at the heart of many trade disputes, as countries naturally have differing perspectives on what is and is not fair. An example is **dumping**, or the sale of goods abroad at below the price charged for comparable goods in the producing country. The GATT **anti-dumping** agreement of 1994 allows anti-dumping duties to be imposed on the exporting country by the importing country, in order to protect local producers from unfair competition. The country making allegations of dumping against another asks the WTO to investigate the matter. The number of investigations initiated by the WTO increased from 163 in 2007 to 208 in 2008. China was the most frequently cited country alleged to be engaged in dumping, and the countries that launched the most anti-dumping complaints were India and Brazil, not – as one might expect – the advanced western economies.

dumping sale of goods abroad at below the price charged for comparable goods in the producing country

anti-dumping rules WTO rules which allow anti-dumping duties to be imposed on the exporting country by the importing country, in order to protect local producers from unfair competition

The Uruguay Round, culminating in the 1994 GATT, laid the groundwork for future trade liberalization, while allowing countries to take limited steps to safeguard national industries. It resulted in worldwide tariff reductions of about 40% on manufactured goods. Less spectacularly, it made strides in the more difficult areas of reducing trade barriers in agricultural products and textiles. It also initiated agreements on intellectual property rights and services, both crucial areas in growing world trade. Finally, the GATT 1994 created the WTO as its successor institution.

Summary points GATT principles

● Under the most-favoured-nation (MFN) principle, a favourable tariff agreed on a specific product with

one country applies to all member countries.

● Other important GATT principles are transparency and fair practices.

WTO and the regulation of world trade

Whereas in 1947 the GATT created only a weak institutional framework, the WTO, which came into being in 1995, was designed on firmer legal footing, with a stronger rule-governed orientation. This approach is reflected in its organizational structure. A Ministerial Conference, consisting of trade ministers of all member states, is the main policymaking body, meeting every two years. A Dispute Settlement Body overseas the dispute settlement procedure for specific trade disputes between countries. This new legal procedure for resolving disputes marks a sharp departure from the GATT procedure, which had no power of enforcement.

► More online ... The Office of the US Trade Representative is at www.ustr.gov

The WTO's dispute settlement procedure aims to resolve trade disputes through impartial panels before they escalate into damaging trade wars in which countries take unilateral action against each other. A country that feels it has suffered because of another's breach of trading rules may apply to the WTO, which appoints an impartial panel for hearing the case within a specified timetable. A country found to be in breach of trade rules by a panel may appeal to the Appellate Body. If it is again found to be in the wrong, the WTO may authorize the country whose trade has suffered as a result, to impose retaliatory trade sanctions.

For the WTO's procedure to succeed, countries must adhere to its decisions, even when they disagree with them. All countries enjoy a recognized right to safeguard national interests, but this principle, as well as interpretation of WTO rules themselves, is subject to considerable latitude in interpretation. If countries impose unilateral sanctions, bypassing the WTO, then WTO procedures, and the authority that underlies them, could be eroded. The US law known as Section 301 is such a provision. Originally enacted in the Trade Act 1974, it authorizes the US to retaliate unilaterally against other countries (as opposed to specific companies) that it judges are violating a GATT provision or unfairly restricting the import of US goods or services. Section 301 was strengthened in 1988, authorizing the US Trade Representative (USTR) to identify 'priority trade practices' of other countries that pose the greatest barriers to US trade, and to single out particular countries which have a history of trade discrimination. Under this legislation a country could lose access to the entire US market, not merely that of the offending product. The legislation has been criticized for its aggressive unilateral approach, which, some argue, is in breach of WTO rules (Sell, 2000). In February 2000, a WTO panel ruled, in what was seen by a number of developing countries as an unsatisfactory decision, that Section 301 is not incompatible with WTO rules, so long as the US refrained from taking unilateral action. Recent monitoring by the USTR has focused on intellectual property rights, relevant to medicines under pharmaceutical patents and copyright material, which are frequently cited as areas in which there is thriving trade in counterfeit goods, produced without permission of legal owners (discussed further in Chapter 10).

Summary points The WTO

● Following in the footsteps of the GATT, the WTO provided a structural and institutional framework for applying multilateral trade rules and negotiating trade agreements.

● The WTO's dispute settlement procedure depends on its perceived fairness and on countries' continued adherence to its rules.

Multilateral trade agreements and the WTO

The WTO has made a dramatic impact in focusing international attention on issues of world trade, but it has also sparked considerable controversy. Since its creation in 1995, issues of globalization and the rise of developing nations have come to the fore, involving the WTO in wider debates. Its meetings have been targeted by demonstrations, from anti-capitalist protesters to environmental activists. In addition, NGOs have been instrumental in vocalizing environmental and human rights issues. Within multilateral negotiations themselves, national interests have remained divergent. Developing and emerging countries seek the opening of markets in rich countries,

▸ More online ... Doha Round issues can be found under 'trade topics' on the WTO's website at www.wto.org

while rich countries wish to export more easily to markets in the developing world. Both developed and developing countries fear that the removal of barriers will open their economies to damaging competition which could jeopardize local industries; hence, all are reluctant to make concessions.

In 2001, a new round of multilateral trade negotiations, known as the Doha Round, commenced in Doha, Qatar. Negotiations continued at several ministerial conferences which followed, but the major policy areas, which had been carried forward from the Uruguay Round, generated sharp divergence of perspectives, mainly between developed and developing countries. It was intended that the new Doha agreement would be in place by the end of 2008, but negotiations faltered once again, and the deteriorating global economic situation at the time seemed to dampen national leaders' appetites for further multilateral talks. Areas in which agreement was sought included agriculture, opening of markets, and access to patented drugs. Other issues were labour standards, environmental protection, and competition policy. Doha was described as a 'development' round, focusing on issues central to developing countries. These countries have been firm in their view that progress must be made by rich countries in reducing farm subsidies and tariffs. A framework agreement on the principle of reducing farm subsidies was reached in 2004, but it lacked detailed provisions. A draft accord on measures to ease access to cheap medicines for poor countries was also agreed in 2004. Welcomed by developing countries, it caused alarm in the pharmaceutical industry.

The Doha Round placed issues of labour standards and the environment on the agenda for future consideration. Environmentalists argue that if issues such as global warming and protection of the rainforests are not brought into the equation, commercial goals will win out and the environment will suffer. Trade unionists in industrialized economies, fearful of job losses, argue for the inclusion of labour standards in trade policy. Moreover, labour standards, including condemnation of practices such as child labour, have come to be included in human rights principles generally. These issues crystallized over China's application for WTO membership: its poor human rights record and weak environmental protection regulation were major hurdles to its eventually gaining WTO membership in 2002. Since then, China's growing strength as a trading superpower has tended to overshadow ethical and environmental concerns in the many countries with which China is developing trading ties. A rift between developed and developing countries seemed to cast a cloud over future multilateral negotiations.

Summary points The Doha Round

● Intended to be a 'development' round, the Doha multilateral negotiations reached only tentative agreements on development issues such as reducing tariffs on agricultural products.

● Other agenda items were labour standards and the environment, but different perspectives of developed and developing countries cast doubt on the future of multilateral negotiations generally.

Regional and bilateral trade agreements

Although the WTO has promoted a multilateral approach to trade liberalization, countries have been active in making their own agreements to liberalize trade with

bilateral agreement an
agreement between
two countries, often for
reciprocal trade terms

**free trade agreement
(FTA)** any agreement
between countries which
aims to liberalize trade
among them; often
bilateral or regional

**regional trade
agreement (RTA)** free
trade agreement among
a number of countries
in the same broad
geographic region

trading partners, both within their own geographical regions and beyond. It is common to make a distinction between a **bilateral agreement**, between just two countries, often just called a **free trade agreement (FTA)**, and a **regional trade agreement (RTA)** among a number of countries in the same broad geographic region. However, from the WTO's perspective, both types of agreement, which lie outside the multilateral system, are treated broadly as regional trade agreements. The RTA is often referred to as a 'preferential trade agreement' (PTA), reflecting the fact that its terms give preference to goods and services from countries which are parties to the particular agreement. The number of RTAs (including bilateral agreements) notified to the WTO has grown dramatically in recent years, now reaching over 400, as Figure 4.8 shows. Although they are not all active, this rise shows a marked trend towards trade initiatives outside the multilateral system. Here, we look at these initiatives, distinguishing between regional and bilateral agreements, and then assess their impacts on the global economy.

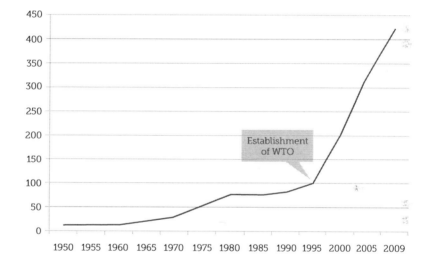

Figure 4.8 **Regional
trade agreements
notified through the
GATT and WTO in the
post-war era**

Source: WTO (2009) RTA
notifications, RTA portal at
www.wto.org

Categories of regional trade agreement

Countries look naturally to trade with their neighbours. Not only does regional trade make sense in terms of costs, firms are likely to have greater familiarity with firms and industries in their own region than with those oceans away. RTAs are designed to bring down trade barriers among their member states, thus opening up regional markets for national producers. A group of countries that have joined in an RTA are sometimes referred to as a **free trade area or bloc**. The RTA can cover a range of issues besides trade, including investment, intellectual property protection and environmental protection. Political considerations can play a key role, as economic integration is inseparable from the political power balance within any region, and regional trading blocs are influential in global politics. We begin by looking at the categories of regional groupings, expanded from the one originally devised by Bela Balassa in *The Theory of Economic Integration* (Balassa, 1962). They can be categorized accordingly:

free trade area or bloc
a group of countries
which have joined in a
regional trade agreement

* **Free trade area** – Member states agree to remove trade barriers among themselves, but keep their separate national barriers against trade with non-member states.

- **Customs union** – Member states remove all trade barriers among themselves and adopt a common set of external barriers.
- **Common market** – Member states enjoy free movement of goods, labour and capital.
- **Economic union** – Member states unify all their economic policies, including monetary, fiscal and welfare policies.
- **Political union** – Member states transfer sovereignty to the regional political and law-making institutions, creating a new 'superstate'.

Most of the world's nations belong to at least one regional grouping, the vast majority of which fall into the first two categories – free trade area and customs union (see Table 4.2). The categories can be seen as successive steps towards deepening economic integration. Only the EU has reached the stage of economic union. Political union is still some way off, but reforms in 2009 have enhanced the role of the European Parliament, discussed in Chapter 7. Free trade areas are now in place in all the world's regions, although with less regional economic integration than in Europe.

Table 4.2 **Regional trade groupings**

Region	Group	Current member countries	Date of formation	Type of agreement
South America	Mercosur (Southern Common Market)	Argentina, Brazil, Paraguay, Uruguay	1991	Common market
South America	Andean Community	Bolivia, Colombia, Ecuador, Peru	1969	Free trade area
Asia-Pacific	Apec (Asia-Pacific Economic Cooperation Group)	21 countries: Australia, Brunei, Canada, Indonesia, Japan, South Korea, Malaysia, New Zealand, Philippines, Singapore, Thailand, US, China, Hong Kong, Taiwan, Mexico, Papua New Guinea, Chile, Peru, Russia, Vietnam	1989	Free trade area to be in place by 2020
South East Asia	Asean (Association of South East Asian Nations)	Indonesia, Malaysia, Philippines, Singapore, Thailand, Brunei, Cambodia, Laos, Myanmar (Burma), Vietnam	1967	Co-operation agreement, free trade by early 2010
Caribbean	CARICOM (Caribbean Community)	15 Caribbean nations: Antigua and Barbuda, Bahamas, Barbados, Belize, Dominica, Grenada, Guyana, Haiti, Jamaica, Monserrat, St Lucia, St Kitts and Nevis, St Vincent and the Grenadines, Suriname, Trinidad and Tobago	1973	Common market
Europe	EFTA (European Free Trade Area)	Iceland, Switzerland, Norway, Liechtenstein	1960	Free trade area
	EU (European Union)	Austria, Belgium, Denmark, France, Finland, Germany, Greece, Ireland, Italy, Luxembourg, the Netherlands, Portugal, Spain, Sweden, UK, Czech Republic, Poland, Hungary, Slovenia, Slovakia, Estonia, Lithuania, Latvia, Cyprus, Malta	1957	Economic union, moving towards political union
North and Central America	Nafta (North America Free Trade Agreement)	Canada, Mexico, US	1994	Free trade area

▸ More online ... The WTO has a web page on regional trade agreements, under 'trade topics' at www.wto.org

Region	Group	Current member countries	Date of formation	Type of agreement
Africa	Ecowas (Economic Community of West African States)	15 members: Benin, Burkina Faso, Cote d'Ivoire, Gambia, Ghana, Guinea, Guinea Bissau, Liberia, Mali, Niger, Nigeria, Senegal, Sierra Leone, Togo, Cape Verde	1975	Customs union
Africa	East African Community (EAC)	Kenya, Tanzania, Uganda, Rwanda, Burundi	2001	Common market

Summary points Levels of regional integration

● The free trade area, in which customs barriers are reduced among member states, is the commonest type of regional free trade agreement.

● The RTA can, and often does, cover many areas in addition to trade, including investment and intellectual property protection.

● Moves to achieve greater integration, involving economic and political union, have occurred mainly in the EU.

Focus on regions

In this section we look in turn at the major geographic regions of the world, describing the free trade groupings in each, along with regional variations and prospects for the future.

Europe

As early as the Treaty of Rome in 1957 the founding six members of the European Economic Community, later the EU, envisaged both economic and political integration (see Chapter 3 for a discussion of EU economic goals). The institutions set up, dominated by the Commission and Council, have remained the structural foundations, and the European Court of Justice has established its legal supremacy (see Chapters 7 and 8). No other regional grouping begins to approach this level of structural autonomy. However, the goal of Single European Market, which was the cornerstone of European economic integration, has come about only gradually, and amid a good deal of political and bureaucratic stalemate. The Single European Act of 1987 aimed to dismantle internal barriers and establish a single market by 1992. Businesses would be able to move seamlessly from one member country to another without bureaucratic frontier procedures. Product standards would be recognized between member states. Financial services would be liberalized, so that firms such as banks and insurance companies could compete across national borders.

In reality, progress in internal liberalization has been neither as swift nor as easy as many predicted back in 1987. Liberalizing of financial services began in the mid-1990s. Banks and investors urged speeding up of the necessary legislation, which has taken years, and there are still national barriers to cross-border financial services. Telecommunications deregulation and deregulation of utilities such as water, gas and electricity have been uneven. Histories of protected industries and varying degrees of state ownership have slowed progress. Deeply rooted national cultural differences were underestimated, and domestic political considerations have loomed large. The latter have sparked continuing debate on principles of sovereignty and national identity, and also the economic interests of groups of workers affected by liberalization.

▶ More online ... The EU's main portal is http://europa.eu.int
Mercosur is at http://www.mercosur.org

For agriculture, the effect of the GATT Agriculture Agreement of 1994 was to reduce the CAP budget, but it is still nearly half the EU's annual budget (see Chapter 3). Liberalization has taken on renewed urgency in negotiations on EU enlargement, as the countries waiting in the wings are concerned to protect farming interests, creating more strain on the CAP in propping up relatively inefficient agriculture.

As Table 4.2 shows, Europe has long had a free trade area co-existing with the EU. The **European Free Trade Area (EFTA)** was formed in 1960 by countries not signed up to the Treaty of Rome. They were Austria, Denmark, Norway, Portugal, Sweden, Switzerland and the UK. They were later joined by Iceland and Finland. As most of these countries joined the EU, EFTA has four remaining members, as shown in the table. With the exception of Switzerland, EFTA members have joined the EU in a wider **European Economic Area (EEA),** which is a free trade area.

European Free Trade Area (EFTA) grouping formed in 1960 by countries not signed up to the Treaty of Rome (which created what is now the EU)

European Economic Area (EEA) grouping of the European Free Trade Area (EFTA) and the EU

Andean Community South American free trade area

Mercosur South American common market

The Americas

The Andean Pact, later changed to the **Andean Community**, is the oldest of the regional trade groupings in the Americas. Political instability in the 1970s set back plans to establish a customs union. With the upsurge in global commodities markets, which occurred in the 1980s, South American countries saw economic gains from commodity exports. The two largest traders, Brazil and Argentina, joined forces in 1988 to form a grouping which became **Mercosur**, with the addition of Paraguay and Uruguay. These countries are all associate members of the Andean Community. Similarly, Andean Community member countries are associate members of Mercosur. Efforts to bring the two groupings together in a Free Trade Area of the Americas have taken place partly as a response to US moves to expand Nafta southwards. Venezuela, one of the continent's largest trading nations, and also an oil exporter, applied to join Mercosur in 2006. Its application had to be approved by member states, the key to which has been approval by Brazil, the region's largest economy. Within Brazil, there was considerable opposition to Venezuela's membership, for fear that Venezuela's outspoken left-wing president, Hugo Chavez, well known for his anti-US sentiment, would jeopardize free trade initiatives. Approval by Brazil's Senate came in 2009, removing a major hurdle to full membership for Venezuela.

North American Free Trade Agreement (Nafta) free trade area comprising the US, Canada and Mexico

The **North American Free Trade Agreement (Nafta)**, which came into effect in 1994, comprises the US, Canada and Mexico. While Nafta does not envisage the degree of economic integration of the EU, its provisions and future developments raise similar issues, including political concerns and the question of sovereignty. In contrast to the EU, Nafta is centred on one dominant power, the US, whose GDP is ten times that of Mexico – a much bigger gap than that between the rich and poor EU members. Fear of economic dependence on the US has bred nationalism in both Canada and Mexico, although rather more virulent in nature in its Mexican form. In the post-war period their economies became increasingly integrated with that of the US, as US companies set up branch plants and subsidiaries to export to US markets. A free trade agreement, securing free access to markets, offered advantages to all three countries. The US looked for advantages of low-cost labour in Mexico, the opening of Canada and Mexico to US financial services, and improved access to oil in Canada and Mexico. For the two smaller states, the main advantage consisted of negotiated rules to put their access to US markets on a more secure footing, replacing the informal relationships of the past. Still, some Canadians have considered that their trade relations with the US are being constrained by having to work within a tripartite arrangement with Mexico, which is a

► More online ... The Nafta website is http://www.nafta-sec-alena.org/en/view.aspx

much poorer country than itself. They would like to see Canada negotiating a bilateral agreement with the US (*The Economist*, 2009c).

Market access provisions were the main substance of Nafta, by which the parties agreed to eliminate tariffs on most manufactured goods over a 10-year period. Nafta's investment rules allow investors from any of the three countries to be treated in the same way as domestic investors. These rules apply to both FDI and portfolio investment. For matters other than investment, Nafta introduced a dispute settlement procedure. While it aimed to satisfy the worries of the smaller partners that the stronger partner always has the upper hand, there is still the problem for smaller countries that US pressure may be backed up by retaliatory actions such as anti-dumping measures to restrict imports into the US. Two 'side accords' of Nafta concern labour standards and environmental standards, stemming from concern in the US over firms moving production to Mexico in order to avoid the higher US standards. Commissions were set up in both areas to monitor and enforce national standards (rather than international ILO standards), but enforcement procedures are weak.

Unlike the EU, Nafta operates no common external trade policy. Also in contrast to the EU, it has no institutions for dealing with exchange rates. The Mexican peso crisis of the mid-1990s was left to individual governments to resolve. At its inception, Nafta aimed to increase exports between partners, who already traded heavily with each other, and to create jobs in all three countries. Fifteen years later, Mexico remains a poor country, with GDP per capita only one-fifth that of the US. More than 80% of Mexico's exports are to the US, making it vulnerable to economic downturn in America. An additional concern has been rising protectionism in the US. During the recession of 2008–9, Canada and Mexico feared that their exports would be adversely affected by the 'Buy American' law introduced by the US Congress. American proposals to expand Nafta to include South American countries made some progress, but have been rather stalled since 2006, having met resistance from leading players such as Brazil.

Asia

Asia's economies vary from the small city-state (Singapore) to the industrial giants (China and Japan). Despite some cultural affinities among the many Asian countries, they are diverse in their economies and political systems. The **Association of South East Asian Nations (Asean)** brings together ten South East Asian countries (see Table 4.2). Even among these economies, there is considerable diversity and differing levels of economic development. Singapore has developed as an FDI-oriented market economy with rather autocratic political rule, while Vietnam is a poorer country, whose communist leadership is keen to foster economic growth and market reforms. For these countries, links in global supply chains are key to development. A new free trade agreement has been made between China and the six founder members of Asean (Brunei, Indonesia, Malaysia, Philippines, Singapore and Thailand). This agreement, which came into effect in January 2010, is the world's largest free trade agreement, covering a population of 1.9 billion people. It eliminates tariffs on 90% of imported goods. The smaller countries have concerns that they will be unable to compete with China. China will benefit from the free flow of raw materials from Asean countries to its factories. Asean countries also stand to gain, specifically from the flow of parts and components from China to their own assembly plants.

The **Asia-Pacific Economic Cooperation Group (Apec)** is the other large regional grouping, although it lacks the coherence of most free trade areas. It is hardly regional, as its members, all bordering the Pacific, are located on three different continents. As

Association of South East Asian Nations (Asean) co-operation agreement of South East Asian countries

Asia-Pacific Economic Cooperation Group (Apec) co-operation agreement of economies bordering on the Pacific

► More online ... Apec's home page is http://www.apecsec.org.sg/
The Asean Secretariat is at http://www.aseansec.org/
The Ecowas Commission is at www.ecowas.int
The East African Community is at www.eac.int

yet, it does not function as a free trade area, and its large size, encompassing more than half of the world's economic output, makes it rather different from regional groupings. Its members attend regular summits, at which bilateral agreements are negotiated. The presence of the US, China and Japan in Apec have led some to see it as a kind of multilateralism, or 'open regionalism', potentially rivalling the WTO (Bhagwati, 2006). As with all RTAs, the preferential status afforded to members contrasts with the treatment of non-members, which would amount to discrimination within the WTO's framework. A free trade area of the Asia-Pacific which would exclude the EU, India and Brazil, would be viewed by many as a threat to multilateralism.

Africa

African countries, many of which are rich in oil and other natural resources, are becoming increasingly important in world trade. Co-operative agreements focusing on regional trade in the western, southern and eastern regions, have not as yet led to deepening regional integration. Poverty and poor governance have combined with internal instability in many countries, which has spilled over into regional conflicts. These have all been factors in slowing the economic development that Africans had hoped for in their post-colonial period. A number of regional co-operative agreements have been entered into, often with overlapping membership. One of the oldest and most developed at the institutional level is the **Economic Community of West African States (Ecowas)**, which has a Commission, Parliament and Court of Justice. The Commission's specialized agencies focus on development projects in areas such as health and sport. A first-ever Ecowas cycling tour, modelled on famous western tours such as the Tour de France, was held in 2009. It went through 12 countries and featured 12 national teams.

Economic Community of West African States (Ecowas) organization for co-operation among West African states

East African Community (EAC) common market of East African countries

The **East African Community (EAC)**, which started as a free trade area, became a customs union and is now being transformed into a common market. From mid-2010, goods have flowed tariff-free across the national borders of five of its member countries (Burundi, Kenya, Rwanda, Tanzania and Uganda). Kenya is the largest of these economies, with well-positioned retailers, manufacturers and banks, which hope to gain from the common market. The smaller countries also stand to gain, with better transport and the opportunity to build more competitive manufacturing industries than they could achieve individually. By coming together, these countries' manufacturers could begin to compete with imports from China. EAC members hope to set up a monetary union as a next step, and envisage joining free trade blocs in western and southern Africa in the future.

Summary points Region-by-region focus

● The EU is an economic union, and EFTA is the wider free trade area.
● In the Americas, two important free trade areas are Nafta and Mercosur. There have been proposals to combine these into a north–south free trade area.

● In Asia, there are two main groupings, Asean and Apec, but the growth of China as a regional superpower, challenging Japan's longstanding strength, is a major factor in future free trade initiatives.

● Among African countries, the creation of regional free trade areas is gradually taking place, with potential for cross-border business which could aid economic development.

> **Critical thinking**
> Regional integration: some more equal than others?
> Free trade agreements are generally applauded for bringing down barriers to trade, benefiting all members. But where the member countries are unequal, as in Nafta, this assumption does not necessarily hold. What are the benefits and drawbacks of free trade agreements from the perspective of a weaker partner?

Multilateralism at the crossroads

As bilateral and regional initiatives proliferate, the multilateralism promoted by the WTO has foundered, calling into question its future for the regulation of world trade. The breakdown of the Doha Round, economic recession in many countries, and rising protectionist sentiments have weakened governments' commitment to the WTO's multilateral trade agenda. In this context, governments see bilateral agreements as more attractive and potentially more advantageous in terms of their own national interests. There has been a proliferation of free trade agreements (FTAs), usually bilateral in conception. Pascal Lamy, the WTO's Director-General, concerned about the threats to multilateralism, has highlighted some of the aspects of bilateral agreements which appeal to governments (Lamy, 2007):

- They can be concluded much more quickly than multilateral agreements.
- They can go into areas beyond trade, such as investment, technical standards and environmental standards, which can be designed for the interests of the countries involved.
- In circumstances of inequality, such as agreements between a poor developing country and a rich one (which is common in bilateral agreements), development assistance and other benefits to the developing country can be written in.

Lamy argues that, despite these apparent benefits, the rise of preferential trade agreements constitutes a threat to global trade. He cites four causes for concern:

- The preferential terms contained in a bilateral agreement discriminate against outsiders. A country outside such an agreement will try to conclude an agreement with one of the partners inside, to avoid discrimination, leading to a 'bandwagon' effect of multiplying bilateral agreements. The result is that the preferential positions contained in the first agreement tend to be short-lived: 'the more agreements you have, the less meaningful the preferences would be' (Lamy, 2007).
- Many issues cannot be dealt with at the bilateral level. These include anti-dumping and subsidies to farmers, which must be agreed on a multilateral basis.
- The proliferation of bilateral agreements greatly complicates the international business environment, creating a 'spaghetti bowl' effect for companies to wade through.
- The inequality of bargaining power between a small, weak country and a large, powerful one can be immense. The smaller country will have neither the legal and technical expertise of the more powerful partner, nor the in-depth resources to support negotiating teams to match those of the richer partner. The small partner is likely to be at a greater disadvantage in negotiating than it would be in multilateral talks.

Lamy concludes that a strong multilateral trading system should be at the centre of world trade, and that RTAs should complement, rather than undermine, the WTO

► More online ... See the G20's website at www.g20.org

approach. In practice, the major economies, including the large emerging economies, are expending considerable effort in forging bilateral ties while multilateral negotiations to conclude the Doha Round are on hold.

The US has concluded FTAs (including bilateral and regional agreements) with 17 countries: Australia, Bahrain, Canada, Chile, Costa Rica, Dominican Republic, El Salvador, Guatemala, Honduras, Israel, Jordan, Mexico, Morocco, Nicaragua, Oman, Peru and Singapore. A number of others, including one with Columbia, are pending. The foreign partner in all these agreements is a weaker partner, which is targeted by the US largely as an export market for US business. However, many of these agreements have not been as quick and uncomplicated as one might expect in a situation where there are only two partners, in contrast to the WTO's 153 members. The American trade agreements with Peru and Columbia were signed in 2006. Both run to over 20 chapters and nearly 1500 pages of text, challenging even technical and legal experts to fathom. The US–Peru agreement came into force in 2009, and the Columbia agreement was still pending in 2010. The presence of US military bases in Columbia, with defence agreements pending for their expansion, suggests that military and trade considerations are connected.

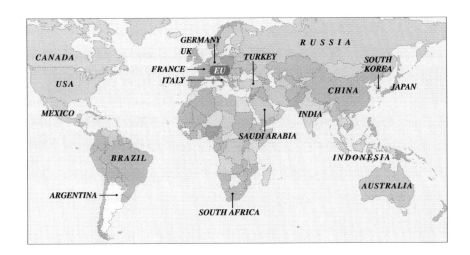

Figure 4.9 **G20 members**

G20 grouping of 20 developed, developing and emerging economies, brought together by the IMF in 1999, which meets regularly, focusing mainly on financial stability

Group of Seven (G7) grouping of 7 advanced economies (US, Canada, UK, France, Germany, Italy, and Japan); with the addition of Russia, it is known as the G8

The future of multilateralism will be influenced by the relatively recent grouping of countries known as the **G20**. Brought together by the IMF in 1999, in the wake of financial crises, this grouping is more representative of the current global economy than the **Group of Seven (G7)**, which represents only the advanced economies (US, Canada, UK, France, Germany, Italy and Japan). The G20 is a diversified group, with members representing all continents, as shown in Figure 4.9. These countries account for 80% of world trade. Although advanced economies are heavily represented and the EU is a member in its own right, emerging economies are also well represented. The IMF and World Bank are also involved.

Envisaged initially as a gathering of finance ministers, the G20 members attend regular summit meetings on both finance and wider issues, but have no permanent secretariat. Meeting in the aftermath of the global financial crisis of 2008–9, member countries raised concerns that rising protectionism could jeopardize economic recovery. Nonetheless, their governments implemented numerous protectionist measures in the months that followed, in efforts to aid their individual economies' recovery. As the emerging economies were not as severely affected by the financial crisis as the US, it is possible that protectionist pressures are receding and governments will once again recognize the importance of multilateral agreements on trade and other issues. Larger members of the G20 featured in the climate change conference held in Copenhagen in 2009 (see Chapter 11). Although environmentalists were disappointed because no binding targets were set, the meeting did establish that governments of the large economies, both developed and developing, recognize the need for multilateral solutions.

Summary points The future of multilateralism

● The rise of regional and bilateral trade agreements poses threats for future multilateral agreements. However, their proliferation has occurred partly as a reaction to the failure of the Doha Round of multilateral talks.

● Although bilateral agreements look an attractive alternative in principle, they tend to be lopsided, favouring the stronger country.

● A prospect for future multilateral agreements could lie with the G20 countries, which represent a wide range of developed and developing countries.

Critical thinking

Bilateralism and international business

For international managers, which type of trade agreements would be preferred: multilateral or bilateral?

Globalization and world trade

Trade, as this chapter has highlighted, involves both political and economic considerations. Nation-states have traditionally relied on tariffs, quota restrictions and other policies which rested on the assumption that protection and economic development naturally went together. In modern economies, the levels of productivity, technological innovation and investment are more than ever dependent on participation in the global economy. Participation no longer simply means increasing trade, although expansion of trade has been one of the major trends of the post-war era. Increasingly, through the global strategies of MNEs, foreign investment has been the driver of trade. The processes of globalization in integrating national economies can largely be attributed to MNEs' global production networks.

The 1980s and 90s saw a tension between two apparently contradictory trends: trade liberalization, sponsored by the WTO, on the one hand, and growing regional and bilateral arrangements on the other. Economists have argued that regional agreements put up barriers to free trade with outsiders, but predictions of a regionalized world economy have not yet come to fruition (see Castells, 2000). As we have seen, few of these groupings are homogeneous or cohesive. Apart from the EU, institutional structures are limited. And even in the EU, which is the most economically integrated, nation-states have not yet been superseded as defining units for a population's economic interests. But those interests are now played out in regional, as well as multilateral, institutions. Moreover, bilateral free trade agreements are a continuing trend.

Conclusions

1 The post-Second World War period has seen a growth of international trade and a trend towards liberalization of the world trading system.
2 A recent trend has been the rise of China as a trading superpower.
3 International trade theories offer explanations of why countries, as well as companies, compete, and how comparative and competitive advantages can be exploited.
4 Government policies, highly influential in international trade, rest on concerns of national producer and consumer interests.
5 Tools of government trade policy include exchange rate manipulation, tariffs and non-tariff barriers to trade. However, the growth of the multilateral trading system, initiated by GATT, has limited the scope of governments to act unilaterally in managing trade.
6 The World Trade Organization, successor to GATT, has strengthened the rule-governed system of international trade regulation, particularly in regard to dispute settlement. Tensions nonetheless remain over the processes and implementation of WTO decisions in trade disputes.
7 The Doha Round of negotiations has made progress in some respects, such as a framework for reductions of agricultural subsidies, but differences between developed and developing countries have slowed negotiations. Outstanding issues facing the WTO remain whether to link issues such as core labour standards and environmental protection to trade policies.
8 The trend towards regional trade agreements since the Second World War represents growing regional economic integration. However, regional groupings differ considerably in their internal cohesiveness and structures, the European Union being the most integrated.
9 Bilateral free trade agreements, which have proliferated in recent years, raise questions of the benefits to the two parties, especially where they are unequal in bargaining power and resources.
10 World trade can best be viewed in the context of globalization, in which the large MNEs with globalized production capacities have been major players.

Review questions

1 How relevant is the theory of comparative advantage to modern trade patterns?
2 What are the main contributions of Porter's theory of competitive advantage?
3 What is meant by strategic trade policy?
4 Outline the motivations underlying government trade policy.
5 Summarize the arguments for and against free trade.
6 What are the main tools of government trade policy?
7 Define the GATT principles of most-favoured nation and national treatment.
8 In what ways does the WTO represent a step on from GATT?
9 What progress has been made in the Doha Round of trade negotiations?
10 What are the outstanding issues facing the WTO, and why has it struggled to arrive at a consensus?
11 Why have regional trade groupings become popular, and in what ways, if any, do they undermine multilateral trade liberalization efforts?
12 Contrast the European Union and Nafta in terms of regional integration.
13 Why do developing countries have ambivalent feelings about trade liberalization?

Key revision concepts

Comparative advantage, p. 73; Competitive advantage, p. 75; Export/import, p. 73; Free trade agreement (FTA), p. 91; Multilateralism, p. 87; Protectionism, p. 78; Subsidies, p. 82; Tariffs, p. 82; Voluntary export restraint (VER), p. 82

Assignments

◆ Assess the contrasting perspectives and interests of developed countries, the large emerging economies and the weaker developing countries with respect to global trade liberalization.

◆ Is regionalism a 'stepping stone' or 'stumbling block' to free trade? Compare the progress of regional integration in three regions: Europe, North America and Asia.

Further reading

Berry, B., Conkling, E. and Ray, D. (1997) *The Global Economy in Transition*, 2nd edn (New Jersey: Prentice Hall).

Frieden, J. and Lake, D. (1999) *International Political Economy: Perspectives on Global Power and Wealth* (Oxford: Routledge).

Gilpin, R. (2000) *The Challenge of Global Capitalism* (Princeton: Princeton University Press).

Gilpin, R. (2001) *Global Political Economy: Understanding the International Economic Order* (Princeton: Princeton University Press).

Hirst, P. and Thompson, G. (1999) *Globalization in Question*, 2nd edn (Cambridge: Polity Press).

Mattli, W. (1999) The *Logic of Regional Integration: Europe and Beyond* (Cambridge: Cambridge University Press).

Oatley, T. (2009) International Political Economy, 4th edn (New Jersey: Pearson Education).

Michie, J. and Kitson, M. (eds) (1995) *Managing the Global Economy* (Oxford: Oxford University Press).

Volkswagen builds on strengths in global markets

Volkswagen (VW) once toyed with the idea of building a 'global car', one model suited for all markets, whether Europe, the US, China or India. Those days are now gone, and the company's strategy is to build cars tailored to consumer needs in each market, using its strengths as a global company to be competitive in each. Its engineering strengths are formidable, centred in its home market in Germany. It is headquartered in Wolfsburg in the State of Lower Saxony, where it operates six factories. As Lower Saxony is also one of its main shareholders, VW's strategy is partly influenced by domestic political concerns. It operates 15 factories altogether in Germany, employing 195,000 people, 47% of its global workforce. Its factories have built up specialist expertise in component manufacturing for the whole network: they include specialist makers of engines, gearboxes and steering units for the group. Its strengths in component manufacturing – some for other car manufacturers – have helped Germany to gain pre-eminence in export markets. Germany is a high-cost location, but the company has implemented agreed cost reductions, including wage freezes. VW has also maintained its competitiveness by globalizing

production in lower-cost locations, from where it exports to other markets.

Mexico is home to the largest VW plant outside Germany. It has been manufacturing cars in Puebla, Mexico since 1965, but the focus of these operations has changed over the years. Initially, it produced small cars mainly for the Mexican market, but it gradually shifted to production for export: 80% of its output is now exported. Following the Nafta agreement of 1995, VW was able to export its Mexican-made cars freely into the US. Puebla now manufactures a range of models, including the New Beetle and Jetta models, for export globally. Europe remains VW's biggest market, and it has trailed behind other foreign manufacturers in the US (see figure). Japanese carmakers, as well as German luxury rivals, such as BMW, invested in greenfield sites in the US from the 1980s onwards, and have built market share. VW has now, belatedly, followed in their footsteps, with a factory in Chatanooga, Tennessee. Its location is close to a network of supplier companies which serve existing BMW and Mercedes plants. The current climate in the car industry, which has seen falls in global sales, is perhaps not the best time for new greenfield

On show at the Shanghai Expo: Volkswagen sees a bright future in emerging markets such as China

Source: Volkswagen

▶ More online ... Volkswagen's corporate website is www.volkswagenag.com

investments, but VW feels in a strong position. It has been less exposed than its rivals to the downturn in the US market, and the shifts in consumer tastes in America, towards smaller, cleaner cars, have opened up opportunities for VW. It is also optimistic about growing sales in the large emerging markets, Brazil, China and India. In India, it set up a Skoda plant, its first in the country, in 2001. It now has another new plant in India, producing the Polo model.

VW has become adept at producing a range of models that share design and engineering, using 'platforms' which can form the basis of a number of models, from the modest to the luxurious. For example, it can use the Polo small-car platform to build a bigger car for the American market. The Skoda and the Seat utilize basic parts found in the more expensive VW Golf, but these more modest brands have their own distinctive fittings and finishes. At the more luxurious end of the market, the Audi brand also benefits from VW's platform strategy. VW is now seeking to expand the Audi brand, hoping to topple BMW as the world's largest premium brand. The strength of VW's formidable expertise in other consumer segments will be an asset.

VW's strategic focus in recent years has been clouded by ownership and corporate governance disputes, which now seem to be resolved. VW's roots go back to Ferdinand Porsche, who designed the original Beetle, which became symbolic of Germany's post-war development. The Porsche family also founded the sports-car company, which became a major VW shareholder. In a series of audacious moves, Porsche attempted to take over VW in 2008, but the attempt failed, and the sports-car company was left nursing large debts. VW then orchestrated a merger of the two companies, also involving an investment by a Qatari sovereign wealth fund. The merger would see all VW and Porsche brands under the same roof, in an

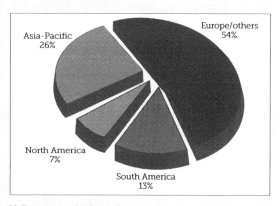

Volkswagen sales by region
Total: 6,310,000 vehicles
Source: Volkswagen Annual Report 2009, at www.volkswagenag.com

'integrated car-manufacturing group' (Schafer, 2009a). The dominant families will own 40% of the newly merged company, and Lower Saxony will retain its 20% stake, from which it is able to influence strategic and operational decisions. Lower Saxony's stake has long been a subject of contention, having been enshrined in Germany's so-called 'VW law', which deters a would-be takeover by capping any shareholder's voting strength at 20% regardless of the size of its shareholding. Although the German government had contemplated relaxing the law as part of its liberal market reforms, the law has remained in place. In addition, employee representation of 50% of VW's supervisory board helps to ensure that domestic employment remains a strong element of future VW strategy.

Sources: Schafer, D. (2009a) 'Saxony firm on keeping its blocking power at VW', Financial Times, 8 May; The Economist (2009) 'My other car firm's a Porsche', 22 August; Schafer, D. (2009b) 'VW flexes its muscle ahead of Porsche merger', Financial Times, 13 May; Schafer, D. (2009c) 'VW small vehicle focus to take on Toyota in the US', Financial Times, 16 September; Kierman, P. (2009) 'Workers strike at VW plant in Mexico', Wall Street Journal, 19 August; Volkswagen Annual Report 2009, at www.volkswagenag.com

Questions for discussion

◆ What are Volkswagen's main strengths as a company?
◆ How has Volkswagen managed to expand into differing national markets, even in times of economic downturn?
◆ To what extent do Volkswagen's ownership and corporate governance suggest German protectionism?

CHAPTER 5

STRATEGIES IN A GLOBALIZED WORLD

Outline of chapter

Introduction

Overview of strategy

Theories of business strategy
SWOT analysis
Porter's theory of competitive strategy
Resource-based and competence-based theories
Process-based theories

Levels of strategy

Internationalization strategies
Exporting
Licensing
FDI
Emerging-market MNEs and internationalization

MNE structures
The functional approach
The divisional structure
The matrix structure
Evolution of the transnational organization
Inter-organizational networks

Rethinking globalization

Conclusions

Learning objectives

1 To appreciate the ways in which corporate strategy is formulated and implemented in the international context
2 To assess internationalization strategies of MNEs from a variety of national environments
3 To identify organizational structures through which MNEs achieve their aims
4 To critically assess corporate strategic objectives in terms of the changing global environment, including opportunities and risks

Critical themes in this chapter

- **Globalization – internationalization strategies of MNEs**
- **Multilayered environment – corporate structures and strategies for managing subsidiaries in differing locations**
- **International risk – market entry strategies; joint ventures**
- **Multidimensional environment – entry strategies and operations in different cultural environments**
- **Emerging economies – emerging-market MNEs**

Shanghai has become an emblem of China's growing prosperity and global ambitions

Source: Istock

South Korea's Kepco: the new global force in nuclear power stations

Building nuclear reactors is a complex, specialist business, in which projects can last many years and cost billions. Only a handful of companies worldwide can offer a full service, designing, building and running nuclear power stations. Yet, because of its low emissions, most governments now see nuclear power generation as having a vital role in meeting energy needs of the future. The dominant companies in the nuclear industry have tended to travel in groups, or 'consortiums', which come together in joint ventures to bid for large projects. The two main groups have been a GE-led one, which includes Hitachi Heavy Industries of Japan, and a French one, which includes Areva and EDF, both French national champions, and both largely state owned. Now, a newcomer has arrived on the scene: Korean Electric Power Company (Kepco). Kepco sprang a surprise by beating its two heavyweight rivals and winning a $20 billion contract to build and run nuclear reactors in the United Arab Emirates (UAE), the oil-rich state now seeking to develop peaceful nuclear power. The bidding process was led by Abu Dhabi, the richest of the emirates, and the project was for four nuclear plants. A simple explanation for Kepco's success would be that its bid was cheaper, but this explanation would overlook the other benefits which the Koreans brought to the table.

For 20 years, Kepco has been building and running nuclear power stations in South Korea, where it is the state-owned monopoly electricity provider. It has an enviable safety record and a history of building quickly, efficiently and within budget. Its CEO says, 'We're cheap, durable and dependable' (*The Economist*, 2 January 2010). This is in contrast to some of its rivals. Japanese reactors have a weaker safety record, for example. In addition, there are perhaps organizational and managerial explanations for Kepco's success. Kepco works with a consortium that includes Hyundai and Samsung, two of the country's big conglomerates,

and also uses Westinghouse technology. The Kepco group has worked together for many years, and has expertise not just in building the reactors, but in running them. South Korea's president, Lee Myung-bak, was a knowledgeable advocate for the Korean group, being himself formerly of Hyundai Construction. His travelling to the UAE to encourage the bid did no harm. The French president, Nicholas Sarkozy, also stepped in to back the French bid. But by contrast, the two French companies involved, Areva and EDF, although in the same consortium, offer rival reactors in global markets. Similarly, GE and Hitachi are promoting separate reactors, and have also developed a third design. Meanwhile, Areva and Mitsubishi Heavy Industries, although each has its own design, have come together in a joint venture to promote yet another different design. The web of alliances and joint ventures in the industry makes it difficult to discern where ownership and control lie. In this environment, Kepco's relative simplicity and government backing are assets.

Kepco has gone on from its success with the UAE contract to take part in a consortium that won a $6 billion wind and solar farm project in Canada. It now has its eyes focused on Vietnam, where there is a big project. And, further ahead, it hopes to invest in countries such as Turkey, Indonesia and South Africa – all middle-income countries. Kepco has become an emerging-market national champion, signifying its country's new confidence in international business. South Korea's car companies, such as Hyundai, and electronics firms, such as Samsung, are notably gaining competitive advantage, while Japanese counterparts, Toyota and Sony, have seen their reputations suffer due to quality problems. South Korea's conglomerates have restructured and revitalized their organizations, and are now focusing on global markets.

▶ More online ... Kepco is at www.kepco.co.kr/eng

The UAE is the first Gulf state to invest in civilian nuclear power, but other Middle Eastern countries might follow, especially in light of Iran's nuclear programme, which is looked on with some disquiet in the region. The UAE has pledged not to engage in domestic nuclear enrichment or reprocessing – technologies which can lead to nuclear weapons. The UAE is an ally of the US, which keeps a careful eye on Middle East relations. US and Japanese companies in the nuclear industry now realize there is a formidable new competitor in building nuclear capacity globally. The South Korean government also feels more confident of its global role, hosting the G20 in 2010.

Sources: England, A., Hollinger, P. and Song, J. (2009) 'South Korea wins $20bn UAE nuclear power deal', *Financial Times*, 28 December; Oliver, C. and Pilling, D. (2010) 'Into position', *Financial Times*, 17 March; *The Economist* (2010) 'Unexpected reaction', 6 February; *The Economist* (2010) 'Atomic dawn', 2 January

Nuclear energy is becoming crucial for governments seeking to meet future energy needs, offering opportunities for energy companies to compete for large projects such as this nuclear power station

Source: Istock

Questions for discussion

◆ Why is nuclear energy gaining more attention from governments?

◆ What were the strengths of Kepco and its partners in their UAE bid?

◆ In what ways does the success of the South Korean company symbolize the shifting international competitive environment?

Introduction

A now-familiar aspect of globalization is the driving force of MNEs seeking competitive edge. They juggle with a number of aims: to reduce production costs (including raw materials and operations), to improve efficiency, to improve technology and to respond quickly to changing demand from customers. In fact, many of these goals overlap. For example, improving efficiency often involves improved technology, which brings down costs. For the MNE, the ability to shift location relatively easily has become a key factor in achieving these goals. Using the concept of the value chain (introduced in Chapter 2), the MNE can identify priorities for each stage of production, and is then in a position to choose locations and design operations to meet corporate goals. This journey from identifying corporate objectives to delivering products to customers depends crucially on the right strategy. We have already stressed the importance of environmental factors in strategy formation (in Chapter 2). Here, we focus on strategy from the firm's perspective.

The chapter begins with a broad overview of corporate strategy. We highlight influential theories which provide the guideposts for decision-makers within companies generally. We then turn to internationalization strategies, looking at alternative entry modes in the context of different environments. Because MNE strategies are closely linked to organizational issues, we discuss organizations in the international environment. Is there one best type of business organization for international operations, or must organizations respond constantly to changing environments? While the network organization and an array of inter-organizational networks have been generally thought to present the optimum balance between control and flexibility, networks are being rethought in the constantly changing global environment. The rise of emerging markets and emerging MNEs is changing the competitive landscape, as these new players becoming catalysts for all international businesses to refocus on strategy. In particular, the impact of differing corporate cultures on strategy and organizations is making for a richer range of strategic perspectives, and posing new challenges for MNEs.

Overview of strategy

Back at the start of Chapter 1, we posed the question, 'What does the business enterprise exist to do?' We found that enterprises aim to achieve a variety of purposes, among them, to satisfy customers, to make money and to contribute to communities in which they operate. At the broadest level, strategy is about the firm's goals and means to achieve them. A large MNE is guided by its global corporate strategy, which sets overall goals and envisages how each of the units in different locations contributes to achieving them. Strategy of the subsidiary is linked to that of the parent company, which has an overall framework for allocating roles to different subsidiaries in its global activities. Companies differ considerably both in their ultimate goals and in the means to achieve them, that is, the organizational and operational aspects of their business.

No firm sets out with a completely 'blank slate' to formulate strategy. Both internal and external factors play a part, as the following discussion of theories will show. Even in a start-up firm, the owners will bring their own cultural background and ways of doing things into the business, along with their technical expertise. In some firms, the owners determine strategy and exert a firm grip on operations, through which a strategic plan is implemented. One might expect SMEs to be the main type of business that is centred on the owner, but some large MNEs are also run in this way, especially where the founder's strategic vision is strong and shapes the corporate culture of the firm. The home country of the company is also important, as we have seen in Chapter 1. Some countries and companies are more likely to look beyond their home environment and values, whereas others seek to stamp their national values and ways of doing things on operations worldwide.

Formulating strategy in a changing external environment is one of the supreme challenges of the MNE. A number of 'balancing acts' must take place. It must strike a balance between flexibility and control. It desires the benefits of customization, but these must be weighed against the scale economies of standardized products. The firm seeks to carry out activities in the best location for production costs, but manufacturing in China for western markets, although low-cost in terms of production, involves higher transport costs: the risks associated with shipping and the need for a long lead time, make it difficult to respond quickly to changes in demand. Every company chief executive probably dreams of the 'killer' product in global markets, produced in low-cost locations with high quality standards and able to adapt to changing demand at short notice. Turning the dream into reality is partly a matter of luck and having talented people in the company, but mainly it is about strategy.

Summary points Strategy overview

◆ Strategy is about the firm's goals and ways of achieving them.

◆ Firms must strike a balance between flexibility and control, and between customization and standardization.

Theories of business strategy

Theorists of strategy offer a variety of perspectives on both how businesses should formulate strategies and what they should focus on. Generally, these theories concentrate on one or more of the following perspectives: the external dimension, the internal dimension and the process of strategy formation. The discussion here will roughly follow these categories. In Chapter 1, a common analytical tool, the PEST analysis, was presented. The PEST analysis is a good starting point for assessing the external environment, especially for companies looking for the best location for international expansion. However, internal capabilities are also important, and these are highlighted in the SWOT analysis.

SWOT analysis

SWOT analysis
strategic tool used by businesses to assess the organization's strengths, weaknesses, opportunities and threats

The **SWOT analysis** is a familiar analytical tool, highlighting a firm's strengths, weaknesses, opportunities and threats. Strengths and weaknesses relate to the firm itself (the internal environment), while opportunities and threats relate to the external environment. The SWOT analysis is usually depicted in the form of a matrix, as shown in Figure 5.1. The top boxes represent the internal environment, and the bottom boxes, the external environment.

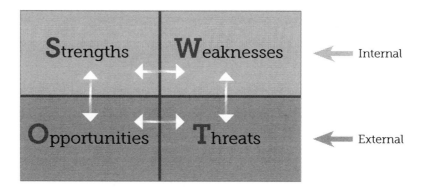

Figure 5.1 **SWOT analysis**

The interactions that are highlighted by arrows in the figure show how the firm can glean strategic insight, aiming to build distinctive competencies, which will enable it to gain competitive advantage.

Some of the key issues addressed in a SWOT analysis are listed below:

1 *External environment: opportunities and threats:*

- What are the main factors in the societal environment (political-legal, economic, sociocultural and technological)?
- What is the market strength of competitors?
- What new products or services, including both those of the firm and those of competitors, are in the pipeline?
- What is the level of consumer demand, and can it be expected to remain stable?
- What is the likely threat of new entrants in the market for the firm's products?

2 *Internal environment: strengths and weaknesses:*

- Does the organization have a structure that helps it to achieve its objectives?
- Does it have clear marketing objectives and strategy?
- Does the organization use IT effectively in all aspects of its activities?
- Does its investment in R&D match or exceed that of competitors?
- Does the organization meet its financial objectives?
- To what extent does the firm have clear HRM objectives and strategies in areas such as employee motivation, turnover of staff, and provision of training?

The SWOT analysis can be carried out in teams or by groups of executives (Piercy and Giles, 1989), and their impressions can be quite different. It has been found that higher-level managers tend to take a broad overview, seeing organizational factors as strengths, while lower-level ones single out marketing and financial factors (Mintzberg, 2000: 276). This suggests that people's views are influenced by their own position in the business. The SWOT exercise can serve to widen the perspectives of participants, which raises awareness of strategy for all employees of the company. However, it is rather limited in that it does not give any direct pointers as to how a firm should achieve its goals.

Summary points SWOT analysis

- The SWOT analysis focuses on both internal environment (strengths and weaknesses), and external environment (opportunities and threats).

- The theory is limited in that it does not address the process of strategy formation.

Porter's theory of competitive strategy

Porter's approach to firm strategy concentrates on the competitive forces in any industry. Analysis of these forces is necessary to achieve profitability (Porter, 1998c; 2008). The five forces are industry competition, buyers, suppliers, potential entrants and possible substitute products. They are depicted in the **five forces model**, shown in Figure 5.2.

five forces model in Porter's theory of competitive strategy, an analysis of an industry based on buyers, suppliers, potential entrants and possible substitute products

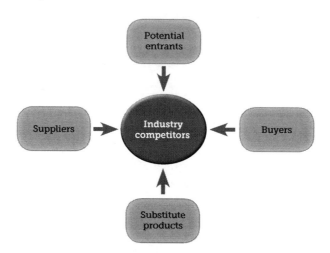

Figure 5.2 **Porter's five forces model**

Source: Adapted from Porter, M. (1998) *Competitive Strategy: Techniques for Analyzing Industries and Competitors* (New York: Free Press)

In Porter's model, buyers and suppliers are key players, with ability to exert bargaining power on the firm. The supplier might be in a strong bargaining position because there are few who can meet the firm's needs for quality or quantity. Alternatively, if there are many potential suppliers of a standardized product, the firm will be in a relatively strong position vis-à-vis any one supplier, and be able to negotiate more favourable terms. Similarly, the purchasing firm will be in a strong position if it is a large company with a large order to place and there are many possible suppliers. In this situation, the buyer is seeking economies of scale and is looking for the lowest cost in the marketplace. On the other hand, the buyer with specialized requirements might find there are few potential suppliers, and will therefore be compelled to pay a premium price. As these examples show, the existence (or absence) of substitute products is a factor which helps to determine the market. Where substitute products are usable and available, buyers are in a stronger position; where a substitute product will not work, the company selling the desired product has the upper hand.

Industry rivalry is at the centre of Porter's model. In every industry, there is a changing scenario of competitors – newcomers, established businesses, some gaining market share and some losing market share. Corporate performance is often envisaged in terms of market share. In Porter's model, the ease (or difficulty) of entry into a market is one of the forces. There can be a variety of barriers to entry. For example, if large capital expenditure is required, as in the oil industry, potential entrants could be deterred. The opposite is the case where little capital outlay is necessary to get started, as in software design. If there are strong global brands in a sector, such as carbonated drinks, then a new entrant will find it difficult to make inroads in markets. For a new entrant in this sector, offering a product to appeal to local tastes in specifically targeted markets could be a better strategy. In this situation, the newcomer would be designing a strategy with a particular focus, to gain competitive advantage.

► More online ... Coca-Cola's corporate website is www.thecoca-colacompany.com

A firm's overall strategy, for Porter, must be based on an analysis of the five forces, addressing the competitive pressures which exist under each heading. This is the highest level of strategy within the company, and is referred to as competitive strategy or generic strategy. Porter sees generic strategies falling into three main types. The first is 'low-cost' positioning, and the second, 'differentiation', referring to the attributes of the product offered. A third type, 'focus', brings the strategic target into the equation. A strategic target can be industry-wide (broad) and a particular segment (narrow). The focused strategy can be based on low cost, differentiation or a combination of the two. We have just seen an example of the focused strategy, in the example of a new carbonated beverage. By targeting a 'niche' market, the competitor can win over a particular group of consumers. Health-conscious or environment-conscious consumers are niche markets, for example. Of course, large MNEs such as Coca-Cola cater for different groups of consumers, offering healthy alternatives to sugary carbonated drinks. It can be all the more difficult, therefore, for niche companies to compete, even if their products have been established for longer. Such a company might pursue one of the other two strategies, but what would be its chances of success?

A low-cost strategy aims to undercut the competitor on price, usually bringing in economies of scale, which act as an entry barrier. In emerging markets where the new middle-class consumers are highly cost-conscious, this is a key strategy. But this does not necessarily mean that only the large MNEs are competitive. On the contrary, smaller local companies are often able to compete on price, which is the main source of competitive advantage in the consumer markets of China and India. They probably do not compete on quality, but that does not matter so much for consumers living on $2 to $10 a day. And this is the fastest growing segment of middle-class consumers globally (Ravallion, 2009). Where consumers have more money to spend and seek out products above the basic level, companies with a differentiation strategy can gain competitive advantage. Not just quality, but brand image, design and high-tech features can give a product a competitive edge in this market.

As an aid to strategy formation, Porter's model is focused on the external competitive environment. Assessing the five forces in an industry can help a firm to identify whether to enter a market or not, and how to position the product. However, national markets must be distinguished from global markets, and in this respect, the model is possibly less helpful. There are not many products in which the market is truly globalized. The oil industry is one. For most products, companies formulate national strategies based on national conditions. Although these are co-ordinated at the global level (as discussed below), the MNE does not pursue a single competitive strategy, such as low-cost positioning, in all markets. The large MNE could well have a portfolio of many brands, and it might well develop a low-cost brand for sale in emerging markets (as we found in the P&G 'Meet the CEO' feature in Chapter 4). Making these decisions involves assessment of the company's own internal strengths as well as external environments.

Summary points Porter's five forces model of competitive advantage

◆ Competition in any industry, according to Porter, can be assessed by examining the five forces he highlights, which are competitor rivalry, potential entrants, buyers, suppliers and substitute products.

◆ Competitive strategies fall into three broad categories: low cost, differentiation of products and focused strategy on a particular group of customers.

Resource-based and competence-based theories

resource-based theory
theory of the firm based on analysis of three sets of resources: physical, human and organizational

A number of theories can be grouped in this category. They share a focus on attributes of the firm itself, from its buildings to its skills. In **resource-based theory,** the starting point is that every firm has three sets of resources: physical resources, such as plants; human resources, such as skills and insight; and organizational resources, such as its formal structures and networks (Barney, 1991). Barney argued that assessment of the firm's strengths in each area will help it build competitive advantage. A set of criteria aids in assessing each resource. These are shown in Figure 5.3.

Figure 5.3 **The resource-based view of the firm**

Source: Adapted from Barney, J. (1991) 'Firm resources and sustained competitive advantage', *Journal of Management*, 17(1): 99–120

The four key attributes of each resource are shown in Figure 5.3. To take an example, firm Q might view its informal network with SMEs as a resource. It is valuable, in that it can generate new ideas to exploit. It is relatively rare, as Q's competitors tend to rely on in-house generation of new ideas. It is not easily imitable, in that the links have been cultivated over time and rely on personal relations between individuals, who have become accustomed to each other's ways of thinking. Such relations would be difficult for a rival firm to put in place mechanically. But would there be another way of achieving the same benefits? The fourth criterion is that there is no strategic equivalent which would yield the same firm-specific benefits. A rival firm with in-house R&D can seek new ideas from outside the company, and, like many large pharmaceutical companies, develop products under licence from their inventors. But it will not be replicating the network benefits enjoyed by Q.

For Q, its network links are a source of *sustainable* competitive advantage, in that new ideas will be likely to flow from this resource over the long term, even in the midst of a changing competitive environment. Indeed, its network links will probably help it to keep to the forefront of advances in technology – one of the major weaknesses of large companies, which can become bureaucratic and fall behind in innovation.

core competencies
capabilities of a firm
to maintain innovative
and competitive edge

Q's competitive advantage could equally be viewed from the perspective of the theory of the firm which focuses on core competencies. Developed by Prahalad and Hamel (1990), the theory rests on the belief that a firm's most important resources are the organization's specialist skills and learning, or **core competencies.** Ideally, a firm will build a portfolio of core competencies. Competencies can be distinguished from products: competencies enable the firm to maintain a pipeline of new products, whereas a product's success could be disappointingly short-lived, especially in fast-moving markets. Three criteria help the firm to identify its core competencies. First, they are critical to a number of the firm's product markets. Secondly, they add value to the end product which reaches the consumer. Thirdly, they are difficult for rivals to imitate. If the company produces a successful product, rivals are certain to imitate it, but, the authors argue, the real source of the product's competitive advantage is not the product itself, but the portfolio of competencies lying behind it, which rivals cannot manufacture overnight.

The implications for strategy contained in these theories are that, first, firms should identify their key resources and competencies at present, assessing which technologies and skills they are strong in, and which are weaker. No firm can build expertise in every relevant aspect of its product development and operations. But, looking at its people and organizational history, it will emerge which activities are more worthwhile concentrating on. Building core competencies takes place over a long period, and corporate strategy can be focused towards these goals. This rather general focus, however, provides only a rough 'roadmap' (Prahalad and Hamel, 1990: 89). There will be relevant specialist areas in which the company has little expertise and which it is not worth investing resources in. There will also be supply-chain issues, such as the need for standardized parts or components which are not worth the company's energy and resources to produce itself. Hence, it will look to a range of suppliers and collaborators outside the company, and probably outside its home country. Building competitive advantage, therefore, relies on these non-core activities as well as the core activities. And these strategic considerations bring us back to the external environment.

Summary points Resource-based and competence-based theories

● These theories focus on the internal environment of the organization, mainly on its

resources in the broadest sense, as key to strategy formation.
● Identifying and building core

competencies is held to be the route to sustaining competitive advantage.

Critical thinking
Core competencies
Recalling some of the case studies of earlier chapters, identify the core competencies of the following companies: Volkswagen, BHP Billiton, Nokia. To what extent have these companies rethought their strategies to sharpen their focus on core competencies?

Process-based theories

In a sense, the theories already discussed in this section would fall under this heading. Porter's theory sees analysis of the external environment as a process, and firm-based theories see development of resources over time as crucial to business strategy. However, these theories mainly focus on the key dimension as they see it, rather than on the process itself. Here, we turn to two theoretical approaches in which the process is central. These are Mintzberg's theory of emergent strategy, and stakeholder management theory.

Mintzberg's theory of emergent strategy

Mintzberg considers a number of ways in which strategy can be envisaged (see Mintzberg et al., 2009). A common view of strategy is found in the 'strategic plan'. This notion of making a plan and simply following it is highly prescriptive and leaves little flexibility for changes in response to external factors. A more flexible approach is to see strategy as a position, that is, to formulate a position in the prospective market for the firm's products. This view takes account of the changing external environment, allowing for strategy to be adapted accordingly. However, Mintzberg criticizes both of these approaches as being too inflexible. Strategy is formed deliberately in both the planning and positioning approaches, which tend to undervalue the need to adapt strategy over time. They also take little account of strategic learning constantly taking place in the firm (Mintzberg et al., 2009). In **emergent strategy**, by contrast, 'a pattern is realized that was not expressly intended' (Mintzberg et al., 2009: 12). Business decisions taken by the firm, when looked at as a series of actions, form a pattern over time.

emergent strategy
theory devised by Mintzberg, which focuses on firm strategy adapting over time. rather than following a deliberate plan

The firm is advised to evolve a combination of deliberate and emergent strategies, recognizing the need to plan for likely eventualities, and also the need to be responsive to changes in the environment. How managers combine these two approaches depends heavily on the company's organizational culture and its approach to organizational learning. For example, the firm might have an open corporate culture, in which people are constantly adapting strategy in small ways. In this type of firm, strategy can emerge from anywhere in the organization: employees feel empowered to take part in strategy formation, and subsidiaries in varied locations contribute to the debate. This broad view of strategy formation, in contrast to Porter's five forces model, takes account of the firm's internal capabilities, giving it an affinity with the resource-based and competence-based theories. Our next theoretical approach builds on this broad view of organizational learning.

Stakeholder management theory

The second of the process-based theories is stakeholder management theory. The concept of the stakeholder was introduced in Chapter 1. Recalling that discussion, we found that stakeholders cover a large and potentially divergent group of interests. It is common to think of stakeholders as external to the firm, when in fact stakeholders are both internal and external. Stakeholder management theory aids in (a) identifying stakeholders; and (b) bringing stakeholders into the strategic management process. It is because of this latter element that we look at stakeholder management in this section.

In Chapter 1, we considered Freeman's definition of stakeholders as those who influence the company or are influenced by it. Direct stakeholders were identified as those who have direct links with the company, such as owners and suppliers, whereas indirect stakeholders are more remote, often resembling aspects of the external environment, such as community groups. Because the first group consists of people and organizations with whom the firm has regular relations, both formal and informal, stakeholder management theory tends to focus on them. This is not to say that the second group of interests is less important, but they are more diffuse, and tend to fall more naturally into theories of ethics and CSR, which will be discussed in Chapter 12.

Stakeholder management theory urges that involving stakeholders in strategy formation can make sense for firm competitiveness and performance (Harrison et al., 2010). In a 'managing for stakeholders' approach, the firm can benefit from allocating value and decision-making influence to its primary stakeholders, both individuals and organizations. Investing in stakeholder relations, by, for example, providing health benefits to part-time employees, involves costs. And some might see this as a waste of money, or 'overinvestment', as the firm is paying more than it would need to simply to keep the stakeholder relationship in existence. However, it can be argued that performance in the long term will be enhanced, leading to sustainable competitive advantage. The authors cite the following ways in which value can be created through managing for stakeholders (Harrison et al., 2010: 67):

- Information gained from stakeholders such as customers and suppliers can lead to improvements in demand and efficiency
- Interactions with stakeholders can lead to innovation and evolving innovation networks
- The firm will be better able to deal with unexpected events, such as changes in technology, if it has built up relationships of trust with stakeholders

The last of these points suggests a link with strategic flexibility. Recalling the example of firm Q above, the firm that has invested in stakeholder relationships possesses a resource which is rare and difficult for rivals to imitate. The rival will not know exactly which relationships yielded advantages and how they functioned. The 'nuanced information' that derives from these relations is not readily quantifiable and becomes blended into its corporate culture. Similarly, the value created is not necessarily reflected in the firm's economic data, as relations are not captured using accounting measures. Market share that a firm enjoys today may be fleeting, as the competence-based theories point out, because today's successful products will soon be superseded. The benefits of managing for stakeholders accrue over time, making this approach a sounder footing for sustainable advantage.

Summary points Process-based theories of strategy

- Mintzberg stresses that strategy can be both deliberate and emergent, and that it involves the whole organization.

- A managing-for-stakeholders approach holds that nurturing stakeholder relations can create value and enhance competitiveness over the long term.

Levels of strategy

The journey through theories of strategy has highlighted numerous important factors: internal capabilities, analysis of industry competition, corporate culture and organizational learning. In an SME with only a few employees, decision-making can be informal, and all can participate in discussion of the way the business is being run, roles, products and locations. In a large organization, however, each of these topics is complex and interlocking with the others. The MNE with multiple subsidiaries requires a coherent strategy for all its operations and markets. It desires the flexibility to make strategic adjustments as needed in differing conditions, but it needs co-ordination at the centre, to ensure that all the units are singing in at least some semblance of harmony, rather than entirely different tunes.

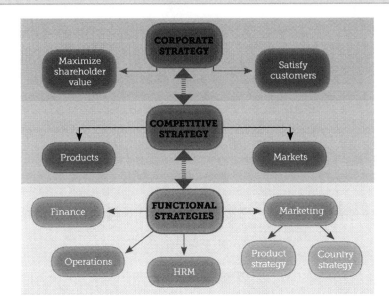

Figure 5.4 **Levels of strategy**

For the MNE, it is helpful to view strategy in levels, beginning with the highest level, which is corporate strategy. Levels of strategy are shown in Figure 5.4. Corporate strategy is the unifying theme, which provides guideposts for lower-level strategies. **Corporate strategy** can be envisaged as the overriding goals of the company, embracing its values and culture. In a sense, the answers to the question we posed in the overview early in this chapter – 'What does the company exist to do?' – form its corporate culture. The answer could be satisfying customers, creating value for stakeholders, or any other goal which gives the company its distinctive character. In liberal market economies, the goal of maximizing shareholder value is often held up as paramount. Corporate goals are set out in company 'mission statements', which typically mention all these goals. However, looking beyond the mission statement, it becomes clearer what the firm's ultimate values are. We therefore turn to further levels of strategy which are less abstract.

Competitive strategy, or business strategy, has been discussed in the context of Porter's five forces model. The firm's competitive strategy concerns its products and markets, which generate its competitive advantage. Porter highlights two generic strategies, differentiation and price, warning that firms are at risk of being 'stuck in the middle' if they do not concentrate on one of these strategies (Porter, 2008). However, there are risks in overspecializing, in that a firm might not be in a position to exploit new opportunities. Many companies target particular markets with low-end products, and target more affluent consumers with high-end products. As markets and competitors change over time, a test of business strategy is whether it is sustainable. Core competencies therefore come into play. If the firm has developed core competencies, these will equip it with the innovation capacity and technological skills to improve its offering, launch new products and meet challenges from competitors' new products. In addition, it must consider the opportunities in new markets. Internationalization strategies, considered in the next section, have profound implications for the way a company is run, including its organizational structure.

As we found in Chapter 1, the firm's activities can be roughly divided into separate business functions. In small firms there are probably no organizational divides. But in a large MNE, these functions take on organizational reality and a feeling of cultural

corporate strategy
strategy which focuses on the overriding goals of the company, embracing its values and culture

competitive strategy
a firm's business strategy which focuses on advantages of particular products and particular markets

functional strategies a firm's strategy pertaining to each functional area, such as marketing, which contributes to achieving corporate goals

distinctiveness, based partly on the professional or management culture involved in each. Ideally, these functions are all co-ordinated, through **functional strategies**. Hence, the marketing strategy will reflect the firm's competitive strategy regarding products and markets; it will also help the firm to achieve its overall goals. For a large MNE, marketing strategy can be designed for its various products and for differing national markets, as Figure 5.4 shows. Hence, a country-specific marketing strategy would need to 'fit' the three strategic levels above it, which are functional, competitive and corporate strategies.

Summary points Levels of strategy

◆ Corporate strategy, representing the company's broadest goals, is the highest level of strategy.

◆ Competitive strategy relates to products and markets, while functional strategies support

both competitive and corporate strategies.

Internationalization strategies

A shift in strategy occurs when a business that has been operating only in its home country decides to add an international dimension to its enterprise. In particular, its competitive strategy changes. Internationalization involves outward expansion in markets and/or production. The firm contemplating a new market or the shift of production to a foreign location can consider a variety of entry strategies. These strategies are often referred to as modes of internationalization, which were introduced in Chapter 2. Here, we look in greater detail at each. The choice of entry strategy depends on both internal and external factors. Internally, the firm's corporate culture influences how it goes about international expansion and also what locations it chooses for foreign operations. External factors include the competitive environment in differing locations as well as country-specific factors, which the PEST analysis reveals.

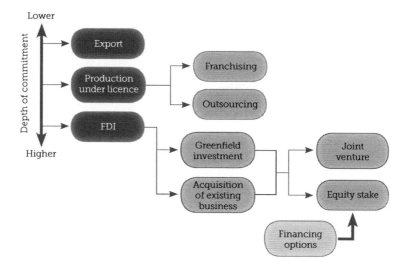

Figure 5.5 **Foreign integration in modes of internationalization**

Entry strategies can be compared according to the depth of involvement that the firm envisages in the new location. This commitment is usually reflected in the

MEET THE CEO

▶ More online ... Carlsberg's website is www.carlsberg.com

Jorgen Buhl Rasmussen CEO of Carlsberg, the Danish brewer

Carlsberg's chairman and CEO, Jorgen Buhl Rasmussen, although Danish by birth, had worked mainly outside the country, in Asia, Eastern Europe and the UK, before joining Carlsberg. These jobs, chiefly with Duracell batteries, were unrelated to brewing, but his focus was always on marketing – an expertise which helped to propel him into the top job at Carlsberg in 2007. He was plunged straight into the 'deep end' at Carlsberg, as the company was in the process of negotiating a huge takeover of Scottish & Newcastle (S&N). That acquisition, mounted jointly with Heineken, was a strategic turning point for the company. S&N was strong in Russia, where it owned the leading brand, Baltika. Acquiring the brand presented an opportunity for further growth in this large market, although Rasmussen realized it also brought challenges. Investors were concerned that the Russian market would now account for about 40% of Carlsberg's overall profits.

Although a large emerging market, Russia has not enjoyed the economic growth of the other Brics, and it was more affected by the global financial crisis. Carlsberg had an impressive market share of 39.1% in the quarter to 31 March 2010, but this was actually down on its market share a year earlier. From his depth of experience in marketing, Rasmussen says, 'Pricing in a big place like Russia is a delicate task ...

This will be different based on brand, packaging, type and region. It will vary from St. Petersburg to Vladivostok' (Anderberg, 2010). The financial crisis has had a negative impact in all the company's markets, in many of which it is competing with strong local brands. He says, 'in Carlsberg we often talk about being "glocal", and for us that's being global and local. Ideally, we need strong, local power brands – as we call them – and then some international, global brands on top' (*Financial Times*, 2009).

Carlsberg is famous for its advertising – 'probably the best lager in the world' – as well as for its brands, which, apart from Carlsberg itself, include Tuborg and Kronenbourg. With sales lacklustre in western markets, Rasmussen is banking on growth in Russia, but is also making acquisitions in Asia. He is alert to the fact the Russian government is concerned about alcohol consumption, and is intending to regulate advertising and sales more closely. Rasmussen feels the key to success is keeping in touch with people, whether employees or consumers. Marketing has been the force that drives him, but he welcomed the opportunity to take on greater responsibility for the business. He says, 'Having responsibility for the business, working with a team ... it becomes more important than just doing marketing because this is suddenly people' (Wiggins and Anderson, 2008).

Sources: Anderberg, J. (2010) 'Interview: Carlsberg to up market share in Russia – CEO', *Wall Street Journal*, 11 May; Wiggins, J. and Anderson, R. (2008) 'Brewery chief's thirst for success', *Financial Times*, 24 November; *Financial Times* (2009) 'View from the top: interview with Jorgen Buhl Rasmussen', 5 June

Jorgen Buhl Rasmussen
Source: Carlsberg

▸ More online ... Chery's website is www.cheryinternational.com
Carrefour is at www.carrefour.com

extent of ownership and control that the firm exerts over foreign assets. A comparison of entry modes is shown in Figure 5.5. It is common for a firm to begin with export, and to expand through other modes which involve greater presence in the foreign location.

Exporting

The manufacturing firm contemplating foreign expansion for the first time will be attracted to the relatively low-risk option of exporting. It will need to choose carefully which products to export to specific markets, for the greatest chance of success. A PEST analysis of likely markets will be an aid. Recall from the last chapter that barriers to imports can be an important external factor: tariffs or non-tariff barriers can make imported goods appear expensive alongside domestic goods in consumer markets. The firm will be relying heavily on the services of other organizations. It must arrange freight and distribution with specialist export companies, and it must choose the retailer carefully, to obtain the best possible exposure for its products.

Although exporting is a low-risk option in terms of financial commitment, with minimal organizational impact on the firm's home activities, there are numerous pitfalls due to the heavy reliance on others in the supply chain. Without a presence in the market, designing marketing strategy is likely to be contracted out to a local company. Because of the distance between the home production and the end consumers, after-sales service will probably be handled by other firms, again adding a potential weakness in the delivery of value to the consumer. The use of external organizations adds to transaction costs, which must be factored in when considering the firm's pricing policy. There are also foreign exchange risks to be considered. Nonetheless, if the firm's products prove successful, it will probably contemplate setting up a sales office in the country, establishing an organizational presence. It could then think about establishing production in the country, depending on its assessment of the market potential. An example is Chery Automobile of China, which has been exporting vehicles, and now plans FDI projects on greenfield sites in Eastern Europe, the Middle East and South America.

Exporting is an obvious entry mode for a manufacturing company with operations concentrated in its home country. Is there an equivalent of the export option for firms in other sectors? The retailer wanting to expand abroad is almost compelled to establish a presence in the foreign location. An example is Carrefour, the French hypermarket retailer, which has expanded in Asia. Similarly, the service provider, in, for example, financial services, must usually have some presence in the target country, even if its computing system is integrated with that in the home country. For firms in these other sectors, international expansion can involve the acquisition of assets (such as buildings) in overseas locations, but there are other legal alternatives available, such as the franchise, considered in the next section.

Summary points **Exporting**

⬥ Exporting as an entry mode offers the firm possibilities of wider markets with minimal investment in assets and operations in the foreign location.

⬥ The exporter will entail considerable costs, especially over long distances, and could face trade barriers in some markets.

▶ More online ... Danone is at www.danone.com

Licensing

Operations in a foreign location are often carried out through organizations linked by contractual arrangements short of outright ownership. In manufacturing sectors in today's globalized world, even SMEs consider foreign production as a strategy from early on, carried out by other companies under licence. The **licence** is a legally enforceable agreement by which a firm (the licensor) grants permission to use its property (mainly intellectual property such as patents and trademarks) to another firm (the licensee). The owner of a patent essential to the manufacture of a product can license a firm to produce the product in a foreign location, either the relevant market or a low-cost country. This is the typical arrangement with outsourced production. A manufacturing company that has operated its own factories in a high-cost country might decide to shift manufacturing to a low-cost country, in order to become more competitive in global markets.

licence legal agreement by which a firm (the licensor) grants permission to another firm (the licensee) to use its property, notably intellectual property such as patents and trademarks

The company need not set up a greenfield operation in the new location, but can license a locally registered company (which could be foreign owned) to manufacture the product. This type of strategy is often called **offshoring**, which carries rather negative connotations, as it suggests that jobs are being lost in the firm's home country. The firm might also face allegations that local people are being exploited in the production of its branded products, even though they are employed by an independent company. Clothing and sportswear are industries in which the cost of labour is a major factor, and these industries are often relocated to low-cost economies, as we saw in Chapter 2. Where the firm licenses a manufacturer in a country near to a major market, such as manufacturing in Mexico for the US market, this arrangement is known as **nearshoring**. Nearshoring, similarly, can be seen as a cost-reduction exercise. Perceptions vary according to the prevailing approach to stakeholders. Where maximizing shareholder returns is the guiding goal, reducing costs of production is welcomed, whatever the location of manufacturing.

offshoring contracting out of a business process, usually to a low-cost location; often carrying negative connotations

nearshoring type of FDI or outsourcing by which a firm invests in operations in a lower-cost location near to a major market

Although it might be assumed that the licensor has the upper hand in licence arrangements, the relationship can be quite complex, requiring trust and co-operation on both sides. In the pharmaceutical industry, the licensor can be an SME, which licenses a large MNE to manufacture and market a medicine. This occurs where the SME's researchers have come up with a product that is patentable, but lack the resources to exploit the patent. The reverse situation is also possible: large pharmaceutical companies license local companies to manufacture their medicines for local markets. In these situations, both the patent and the brand are involved. However, there are inherent risks with any licensing of IP rights. The licensor is concerned that quality of production is maintained and that no misuse of its brand takes place. These are difficult to monitor from a distance. Similarly, there could well be problems where the local company is accused of misusing the brand or patent for its own purposes. Danone, the French food company, endured a number of years of difficulties, including lengthy legal proceedings against a Chinese firm, Wahaha, which made its products in China. Finally, in 2008, the disputes were settled and the relationship was dissolved.

The franchise is a particular type of licensing agreement, whereby the franchisee, or business owner, agrees with the franchisor, the owner of a branded product, to deliver the product in the franchisee's local market. This type of arrangement is often suitable for entrepreneurs, as mentioned in Chapter 1. The entrepreneur benefits from the brand, know-how, marketing and quality proceedures of the brand owner. Some companies specialize in the franchise, acquiring numerous outlets from the same franchisor. McDonald's decided to pull out of Iceland in 2009, following the country's financial collapse. The owner of its three outlets in the country decided to carry on in business. Although no longer able to brand his products with the McDonald's logo, he was confident he could produce appetizing meals for less money by using Icelandic ingredients. His franchise agreement had required him to import basic products such as onions from Germany, which became prohibitively expensive when the Icelandic currency collapsed.

Nonetheless, McDonald's reported healthy profits for 2009, growth stemming largely from foreign markets. The benefits of licensing, from the MNE's point of view, are that it can exit the country relatively smoothly, as the investment commitment is made by the local business owners rather than the brand owner.

Summary points Licensing

◆ Licensing agreements cover a wide range of international business situations, including manufacturing and service provision.

◆ Licensing allows MNEs to deliver products and services in local markets based on contractual relations with firms in the target market.

◆ Production under licence in low-cost economies is associated with globalization.

Critical thinking
Licensing and globalization
Manufacturing under licence in low-cost locations has acquired a negative image in many consumer markets. How can it be criticized from a stakeholder perspective?

FDI

FDI represents a deeper level of commitment to a foreign location than the alternatives discussed above. In Figure 5.6, greenfield investment and acquisition of an existing business are highlighted as examples of FDI. Both involve capital investment and a planned long-term commitment to the foreign location. Recalling the discussion of motives for FDI in Chapter 2, MNEs are influenced by both push factors and pull factors, which can be mutually reinforcing. Saturation in the firm's home market might be felt by companies in the western advanced economies. At the same time, the large emerging markets attract investors because of the good prospects of growth. But how does the investor choose which route to follow? Figure 5.6 gives a breakdown of the advantages and disadvantages of each.

The ability to design and control operations is an advantage of the greenfield project, but there could be a long wait before production becomes a reality. It will have required patient dealing with regulatory and planning bodies, and it will be an even longer wait before the firm begins to see profit from the investment. It is not difficult to see, therefore, why acquisition of an existing business is an attractive option. The acquired company can be integrated into the acquirer's strategy for the region, and could well have an existing customer base on which to build. Acquisition thus seems like a lower-risk alternative to greenfield investment. However, integration of the two firms can be slow, requiring give-and-take on both sides.

Greenfield investments

The type of industry is one of the main factors in choosing an entry strategy. Where the manufacturing process involves specialist plant and skills, the greenfield site is

Greenfield or acquisition?

Greenfield	Acquisition
• Customized design of plant • Control over build and operations (including IP), *but ...* • Slow to get going • Large capital investment • Lack of local knowledge a drawback • No pre-existing customer base	• Quicker to get up and running • Local company has local knowledge, existing workforce and customer base, *but ...* • Cultural tension between acquirer and local firm • Weaker control over quality, delivery and IP

Figure 5.6 **FDI options**

attractive. Some governments, keen to attract greenfield investors, offer incentives such as tax concessions. Southern states in the US attracted foreign carmakers through incentives, hoping to create new jobs as the region shifted away from agriculture to industrial activities. The carmaking industry in the US has been transformed by the success of foreign manufacturers setting up production on greenfield sites outside the traditional carmaking regions of the country, notably Michigan, where American carmakers were strong. Japanese, South Korean and German companies, in particular, set up to serve the US market. They benefited from being close to the consumer. They were able to undercut American car companies on price partly because they set up in regions without the strong trade unions which have dominated the American motor industry (see case study in Chapter 2).

Greenfield investment is appropriate in manufacturing industries that require new plants to be built, but FDI in the extraction industries is similar, requiring large capital investment in the foreign location before production can begin. This entails dealing with governments and other stakeholders, and complying with local environmental laws. The greenfield investor becomes part of the local community in a way that the brand-owning company which outsources production does not. Still, putting down roots does not mean that the MNE will stay permanently in the country. There are numerous examples of companies that have built factories in countries for cost savings, and, when the costs grew and new markets opened up, moved on to build factories in these newer markets. Spain's car industry, which attracted FDI for its proximity to European markets and relatively low costs in the 1990s, saw the departure of a number of these companies in the 2000s, to Slovakia and other lower-cost destinations. Similarly, Slovakia must compete with countries where costs are even lower, such as Romania, Turkey and India, all of which have growing car industries.

Where the MNE contemplates greenfield investment in a new environment, the joint venture can provide a means of sharing the financial burden – and the risk. If a local partner is chosen, its local knowledge can be beneficial in navigating the process of building up a business from scratch. The joint venture can be a new company, with participating investors each contributing capital. If successful, the joint venture company can gradually become more independent of its parent companies. However, success depends not just on environmental factors in the new market, but on relations between the parent companies, which must develop a coherent strategy for the venture. The joint venture must have a clear position in the strategy of the parent companies, as the opening case study showed. A company that invests in a number of joint ventures risks blurring its strategic vision.

Acquisitions

In many industries, acquiring a local company is an attractive alternative to the greenfield operation. The local company can be wholly bought out by the acquirer, but it is also possible for the investor to acquire a sizeable equity stake, which can be raised at a later date. In many industrial and extraction industries, acquisition is a common expansion strategy. The growth of ArcelorMittal, the steelmaking company, has been largely by acquisition. The MNE wishing to expand by acquisition is looking for quick growth, and benefits from the fact that the acquired company already has a presence in the market. It has local knowledge and knows local business practices. It might also have good links with governmental authorities, which can be important. However, there are disadvantages in expansion by acquisition, as Figure 5.6 highlights. If the corporate cultures of the two companies are quite different, the acquirer must decide what type of integration strategy to pursue. It might attempt **integration** of the companies, blending the cultures of both. Alternatively, if the acquiring company's culture is paramount, the acquired company will be compelled to conform with the new owner's culture and practices, through an **assimilation** process. However, assimilation can be difficult if the two cultures are very different: sensitivity and a willingness to adapt can be needed to smooth the process. The polycentric organization is more likely to be successful in managing integration than the ethnocentric organization. (These issues are discussed in Chapter 6.) Productivity can suffer in the meantime, as the participants focus on internal issues, and give less attention to the market.

Growth by acquisitions has been a widely used strategy in the era of globalization. In sectors ranging from banks to telecommunications, some MNEs, such as General Electric (GE), have built business empires largely through acquisition (see Figure 5.7). Acquisition strategy varies from sector to sector, and company to company. It is common for companies to buy up smaller rivals in the same industry. In this way, industries become **consolidated** over time. With fewer players, economies of scale are achievable. In such industries, for example mining and shipping, which are globally consolidated, the size of the players can act as a barrier to entry.

A **diversification** strategy is also favoured, whereby MNEs acquire companies in other sectors, often those which are complementary to their existing portfolio of products. For example, Google, the search engine company, diversified into operating systems for mobile phones, then into its own branded phone. This would seem to be akin to an emergent strategy in the case of Google: one product succeeds, and the firm then thinks of ways of building on this success (Mintzberg et al., 2009). From the marketing perspective, diversification is a means of brand extension, whereby success with one branded product can be transferred successfully to a range of others. This strategy does not always work: the products in the newer categories must live up to the reputation of the first one, or the brand as a whole could suffer. If the company is starting from scratch in the new product area, it must learn quickly to compete against existing specialist players, and it will take more than simply a well-known brand to maintain consumer loyalty.

integration in an acquisition of one firm by another, the blending of the two cultures into a single organizational culture

assimilation in an acquisition by one firm of another, compelling the acquired company to conform to the culture and practices of the new owner

consolidation in an industry, a pattern of larger firms taking over smaller ones, which results in a few large companies

diversification corporate strategy whereby a company acquires businesses in a range of different sectors

▶ More online ... GE is at www.ge.com

Figure 5.7 **General Electric (GE) businesses in 2009**

Some firms possibly take diversification too far, losing sight of core competencies. The highly diversified multidivisional company might benefit if there is a downturn in one sector, as it can compensate with healthy earnings in other sectors. The strategy is thus defensive to some extent. The large, diversified company is often referred to as a **conglomerate**, indicating that there is no one single identifiable core business. General Electric (GE) of the US, whose separate businesses are shown in Figure 5.7, is essentially an industrial company, having been founded to produce light bulbs. As the figure shows, it now produces a wide range of industrial products for businesses and consumers. Some might find its industrial range alone rather too diverse to be coherent. It should be remembered, too, that GE is involved in numerous joint ventures. GE's financial and media businesses are the sectors that stand out as not fitting with its industrial legacy. The financial business, once part the GE Capital division, has been largely scaled back. The media and entertainment businesses, shaded in Figure 5.7, retain their own brand identities. In late 2009, GE decided to gradually reduce its stake in these businesses by placing them in a joint venture with Comcast, a media company.

conglomerate large, diversified company, in which there is no single identifiable core business

Conglomerates are not confined to western MNEs. MNEs in many emerging markets, India in particular, have grown to become sprawling conglomerates, whose businesses are only tenuously linked to each other. We look next at emerging MNEs and ask in what ways their internationalization strategies are distinctive.

Summary points FDI strategy

◆ Greenfield investment indicates a desire to commit extensive resources in the new location, reflecting its

importance as a potential market for the firm.

◆ Acquiring companies in new markets is a relatively quick means

of market entry, and benefits from existing operations of the acquired company.

Emerging-market MNEs and internationalization

Ford Motor Company of the US purchased Jaguar, the upmarket British carmaker, in 1989 and Land Rover in 2000. Both companies were sold to Tata Motors of India in 2008 (see closing case study in Chapter 3). In 1990, developing countries accounted for 5% of outward FDI in the world. This percentage was up to 14% in 2006, and 18.9% in 2008. And this figure does not include companies like ArcelorMittal, the steel-making empire of Lakshmi Mittal, whose roots are in India, although the company is registered in Luxembourg. Mittal bought steelmaking plants in developing countries around the world, many of which, such as those in Mexico, were privatizations. His largest acquisition, however, was the purchase of Arcelor, the European steelmaker, in 2006. How does emerging MNEs' expansion compare with that of existing globalized MNEs, in whose footsteps they are following?

The history of MNE expansion, along with the theoretical insights which have developed simultaneously, provides guidance for today's emerging-market MNEs. They are probably more acutely aware of the risks of rapid expansion, and will have bigger and better resources for researching potential markets than their predecessors. But these advantages are true of *any* company internationalizing today. For emerging-market companies, there are some distinctive aspects of the home environment which can be viewed as advantages. Their MNEs have grown quickly in fast-growing economies which combine large potential markets with low costs. These are ideal platforms for future growth. Most of them, including Brazil, India and China, have seen liberalization in their home markets, bringing in foreign competitors, which have forced them to sharpen up their products and performance. Hence, there are both push and pull factors at work. As they have gained in competitiveness, they have felt better able to take on rivals in both developing and developed countries, including the home markets of their biggest competitors.

Emerging MNEs have also learned the lesson of the importance of innovation in global markets. They have been early to see the importance of collaborative partnerships in R&D, often with other MNEs. Western MNEs, in comparison, were slow to internationalize R&D, this function often remaining concentrated in the home country long after the parent company had become globalized.

The home background in a developing country can be frustrating. Poor infrastructure, heavy-handed regulation, weak skills in the workforce and lack of supporting services pose challenges for new businesses, especially those in the private sector in countries which have widespread state ownership, as in China. However, the skills developed in coping with the difficulties can make managers more resilient, adaptable and imaginative in facing problems. In particular, companies in developing countries are accustomed to the need to keep costs and prices low – disciplines which hold them in good stead in global markets. On the other hand, these companies are entering markets in which globalization is already advanced, and existing MNEs enjoy economies of scale, along with well-oiled global supply chains. Breaking into this competitive landscape is a huge challenge. Often, the lack of management expertise and experience is a stumbling block, and these competencies are difficult to acquire overnight. Years of organizational learning in global markets benefit the western MNE, but the emerging MNEs are catching up quickly. Recall Cemex of Mexico (featured in the closing case study of Chapter 1), which has become globalized rapidly.

We have noted that the emerging MNEs aim to grow quickly, implying ambitious acquisitions in diverse locations, seemingly undaunted by the cultural differences

Mexico: the lagging OECD economy

In recent years, Mexico has tended to capture media headlines for a disparate variety of reasons, many unfavourable. The billion-dollar drugs cartels, whose violent activities are regularly reported, lead to perceptions of general lawlessness, although their activities are mainly concentrated in the area along the US border. Mexico stresses that, in fact, it has a lower murder rate than its Latin American neighbours. Brazil, often applauded for its improvements in social development, has a murder rate twice that of Mexico. Mexico also features in development data for its high levels of inequality and poverty. This picture contrasts sharply with the 2010 ranking of a Mexican tycoon, Carlos Slim, as the world's richest individual, overtaking Bill Gates, the Microsoft founder. Slim's fortune, estimated at $53.5 billion, about 5.4% of Mexico's GDP, grew $18.5 billion in the previous year, largely thanks to the financial performance of his telecoms empire. In

that year, Mexico's economy shrank about 6.5%. To add to a bad year, Mexico's coastal resort area was struck by a swine flu epidemic in 2009.

The year 2010 is Mexico's bicentenary as an independent country, and the centenary of Mexico's 1910 revolution, which marks the beginning of modern Mexico. But Mexicans might feel there has been little to celebrate of late. A severe contraction in the economy followed recession in the US, as four-fifths of its exports are destined for the US. As the US economy resumed growing in 2010, Mexican firms stood to benefit. Another source of optimism is that, as costs have risen in China, Mexico, which had lost out to Chinese imports in some sectors in the US, is now becoming more competitive again. This is largely thanks to the effects of Nafta, which has led to a burgeoning of export-oriented businesses in the northern regions of the country. On the other hand,

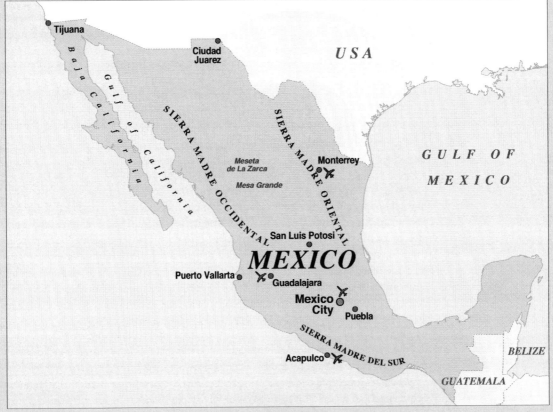

Map of Mexico

► More online ... See the World Bank's page on Mexico, under 'countries' on the World Bank's website at www.worldbank.org

Mexico's finance minister has stressed that the country still needs to diversify the economy, away from the reliance on American exports. Mexico's business environment is ranked only 51 in the World Bank's 'Doing business' rankings of 183 countries, whereas Brazil is ranked 26 (World Bank, 2010). Mexican SMEs, in particular, find it difficult to get bank loans and cope with bureaucratic regulation. The government is also concerned that oil, which has been a valuable source of income for Mexico, is now a contracting industry as the oil is running out. Diversification, however, remains more an aspiration than a reality. Part of the reason has been the structure of Mexico's economy.

Mexico's economic development has been dominated by large state-owned enterprises. Although privatization has helped to open the economy, the result in some cases has been to perpetuate near-monopolies in the hands of a few individuals, such as Carlos Slim. Income inequality and poverty are the highest of all OECD countries (OECD, 2008). The percentage of Mexican inhabitants living in poverty (defined as less than 50% of the median income) has fallen to 18%, from a high of 22.5% during the 'peso' financial crisis of the mid-1990s, but this is double that of the OECD generally. Worryingly, there are significant differences between the more prosperous north and mainly rural south of the country. The Mexican government does calculations on a broad measure of poverty, *pobreza de patrimonio*, which is the ability to afford basic food, clothing, health, education, housing and public transport. On this measure, 54.7% of rural inhabitants fall below the poverty line, a reduction from nearly two-thirds in 1992, but still over half the rural population. In urban areas, 35% live in poverty, a reduction from 44.3% in 1992 (CONEVAL, 2008). While the impacts of Nafta were beneficial to firms in the north, the grain producers in southern Mexico have suffered, especially small farmers, who have lost out to large producers and imported grains from subsidized US producers.

Mexico's tourist industry has been a source of optimism. In the 1970s, the government invested large sums in developing the Yucatan peninsula, with aid from the Inter-American Development Bank. The resort of Cancun became the country's largest, but suffered a devastating setback in May 2009, with an outbreak of swine flu, which grabbed media headlines around the world. It was particularly unfortunate, occurring in the same year as the US recession. The authorities closed all hotels and services, emptying the beaches, which should have been packed with visitors. The tourism sector is gradually recovering, and there are plans for more developments. Are there more clouds on the horizon? Violent storms are a risk in coastal areas, and the oil slick in the Gulf of Mexico in 2010, which BP struggled to control, illustrated another kind of risk to which coastal resorts are susceptible.

Sources: OECD (2008) *Growing Unequal? Income Distribution and Poverty in OECD Countries* (Paris: OECD); Thomson, A. (2010) 'Eager to shut the door on a bad year', *Financial Times*, 31 March; Buchanan, R. (2010) 'Business unfazed by drugs bloodshed', *Financial Times*, 31 March; Forbes (2010) World's richest rankings, at www.forbes.com; World Bank (2010) Doing Business rankings, at www.doingbusiness.org, CONEVAL (Consejo Nacional de Evaluación de la Política de Desarrollo Social) (2008) 'Informe de Evaluación de la Política de Desarrollo Social en México 2008', at www.coneval.gob.mx

Questions for discussion

◆ How would you rank Mexico's economy in terms of economic sustainability?

◆ Why does Mexico receive a rather low rating in the 'Doing business' rankings?

◆ What should be the Mexican government's priorities for diversification of the economy and social development?

which arise. Can their organizations keep up with their strategic ambitions, and are there lessons to be learned in this respect from the more traditional MNEs? Corporate governance is perceived as a crucial issue in western MNEs, as it is gradually becoming accepted that structures and processes should comply with best practice internationally (see Chapter 1). However, MNEs from emerging markets are often perceived as close-knit and opaque in their governance, despite their growing international presence. Some are largely state owned and seen as 'national champions' in their home countries. As these companies become more internationalized, it is arguable that their structures and governance should reflect this diversity. MNEs from developed countries present a variety of organizational models, discussed in the next section.

Summary points Emerging-market MNEs go global

◆ MNEs from fast-growing emerging economies are new global players, showing ambition and agility in the fast-changing competitive environment.

◆ These MNEs are keen to establish themselves globally, often pursuing acquisition strategies to enter new markets.

MNE structures

organization two or more people who work together in a structured way to achieve a specific goal or set of goals

An **organization** may be defined as 'two or more people who work together in a structured way to achieve a specific goal or set of goals' (Stoner and Freeman, 1992: 4). This broad definition encompasses many types of organization. It includes, for example, police forces, hospitals and schools, as well as all types of business enterprise. The structure and operations of an organization within national borders are much less complicated than those of organizations which operate across borders. The MNE parent company, introduced in Chapter 1, is at the pinnacle of its organization, usually located in the company's home country. Structures of subsidiaries and links between them must be co-ordinated through structures designed to serve the organization's corporate strategy. Physical resources, including plant, machinery and offices must be organized, and functions such as finance, purchasing and marketing must be co-ordinated, to enable the entire enterprise to function smoothly as a unit.

structure the design of organization through which the enterprise is administered

While every organization wishes to make the most of its expertise and resources, there is no one type of organization which can be said to be an ideal model that suits all businesses. There is a large body of organization theory, which studies 'the structure, functioning and performance of organizations and the behaviour of groups and individuals within them' (Pugh, 1997: xii). **Structure** has been defined as 'the design of organization through which the enterprise is administered' (Chandler, 1990: 14). It includes both formal and informal lines of authority. Organizational structures can be divided into three broad categories. The first is organization based simply on function. The second is the divisional structure, based on products, brands or regions. Thirdly, there is the organizational structure based on a matrix, the aim of which is to bring together the benefits of the other types. We look at each in turn.

functional approach organizational structure based on business functions, such as finance, HRM and marketing

The functional approach

Business functions were introduced in Chapter 1. In the **functional approach** to organization, business functions determine organizational structure. The importance of particular functions depends in part on the type of business. Product design and production, along with research and development, feature mainly in manufacturing firms, whereas all firms have need of finance, HRM and marketing functions.

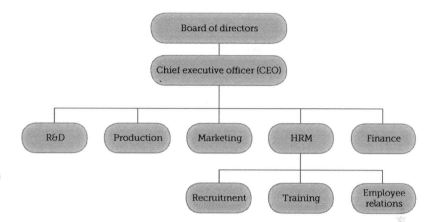

Figure 5.8 **Organization based on functional departments**

The functional organizational approach is depicted in Figure 5.8. There is a risk in this type of structure that each functional department will become inward-looking, evolving its own culture and losing sight of organizational goals. Within the formal structure, the functional specialists must blend into a smooth-running whole. Central management and, in particular, its chief executive officer (CEO) is at the pinnacle of the organization, and is therefore crucial in co-ordinating the departments. This is one of the main management challenges. **Management** is the:

management
process of planning, organizing, leading and controlling the work of organization members

> process of planning, organizing, leading and controlling the work of organization members, and of using all available organizational resources to reach stated organizational goals. (Stoner and Freeman, 1992: 4)

Head-office managers seek to reap the benefits of specialized staff in each functional area, but must also keep organizational goals in focus, which can mean making tough decisions on budgets of particular departments. For example, the marketing budget could be cut in order to boost spending on R&D, or vice versa. The larger the company, the more cumbersome this structure becomes. This type of structure is suitable for domestic companies, but does not necessarily lend itself to companies which are becoming internationalized. The MNE that produces a number of different products for different markets will require a structure accommodating these aspects of the business – one that combines central guidance and local responsiveness. The more decentralized divisional structure has developed in conjunction with international expansion.

Summary points The functional structure

- A structure based on separate functional areas is commonly adopted by companies which operate in a limited range of activities and in a single national environment.
- The functional structure risks becoming inward-looking, each function evolving its own culture, and losing sight of organizational goals

▶ More online ... DuPont is at www.dupont.com
PepsiCo is at www.pepsico.com

The divisional structure

When a company has grown to the extent that it has a number of successful products in different regions, it tends to structure the organization into business units or divisions, which may be based on product, brand, or geographical region (see Figure 5.9). Known as the **multidivisional structure**, this has been one of the major structural innovations of modern corporations, seeking to solve the problems of how to decentralize a large company while still maintaining overall co-ordination of the parts. A full account of its development is given in Alfred Chandler's *Strategy and Structure* (1990). In it he recounts the experiences of General Motors and the American chemical corporation DuPont, which adopted the multidivisional structure in the early 1900s. The principle is that each division is headed by a division manager who has responsibility for managing the division as a profit centre in its own right. The division itself may be a subsidiary company whose major shareholder is the parent company. The company's executives at the head office concentrate on the broader corporate aims, leaving the divisions considerable independence. The head office will house centralized functional departments, such as finance, for the group as a whole.

multidivisional structure organizational structure with decentralized divisions based on product lines or geographical areas

A divisional structure based on **product divisions** has been adopted by a number of global companies, including General Electric (GE), British Telecom (BT), and Ericsson. An advantage of this approach, in theory, is the ability to co-ordinate activities to produce and market a particular line worldwide, but a drawback tends to be that its standardized approach overlooks differences in national markets (Birkinshaw, 2000). Some companies combine product divisions and an international division, which is responsible for the firm's products in all markets other than its home country. PepsiCo is an example.

product divisions company divisions based on products, which co-ordinate product strategy globally

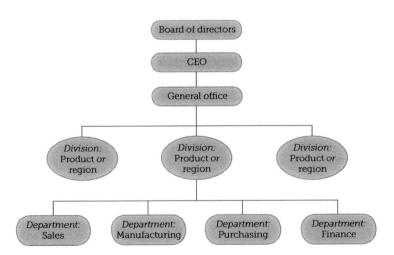

Figure 5.9 **The multidivisional structure**

area divisions company divisions based on geographical regions of the world, adapting strategy to local conditions

The **area division** is a way of addressing different regional conditions. In this type of organization structure, country or regional managers preside over area divisions, and are responsible for all of the company's activities in that area. The area may be, for example, Asia-Pacific, in which case the area manager has charge of operations in that region, including control over resources. For many US companies, Europe, the

► More online ... Unilever is at www.unilever.com

Middle East and Africa (EMEA) form a division, although these markets are highly diverse. A main advantage of the area division structure is that it is able to respond to regional needs. It also lends itself to decentralization, that is, the delegating of decision-making down to the divisions. Many global companies, including Nestlé and Unilever, have been organized in this way, although they have found that it is difficult to achieve economies of scale in development and production (Birkinshaw, 2000). They have tended to move towards global product divisions or a combination of geographical regions plus product divisions, as Unilever has done.

holding company
company, often referred to as the 'parent' company, which owns a number of subsidiaries

The **holding company** may also be said to be based on divisions, in that a parent company is the owner of a diverse array of subsidiary companies. However, unlike the multidivisional companies described above, the holding company usually exerts little control over the separate companies and provides few general functions for the group as a whole. The companies within the group operate, in effect, as independent organizations.

Summary points The divisional structure

◆ The divisional structure facilitates decentralized product units or regional units.

◆ This structure has been widely adopted by MNEs, and adapts to expanding international operations.

The matrix structure

matrix structure
organizational structure involving two lines of authority, such as area and product divisions

The **matrix** is a way of structuring the organization to incorporate the benefits of other types of structure, including the functional organization, product divisions and area divisions. It involves two lines of management, as indicated in Figure 5.10. The product manager must co-ordinate with the area manager for the launch of a new product in that region. In theory, this allows the company to respond to local trends, and also to derive the benefits of globally co-ordinated product management. In

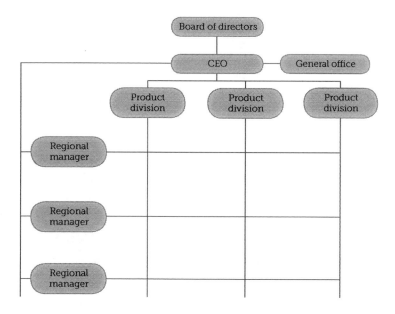

Figure 5.10 **The global matrix**

practice, however, it is difficult to reconcile these different lines of authority, and the system can lead to deadlock in decision-making (Bartlett and Ghoshal, 1990). Thus, although the matrix should theoretically provide flexibility, it can lead to inefficiency.

Some companies adopt a compromise, using product divisions, but adding country management where it is specifically needed (Birkinshaw, 2000). In the early 1990s, the Swiss-Swedish electrical engineering company ABB put in place a matrix structure, but changed to a divisional structure based on products and technologies in 1998. The company has undergone further restructuring since then, in which the divisions were replaced by four 'consumer segments', aimed at developing a greater customer orientation. The structural design journey of ABB reflects the challenges of MNEs in balancing the need for central control with local responsiveness.

Summary points   The matrix structure

◆ The matrix structure aims to combine co-ordinated product management and regional centres.

◆ In practice, the matrix structure is difficult to manage, due to crossing lines of communication.

Critical thinking

Growing too big?

The large, often highly diversified, MNE has come in for criticism for being so unwieldy that it is unable to make efficient use of the economies of scale which its large size should bring. Think of some large organizations that you know or that have featured in this book. What have they done to enhance their competitiveness in recent years?

Evolution of the transnational organization

As experiments with matrix structures suggest, designing organizational structures is only part of the story for an organization to achieve its aims. The parts must function efficiently, focusing on corporate goals while remaining agile in local markets. Degrees of autonomy of local units vary from one company to another: some are highly centralized while others are decentralized. Bartlett and Ghoshal have devised a typology of international organizations that highlights these features and emphasizes the importance of the firm's own corporate culture and legacy in influencing its structures (Bartlett and Ghoshal, 1998). These models are shown in Figure 5.11.

Figure 5.11 **Models of the international organization**

Source: Based on Bartlett, A. and Ghoshal, S. (1998) *Managing Across Borders: A Transnational Solution*, 2nd edn (London: Random House)

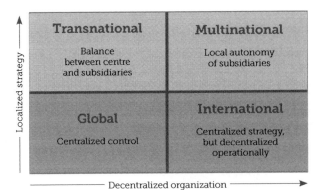

multinational model in Bartlett and Ghoshal's typology, a model of the international company based on autonomous national units

international model in Bartlett and Ghoshal's typology, a model of the international company based on decentralized subsidiaries

global model in Bartlett and Ghoshal's typology, a model of the international company based on centralized control

Fordism approach to an industrial organization based on large factories producing standardized products for mass consumption, named after the automobile magnate Henry Ford

transnational model in Bartlett and Ghoshal's typology, a model of the international company balanced between the centre and subsidiaries

flexible mass production model of manufacturing which combines the benefits of flexibility with those of scale economies

lean production systems and techniques of production enabling companies to reduce waste, leading to greater flexibility in production processes

just-in-time (JIT) manufacturing system of manufacturing which relies on a continuous flow of materials

Looking at the models shown in Figure 5.11, the **multinational model** (sometimes called the 'multidomestic' model) is the most decentralized. Subsidiaries are managed as autonomous units, with strategy-making powers for their areas. The **international model** decentralizes operations, but maintains central strategy formation. This model has proved successful for many European companies which have expanded through acquisitions. These businesses have considerable managerial latitude, which allows for local responsiveness, but the lack of strong global strategy might be considered a drawback. By contrast, the global model is highly centralized strategically and operationally. Resource allocation and planning stem from the centre, with little scope for local responsiveness.

The **global model** is typified by the management system known as **Fordism**, deriving its name from the top-down management associated with the Ford Motor Company in its post-war heyday. Ford aimed to produce a basic standardized product in large volumes and at prices affordable by the new middle classes in America's booming post-war period. This vertically integrated system relied on assembly-line processes operated by large numbers of semi-skilled workers. In Ford's River Rouge plant, which employed 35,000 under one roof, coal and iron went in at one end, and complete Ford cars rolled out the other. The Fordist system was highly bureaucratic and inflexible. Poor industrial relations characterized Fordist factories, where adversarial relations between highly organized trade unions and inflexible managers lingered long after Fordism as a manufacturing system was superseded.

To meet changing consumer tastes and a diversity of consumer needs, mass manufacturing was compelled to become more flexible, no longer based on a single mammoth factory, but on networks of smaller specialist organizations linked in supply chains. The use of integrated networks characterized the last of the four models, the **transnational model**. The thinking behind this model is similar to that underlying the matrix structure, in that it emphasizes local responsiveness. IBM's CEO speaks of the 'globally integrated enterprise'. He says:

> Unlike the multinational – which created mini versions of itself in markets around the world – this new kind of organization locates work, skills and operations wherever it makes sense, based on access to expertise, on superior economics and on the presence of open environments and technologies. (Palmisano, 2008)

Organizational flexibility and decentralized management, relying on more highly skilled workers to share responsibility, characterized the post-Fordist factory. Japanese companies are credited with the most successful examples of these manufacturing innovations. The Japanese model has been called one of '**flexible mass production**' (Sabel, 1994: 122). The large Japanese manufacturing companies, such as Toyota, the leading automaker, allow for flexibility in production and organization. While producing for mass markets, the system of centralized product development is nonetheless able to respond to changes in demand, making use of technology to reduce development time. New automated manufacturing equipment facilitates the rapid implementation of changes and variations in the product. **Lean production** techniques aim to reduce waste of all types, including time, and rely on a **just-in-time** supply of components, reducing the need for large amounts of stock. This flexibility is reflected in a workforce trained to understand the entire process involved in the new technology, enabling workers to change tasks with ease. High levels of knowledge and training are also essential to the Japanese philosophy of quality control, which emphasizes worker involvement and contribution (summed up in the

► More online ... Information on *kaizen* can be found at www.lean-manufacturing-japan.com
Toyota is at www.toyota.co.jp

kaizen management
philosophy of continuous
improvement, involving
the entire workforce

concept of **kaizen**). A consensus-based system of worker participation is a long way from the confrontational labour relations of classical mass production.

Summary points The transnational organizational structure

◆ Corporate structures differ in the extent of centralization of both strategy and operations.

◆ The transnational model aims to benefit from global strategy and

decentralized networking at the operational level.

Inter-organizational networks

Supply chains depend on co-operation among numerous organizations in the value chain, in which personal relations and ease of communication are crucial. As these ties, both formal and informal, evolve, the boundaries of the firm become 'fuzzy': people might have greater day-to-day relations with key people in other organizations than with people in their own firm. These network ties require a sharing of knowledge and thinking, which can benefit all the firms in the chain. But how does the notion of the network fit into traditional notions of competitive strategy?

Strategic alliances have become important aspects of corporate strategy. By co-operating in R&D, for example, two firms can make greater headway than each would achieve separately (see Chapter 10). In this way, both firms can benefit. The firm that co-operates with a competitor in this way can help to build competitive advantage, translating the knowledge into performance, which enhances the firm's core competencies. The idea of benefiting from ties with other firms is not new. Japanese firms have long nurtured inter-firm ties in the loosely formed keiretsu groups (see Chapter 3). Japanese manufacturing companies rely on a constellation of smaller firms to supply components and expertise. As western companies adopted Japanese management principles of lean production and just-in-time systems, they have become more open to co-operative strategies and inter-firm ties. However, just as there are risks in the highly centralized, hierarchical organization, there are risks in the decentralized, networked organization. Toyota has experienced problems in maintaining quality in its global production networks. Having built up expertise in quality management in its domestic production, it has encountered challenges in adapting these systems to globalized production.

The company that works closely with a number of suppliers and customers enhances its ability to satisfy customer needs, but also risks losing sight of its own core competencies. It can even find that its partners are benefiting from shared technology to gain a competitive lead. Hence, perhaps paradoxically, the firm must focus more strongly on its own core competencies, lest its competitive position becomes undermined. On the other hand, if it goes to the opposite extreme and is very reluctant to share technology with partners, it could well find that co-operative agreements bear little fruit. The balance must be struck between openness and control. Where firms are from differing cultural backgrounds, inter-firm networks face challenges in working smoothly and achieving collective goals, as the next chapter will show.

Summary points Inter-organizational networks

◆ The spread of supply chains, involving different companies, has led to the development of inter-organizational networks, involving the sharing of information and operational co-ordination.
◆ Networks are characteristic of post-Fordist organizations, especially in manufacturing based on Japanese-pioneered flexible mass production.

Rethinking globalization

MNEs from the developed economies have been at the forefront of globalization in the post-war period. Various strategies have played a part. Some companies have focused on vertical integration, acquiring ownership of key assets in a variety of locations. Others have acquired a diversity of different businesses, building sprawling conglomerates. More recently, companies have become more 'asset light', collaborating in complex supply chains. All three responses reflect globalization processes, as communications technology makes cross-border business easier to manage. National governments have played a big role, too, bringing down obstacles to cross-border business activities. However, national governments have revealed rather ambivalent approaches to globalization. They have liberalized trade and facilitated cross-border capital movements and FDI. However, in times of domestic economic stress, some governments have reacted by raising barriers to trade and investment, in order to protect domestic industries and jobs. At the same time, they express disappointment when foreign MNEs, once welcomed for their FDI, have exited countries in which performance has been disappointing.

For MNEs, keeping ahead in the global competitive environment requires a willingness to seize new opportunities and seek new markets. However, firms can find that they become overstretched, hanging onto units and activities which are not viable. Inevitably, from time to time, they will close factories or sell whole businesses, as part of their ongoing realignment of corporate strategy. If an acquired business or joint venture turns out not to be a good fit with the parent company's product portfolio, or if problems of integration emerge, the company must take hard decisions on where to let the axe fall. CEOs must take into account the views and interests of stakeholders. Key shareholders, in particular, are vigilant in cases where they feel the overall value of the parent company might be eroded.

In periods of rapid expansion, some MNEs have enjoyed acquisition sprees, acquiring dozens of companies around the globe in a single year. Nowadays, MNEs from developed countries are inclined to weigh up expansion plans more carefully, thinking more of the long-term benefits – and possible drawbacks. MNEs from emerging economies, keen to catch up with more established competitors, are approaching internationalization from slightly different perspectives. Their foundations in strong-performing economies encourage them to internationalize quickly. Some are family empires, unencumbered by the concerns of diverse shareholders and other stakeholders which have helped to shape western MNEs' approaches to strategy. In addition, many emerging-market MNEs are backed by state governments and approach internationalization as national champions. The notion of the globalized national champion might seem a contradiction. However, as we noted in Chapter 2, the truly global company, with little sense of national roots, is a rarity. Most reflect to some extent the cultural background in which they have emerged, even when their operations take place mainly outside their home countries. The cultural dimension remains strong in MNEs, as we discuss in the next chapter.

Summary points Rethinking globalization

◆ Expansive MNE strategies have propelled globalization, largely through FDI and the growth of global supply chains.

◆ National governments have facilitated MNE expansion, for example by welcoming FDI, but can show a reverse side, by discouraging and constraining investment when domestic interests are perceived to be at stake.

◆ Emerging-market MNEs have expanded quickly, often encouraged by generous state support and the underpinning of strong domestic economies.

Critical thinking

Globalization perspectives

In what ways do the perspectives of established western MNEs and emerging-market MNEs differ in respect of globalization?

Companion website

Remember to check the companion website at **www.palgrave.com/business/morrisongbe3** where you will find a searchable glossary, updated weblinks, video interviews with CEOs and extra guidance on the case studies in this book, all designed to help you get to grips with the global business environment.

Conclusions

1 Formulating strategy involves examining the organization's goals and how to achieve them.
2 The SWOT analysis, highlighting the firm's strengths, weaknesses, opportunities and threats, is an aid to formulating strategy, which takes in both internal and external aspects of the firm's environment.
3 Porter's five forces model focuses mainly on the competitive environment in a particular industry.
4 The resource-based view of the firm assesses the firm's internal strengths, including core competencies, in relation to those of competitors and potential competitors.
5 The emergent strategy approach allows for a firm's strategy to evolve as it grows and responds to the changing environment.
6 The stakeholder management approach focuses on the need to involve a range of stakeholders in the strategy process.
7 Strategy can be viewed at three different levels: the highest is corporate strategy, involving the firm's ultimate goals. Competitive strategy focuses on achieving success in different markets. Both help to determine functional strategies, such as marketing strategy.
8 Of internationalization strategies, export is the mode that entails the least involvement in the host environment, while FDI involves greater integration in the host country.
9 Greenfield investment can be contrasted with acquisition, the latter of which is a quicker way to gain a foothold in the host country, often implying existing market share.
10 Licensing, especially to outsourcers, is a favoured option in many manufacturing sectors, but terms of agreements and management relations need to be carefully handled, in order to succeed.
11 Emerging-market MNEs have become powerful players in global markets, demonstrating ambition and flexibility in adapting to changing environments.
12 MNE organizational structures vary according to the degree of latitude which foreign subsidiaries enjoy. In the multinational structure, they enjoy considerable latitude, while the global model is highly centralized.
13 The transnational model combines centralized strategy with local responsiveness.
14 The benefits of inter-firm networks, which develop relational ties between firms, have become more apparent with the advances in global supply chains.
15 Some MNEs have embraced globalization by going on acquisition sprees, especially when financing posed few obstacles. Now, as finances have become tighter and the competitive environment has become more challenging, firms are rethinking global strategies with a view more focused on core competencies.

Review questions

1 What factors must a firm balance in formulating strategy?
2 Explain the different elements of the SWOT analysis, giving an example of each.
3 In what ways does Porter's five forces model aid the firm in identifying strategic opportunities?
4 Define the key attributes of a resource according to the resource-based view of the firm.
5 Give an example of a core competence, and explain how it would help to achieve competitive advantage.
6 What are the advantages of an emergent-strategy approach, as opposed to a strategic-planning approach?

7   What long-term benefits are arguably achievable through the stakeholder management approach to strategy?

8   Explain the different approaches to competitive strategy.

9   What type of firm and product would be likely to benefit from export as an internationalization mode?

10 What are the advantages and disadvantages of licensing as an entry mode?

11 What are the advantages of acquisition over FDI as an entry mode? What are the drawbacks?

12 What degrees of decentralization are associated with each of the following organizational structures: (a) the multinational model; (b) the global model?

13 Why are multidivisional companies increasingly opting for global product divisions?

14 The matrix organizational structure is often held up as ideal in theory, but unworkable in practice. Why?

15 What advantages and disadvantages do emerging-market MNEs have in their internationalization strategies?

Key revision concepts

Core competencies, p. 113; Diversification, p. 123; Emergent strategy, p. 114; Five forces model, p. 110; Flexible mass production, p. 133; Fordism, p. 133; Integration, p. 123; Management, p. 129; Multidivisional structure, p. 130; Resource-based theory, p. 112; SWOT analysis, p. 108

Assignments

◆ The large conglomerate has traditionally relied on its diverse businesses as a strength in global markets. These supposed benefits are now not so obvious. Assess the advantages and disadvantages of the large diversified organization in today's global environment.

◆ Assume you are the CEO of a large retailer in a western country. Your shareholders wish to see the company expanding into large emerging markets. How would you go about formulating an internationalization strategy to maximize the chances of success and minimize the risks?

Further reading

Barney, J. and Hesterley, W. (2007) *Strategic Management and Competitive Advantage: Concepts and Cases*, 2nd edn (Prentice Hall).

Bartlett, C.A. and Ghoshal, S. (2002) *Managing Across Borders: The Transnational Solution*, 2nd edn (Boston, MA: Harvard Business School Press).

Johnson, G. and Scholes, K. (2006) *Exploring Corporate Strategy*, 7th edn (Financial Times Prentice Hall).

Lasserre, P. (2007) *Global Strategic Management*, 2nd edn (Basingstoke: Palgrave Macmillan).

Mintzberg, H., Ahlstrand, B. and Lampel, J. (2009) *Strategy Safari*, 2nd edn (Harlow: Pearson Education).

Mullins, L. (2009) *Management and Organizational Behaviour*, 8th edn (Financial Times Prentice Hall).

Wheelen, T. and Hunger, J. (2009) *Strategic Management and Business Policy*, 12th edn (Pearson Education).

Sony seeks to revive profitability

Few brands in electronics have the enduring brand reputation that Sony enjoys. Yet the Japanese company has found it difficult to maintain profits in an increasingly competitive environment. Its history of innovative products goes back to the Walkman in 1979. It invested heavily in flatscreen televisions, but competitors such as Samsung and LG have challenged it in quality and price. Sony has not been an inward-looking company. It was among the first Japanese companies to have foreign board members, and its chairman and CEO, Sir Howard Stringer, is British. It has globalized production and sought to locate manufacturing facilities near markets. However, competitive pressures and global economic downturn have taken their toll. Sony's CEO has embarked on a widespread restructuring programme, targeting its television factories in particular.

Sony started manufacturing televisions in Slovakia in 2006, and built up production capacity, but it has now decided to slim down its operations to save costs. Overall, Sony's electronics business, which includes audio, video and televisions, is being reduced from 57 factories to 42. It is shedding four of its eight TV factories. The Nitra plant in Slovakia was sold to Hon Hai (Foxconn) of Taiwan, an outsource manufacturer making TVs under licence (although Sony retained a 10% stake). Hon Hai also bought Sony's TV factory in Mexico. Hon Hai's attractiveness as an outsourcer stems partly from its acquisition of an affiliate specializing in liquid crystal display (LCD) panels. Hon Hai should thus be a strong competitive position in TV assembly, as it can

benefit from transaction costs savings. Still, competition from Samsung is stiff, and Samsung has an in-house supply of LCD panels.

Sony's loss-making Barcelona factory posed another challenge. The Barcelona operation is small in comparison to Nitra, and therefore a natural candidate for closure, but it would be costly. The factory is unionized, and Spain has strong employment protection laws. Who would buy the Barcelona factory? An outsourcing manufacturer would be deterred by the small scale and high costs. Late in 2010 a provisional deal was done to sell the Barcelona factory to two local Spanish firms, one concentrating on manufacturing operations and the other on development and engineering. Sony had thus disposed of all its European TV plants. It is still intent on keeping the 'mother factory' in Japan, which is important in design and feedback. Its factories in Brazil and China, both growing markets, will also be kept: these are large markets and both countries have high import duties on TVs.

Small LCD panels for use in mobile phones and digital cameras are still manufactured at Sony factories in Japan, even though they are not profitable. It sold one of these factories to Kyocera, but has kept two. Its reasoning is that it wishes to

Watching the screen: Sony has become a global leader in technology, but despite its fame as a global brand, it faces stiff global competition

Source: Sony

develop display technologies for the future, as these help to differentiate its products. Sony has faced criticism that it has lost its leadership role in innovation as other companies, such as Apple, with its iPad, have taken the limelight. Sony is producing a rival to the iPad, and it has been somewhat cheered by increased sales of its Vaio PCs. However, quality problems with the new PS3 PlayStation were disappointing, especially coming at a time when Toyota was also experiencing quality problems. Production of the PS3 is outsourced to China. Sony has traditionally justified its premium prices on its reputation for quality. With its TV manufacturing increasingly outsourced, will consumers still be willing to pay for the Sony brand, even though someone else has made the product? Sony executives are hoping the answer is 'yes'.

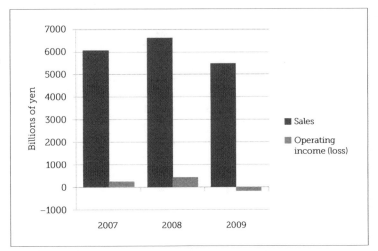

Sales and operating income (loss) in Sony's electronics division

Source: Sony Annual Report 2009, at www.sony.net

Sources: Harding, R. and Soble, J. (2010) 'Japanese fret over quality of manufacturing', *Financial Times*, 3 March; Harding, R. (2010) 'Stringer's Sony restructuring has unfinished business', *Financial Times*, 1 April; Harding, R. and Gelles, D. (2010) 'Sony plans to compete against the Apple iPad', *Financial Times*, 5 February; Sony Annual Report 2009, at www.sony.net

Questions for discussion

● What trends are apparent in the global electronics industry, which are having adverse effects on Sony?
● What are Sony's core competencies?
● What are the risks of outsourcing from Sony's perspective?

Chapter 6

Competitive advantage and strategy

Introduction and chapter overview

The key challenge for any organization is the ability to gain and sustain a competitive advantage in the market or industry. This advantage can be based on alignment to environmental and industry structures, or by the continual adaptation, creativity and innovative use of organizational resources and networks. This chapter explores the means by which organizations can gain and sustain a competitive advantage through the use of positioning or the creative use of resources. The schools of strategic thought are examined before focusing on the identification of generic strategies as building blocks for the overall strategic direction of the organization. Once the generic strategies have been determined, the chapter explores the nature and role of competences and core competences. This sets up the alternative forms of strategic direction, strategic frameworks, and management of strategic risk, which are discussed in Chapter 14, as well as the methods for growth developed in Chapter 15.

Learning objectives

After studying this chapter, you will be able to:

- describe the different schools of strategic thought relating to competitive advantage
- explain the concept of competitive advantage, and identify sources of competitive advantage
- describe and demonstrate the application of Porter's generic strategies
- explain low-cost, differentiation, focus and hybrid strategies
- define core competences and explain sources of competence

6.1 Sources of competitive advantage

The main goal of strategic management is to produce sustainable competitive advantage for a business. Competitive advantage can arise from deliberate, planned strategies and emergent strategies, which arise from opportunistic moves by the business. Competitive advantage is not easy to achieve and is even more difficult to sustain. Superior performance is built and sustained through continuous organizational learning and results in a constant process of new strategy development and improvement in the way in which business activities are carried out.

The rapid pace of technological, political, economic and social change, the increasing turbulence of the business environment, the growing sophistication of customer needs and the drastic shortening of product life cycles that typifies 'hypercompetition' all mean that competitive advantage is often contestable rather than sustainable. In other words, the search for strategies that produce and sustain superior performance over a long period of time has become increasingly difficult. Competitive advantage can only be developed and sustained through the creation of new business knowledge based on continuous organizational learning and the deployment of dynamic capabilities (Teece, 2009).

In Chapter 1, we learned that the different strands of theory in strategic management offer several explanations and potential methods by which competitive advantage can be achieved.

The 'competitive positioning' theory is based on the structure-conduct-performance paradigm and is typified by Porter's five forces, generic strategy and value chain frameworks (Porter, 1980, 1985), which have subsequently been augmented by the concept of a hybrid strategy. While dated and arguably inflexible, Porter's work still forms an excellent platform for understanding the positioning school. For Porter, the first question to be answered was: 'in which industry should the business compete?' Potential industry profitability, and hence **industry attractiveness**, was established through five forces analysis (Chapter 10). The factors that lead to industry attractiveness are:

> **Industry attractiveness** represents the potential to make a profit or gain strategic rent from a specific industry configuration.

- Industry's market size and growth potential
- The impact of environmental forces on the industry structure and dynamics
- Potential for entry and exit, and mobility in the industry
- Stability and dependability of demand
- Asset specificity, switching costs and capital costs
- Degree of risk and uncertainty in the industry's future
- Knowledge of the industry.

Once the choice of industry was made, the organization had to determine which generic strategy to pursue, and then decide the optimum configuration of its value-adding activities to support the chosen generic strategy. The approach is essentially 'outside-in', with choices initially being concerned with which industry was likely to prove the most profitable. As such, the competitive dynamics revolved around the degree to which perfect information or knowledge could be achieved and how barriers to entry and mobility could be exploited.

As an alternative, the resource-based school (Prahalad and Hamel, 1990; Barney, 1991; Grant, 1991) emerged on the basis that competitive advantage results from the development and exploitation of core competences by individual businesses, whatever industry they are in. This theory is built on the notion that certain firms outperform their competitors in the same industry. If this is the case, competitive advantage cannot be explained entirely by different industry conditions. The explanation for competitive advantage must rest, at least in part, within the firm itself. For this reason, the approach to strategy is best regarded as 'inside-out', and explains why firms in the same industry experience different levels of success and performance.

The third, knowledge-based school (Sveiby, 1997, 2001) suggests that competitive advantage arises from the creation, development and exploitation of new knowledge through a process of organizational learning. Interestingly, the competitive positioning, core competence and knowledge-based approaches need not be viewed as mutually exclusive. Knowledge can be viewed as the basis of an organization's core competences and generic strategy, leading to innovation, the ability to adapt and adopt. Equally, a generic strategy can be viewed as being dependent on a particular set of core competences underpinned by an appropriate configuration of value-adding activities or dynamic capabilities (Teece, 2009).

GURU GUIDE

Karl-Erik Sveiby is a professor of knowledge management at the Hanken Business School in Helsinki, Finland. He is a subject expert in knowledge management and is often regarded as one of the founding fathers of knowledge management. He has considerable management experience, having worked with several international firms and was the proprietor of one of Scandinavia's leading publishing houses. Dr Sveiby has also extensive consultancy experience, and is the founder of Sveiby Knowledge Associates (www.sveiby.com), a consultancy firm specializing in providing knowledge management solutions to global firms.

His work in measuring the value of intangible assets has been extensively adapted by Swedish companies and has become part of a international standard in this field.

The development of a strategy will inevitably draw on some analysis of the business, its objectives, its resources, competences, activities and its competitive environment. Even in the context of an emergent approach to strategy, managers still require an understanding of the business and the consequences of alternative courses of action.

This chapter provides tools that can be employed in developing our understanding of current strategy and future strategic alternatives. The frameworks are first explored separately and then the linkages between them are developed. It is important to note that there is no universal prescription for building competitive advantage. Competitive advantage is, however, more likely to result from doing things differently from competitors and doing them better rather than from trying to emulate them. Hamel and Prahalad (1985) made a strong case that organizations should develop a 'strategic intent' to stretch their resources and competences to the limits in order to achieve superior performance. Similarly, superior performance is more likely to result from an informed approach to management based on an understanding of the firm, the environment in which it operates and the strategic alternatives available to it. This chapter provides the basis of an informed approach to the development of corporate strategies.

Competitive and collaborative advantage

Competitive advantage will depend on the ability of a firm to outperform its competitors. Sustainable competitive advantage requires that the firm outperforms its rivals over a long period of time. While there is no recipe or formula that can guarantee sustained superior performance, there are certain organizational behaviours that have been shown to make success more likely:

- *strategic intent:* constantly stretching the organization to its limits

- *continuous improvement and innovation:* continually trying to improve products and services, relationships with customers and suppliers, and the way that activities are organized and carried out
- *doing things differently from competitors:* devising ways of doing business that are different from and better than the approaches adopted by competitors
- *being customer oriented:* always seeking to meet customer needs
- *building knowledge-based core competences and distinctive capabilities*
- *developing clear and consistent strategies* that are understood by managers and customers
- *awareness of factors in the business environment,* potential changes and their likely implications for the business
- *collaborating with other businesses and customers* to improve agility and flexibility.

Any strategy ought to take these factors into account, as by doing so, it is more likely that the strategy will be more difficult for competitors to emulate. Collaboration with suppliers, distributors and customers can be particularly important for building competitive advantage that is sustainable, as collaboration can be particularly difficult for competitors to replicate. For example, the association of Ferrari's Formula One team with Shell has led the team to win a number of world titles. Ferrari engines are powered by high performance race fuels developed by Shell, and their partnership has been a crucial factor in Ferrari's successful campaign in winning constructor and driver titles at Formula One world championships.

6.2 Michael Porter's generic strategies

Perhaps the oldest and best-known explanation of competitive advantage is given by Porter in his generic strategy framework. Although this framework has increasingly been called into question in recent years, it still provides useful insights into competitive behaviour. The framework and its limitations are considered in this section.

According to Porter (1985), competitive advantage arises from the selection of the generic strategy that best fits the organization's competitive environment and then organizing value-adding activities to support the chosen strategy.

There are three main alternatives:

- *cost leadership:* being the lowest cost producer of a product so that above-average profits are earned even though the price charged is not above average
- *differentiation:* creating a customer perception that a product is superior to that of competitors' products so that a premium price can be charged
- *focus:* utilizing either a differentiation or cost leadership strategy in a narrow profile of market segments (see Figure 6.1).

Porter argued that an organization must make two key decisions on its strategy:

1 Should the strategy be one of differentiation or cost leadership?
2 Should the scope of the strategy be broad or narrow?

In other words, the organization must decide whether to try to differentiate its products and sell them at a premium price, or whether to gain competitive

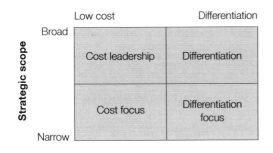

Figure 6.1 The generic strategy framework

Source: Adapted from Porter, 1998

advantage by producing at a lower cost than its competitors. Higher profits can be made by adopting either approach. Second, it must decide whether to target the whole market with its chosen strategy or whether to target a specific segment or niche of the market. Figure 6.1 shows cost focus and differentiation focus as two ends or extremes of a continuum. This is because actual strategies can exist at or anywhere in between the extremes. The same applies to the vertical direction. Broad and narrow are general extremes, where a broad strategy targets many markets and a disparate cross-section of customers, while a narrow or highly focused strategy may target a small number of segments (or possibly just one).

The point of Figure 6.1 is that it is best understood as a map. Companies in an industry can all be successful if they each choose different strategies. If, however, two or more competitors choose to compete in the same part of the map (that is, adopting the same or similar generic strategy), competition will become intensified among those pursuing the same strategy. By plotting competitors on the map, we can get an idea of where the most intense competition will occur. Sections containing only one competitor will experience the least competition.

Cost leadership strategy

> A **cost leadership strategy** is based on a business organizing and managing its value-adding activities so as to be the lowest cost producer of a product (a good or service) within an industry.

A **cost leadership strategy** is based on a business organizing and managing its value-adding activities so as to be the lowest cost producer of a product (a good or service) within an industry.

There are several potential benefits of a cost leadership strategy:

- the business can earn higher profits by charging a price equal to, or even below, that of competitors because its unit costs are lower
- it allows the business the possibility to increase both sales and market share by reducing price below that charged by competitors (assuming that the product's demand is price elastic in nature)
- it allows the business the possibility of entering a new market by charging a lower price than competitors
- it can be particularly valuable in a market where consumers are price sensitive
- it creates an additional barrier to entry for organizations wishing to enter the industry.

A successful cost leadership strategy is likely to rest on a number of organizational features. Such features will relate to the means by which a cost advantage can be gained and maintained in the long run (although cost-based strategy tends to be difficult to sustain). As such, features such as lean supply chain, efficient production processes, aligned value systems, dedicated (tied in) supply, customer loyalty and price awareness of competitors are all critical.

Value chain analysis is central to identifying where cost savings can be made at various stages in the value chain and its internal and external linkages. Attainment of a position of cost leadership depends on the arrangement of value chain activities, so as to:

- reduce unit costs by copying rather than originating designs, using cheaper materials and other cheaper resources, producing products with 'no frills', reducing labour costs and increasing labour productivity

- achieving economies of scale by high-volume sales, perhaps based on advertising and promotion, allowing high fixed costs of investment in modern technology to be spread over a high volume of output
- using high-volume purchasing to obtain discounts for bulk buying of materials
- locating activities in areas where costs are low or government help, for example grant support, is available
- obtaining 'learning curve' economies.

> The term **price elasticity of demand** describes the extent to which the volume of demand for a product is dependent upon its price.

A cost leadership strategy, coupled with low price, is best employed in a market or segment where **price elasticity of demand** exists, that is, where volume is relatively responsive to price. Under such circumstances, sales and market share are likely to increase significantly, thus increasing economies of scale, reducing unit costs further, so generating above-average profits. Alternatively, if a price similar to that of competitors is charged accompanied by advertising to boost sales, similar results will be obtained.

Example   Price elasticity of demand

The coefficient of elasticity is expressed in a simple equation:

PED = percentage change in quantity/percentage change in price.

The value of PED (price elasticity) tells us the price responsiveness of the product's demand. If, for any given price change, PED is more than −1, it means that the change in price has brought about a higher proportionate change in volume sold. This relationship between price change and quantity is referred to as 'price elastic demand'.

Demand is said to be 'price inelastic' if the quantity change is proportionately smaller than the change in price (resulting in a PED of less than −1). The larger the value of PED, the more price elastic the demand, and the nearer PED is to 0, the more price inelastic the demand.

The price elasticity of demand (the value of PED) depends on the market's perception of a product. Products tend to be price elastic if the market sees a product as unnecessary but desirable. Products will have a price inelastic demand if the customer perceives a *need* for a product rather than a *want* (such as the demand for most medicines, or tobacco).

Companies whose activities include high-volume standardized products are often cost leaders. The no-frills airlines are good examples. A basic product is offered and costs per sale are minimized by online booking, faster aircraft turnaround between flights, and no on-board free food.

Example   Ryanair: a cost leader

Ryanair has proved to be one of the most, if not the most, successful low-cost airlines. Despite the economic downturn of 2009, Ryanair maintained its performance and profitability. How it achieved this is well articulated in an interview by Tom Chesshyre (2002) of Michael O'Leary, chief executive of the Irish-based, low-cost airline Ryanair, which appeared in *The Times*.

In the article, Tom Chesshyre explains that *The Times* travel desk receives more complaints about Ryanair than any other airline and that complaints about delays, poor in-flight service, damaged luggage and lengthy check-in queues are common. Yet, O'Leary is quick to recognize that Ryanair rarely apologizes or offers compensation for these complaints.

When the interviewer questions this

attitude, O'Leary responds: 'Our customer service is about the most well-defined in the world. We guarantee to give you the lowest airfare. You get a safe flight. You get a normally on-time flight. That's the package. We don't and won't give you anything more on top of that.' He adds: 'Listen, we care for our customers in the most fundamental way possible: we don't screw them every time we fly them. We care for our customers by giving them the cheapest airfares. I have no time for certain large airlines which say they care and then screw you for six or seven hundred quid almost every time you fly.'

However, the article states that many people are now tiring of this attitude and the Air Transport Users Council, which monitors airline complaints, testifies that Ryanair is one of the worst offenders. It explains that several of Ryanair's customers have complained about how difficult it is to talk to anyone when they have a problem, as they have to ring several times before eventually being put through to an operator. In response to this, O'Leary states that: 'Generally speaking, we won't take any phone calls ... because they keep you on the bloody phone all day. We employ four people in our customer care department. Every complaint must be put in writing and we undertake to respond to that complaint within 24 hours. Anyway, do you know what 70 per cent of our complaints are about? They're about people who want to make changes to what are clearly stated as being "non-changeable, non-transferable and non-refundable" tickets.'

Asked if he thinks people should be able to get refunds for his airline tickets, he replies: 'No ... because even if you can't change your ticket and you've got to buy a second one, you're still going to save money compared with buying a single ticket from the major airlines. Anyway, with our new system you can make some changes. If you pay 20 euros (at that time £12.30), you can change the time of your flight, but not the name on the ticket.'

Which, as the article correctly states, is a start.

Differentiation strategy

A **differentiation strategy** is based on persuading customers that a product is superior to that offered by competitors.

A **differentiation strategy** is based on persuading customers that a product is superior to that offered by competitors. This relies on creating added value for the consumer, be it real value or perceived. Value can be in terms of social, economic, political, belonging, emotional or situational, and is at the heart of understanding consumers reserved price for goods and services, or their willingness to pay a premium.

Differentiation can be based on premium product features or simply by creating consumer perceptions that a product is superior. The major benefits to a business of a successful differentiation strategy are:

- its products will command a premium price
- demand for its product will be less price elastic than that for competitors' products
- above-average profits can be earned
- it creates an additional barrier to entry to new businesses wishing to enter the industry.

A business seeking to differentiate itself will organize its value chain activities to help create differentiated products and to create a perception among customers that these offerings are worth a higher price.

Differentiation can be achieved in several ways:

- by creating products that are superior to competitors by virtue of design, technology, performance and so on
- by offering superior after-sales service
- by superior distribution channels, perhaps in prime locations, especially important in the retail sector
- by creating a strong brand name through design, innovation or advertising
- by distinctive or superior product packaging.

A differentiation strategy is likely to necessitate emphasis on innovation, design, R&D, awareness of particular customer needs and marketing. To say that differentiation is in the eyes of the customer is no exaggeration. It could be argued that it is often the brand name or logo that distinguishes a product rather than real product superiority. For example, men's shirts bearing the logo of Ralph Lauren, Calvin Klein or Yves St Laurent command a price well above that of arguably similar shirts that bear no logo. There is little empirical evidence of objectively better design or better quality materials. Differentiation appears merely to be based on the fact that the designer's name is fashionable and that their products bear the logo.

This strategy is employed in order to reduce price elasticity of demand for the product so that its price can be raised above that of competitors without reducing sales volume. This will, in turn, generate above-average profits when measured against sales (return on sales).

Figure 6.2 provides a simplified understanding of cost and differentiation strategies.

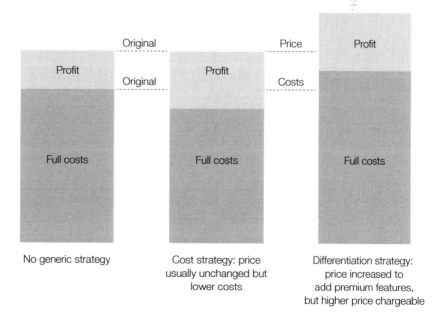

Figure 6.2 A simplified understanding of cost and differentiation strategies

Note: price = full costs plus profits

Focus strategy

A focus strategy is aimed at a segment of the market for a product rather than at the whole market or many markets. A particular group of customers is identified on the basis of age, income, lifestyle, sex, geographic location, some other distinguishing segmental characteristic or a combination of these. Within the segment, a business then employs either a cost leadership or a differentiation strategy.

The major benefits of a focus strategy are:

- it requires a lower investment in resources compared to a strategy aimed at an entire market or many markets
- it allows specialization and greater knowledge of the segment being served
- it makes entry to a new market less costly and simpler.

A focus strategy will require:

- identification of a suitable target customer group, which forms a distinct market segment
- identification of the specific needs of that group
- establishing that the segment is sufficiently large to sustain the business
- establishing the extent of competition within the segment
- production of products to meet the specific needs of that group
- deciding whether to operate a differentiation or cost leadership strategy within the market segment.

An example of a business that pursues a focus strategy is Ferrari, which targets the market for high performance sports cars (a relatively small number of customers in relation to the total market for cars). Ferrari, unlike Toyota or Fiat, does not produce family saloons, minis, off-road vehicles or people carriers. It only produces high performance cars. Its strategy is clearly one of differentiation based on design, superior performance and its Grand Prix record, which allows it to charge a price well above that of its competitors.

Many businesses use a focus strategy to enter a market before broadening their activities into other related segments.

6.3   Porter's global generic strategies

We learned in Chapter 11 that a global context is important. In parallel, Porter (1980) has argued that competitive advantage rests on a business selecting and adopting one of the three generic strategies (differentiation, cost leadership or focus) to modify the five competitive forces in its favour so as to earn higher profits than the industry average. In this section, we look at how Porter extended the generic strategy framework to global business. The model suggests that a business operating in international markets has five strategy alternatives (Figure 6.3), which are defined according to their position in respect to two intersecting factors; the extent to which the industry is globalized or country-centred (horizontal axis) and the breadth of the segments served by competitors in an industry (vertical axis).

The five strategic positions are:

1 *Global cost leadership:* the business seeks to be the lowest cost producer of a product globally. Globalization provides the opportunity for high-volume sales and greater economies of scale and scope than domestic competitors.

CASE STUDY   Mattel

If you are to stand the best possible chance of making and delivering products and services that your customers need and want from you, then you need to know what customers' needs and wants are.

However, knowing what your customers genuinely need and want from you, how much they are prepared to pay for this, and how often they are prepared to do business with you are the foundations of success, and, as such, distinguish the successful from the less so and the failures.

The Barbie organization was one of the first to recognize the importance of this, and, crucially, to take the next step and integrate the management of market and customer information into its product and brand development strategy. The Barbie organization was founded by Ruth Handler, who came across a German toy doll called Bild Lilli and reworked the design of the doll and named it after her own small daughter Barbara's family nickname – Barbie. The doll went into production and the company started operations in 1956.

The company set out to know everything that it possibly could about its customers – their buying habits, frequency of purchases, attitudes and values. They sought to understand the kinds of products that customers would and would not buy, and the life span of the dolls and their accessories. The result was akin to military intelligence gathering in its coverage and comprehensiveness, and both Ruth Handler and the Mattel organization (which took over the Barbie range of products in 1961) subsequently always boasted that they knew more about their customers than anyone else in the world.

The result was that when the first dolls arrived on the shelves of the world's toy shops in 1959, everyone was eagerly anticipating what they would look like and how the venture would go from a business point of view – quite literally: 'how it would play'. It became clear that there was a huge demand, not just for the dolls as they were, but also for products that would go with them – clothes, accessories and other add-ons.

From all of this grew what has come to be known as 'the eleven-inch doll market'. There was (and remains) a clear structure to this market:

- the products are bought by mothers and aunts for girls aged two and over
- the products are of value to girls

aged two and over, as well as being acceptable and of value to those who buy them

- the products are played with and enjoyed by girls, and they also have to be acceptable to her friends and others whose opinions they value and respond to
- the products have a limited useful life, and the clothes, accessories and add-ons are a fundamental part of product effectiveness and value and brand development.

To remain successful, the company needed a regular flow of new products coming on stream all the time. It therefore needed to know and understand the kinds of products that would keep the customers coming back again and again. Part of the problem that had to be overcome was the availability of choices, both within the eleven-inch doll market, and also outside it (nobody likes to be limited to any one thing, and the buyers and consumers of Barbie dolls are no different). So the brand logo and distinctive colour scheme (a bright pink) were developed so as to be capable of being attached to every product that came out. Also, the core range of products had to be universally available, and at prices that would allow for unconsidered, whim and largely cash purchases to be made. So the products were made available at all possible outlets, including supermarkets, department stores and independent corner shops. In the UK and many parts of the USA and the EU, the decline of independent toy shops made this range of outlets essential.

As the result, the product range now covers themed toys (castles, stables, cars, accessories for dolls' houses), films and video productions, cards and books, and other dolls (Barbie now has a large circle of

friends and acquaintances, and a boyfriend Ken, who she separated from in 2004, but in 2006 they were hoping to rekindle their relationship, after Ken had a makeover). There is also a large range of accessories and add-ons for girls to use, including shoes, bracelets, bags, and hair and cosmetic products, which all carry the Barbie brand. There are limited editions, Christmas and seasonal specials, collectors' items and other exclusives. Barbie has had many careers, including surgeon, nanny, show jumper and schoolteacher, and each career has carried its own range of clothes and accessories. She has had over 40 pets and owned a wide range of vehicles. The first Barbie department store opened in Shanghai in 2009, and more are expected to follow.

The company carefully evaluates everything that carries the Barbie brand for compatibility as well as acceptability, and this remains a core priority of the market intelligence operation as well as product design. The fundamental wholesomeness of the products,

and especially the images of girls and women that are portrayed, continues to be debated. Nevertheless, it is estimated that over a billion Barbie dolls have been sold worldwide in over 150 countries and the company states that it sells one Barbie product every seven seconds somewhere in the world. The overall strategic approach is structured so as to produce an income per customer in the UK of £80 per annum.

Case study questions

1   Where does the source of competitive advantage lie for products such as these?
2   Identify in detail the elements of strategy necessary to ensure that the product remains viable for the next two, five and ten years.
3   What are the main lessons for leaders and managers in all organizations to be learned from the experience and success of the Barbie product and the Mattel organization?

---

2   *Global differentiation:* the business seeks to differentiate products and services globally, often on the basis of a global brand name.
3   *Global segmentation:* this is the global variant of a focus strategy, when a single market segment is targeted on a worldwide basis employing either cost leadership or differentiation.
4   *Protected markets:* a business that identifies national markets where its particular business is favoured or protected by the host government.
5   *National responsiveness:* the business adapts its strategy to meet the distinctive needs of local markets, that is, not a global strategy. Suitable for purely domestic businesses.

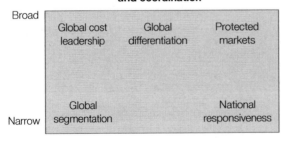

The model suffers from some flaws, in that a hybrid can be adopted rather than falling neatly into one of the areas. As in the case of the conventional understanding of generic strategy, it is possible for a business to pursue a hybrid international strategy. Nissan, for example, concentrates on cost control but also ensures that it differentiates its products on the basis of their reliability.

Figure 6.3 Porter's global strategy framework
Source: Adapted from Porter, 1986

Configuration and coordination of internal activities

One of Porter's most important contributions to understanding global strategy is his work on the global value chain (1986, 1990). Porter makes the case that global competitive advantage depends on configuring and coordinating the activities of a business in a unique way on a worldwide basis. To put it another way, competitive advantage results from the global scope of an organization's activities and the effectiveness with which it coordinates them. Porter (1986, 1990) argues that global competitive advantage depends on two sets of decisions:

1 *Configuration of value-adding activities:* managers must decide in which nations they will carry out each of the activities in the value chain of their business. Configuration can be broad (involving many countries) or narrow (one country or just a few).

2 *Coordination of value-adding activities:* managers must decide the most effective way of coordinating the value-adding activities that are carried out in different parts of the world.

Configuration of activities

	Geographically dispersed	Geographically concentrated
High	High degree of dispersal of activities with a high degree of coordination among subsidiaries	Purest global strategy (high degree of concentration of activities and coordination)
Low	Country-centred strategy for company with several national subsidiaries, each operating in only one country. Activity dispersed and little cooperation	Strategy based upon exporting of product with decentralised marketing in each host country – activities concentrated but not coordinated

*(vertical axis label: **Coordination of activities**)*

Figure 6.4 Configuration and coordination for international strategy

Source: Adapted from Porter, 1986

Configuration and coordination present four broad alternatives, as illustrated in Figure 6.4. In the case of configuration, an organization can choose to disperse its activities to a range of locations around the world or it may choose to concentrate key activities in locations that present certain advantages. Many businesses concentrate the manufacture of their products in countries where costs are low but skill levels are good. Many clothing manufacturers manufacture their products in East Asia where labour costs are low but tailoring standards

Coordination of value-adding activities: garment manufacturing abroad

are high. An organization can decide to coordinate its worldwide activities or to mange them locally in each part of the world. The latter approach misses the opportunity for global management economies of scale. For Porter, the 'purest global strategy' is when an organization concentrates its key activities in locations giving competitive advantages and coordinates activities on a global basis. In the long term, according to Porter, organizations should move towards the 'purest global strategy' as far as is practicable.

Hybrid strategies

There is a body of evidence that suggests that successful strategy can be based on a hybrid (mixture) of differentiation, price and cost control. The hybrid strategy framework developed here is based on the following assumptions:

- strategy can employ a combination of differentiation, price and cost control
- differentiation can be used as the basis for charging a premium price or to increase sales and/or market share
- there are clear linkages between core competences, strategy and value-adding activities
- the framework is not intended as a recipe for competitive advantage, but rather as way of grouping different strategies.

Market price responsiveness

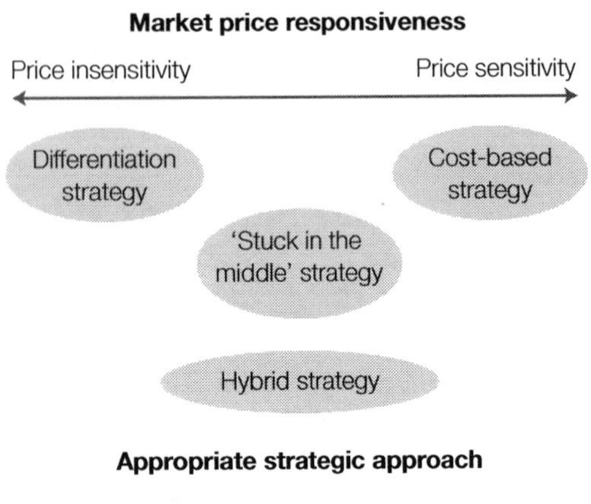

Figure 6.5 **Hybrid strategy**

The extent of differentiation, price and cost control will depend on the nature of the market in which the business is operating. In markets where consumers show a preference for quality, the emphasis will be less on price and costs, while in markets where demand is price sensitive, the emphasis will be on keeping both prices and costs as low as possible (Figure 6.5). Of course, organizations may also seek to shape customer attitudes by advertising and promotion so as to modify market conditions. Supermarkets like Tesco and Sainsbury's operate with a hybrid strategy; their product price range varies with quality and consumer choice. For example, Tesco has four cola varieties ranging from normal to diet to sugar-free versions. Each of them is priced differently, so Tesco fulfils the needs of both cost- and quality-conscious consumers.

6.4   Competence-based competitive strategy

The generic strategy model is not the only one that seeks to provide an explanation of the sources of competitive advantage. The competence or resource-based model emphasizes that competitive edge stems from the competences of an organization, which distinguish it from its competitors, allowing it to outperform them (see Chapter 3).

Part 2 of this book explained the ways in which internal analysis makes it possible to better understand core competences by a process of deconstructing them into the component resources and competences that act as their foundation. Here we build on this analysis to explore the ways in which existing competences can be extended and new ones cultivated, and examine how and where these core competences can be exploited so as to acquire and sustain competitive advantage. Much of the recent attention to the concept of core competence is based on the work of Prahalad and Hamel (1989, 1990) and Stalk et al. (1992), who advocated the idea of competing on the basis of capabilities. Similarly, Kay (1993) advanced the idea that competitive advantage is based on distinctive capability.

Perhaps the best-known explanation of core competence is that provided by Prahalad and Hamel (1990, p. 79):

> Core competencies are the collective learning of the organization, especially how to co-ordinate diverse production skills and integrate multiple streams of technologies.

Prahalad and Hamel specified three tests to be applied in the identification and development of core competence. A core competence should:

- equip a business with the ability to enter and successfully compete in several markets
- add greater perceived customer value to the business's products than that perceived in competitor's products
- be difficult for competitors to imitate.

According to Prahalad and Hamel, there are many examples of core competence resulting in competitive advantage. Philips' development of optical media, including the laser disc, has led to a whole range of new hi-fi and IT products. Honda's engine technology has led to advantages in the car, motorcycle, lawn mower and generator businesses. Canon's expertise in optics, imaging and microprocessor controls has given it access to diverse markets including those for copiers, laser printers, cameras and image scanners.

Prahalad and Hamel argued that, in practice, competitive advantage is likely to be based on no more than five or six competences. These competences will allow management to produce new and unanticipated products, and to be responsive to changing opportunities because of production skills and the harnessing of technology. Given the turbulent business environment in many industries, this adaptability is essential if competitive advantage is to be built and sustained.

Kay (1993) took the concept of capability, initially identified by Stalk et al. (1992), to develop a framework that explains competitive advantage in terms of what he defines as 'distinctive capability'. This idea of distinctive capability has much in common with that of core competence, in that it views competitive advantage as being dependent on the unique attributes of a particular business and its products.

According to Kay (1993), distinctive capability results from one or more of the following sources:

- *Architecture:* the unique network of internal and external relationships of a business that produces superior performance. These can be unique relationships with suppliers, distributors or customers that competitors do not possess. Equally, the unique relationships may be internal to the business and based on the way that it organizes its activities in the value chain.
- *Reputation:* this stems from several sources, including superior product quality, characteristics, design, service and so on.
- *Innovation:* the ability of the business to get ahead and stay ahead of competitors depends on its success in researching, designing, developing and

marketing new products. Equally, it depends on the ability of the business to improve the design and organization of its value-adding activities.

- *Strategic assets:* businesses can also obtain competitive advantage from assets such as natural monopoly, patents and copyrights, which restrict competition.

So what do the concepts of core competence and distinctive capability add to our understanding of competitive advantage? First, they provide us with insight into how a business can build attributes that can deliver superior performance. Second, they inform the process of determining where such competences and capabilities can be exploited.

The process of building new core competences or extending existing ones must take into account the following considerations:

- *Customer perceptions:* competences, capabilities and products must be perceived by customers as being better value for money than those of competitors. The business's reputation can be particularly important in this regard.
- *Uniqueness:* core competences must be unique to the business and must be difficult for competitors to emulate. Similarly, there must be no close substitutes for these competences.
- *Continuous improvement:* core competences, goods and services must be continuously upgraded to stay ahead of competitors. Product and process innovation are particularly important.
- *Collaboration:* competitive advantage can result from the business's unique network of relationships with suppliers, distributors, customers and even competitors. There is the potential for 'multiplier effects' resulting from the complementary core competences of separate businesses being combined.
- *Organizational knowledge:* competences must be based on organizational knowledge and learning. Managers must improve the processes by which the organization learns, builds and manages its knowledge. Today, knowledge is potentially the greatest source of added value.

Core competence, generic strategy and the value chain: a synthesis

It has been argued (see for example Heene and Sanchez, 1997) that the resource or competence-based approach is largely incompatible with the competitive positioning or generic strategy approach advocated by Porter (1980, 1985). Mintzberg et al. (1995), however, make the case that the two approaches are in many respects complementary rather than mutually contradictory. Perhaps the best way of illustrating the linkages between the approaches is through the value chain of the organization.

As competitive advantage is based on the unique approach of the individual business to its environment, it is not possible to identify a one-for-all prescription that will guarantee superior performance in all situations. Both the competitive positioning and the resource-based approach, however, provide frameworks that allow broad sources of competitive advantage to be categorized for the purposes of analysis and development of future strategy. A differentiation strategy, for example, will be likely to be dependent on core competences in areas of the value chain like design, marketing and service. Similarly, a cost or price-based strategy may well require core competences in value chain activities like operations (production), procurement and perhaps marketing. It is much less likely that a cost leader will have core competences based on design and service. The possible relationships between core competences, generic strategies and the value chain are shown in Table 6.1.

Table 6.1 Core competences, generic strategies and the value chain

Value chain activity	Areas of competence associated with differentiation strategies	Areas of competence associated with cost/price-based strategies
Primary activities		
Inbound logistics	Control of quality of materials	Strict control of the cost of materials. Tendency to buy larger volumes of standard inputs
Operations	Control of quality of output, raising standards	Lowering production costs and achieving high-volume production
Marketing and sales	Sales (and customer relations) on the basis of quality technology, performance, reputation, outlets and so on	Achieving high-volume sales through advertising and promotion
Outbound logistics	Ensuring efficient distribution	Maintaining low distribution costs
Service	Adding to product value by high-quality and differentiated service	Minimal service to keep costs low
Support activities		
The business's infrastructure	Emphasis on quality	Emphasis on efficiency and cost reduction
Human resource development	Training to create a skills culture, which emphasizes quality, customer service, product development	Training to reduce costs
Technology development	Developing new products, improving product quality, product performance and customer service	Reducing production costs and increasing efficiency
Procurement	Obtaining high-quality resources and materials	Obtaining low-cost resources and materials

GURU GUIDE

James **Brian Quinn** received a BSc from Yale University in 1949. Professor Quinn is currently the Emeritus Professor of Management at Amos Tuck School of Management at Dartmouth College, Hanover, New Hampshire. During his distinguished academic career, Professor Quinn has taught courses in technology management, entrepreneurship and business policy. He is a well-known authority in the fields of management of technological change, outsourcing and strategic planning. He is a respected lecturer and has acted as consultant for numerous leading US and foreign corporations, the US and foreign governments, and small enterprises. His work has been widely appreciated and has won several prizes, including the McKinsey prize for the most outstanding articles appearing in *Harvard Business Review* and the American Academy of Management's Book of the Year Award for Outstanding Contribution to Advancing Management Knowledge. In 1989, Professor Quinn was awarded the Outstanding Educator award by the Academy of Management, and in a rare gesture, his former students created the James Brian Quinn Chair in Technology and Strategy at Dartmouth College in 1999.

Professor Quinn has been a member of the board on Science and Technology for International Development for the National Academy of Sciences and served as the chairman of National Academy of Engineering committees on the Productivity of Information Technology in Services, Technology in the Services Sector, and Environmental Impacts of Services. He is also a visiting professor at various universities, including Monash University, Dalien University, University of Western Australia and the International University of Japan.

Where to exploit core competences and strategies

As core competences and business strategies are developed, it is necessary to decide where they should be exploited. Core competences and strategies can be targeted on existing customers in existing markets or it may be possible to target new customers in existing markets. Alternatively, it may be possible to target new customers in new markets. These markets may be related to markets currently served by the organization or they may be unrelated markets. The organization may also consider employing its competences in a new industry. These decisions are concerned with determining the 'strategic direction' of the business. Once this decision has been made, decisions must be made on the methods to be employed in following the chosen strategic direction.

The process of exploiting existing core competences in new markets is known as 'competence leveraging'. In order to enter new markets, it is often necessary for the organization to build new core competences, alongside the existing core competences that are being leveraged, so as to satisfy new customer needs. The identification of customer needs to be served by core competences is based on analysis of the organization's competitive environment using the resource-based framework. Chapter 14 considers the alternative strategic directions an organization can pursue and the methods that can be employed in following these strategic directions.

STRATEGIC
PLANNING SOFTWARE

This is a helpful chapter to refer to when completing 1.1.3 Industry Life Cycle and 1.1.4 Porter's Five Forces within the External Analysis section and 1.2.2 Value Chain within the Internal Analysis section in Phase 1 of the **Strategic Planning Software** (www.planning-strategy.com). It would also be useful to recap the chapter before attempting to complete section 2.2 Competitive Strategy in Phase 2 of the **Strategic Planning Software** (www.planning-strategy.com).

For test questions, extra case studies, audio case studies, weblinks, videolinks and more to help you understand the topics covered in this chapter, visit our companion website at www.palgrave.com/business/campbell.

VOCAB CHECKLIST FOR ESL STUDENTS

Coefficient	Logistics	Outsourcing
Distribution channel	'No frills'	Procurement
Hypercompetition (see 'hypercompetitive')	Opportunistic	Synthesis
	Optical media (see 'optical' and 'media')	Unit cost
Infrastructure		Whim

Definitions for these terms can be found in the 'Vocab Zone' of the companion website, which provides free access to the Macmillan English Dictionary online at www.palgrave.com/business/campbell.

REVIEW QUESTIONS

1 Explain what is meant by competitive advantage and where it comes from.
2 Describe how Porter's generic strategies can be used by an organization.
3 Explain what is meant by low-cost, differentiation, focus and hybrid strategies.
4 Define what a core competence is and how it can be used to gain competitive advantage.

DISCUSSION TOPIC

Porter's generic strategies related to the 1970s and 80s, and they are simply not applicable to 21st-century organizations. Discuss.

HOT TOPICS – Research project areas to investigate

For your research project, why not investigate …

- … which generic strategies are adopted by airlines operating in Continental Europe.
- … which core competences lead to the greatest cost focus advantage.
- … managers' attitudes to the applicability of hybrid strategies in music retail companies in your region.

Recommended reading

Grant, R.M. (1996) 'Prospering in dynamically-competitive environments: organizational capability as knowledge integration', *Organization Science*, **7**(4): 375–87.

Kay, J. (1995) 'Learning to define the core business', *Financial Times*, 1 December.

McKiernan, P. (1997) 'Strategy past; strategy futures', *Long Range Planning*, **30**(5): 790–8.

Newbert, S. (2005) 'New firm formation: a dynamic capability perspective', *Journal of Small Business Management*, **43**(1): 55–77.

Rumelt, R. (1991) 'How much does industry matter?', *Strategic Management Journal*, **12**(3): 167–85.

Teece, D.J., Pisano, G. and Shuen, A. (1998) 'Dynamic capabilities and strategic management', *Strategic Management Journal*, **18**(7): 509–33.

Chapter references

Barney, J.B. (1991) 'Firm resources and sustained competitive advantage', *Journal of Management*, **17**(1): 99–120.

Chesshyre, T. (2002) 'It's cheap but why not more cheerful?', *The Times*, 5 January.

Grant, R. (1991) 'The resource based theory of competitive advantage: implications for strategy formulation', *California Management Review*, **33**(3): 114–35.

Hamel, G. and Prahalad, C.K. (1985) 'Do you really have a global strategy?', *Harvard Business Review*, **63**(4): 139–48.

Heene, A. and Sanchez, R. (eds) (1997) *Competence-based Strategic Management*, London: John Wiley.

Kay, J. (1993) *Foundations of Corporate Success*, Oxford: Oxford University Press.

Mintzberg, H., Quinn, J.B. and Ghoshal, S. (1995) *The Strategy Process: Concepts, Contexts and Cases*, Englewood Cliffs, NJ: Prentice Hall.

Porter, M.E. (1980) *Competitive Strategy: Techniques for Analysing Industries and Competitors*, New York: Free Press.

Porter, M.E. (1985) *Competitive Advantage*, New York: Free Press.

Porter, M.E. (1986) 'What is strategy?', *Harvard Business Review*, **74**(6): 61–78.

Prahalad, C.K. and Hamel, G. (1990) 'The core competence of the corporation', *Harvard Business Review*, **68**(3): 79–91.

Stalk, G., Evans, P. and Shulmann, L.E. (1992) 'Competing on capabilities: the new rules of corporate strategy', *Harvard Business Review*, **70**(3): 57–69.

Sveiby, K.E. (1997) *The New Organizational Wealth: Managing and Measuring Knowledge-based Assets*, San Francisco, CA: Berrett-Koehler.

Sveiby, K.E. (2001) *What is Knowledge Management?*, www.sveiby.com.au/KnowledgeManagement.html.

Teece, D. (2009) *Dynamic Capabilities and Strategic Management: Organizing for Innovation and Growth*, Oxford: Oxford University Press.

Chapter 7
Change management and leadership

Introduction and chapter overview

This chapter deals with two critical elements of implementing strategy. The first is change and how change can be managed, and the second is leadership. In this chapter we explore what change is and what the change management process involves. In doing so, we examine different models for managing change and highlight the issues associated with change management. In terms of leadership, we consider the different schools of leadership theory and highlight key theories for further study.

Learning objectives

After studying this chapter, you should be able to:

- explain the nature of change and what models exist for managing the change process
- identify issues associated with managing change
- recognize the role of leadership in the change management process
- identify the different schools of leadership theory
- determine different leadership theories and the nature of leadership styles and approaches
- recognize the importance of leadership and change in the strategy process

7.1   The nature of change

In Chapters 9 and 10, we discussed the nature of the environment and how changes in the environment can change the industry structure, operating environments and overall dynamics of the markets. In Chapter 2, we learned about planned and emergent change. As such, change shapes the environment (both external and internal) and impacts on the nature of, as well as shaping, strategic decisions. However, we are interested in change that is managed and deliberate, in effect, changes being imposed on the organization, by the organization.

Change can be cyclical or structural in impact:

- *Cyclical changes* are reoccurring changes that can often be predicted and require temporary reactions or measures

* *Structural change* is permanent in nature and requires responses to deal with the permanent reconfiguration of the industry, company or technology base.

Change can relate to various organizational dimensions, systems/procedures, processes, and organizational configuration or structure:

* Changes to systems or procedures usually represent a refinement of procedures and are geared towards streamlining bureaucracy or layering bureaucracy to tighten control over resources or 'quality'.
* Changes to processes are often exemplified by business process redesign or restructuring, lean, value management and various quality regimes. The change relates to how the organization operates and how it configures its activities through the value and supply chain.
* Organizational configuration/structure refers to how the administration of the organization is put together and is often called the organizational chart or structure. It relates to the formal and informal relationships, power and authority lines.

Types of change can also relate to the pace of change and magnitude of such change. This is captured well by the work of Ansoff, Andrews, Mintzberg and others. In essence, there are different forms of change, ranging from continuity (no change), to incremental change (Ansoff's science of muddling through, or Quinn's logical incrementalism), to flux (oscillating changes back and forth) to transformational or fundamental change, which is usually a major event for an organization and involves a shift in mindset or resource base beyond the comfort zone.

7.2 Managing the change process

At its simplest, strategy is all about change. In this book, we have encountered the importance of an organization's resource base, its culture and its structure. In order to bring about strategic repositioning, say, in respect of products and markets, all these may need to be changed.

Different organizations exhibit differing attitudes to change. We can draw a parallel here with different types of people. Some people are very conservative and fear change and resist it. They configure their lives so as to minimize change. Other people seem to get bored easily and are always looking for new challenges, new jobs and so on. Organizations reflect this spectrum of attitudes. It is here that we encounter the concept of 'inertia'.

Inertia: identifying barriers to change

Inertia refers to the force that needs to be exerted on a body to overcome its state in relation to its motion.

Inertia is a term borrowed from physics. Inertia refers to the force that needs to be exerted on a body to overcome its state in relation to its motion. If a body is stationary (at rest), then we would need to exert a force on it to make it move. The size and shape of the body will have a large bearing on its ability to be moved – compare the inertia of a football to that of a train. In the same way, different organizations present management with varying degrees of inertia. Some are easy to change and others are much more reluctant. The willingness to change may depend on the culture of the organization, its size, its existing structure, its product and/or market positioning and even its age – how long it has existed in its present form.

For most purposes, we can say that resistance to change on the part of employees can be caused by one or more of the following attitudes:

- *lack an understanding:* they may not have had the reasons for the change explained to them or they may not be aware of how they will personally be affected. This can normally be overcome relatively easily by management taking the requisite measures to close the information gap
- *lack of trust:* on the part of employees in respect of management
- *fear:* particularly in respect of their personal position or their social relationships. Those affected by the change may fear that the proposed changes will adversely affect their place in the structure or the relationships they enjoy in the organization
- *uncertainty:* some inertia is driven by uncertainty about the future. Attitudes to uncertainty vary significantly between people, with some showing a much more adverse reaction to it than others.

Lewin's three-step change model

Lewin (1947) suggested that organizational change could be understood in terms of three consecutive processes: unfreezing, changing and refreezing:

- *Unfreezing:* This involves introducing measures that will enable employees to abandon their current practices or cultural norms in preparation for the change. In many organizations, nothing has changed for many years and unfreezing is necessary as a 'shaking-up' phase. The impetus for unfreezing can come from inside or outside the organization. Changing market conditions, for example, sometimes give employees warning that change will be imminent. A particular market crisis may precipitate the expectation among employees that change must happen as a result. Internally, a management shake-up, a profit warning or talk of restructuring may bring about similar expectations.
- *Changing:* This transition phase involves bringing about the requisite change itself. The time period for this phase varies widely. Structural change can usually be brought about relatively quickly. Changes in internal systems sometimes take longer, such as the introduction of new quality or information systems, while changing culture can take years.
- *Refreezing:* This is necessary to 'lock in' the changes and prevent the organization from going back to its old ways. Again, we would usually take cultural changes to require more 'cementing in' than some other changes and some resolve might be required on the part of senior management.

Step and incremental change

The pace at which change happens can usually be divided into one of two categories – step and incremental (see Figure 7.1). There are two factors that determine which is the most appropriate (Quinn and Voyer, 1998):

1. How urgent the need for change is. A market crisis will typically bring about an urgent need for rapid change, whereas preparing for the introduction of a new legal regulation in five years' time will usually allow change to be brought about more slowly and perhaps more painlessly.
2. How much inertia is resident within the organization's culture. The time taken to unfreeze the inertia will necessarily take longer in some organizations than in others.

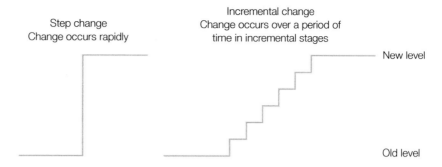

Figure 7.1 **Step and incremental change**

Step change offers the advantage of 'getting it over with', and enables the organization to respond quickly to changes in its environment.

Incremental change offers the advantage of a step-by-step approach to change, and enables management to gain acceptance before and during the change process.

Step change offers the advantage of 'getting it over with'. It enables the organization to respond quickly to changes in its environment and thus conform to new conditions without lagging behind. Its disadvantages include the 'pain' factor – it may require some coercion or force on the part of management, which in turn may damage employee–management relationships.

Incremental change offers the advantage of a step-by-step approach to change. For organizations with high inertia, incremental change enables management to gain acceptance before and during the change process, so it tends to be more inclusive. The process is divided into a number of distinct phases and there may be periods of 'rest' between the phases. It would be an inappropriate technique to use in situations of rapid environmental change.

7.3 Models for managing change

The process of actually managing strategic change brings us to consider a number of managerial approaches and their appropriateness in various contexts. Writers in this area have tended towards two complementary approaches, managerialist and change agent.

Managerialist approaches

Some writers have suggested that change can be successfully managed by employing a range of managerial practices. We can conceive of this approach as an 'if this doesn't work, try this' mechanism.

Most academics and managers have agreed that the process should begin with *education* and *communication*. The purpose of this is to inform those (usually internal) stakeholders who will be affected by the change. The message communicated will usually contain an explanation of the reasons for the change and an overview of its timescale and extent. In some organizational contexts, this procedure alone will be sufficient to overcome inertia and get the change process underway. In others, this will not be enough.

The next step will be to progress to *negotiation* and *participation*. Affected stakeholders will be invited to contribute to the process and participate in its execution. It is hoped that this process will bring employees 'on board' – they will feel some sense of ownership of the change. Some managers may introduce some degree of manipulation of employees in this stage, possibly by appealing to the emotional responses of employees or by over- or understating the reality of the changes in the environment.

Finally, if all else has failed to bring about the willing participation of employees, management may be able to introduce some degree of *coercion*. This tactic is far from being appropriate in all contexts, but where it is possible, it can be used to significant effect. Coercion is the practice of forcing through change by exploiting the power asymmetry between executive management and 'rank-and-file' employees. It is usually only used as a last resort – it can have a negative effect on management–employee relationships after the change.

The change agent approach

Some texts refer to the change agent approach as the 'champion of change' model. Here, the change process is managed from start to finish by a single individual (change agent), who could be a key manager within the organization or someone who is brought in as a consultant for the duration of the process.

The change agent approach offers a number of advantages:

1   It provides a focus for the change in the form of a tangible person who becomes the personification of the process. A 'walking symbol' of change can act as a stimulus to change and can ensure that complacency is avoided.

2   In many cases, the change agent will be engaged because they are an expert in their field. They may have overseen the same change process in many other organizations and so are well acquainted with the usual problems and how to solve them.

3   The appointment of a change agent sometimes means that senior management time need not be fully occupied with the change process. The responsibility for the change is delegated to the change agent and management gain the normal advantages of delegation. Thus senior management are freed up to concentrate on developing future strategy.

7.4   Issues in managing change

Issues in managing change are usually associated with 'people' issues. Work by Andrews (1987) highlighted the importance of communication in attempting to implement any strategy and enforce any change. In a similar way, barriers to change can be seen to revolve around 'soft' factors such as staff (and management) perceptions and emotions, or cultural barriers, and 'hard' issues such as the business environment and resources.

Soft factors

Perception and emotion problems are often embedded in the emergent and cyclical approaches to strategy where, it could be argued, implementation issues are actually part of the strategy formulation process. As such, the perceptions of a strategic situation will impact on the ability to manage the change. These perceptions and emotions may lead to poor proposed solutions that do not address the heart of the problem, as they are too sensitive to company history, staff or sentiment. The issues relating to perceptions can be seen to be:

- We do not seek real change, we merely tinker around the edges of the problem and avoid elements close to us or deemed as embedded in our belief system or culture

- We only see what we want to see and so do not identify the core of the problem, resulting in too narrow a focus
- A narrow focus often results in scapegoating or protection of a particular area of the business
- On occasion, too much information and data are sought to justify and defend decisions. This can result in information overload and, ultimately, change fatigue.

As we saw in Chapter 5, culture drives the way an organization thinks, acts and behaves. Thus, the culture of the organization will impact on the ability to change and so poses an issue for managing change. This may involve the accepted norms of the organization, rituals, beliefs, attitudes and personalities. Often, change management involves changing ways of thinking and doing and, in essence, changing culture. However, as the phrase often attributed to Peter Drucker claims: 'Culture eats strategy for breakfast.'

Hard factors

Hard factors are typified by an organization's structure, systems, resources and general support for the change process. Problems may include a lack of support from all levels in the organization, where staff and management perceive changes as a threat to them and their personal status. This results in a lack of cooperation and the creation of barriers to prevent the process occurring, or perhaps questioning the legality and governance of the process. As mentioned earlier, changes move the whole organization, individuals included, out of their comfort zone, the result being that some staff will not comply or engage but seek to actively or passively resist change.

The most obvious hard factors include a lack of physical resources to support the change process, a lack of senior management support, and the impact of rushed and unplanned change on customers, staff and suppliers.

7.5 Leadership styles and approaches

Leaders play a critical role when any change is imposed. Theory and experience highlight that the change is secondary in importance to subordinates' views and perceptions of the leader, and confidence in them. Many studies highlight the critical role played by senior management in implementing strategy and leading change programmes. As organizations flatten and responsibility is driven to all levels of the organization, knowledge of leadership styles, traits and theories is useful in understanding the position of leadership in the overall process.

To understand leadership styles and approaches, it is useful to look at the various theories of leadership. Leadership theory has evolved significantly since 1947 and the formalization of the great man theory, through trait theory and to current thinking around service leadership, strategic leadership, authentic leadership and spiritual leadership. This section examines the key theories that have led to current thinking. We provide an overview to understanding, but it is important to note that the various theories can be viewed as a continuum and that there is no smooth transition from one to the other. Scholars and managers believe in their own stance and often such a stance can be a combination of schools. The subject of leadership is rich and deep in details. It is worth taking time to read some of the source materials for a more specialist understanding of the field.

Table 7.1 shows the key schools of thinking, and is presented in roughly chronological order of how each school evolved. Each theory is then explored below.

Table 7.1 **Theories of leadership and key authors**

Theory	Key authors
Great man theory	Popularized in the 1840s by Thomas Carlyle
Trait theory	Stogdill 1974 McCall and Lombardo 1983 Bennis and Biederman 1998
Behaviourist theories	Merton 1957 McGregor 1960 Blake and Mouton 1961, 1964 Pfeffer and Salancik 1975
Situational leadership	Lewin et al. 1939 Maier 1963 Likert 1967 Hersey and Blanchard 1969 Adair 1973 Vroom and Yetton 1973 House and Mitchell 1974 Yukl 1989
Contingency theory	Tannenbaum and Schmitt 1958 Fiedler 1967 Hickson et al. 1971 Adair 1973 Fiedler and Garcia 1987
Transactional theory	Dansereau et al. 1975 Graen and Cashman 1975
Transformational theory	Burns 1978 Bass 1985, 1990 Tichy and Devanna 1986 Covey 1992 Bass and Avolio 1994 Hooper and Potter 1997 Bass and Steidlmeier 1998 Adair 2002 Kouzes and Posner 2003

Robert Tannenbaum

Great man theory

The **great man theory** of leadership is based on the premise that leaders are born and not made.

The great man theory is based on the premise that leaders are born and not made. This probably stems from the fact that most studies conducted into leadership focused on existing great leaders. These existing leaders tended to emerge from the nobility or aristocracy and led to the misconception that breeding influenced leadership ability.

Trait theory

Trait theory extended the great man theory by recognizing that perhaps natural leaders exhibited inherent skills and abilities, which did not necessarily stem from breeding and bloodline. Again, trait theory is based on the premise that leaders are born rather than made but shifted the focus of research to identifying and examining the traits. A key study in this area was carried out by Stogdill (1974), who identified the skills and traits described in Table 7.2.

Trait theory is based on the premise that leaders are born rather than made and focuses on identifying the traits.

Table 7.2 **Skills and traits critical to leaders**

Traits	Skills
Energetic	Intelligent
Alert and sensitive to the social environment	Organized
Cooperative	Knowledgeable about group task
Adaptability to different context and situations	Technically and conceptually skilled
Dependable	Creative and innovative
Achievement oriented	Persuasive and convincing
Persistent	Diplomatic, politic and tactful
Dominant	Excellent intercommunication
Self-confident	
Able to tolerate stress	
Decisive and willing to assume responsibility	
Assertive	

Source: Adapted from Stogdill, 1974

GURU GUIDE

Warren G. Bennis was born in 1925. He graduated with a BA in psychology from Antioch College in 1951 and obtained his PhD in social sciences and economics from MIT in 1955. He is currently the Distinguished Professor of Business Administration at the University of Southern California. Professor Bennis has served on the faculties of Harvard Business School, Indian Institute of Management Calcutta, Boston University, INSEAD and Sloan School of Management at MIT. He was also an adviser to four US presidents and was the founding chairman of the Leadership Institute at the University of Southern California. He has acted as a consultant for several multinational firms and is the chairman of the Centre for Public Leadership at Harvard University's Kennedy School.

Professor Bennis has honorary doctorates from the LSE, the University of Cincinnati and the University of Buffalo. He is also the recipient of the International Leadership Association's Distinguished Leadership Award and the Marion Gislason Award for Leadership in Executive Development from Boston University School of Management. He is a senior fellow at UCLA and a visiting professor of leadership at the University of Exeter, UK.

Professor Bennis is regarded as an influential authority in the field of leadership studies. His work was pioneering in thinking in terms of the need for 'adhocracy', that is, free-moving project team approaches to work ideas, later developed by Toffler and Mintzberg, and in considering the leader as a 'social architect', a transformer of organizations.

Stogdill's study was followed up by other researchers such as McCall and Lombardo (1983) and Bennis and Biederman (1998). McCall and Lombardo (1983) identified four primary traits of leaders. These were:

- emotional stability and composure (confidence, consistency)
- admitting error

- good interpersonal skills (empathy)
- intellectual breadth (knowledgeable about a wide range of areas).

Bennis and Biederman (1998) see the leader as the person who transforms an organization through their ability to bring about change by positive motivation and the four key abilities of the management of attention, meaning, trust and self.

Behaviourist theories

The **behavioural theory** of leadership believes that leaders can be made rather than born, so leadership can be learned if the behaviours can be isolated and taught.

The behavioural theory represents a shift in thinking, away from leaders being born and already having leadership ability, traits and skills, to a perspective that believes that leaders can be made rather than born. As such, leadership could be learned if the behaviours could be isolated and taught. The focus of research in this area therefore became more about what leaders do rather than what they are. The result of this stage in leadership theory was the development of profiles of leadership styles. This is evident by the emergence of theories such as McGregor's theory X and theory Y, Blake and Mouton's managerial grid, and role theory.

McGregor's theory X and theory Y (1960) summarized two contrasting sets of assumptions made by managers in industry (Table 7.3).

Table 7.3 **McGregor's theory X and theory Y manager**

Theory X managers' beliefs	Theory Y managers' beliefs
The average human being has an inherent dislike of work and will avoid it if possible	The expenditure of physical and mental effort in work is as natural as play or rest, and the average human being, under proper conditions, learns not only to accept but to seek responsibility
Most people must be coerced, controlled, directed or threatened with punishment to get them to work to achieve organizational objectives	People will exercise self-direction and self-control to achieve objectives to which they are committed
Workers prefer to be directed, avoid responsibility, have little ambition, and want security above all else	The capacity to exercise a relatively high level of imagination, ingenuity and creativity in the solution of organizational problems is widely, not narrowly, distributed in the population, and the intellectual potentialities of the average human being are only partially utilized under the conditions of modern industrial life

Source: Adapted from McGregor, 1960

GURU GUIDE

Douglas **Murray McGregor** was born in 1906 in Detroit. He was involved with the family-run McGregor Institute in a part-time capacity but his early career was with a regional gas station, where he started as an attendant before rising to the position of manager.

In 1937, he joined MIT and was instrumental in setting up the university's industrial relations section. In 1953, he rejoined MIT as a faculty member and went to write several influential articles and books on leadership, leadership styles and human relations. In addition to his teaching work at MIT, McGregor took on increasing amounts of industrial relations consultancy work, particularly at Dewey Almy, a local rubber and sealants company.

He was a pioneer in industrial relations and his consultancy work helped him to develop the well-known theory X and theory Y of leadership styles. These theories are expounded in his 1960 bestseller *The Human Side of Enterprise* which gave him instant global fame. In the 1970s, the McGregor School, a graduate level business school, was founded by Antioch College in his honour. He died in 1964.

The managerial grid developed by Blake and Mouton (1961) focuses on task (production) and employee (people) orientations of managers. The theory is represented by a grid, with concern for production on the horizontal axis, and concern for people on the vertical axis. Five basic leadership styles are plotted on the grid depending on the manager's emphasis or perspectives. The grid results in five positions:

- *country club management:* high concern for people, low concern for production
- *team management:* high for both
- *organization man management:* moderate for both
- *impoverished management:* low stance for both
- *authority obedience:* low concern for people, high concern for production.

Blake and Mouton propose that team management is the most effective type of leadership behaviour.

The final element in this area is role theory, explored by Merton (1957) and Pfeffer and Salancik (1975). In organizations, actors (management or staff) will form roles for themselves and expectations of these roles. The leadership behaviour is expected to reflect the role held and is guided by the signals received from staff looking for support and guidance from various roles. This can be a subtle process or may be highly formalized. The shaping of expectations and behaviours becomes a key driver.

Situational and participative theories

The situational and participative theories of leadership view leadership as relating to context and the involvement of others.

The situational and participative theories view leadership as relating to context and the involvement of others, rather than taking autocratic decisions. This collection of theories seeks to involve other people in the process at various levels inside and outside the organization.

There are a number of theories to be considered, some blurring the lines between situational and participative. Here we touch on four sets of writers, Hersey and Blanchard (1969), Lewin et al. (1939), Likert (1967) and Yukl (1989).

The Hersey-Blanchard (1969) leadership model takes a situational perspective of leadership. Their model proposes that the readiness and developmental levels of a leader's subordinates play the greatest role in determining which leadership styles (behaviours) are most appropriate. The model is based on the direction (task behaviour) and socio-emotional support (relationship behaviour) needed by followers, where 'task behaviour' is the degree of instruction required for a particular set of duties and 'relationship behaviour' is the extent to which the leader engages in communications. The resulting 'maturity' is the willingness and ability of a person to take responsibility for directing their own behaviour.

Four leadership styles result:

1. *Directing:* The leader provides clear instructions and specific direction. This is for low follower readiness levels.
2. *Coaching:* The leader encourages two-way communication and helps build confidence and motivation. This is best matched with a moderate follower readiness level.
3. *Supporting:* The leader and followers share decision-making. This is best matched with a moderate follower readiness level.
4. *Delegating:* This style is appropriate for leaders whose followers are ready to accomplish a particular task and are both competent and motivated. This is best matched with a high follower readiness level.

On the other hand, Lewin et al. (1939) identified three styles of leader:

- *autocratic:* leader takes decision without consultation
- *democratic:* leader involves others in the decision-making process
- *laissez-faire:* minimal involvement of leader in decision-making.

Meanwhile, Likert (1967) identified four leadership styles:

- *Exploitive authoritative:* the leader has a low concern for people and uses threats and other fear-based methods to achieve conformance
- *Benevolent authoritative:* the leader adds concern for people to an authoritative position
- *Consultative:* upward flow of information is cautious, although the leader makes genuine efforts to listen carefully to ideas
- *Participative:* the leader makes maximum use of participative methods, engaging people lower down the organization in decision-making.

A leader's behaviour is dependent upon the perception of themselves and other factors such as stress. Yukl (1989) identifies six other variables:

- *Subordinate effort:* the motivation and actual effort expended
- *Subordinate ability and role clarity:* followers knowing what to do and how to do it
- *Organization of the work:* the structure of the work and utilization of resources
- *Cooperation and cohesiveness:* of the group in working together
- *Resources and support:* the availability of tools, materials, people and so on
- *External coordination:* the need to collaborate with other groups.

Leaders here work on such factors as external relationships, acquisition of resources, managing demands on the group and managing the structures and culture of the group.

Contingency theory

The contingency theory of leadership states that a leader's ability to lead is contingent on a variety of situational and behavioural factors. Thus leaders may be very successful in one context, but if they move to a different context or situation, they may not be able to replicate such success.

Fiedler's work makes a considerable contribution to this field, along with the work of Fiedler and Garcia (1987). Fiedler's (1967) contingency theory argues that there is no single best way for managers to lead. Situations will create different leadership style requirements for a manager.

Fiedler (1967) examined three situations defining the leadership condition:

- *Leader–member relations:* loyalty, support and commitment
- *Task structure:* how highly structured the task is
- *Position power:* the manager's level of authority.

These factors determine the degree of contextual or situational control. In a favourable relationship, the manager has a high task structure and is able to reward and or punish employees without any problems. In an unfavourable relationship, the task is usually unstructured and the leader possesses limited authority.

Building on contingency theory, Tannenbaum and Schmidt (1958) suggested that leadership behaviour varies along a continuum of autocratic behaviour to a more devolved mode of leadership (democratic). Seven leadership styles occur across the continuum: tells, sells, suggests, consults, joins, delegates and abdicates:

> The **contingency theory** of leadership states that a leader's ability to lead is contingent on a variety of situational and behavioural factors.

- *Tells:* The leader takes the decisions and announces them. Subordinates carry them out without question
- *Sells:* The leader takes all the decisions without discussion or consultation. On this occasion, however, subordinates will be better motivated if they are persuaded that the decisions are good ones
- *Suggests:* The leader presents ideas and encourages questions
- *Consults:* The leader consults with subordinates before taking decisions
- *Joins:* The leader specifies the problem and invites discussion with subordinates. The leader manages the process and draws together the potential solutions in a joint decision-making fashion
- *Delegates:* The leader defines the limits and asks the group to make the decision
- *Abdicates:* The leader leaves the group to operate within defined limits of responsibility and authority, to identify issues and make decisions independent of the leader.

In this theory, as the categories represent a continuum, there will be situations or contexts when one of the styles is more appropriate than the others. It implies flexibility in leadership and sensitivity to context.

The action-centred leadership model was proposed by Adair in 1973. In this model, leadership represents getting things done through the work team and relationships with fellow managers and staff. According to Adair, an action-centred leader must:

- direct the job to be done (task)
- support and review the individual people doing it (individual)
- coordinate and foster the work team as a whole (team).

These three elements, task, individual, team, are found in his well-known three interlocking circles diagram, representing the intersections and overlaps in human interaction.

GURU GUIDE

John Adair was born in Luton in 1934. After working as a senior lecturer at the Royal Military Academy, Sandhurst, he later worked for the Industrial Society before becoming the first professor of leadership studies at the University of Surrey in 1979. He also worked with ICI to develop an in-house leadership development strategy programme that helped to change the loss-making, bureaucratic giant into the first British company to make a billion pounds profit. He became a fellow of the Royal Historical Society and also an emeritus fellow at the Windsor Leadership Trust. More recently, the People's Republic of China awarded him the title of Honorary Professor of Leadership at the China Executive Leadership Academy.

John Adair is one of the foremost authorities on leadership and leadership development. He has written over 40 books on leadership and change management which have been translated into several languages, he is an experienced teacher, and has acted as a consultant. Over a million managers worldwide have taken part in the action-centred leadership programmes he has pioneered.

Transactional theory

> The **transactional theory** of leadership is based on reward and punishment.

The transactional theory of leadership is based on reward and punishment. The transactional leader works by creating clear structures, whereby it is clear what is required of their subordinates, and the rewards they will gain for following orders. Punishments are not always mentioned, but they are well understood and formal systems of discipline are usually in place. The approach emphasizes the importance of the relationship between leader and followers in the pursuit of mutual benefits.

Transformational theory

The transformational theory of leadership contends that people will follow a leader who inspires them. This requires the leader to have vision, empathy and passion about a shared cause or vision. They will draw on elements of trait and behaviour theory through exhibiting charisma, enthusiasm, energy and personalization. In effect, they care about the people they lead and want shared success.

The **transformational theory** of leadership contends that people will follow a leader who inspires them.

The stages in transformational leadership tend to follow a pattern of:

- Develop a vision
- Sell the vision
- Map the way forward
- Lead the 'charge'.

Burns (1978, p. 103) draws on the humanistic psychology movement in his writing by proposing that the 'transforming leader shapes, alters, and elevates the motives, values and goals of followers achieving significant change in the process'. This requires clarity of values and principles and, to a high degree, respect.

Bass (1990) developed Burns' concept of transforming leadership by suggesting that the leader transforms followers, and so 'transformational leaders' may:

- expand a follower's portfolio of needs
- transform a follower's self-interest
- increase the confidence of followers
- elevate followers' expectations
- heighten the value of the leader's intended outcomes for the follower
- encourage behavioural change
- motivate others to higher levels of personal achievement.

Other authors in the area include Tichy and Devanna (1986), Bass and Avolio (1994), Hooper and Potter (1997), and Covey (1992), who offers a distinction between transactional leadership and transformational leadership (Table 7.4).

Table 7.4 **Transactional leadership and transformational leadership compared**

Transactional leadership	Transformational leadership
Builds on man's need to get a job done and make a living	Builds on a man's need for meaning
Is preoccupied with power and position, politics and perks	Is preoccupied with purposes and values, morals and ethics
Is mired in daily affairs	Transcends daily affairs
Is oriented to hard data and short-term goals	Is oriented towards long-term goals without compromising human values and principles
Focuses on tactical issues	Focuses more on missions and strategies
Relies on human relations to lubricate human interactions	Releases human potential – identifying and developing new talent
Follows and fulfils role expectations by striving to work effectively within current systems	Designs and redesigns jobs to make them meaningful and challenging
Supports structures and systems that reinforce the bottom line, maximize efficiency, and guarantee short-term profits	Aligns internal structures and systems to reinforce overarching values and goals

Source: Adapted from Covey, 1992

In the 1970s, the Swiss wristwatch industry was facing ruin. Swiss watches had always been known for their style, appearance and distinctiveness. Marques such as Tissot and Omega were held in great regard, and customers were prepared to pay very high prices. The centre of the Swiss watch industry was La Chaux-de-Fonds, a small town near the border with France, and the watches were handmade by craftspeople and experts working in small companies in the towns and villages around this region. The rural and prosperous location, the crafting by hand, and the sense of community all added to the overall perceived quality of the industry itself. In particular, the Swiss industry had never felt the need for a mass-market, cheap or good value offering – it survived on its exclusivity and perceived product and brand quality.

Then the digital watch was invented. The digital watch was far more accurate than the handmade version, although it was perceived to diminish the quality of the work, and the expert input necessary. When the digital products were presented to the Swiss industry, they were rejected on the spot. So the idea and technology were sold to Casio and Seiko, the Japanese calculator and digital equipment manufacturing companies. These companies embraced the new approach and began to develop their own ranges of watches. As large companies with mass and batch production capacity, Casio, Seiko and others were also able to produce the watches far more quickly and cheaply than the Swiss companies, which preferred to rely on the traditional methods. The Japanese companies were also able to produce their own distinctive designs, so that their offerings quickly came to be as recognizable as the Swiss products, and with the additional benefits of accuracy. Seiko and Casio also produced ranges of very cheap and good quality watches, and these products now found ready outlets in European and North American markets. They were able to attract large numbers of new customers who had long since sought good quality watches but had never before been able to afford them.

Consequently, the bottom dropped out of the Swiss market, and the small companies found themselves facing ruin. The Swiss industry as a whole had met the challenge from Japan with a combination of disdain, disbelief and arrogance, and only when many of the companies started to go out of business was the problem addressed. The Swiss government was called in, and asked to support what was after all a traditional and well-known domestic industry. First, the government prevaricated and then declined. For a time it seemed as if the whole industry would be sold off to Japanese interests. Then UBS, one of the Swiss industry's main backers, decided to consult Nicolas Hayek.

Hayek was known as a manufacturing and industrial expert. He had made his name advising the Swiss army on its sourcing and choice of weaponry and military hardware, and he was known to deliver high-quality and cost-effective results. He was also known to be straightforward to the point of rudeness; if the watch industry could not be saved, he would not prevaricate, but would say so.

Hayek stated that the industry could be saved, but that it would have to be done his way. The requirement was to create an industry in Switzerland that would be profitable and durable, and able to compete on cost and price with the Japanese competitors. Having gained the agreement and support of the banks and the government, he restructured and reorganized the whole industry. He created a holding company, SMH. He reorganized the entire industry into three separate companies, which would operate under the governance and direction of SMH. One company would manufacture the top and mid-range brands, one would produce a cheap/good value product/brand with which to compete directly against the mass-market products of Seiko and Casio, and the third would manufacture the components for the other two.

Hayek became chief executive of SMH, and he set about assembling a team of the world's best watch designers and engineers. He employed manufacturing experts. He built an expert marketing and sales team, whose remit was to get the Swiss industry back on its feet and into profit.

The designs of the workings of all the ranges of watches were streamlined and simplified, and the numbers of components used were reduced in all the brands. This meant that the top and mid-range brands were now as reliable and accurate as the branded goods.

The component manufacturing facility was capitalized and made accurate to the point at which the components themselves, manufactured in Switzerland, using Swiss labour and staff paid at Swiss labour rates, were cheaper and more cost-effective – and more accurate and a higher quality – than the Japanese alternatives.

SMH then introduced its cheap/good value brand, which it called 'Swatch'. Swatch had two different connotations – it appeared as a contraction of 'Swiss watch', and it also gave a marketing and sales platform for a 'second watch', one to be worn on a daily basis rather than something to be kept for smart and dress occasions. As stated above, this was unheard of in the Swiss watch industry. However, SMH built and reinforced the Swatch brand with regular new designs, including use of new materials, especially wood and plastic, and different colours, logos and images on the watches themselves. There was immediate recognition of the brand, and this was (and remains) reinforced by regular Swatch conventions, sales drives, design competitions and the use of limited editions.

Hayek became actively involved in every aspect of SMH's growth and development, and this led to accusations of meddling and interference. Many of the experts that he hired found themselves able to work for him for short periods of time only. His response was (and remains) always:

> I never want executives who are only good. I want people who are expert and fully involved in every

aspect of what we need to be doing. If they will not do this, and if they will not accept this from me, I do not want them here.

Case study questions

1   What were the barriers to change that had to be overcome?
2   What are the strengths and weaknesses of restructuring a company or industry in crisis?
3   What are the leadership qualities brought by Hayek to this situation? What else would you need to be aware of when appointing a leader to such a situation?

For test questions, extra case studies, audio case studies, weblinks, videolinks and more to help you understand the topics covered in this chapter, visit our companion website at www.palgrave.com/business/campbell.

VOCAB CHECKLIST FOR ESL STUDENTS

Autocratic	Personification	Scapegoating
Comfort zone	Power asymmetry (see 'power'	'Shaking up' phase (see
Democratic	and 'asymmetry')	'shake-up')
Impetus	Prevaricate	Tinker
Ingenuity	'Rank and file'	
Laissez-faire	Reconfiguration	

Definitions for these terms can be found in the 'Vocab Zone' of the companion website, which provides free access to the Macmillan English Dictionary online at www.palgrave.com/business/campbell.

REVIEW QUESTIONS

1   Explain how the nature of change can influence the strategy implementation process.
2   What are the issues associated with the change management process?
3   Explain the role of leadership in managing change.
4   Explain the different leadership theories that are common in business strategy and how each differs.

DISCUSSION TOPIC

Leaders are born not made. Discuss.

HOT TOPICS – Research project areas to investigate

If you have a project to do, why not investigate ...

- ... which leadership styles are adopted in organizations during periods of crisis.
- ... whether national culture/gender influences leadership style.
- ... how rapid growth organizations cope with change.

Recommended reading

Adair, J.E. (2002) *Effective Strategic Leadership*, Basingstoke: Palgrave – now Palgrave Macmillan.

Cartwright, R. (2002) *Mastering Team Leadership*, Basingstoke: Palgrave – now Palgrave Macmillan.

Clawson, J.G. (2003) *Level Three Leadership: Getting below the Surface* (2nd edn), Englewood Cliffs, NJ: Prentice Hall.

Coch, L. and French, J.R. (1948) 'Overcoming resistance to change', *Human Relations*, 1: 512–32.

Covey, S.R. (1999) *Principle Centred Leadership*, London: Simon & Schuster.

Cranwell-Ward, J., Bacon, A. and Mackie, R. (2002) *Inspiring Leadership: Staying Afloat in Turbulent Times*, London: Thomson Learning.

Evans, M.G. (1970) 'The effect of supervisory behavior on the path-goal relationship', *Organizational Behavior and Human Performance*, 5: 277–98.

French, J.R., Israel, J. and As, D. (1960) 'An experiment on participation in a Norwegian factory', *Human Relations*, **13**(1): 3–19.

Gillen, T. (2002) *Leadership Skills for Boosting Performance*, London: CIPD.

Godard, A. and Lenhardt, J. (2000) *Transformational Leadership: Shared Dreams to Succeed*, Basingstoke: Palgrave – now Palgrave Macmillan.

Goleman, D., Boyatzis, R. and McKee, A. (2002) *The New Leaders: Transforming the Art of Leadership into the Science of Results*, London: Little, Brown.

Hesselbein, F. and Johnstone, R. (2002) *On Mission and Leadership: A Leader to Leader Guide*, San Fransisco, CA: Jossey-Bass.

Hughes, R., Ginnett, R. and Curphy, G. (2002) *Leadership: Enhancing the Lessons of Experience*, London: McGraw-Hill.

Johnson, G. (1987) *Strategic Change and the Management Process*, Oxford: Blackwell.

Landsberg, M. (2001) *The Tools of Leadership*, London: HarperCollins.

Lewin, K. (1951) *Field Theory in Social Science*, New York: Harper & Brothers.

Mintzberg, H. (1990) 'The design school: reconsidering the basic premises of strategic management', *Strategic Management Journal*, 11: 171–95.

Moss Kanter, R. (1989) *The Change Masters: Innovation and Entrepreneurship in the American Corporation*, New York: Simon & Schuster.

Nahavandi, A. (2000) *The Art & Science of Leadership* (2nd edn), Englewood Cliffs, NJ: Prentice Hall.

Olmstead, J. (2000) *Executive Leadership: Building World Class Organizations*, Houston, TX: Cashman Dudley.

Parker, B. and Stone, C. (2003) *Developing Management Skills for Leadership*, Englewood Cliffs, NJ: Prentice Hall.

Pettigrew, A.M. (1988) *The Management of Strategic Change*, Oxford: Blackwell.

Quinn, J.B. (1980) *Strategies for Change*, Homewood, IL: Irwin.

Quinn, J.B. (1980) 'Managing strategic change', *Sloan Management Review*, **21**(4): 3–20.

Schein, E.H. (1985) *Organizational Culture and Leadership*, San Francisco, CA: Jossey-Bass.

Shriberg, A., Shriberg, D. and Lloyd, C. (2002) *Practicing Leadership: Principles and Applications*, New York: Wiley.

Stacey, R.D. (1993) *Strategic Management and Organisational Dynamics*, London: Pitman.

Stringer, R. (2002) *Leadership and Organizational Climate*, Englewood Cliffs, NJ: Prentice Hall.

Tannenbaum, A.S. and Alport, F.H. (1956) 'Personality structure and group structure: an interpretive structure of their relationship through an event structure hypothesis', *Journal of Abnormal and Social Psychology*, 53: 272–80.

Topping, P. (2002) *Managerial Leadership*, New York: McGraw-Hill.

Williamson, O. (1975) *Markets and Hierarchies*, New York: Free Press.

Chapter references

Adair, J.E. (1973) *Action-Centred Leadership*, London: McGraw-Hill.

Adair, J.E. (2002) *100 Ideas for Effective Leadership & Management*, Oxford: Capstone.

Andrews, K. (1987) *The Concept of Corporate Strategy*, Homewood, IL: Irwin.

Ansoff, H.I. (1965) *Corporate Strategy: An Analytical Approach to Business Policy for Growth and Expansion*, New York: McGraw-Hill.

Bass, B.M. (1985) *Leadership and Performance Beyond Expectation*, New York: Free Press.

Bass, B.M. (1990) 'From transactional to transformational leadership: learning to share the vision', *Organizational Dynamics*, **18**(3): 19–31.

Bass, B.M. and Avolio, B. (1994) *Improving Organizational Effectiveness Through Transformational Leadership*. Thousands Oaks, CA: Sage.

Bass, B.M. and Steidlmeier, P. (1998) *Ethics, Character and Authentic Transformational Leadership*, http://cls.binghampton.edu/BassSteid.html.

Bennis, W. and Biederman, P. (1998) *Organizing Genius: The Secrets of Creative Collaboration*, Cambridge, MA: Perseus Books.

Blake, R.R. and Mouton, J.S. (1961) *Group Dynamics: Key to Decision Making*, Houston, TX: Gulf Publishing.

Blake, R.R. and Mouton, J.S. (1964) *The Managerial Grid: The Key to Leadership Excellence*, Houston, TX: Gulf Publishing.

Burns, J.M. (1978) *Leadership,* New York: Harper & Row.

Covey, S. (1992) *Principle-centred Leadership*, New York: Simon & Schuster.

Dansereau, F. Jr, Graen, G. and Haga, W.J. (1975) 'A vertical dyad linkage approach to leadership within formal organizations: a longitudinal investigation of the role making process', *Organizational Behavior and Human Performance*, 13: 46–78.

Fiedler, F.E. (1967) *A Theory of Leadership Effectiveness*, New York: McGraw-Hill.

Fiedler, F.E. and Garcia, J.E. (1987) *New Approaches to Leadership: Cognitive Resources and Organizational Performance*, New York: Wiley.

Graen, G. and Cashman, J.F. (1975) 'A role making model of leadership in formal organizaitons: a developmental approach', in J.G. Hunt and L.L. Larson (eds) *Leadership Frontiers*, Kent, OH: Kent State University Press.

Hersey, P. and Blanchard, K.H. (1969) *Management of Organizational Behavior: Utilizing Human Resources*, Englewood Cliffs, NJ: Prentice Hall.

Hickson, D.J., Hinigs, C.R., Lee, C.A. et al. (1971) 'A strategic contingencies theory of intra-organizational power', *Administrative Science Quarterly*, 16: 216–29.

Hooper, R.A. and Potter, J.R. (1997) *The Business of Leadership*, Aldershot: Ashgate.

House, R.J. and Mitchell, T.R. (1974) 'Path-goal theory of leadership', *Contemporary Business*, 3: 81–98.

Kouzes, J.M. and Posner, B.Z. (2003) *The Leadership Challenge* (3rd edn), San Francisco, CA: Jossey-Bass.

Lewin, K. (1947) 'Feedback problems of social diagnosis and action: Part II-B of frontiers in group dynamics, *Human Relations*, 1: 147–53.

Lewin, K., Llippit, R. and White, R.K. (1939) 'Patterns of aggressive behavior in experimentally created social climates', *Journal of Social Psychology*, 10: 271–301.

Likert, R. (1967) *The Human Organization: Its Management and Value*, New York: McGraw-Hill.

McCall, M.W. Jr and Lombardo, M.M. (1983) *Off the Track: Why and How Successful Executives Get Derailed*, Greenboro, NC: Centre for Creative Leadership.

McGregor, D. (1960) *The Human Side of Enterprise*, New York: McGraw-Hill.

Maier, N.R. (1963) *Problem-solving Discussions and Conferences: Leadership Methods and Skills*, New York: McGraw-Hill.

Merton, R.K. (1957) *Social Theory and Social Structure*, New York: Free Press.

Pfeffer, J. and Salancik, G.R. (1975) 'Determinants of supervisory behavior: a role set analysis', *Human Relations*, 28: 139–53.

Quinn, J.B. and Voyer, J. (1998) Logical incrementalism: managing strategy formation, in H. Mintzberg, J.B. Quinn and S. Ghoshal (eds) *The Strategy Process,* Englewood Cliffs, NJ: Prentice Hall.

Stogdill, R.M. (1974) *Handbook of Leadership: A Survey of the Literature*, New York: Free Press.

Tannenbaum, A.S. and Schmitt, W.H. (1958) 'How to choose a leadership pattern', *Harvard Business Review*, 36: 95–101.

Tichy, N.M. and Devanna, M.A. (1986) *The Transformational Leader*, New York: John Wiley.

Vroom, V.H. and Yetton, P.W. (1973) *Leadership and Decision-making*, Pittsburg: University of Pittsburg Press.

Yukl, G.A. (1989) *Leadership in Organizations*, Englewood Cliffs, NJ: Prentice Hall.

Chapter 8
Quality

Introduction and chapter overview

The strategic development of many companies has been marked by recognition that good quality in operations can contribute significantly to competitive advantage, so we have seen the emergence and prominence of concepts such as service quality, Six Sigma, lean sigma and quality frameworks. In particular, total quality management (TQM) is seen by many companies as an important part of this operational emphasis, especially for those that aim to be world-class organizations. In order to recognize the importance of quality, each of the world's major industrialized nations has its own quality award. These awards act as an important strategic tool and can assist in an organization's product and market positioning.

In this chapter, we explain how this emphasis on quality management has come about and explore the main features demonstrated by those organizations that have successfully adopted a TQM philosophy. Key features of the quality award frameworks are discussed and, finally, the chapter explains the various types of operational benchmarking in common use.

Learning objectives

After studying this chapter, you should be able to:

- define quality and total quality management
- explain how TQM evolved
- explain the main principles of TQM
- describe and distinguish between the enablers and results elements of the EFQM excellence model
- describe how self-assessment frameworks are used and say what benefits they can bring to businesses
- distinguish between the different types of benchmarking and explain the benefits of each

8.1 Quality as a strategic imperative

The most important set of factors that impact on any organization's operations strategy are those set by the customers. The purpose of any operation's function is to manage the value-adding activities inside the business in such a way that customer requirements are met in full.

What 'matters' to the customer will, of course, vary from market to market. For each element of product that is of concern to a customer, organizations will have an internal response that facilitates the satisfaction of that concern. The most successful businesses are those that can most effectively configure their operations to meet customer requirements.

The various areas of focus for an organization when developing a competitive strategy are listed in Table 8.1 below. It is notable from this list just how important quality and customer focus become in the overall strategy. The quality of products (goods and services) can be seen to extend from the original design, to on-time delivery, reliability in service, through to after-sales service. This is what we mean by 'customer-driven quality'.

Quality begins with the quality of product design. Do the specifications achieve what the customer wants? Does the company fully understand customers' needs and requirements? Quality extends into the manufacturing or service processes. Can the company deliver the products at the right price? The efficiency of work processes and the competences of employees need to be such that products can be made cost-effectively and consistently to design specifications. Have all wasteful processes, those which do not add value, been eliminated? In the case of service operations, the customer is often in face-to-face contact with the employee providing the service. The customer should feel confident that the service is speedy, professional, efficient and provides value for money.

Product reliability is another important issue. From the customers' perspective, product reliability is measured by the product's functional performance and so the product must perform as expected. Continuous good functional performance over time is also important. The product must continue performing throughout what the customer considers to be a reasonable life expectancy. Reliable, fast delivery of products or off-the-shelf availability of consumer products is also a major consideration. Can the company meet the delivery lead time requirements? Does it do so reliably and consistently? In the case of service industries, the service provided is less tangible than physical products and therefore it is often the customers' perception of the reliability and timeliness of the service provided that is important.

For many businesses, 'what really matters to customers' can be seen to extend beyond the above issues. Customer-driven quality often requires innovation and the use of cutting-edge technologies. This innovation can be applied to materials

Table 8.1 **Factors affecting customer-driven quality and the operating performance characteristics of an organization**

What matters to customers in selecting a product purchase	How a business responds to customer demands
Low price (value for money)	Producing efficiently at low or reasonable unit cost
High-quality products and services	Building quality into processes and products
Fast delivery	Having short manufacturing lead times, finished goods stock or fast distribution
Product and service reliability	Building reliability into products and delivering dependable service
Innovation, using cutting-edge technologies	Keeping abreast of latest developments and emphasizing R&D
Wide product choice	Responding to change and providing a wide product mix
Responsive to changes in customer requirements	Being flexible and responding quickly to volume and delivery changes

and product design, or even to manufacturing processes or the way services and facilities are provided.

KEY CONCEPTS

Stocks are the physical goods that are bought in, converted and then sold to the customers in a manufacturing or assembly business. There are three types of stock, depending on where they are along the production process – raw materials, work-in-progress and finished goods.

Raw materials or purchased parts are stocks in their 'raw' state. Raw materials are those goods that are purchased, before they undergo any processing within the manufacturing process.

Work-in-progress (WIP) is the name given to stocks that are actually being worked on in the manufacturing process.

Finished goods (FG) stocks are those which have passed through the process and are ready for distribution to the customers.

The list in Table 8.1 is useful as a starting point to identifying the wide range of issues that must be addressed by manufacturing and service sector organizations in the quest to become leaders in their own markets. Many 'winning' organizations – those with a competitive advantage in their industry – have arrived at the conclusion that one area of concern in operations is more important than any other – quality.

8.2 Quality and quality management

A number of academics and practitioners have attempted to provide a coherent definition of quality. The fact that there are so many definitions is testimony to the fact that it is a complicated matter on which to agree.

For a common product such as a car, we might think of quality as referring to reliability, build or safety features. For a service such as plastering a wall, we would probably arrive at a different set of things to describe a 'quality' job, such as the finish of the surface, the flushness of the edges and the extent to which it is even. It is the fact that the quality criteria vary from product to product that makes it difficult to agree on a definition.

Some of the most noted thinkers in the field have described quality with respect to 'excellence' or, more accurately, 'perceived excellence'. Although quality means many things to different people, in general, we can consider quality as meeting customer needs or expectations. Table 8.2 summarizes some of the most widely used definitions, while the major thinkers in this area are described in Table 8.3.

Table 8.2 **Some definitions of quality**

Quality guru	Definition of quality
Deming	Quality should be aimed at meeting the needs of the consumer, present and future
Juran	Quality is fitness for the purpose for which the product is intended
Crosby	Quality is conformance to requirements, either customer requirements or the specification predetermined for it
Oakland	Quality is meeting customer requirements

A **quality guru** is someone who has been recognized for their contribution to the management of quality within business and whose messages have led to major changes in the way organizations operate. There are a number people who are highly regarded as major contributors in the field of quality management, including Juran, Deming and Peters.

Table 8.3 **The quality gurus**

Quality guru	Main messages
W. Edwards Deming	Sometimes referred to as 'the father of TQM', Deming believed that bad management is responsible for more than 90% of quality problems. He argued that quality improvement is achieved by continuous reduction in process variation using statistical process control and employee involvement. Later, Deming developed his 'system of profound knowledge', in which he stressed the need for the organization to operate as a coherent system with everybody working together towards the overall aims. Good quality relies in large part on an understanding of the nature of variation (statistical theory), careful planning and prediction based on experience. Finally, he stressed the importance of psychology, recognizing the relationships of extrinsic and extrinsic motivation factors in the workplace
Joseph M. Juran	Juran proposed a general management approach with human elements. He believed that less than 20% of quality problems were due to the workers themselves. He defined quality as 'fitness for use'. Juran recommended a project approach to improvements by setting targets, planning to achieve targets set, assigning responsibility, and rewarding results achieved
Armand V. Feigenbaum	Feigenbaum proposed a systematic approach of total quality control involving every employee and all functions. He emphasized the need for 'quality-mindedness' through employee participation. He made the point that expenditure on prevention costs would lead to an overall reduction in product failure costs
Kaoru Ishikawa	Ishikawa stressed the importance of statistical methods, using his 'seven tools of quality' for problem solving. Also recognized for his contributions to the company-wide quality control movement, involving all staff at all levels through 'quality circles'
Genichi Taguchi	Taguchi developed the 'quality loss function' concerned with the optimization of products and processes prior to manufacture. His methods can be applied in the design phase of products or systems, or in production to optimize process variables
Shigeo Shingo	Shingo introduced a practical approach to achieve zero defects. With careful design of products and tooling systems, he eliminated the need for sample inspection, through his system of mistake proofing known as 'poka-yoke'. He is also acknowledged for his work on fast tooling changeovers. Commonly known as SMED (single minute exchange of dies), this is one of the most important contributions to JIT (just-in-time) operating systems
Philip B. Crosby	Crosby's 14-step approach to quality improvement sets out to achieve conformance to requirements through prevention not inspection. Believing that 'quality is free' and 'zero defects' should be the target, Crosby rejected statistically acceptable levels of quality. He believed in a 'top-down' approach to quality management and proposed his four absolutes of quality: quality is defined as conformance to requirements; the system of quality is prevention; the performance standard is zero defects; the measurement of quality is the financial cost of nonconformance
Tom Peters	Peters' early work stressed the importance of visible leadership and he encouraged MBWA (management by walking about), giving managers the opportunity to listen and solve problems through face-to-face contact with workers. His later work focused on customer orientation and he stressed that managers need to be 'obsessed' with quality, never accepting shoddy goods. He recognized that everyone needs to be trained in quality tools, and supported the use of cross-functional teams. He believed that organizations should overcome complacency by creating 'endless Hawthorne effects' (after the work of Elton Mayo) through the generation of new goals and environments. He also stressed the importance of the role of suppliers and customers in the quest for improvement

Historical perspective of quality

Quality has been an issue for as long as business has been carried out. For traditional crafts such as masons, blacksmiths, tailors, thatchers and carpenters, it was the craftsmen themselves who were responsible for the price, delivery and degree of quality of their wares and services. Reputations were established on the quality of workmanship, which in turn led to more demand for their skills and higher levels of profitability and prosperity for the individual. The more successful 'masters' recruited apprentices and employed other tradesmen, and quality was assured informally and depended on the pride that each individual had in their own work. In Europe, craft guilds were established, which aimed to ensure that adequate training was given and that apprentices 'qualified' only when they were demonstrably capable of producing adequate standards of workmanship. Much of this pride in workmanship was lost during the Industrial Revolution in the late 18th century with the introduction of machinery and high-volume manufacturing. However, large-scale production methods brought about a need to ensure consistent reproduction of parts, manufactured to exacting specifications and so the concept of 'quality control' was born.

In the early 1900s, Frederick W. Taylor introduced his ideas on scientific management. His methodology was to separate the planning (thinking) function from the physical work elements in production. By breaking down each job into smaller elements of work, he was able to train workers to perform simple mechanical tasks, which comprised only a part of the total production process. High-volume repeatability allowed gains in speed and efficiency, and this in turn led to cheaper products. Quality control techniques enabled specially trained inspectors to test finished components against a predetermined specification. This enabled defective parts to be identified and then removed or reworked before they reached the customer.

GURU GUIDE

Frederick **Winslow Taylor** was born in Philadelphia in 1856. His early education was at Philips Exeter Academy in New Hampshire and in 1873 he joined the Midvale Steel Works as an apprentice pattern maker. Later on he became the chief engineer in the firm. Taylor obtained a degree in mechanical engineering from Stevens Institute of Technology. From 1890 to 1893 he was employed as a consulting engineer to management at the Manufacturing Investment Company of Philadelphia.

He joined the faculty of Tuck School of Business at Dartmouth College and was one of the first figures to offer management consultancy services to firms. He was awarded an honorary doctorate from the University of Pennsylvania. Professor Taylor won a gold medal at the Paris Exposition in 1900 for developing high-speed steel and was a recipient of the Elliott Cresson Medal awarded by the Franklin Institute, Philadelphia. He died in 1915.

He is regarded as the founding father of scientific management and is one of the most influential figures in the study of social sciences.

The modern quality movement

The modern quality movement began in the 1950s. The demand for goods and merchandise saw western industrial nations producing higher volumes of product, with a resulting decline in quality. In Japan, during the rebuilding of its industrial base after the Second World War, help was given by a number of management consultants. In particular, the work of Deming and Juran led the Japanese to completely review the accepted views on quality management.

GURU GUIDE

William Edwards Deming was born in 1900 in Iowa. He worked as a mathematical physicist with the US Department of Agriculture for nearly 12 years before becoming a statistical adviser to the US Census Bureau. He has also been a professor of statistics at New York University's Graduate School of Business Administration.

Professor Deming is a quality guru and was instrumental in developing concepts related to the statistical control of processes and overall quality management. He is widely credited for improving production in the USA and is known for his work in revitalizing Japanese industries after the Second World War, contributing to Japan's later reputation for high-quality, innovative products. From 1950 onward in Japan, he taught top management how to improve design (and thus service), product quality, testing and sales. He was a consultant for a number of private firms and was involved in the compilation of American War Standards. He is credited for introducing the concept of total quality management and for the application of statistical methods to improve the design and manufacture of products. He died in 1993.

Statistical quality control techniques were introduced to reduce variation in the production processes. Much emphasis was placed on the way that quality was managed, rather than simply concentrating on the technical issues. The focus shifted from one of quality inspection to one of preventing quality problems. Management began educating and involving all employees to look for ways to improve product quality and work methods. The Japanese developed a new culture of continuous improvement, where everyone was encouraged to believe that they had two jobs – doing the work and improving the work. They called this approach 'kaizen'.

The kaizen process begins with an examination of the work processes and operating practices, continuously looking for improvement opportunities. It is important that every employee strives for improvement and so an acceptance of kaizen by the organizational culture is an important element. Employees are empowered to experiment and make incremental changes and are sometimes provided with their own limited budgets for doing so. It is important that kaizen activities are actively supported by management, who will usually provide additional resources if required, perhaps when ideas for change are complex, requiring technical expertise, extra finance or help in other ways.

This new manufacturing philosophy gradually evolved and led to the Japanese domination in manufacturing industries by the late 1970s. During the 1980s, the rest of the world awoke to this transformation and the TQM movement was born.

Joseph Moses Juran was born in 1904 in Braila, Romania. With his family, he immigrated to the USA in 1912 and graduated with a bachelor's degree in electrical engineering from the University of Minnesota in 1924. As a hedge against the uncertainties of the Great Depression, Juran qualified as a lawyer, although he never practised. He joined the faculty of New York University as an adjunct professor in the industrial engineering department, and after the Second World War became a freelance consultant. His many clients included Gilette, Bausch & Lomb, General Foods and Borg-Warner.

Juran, well known for his work in quality management, was a prolific figure in introducing statistical testing and control chart techniques in manufacturing process. He wrote several books on quality management and his work with Bell Labs in promoting quality control made him one of the most influential figures in TQM. He died in 2008.

KEY CONCEPTS

Kaizen is a culturally embedded concept of continual improvement pioneered in Japanese companies. It concentrates on small gradual changes involving all employees in every area of business. According to Imai (1986), it is 'the single most important concept in Japanese management – the key to Japanese competitive success'. Kaizen is process-oriented change, involving operators continuously searching for better ways to do their job.

Kaizen teams take responsibility for identifying opportunities for improvement. Typically, ideas for change will be investigated, tested and measured by the team. Any savings in job cycle time, even a few seconds, will be introduced as the new standard method of production. Staff are encouraged to participate in kaizen teams and are given full training in problem-solving tools and techniques.

8.3   Total quality management

Total quality management (TQM) is a holistic approach, which provides awareness of the customer–supplier relationship and continuous improvement effort in all departments and functions.

Today, total quality management (TQM) is a holistic approach, which provides awareness of the customer–supplier relationship and continuous improvement effort in all departments and functions. Much has been written on the subject of TQM, and the philosophy means many things to different people.

Some have used an external customer focus, aiming to ensure employee awareness of customer needs and an elimination of faulty goods or services. Others have focused on the use of quality tools, such as brainstorming, statistical tools or control charts, to encourage problem solving and a right-first-time attitude. Many have used teamwork and 'empowerment' in an effort to develop a 'quality' culture, to improve staff motivation and an ongoing cycle of quality improvement.

There are as many approaches to TQM as there are consultants selling their own formula for success, but whatever the approach, the following features of TQM are usually present:

- it is strongly led by senior management
- it is customer oriented
- it recognizes internal customers in the value chain and external customers

- it represents a fundamental change away from *controlling* bad quality to *preventing* bad quality from happening – it *causes* good quality
- it encourages a right-first-time approach to all activities
- everybody is made responsible for quality
- there is an emphasis on kaizen
- training and quality tools are introduced in support of the quality regime
- employees are encouraged to look for ways for improving quality in their own areas, for example by process 'tightening'
- the introduction of measurement systems to eliminate and control waste.

Waste describes any activity in an operations process that is not value adding. It costs money but does not create value commensurate with its cost. Examples include:

- process inefficiency, say, as a result of bad design
- any process that does not add value, such as unnecessary inspection activities or materials handling activities, say, from station to station in the process
- any stock that is not actually being processed and to which value is therefore not being added. This includes all raw materials, all FG and any WIP that is queuing between production stages
- stocks that have failed a quality test, either in-process or at final quality control
- machine 'downtime', that is, production time lost through machines not being operable for any reason such as breakdown or through tooling up or tooling down between batches
- the time and stock involved in producing unsold or unsaleable stocks.

> **Waste** describes any activity in an operations process that is not value adding. It costs money but does not create value commensurate with its cost.

Oakland's model for total quality management

A number of frameworks for TQM have been developed. The earliest were proposed by academics trying to explain and rationalize the TQM concepts, to facilitate implementation by managers in industry. Many business consultants followed with their own ideas and a proliferation of TQM models ensued.

John Oakland developed a relatively simple framework, which usefully described the main features of TQM (Figure 8.1). According to Oakland (1993, p. 30), TQM is 'an approach to improving the competitiveness, effectiveness and flexibility of a whole organization'. TQM is thus a way of managing people and business process to ensure complete customer satisfaction at every stage, resulting in organizations doing things right first time.

Performance

At the heart of Oakland's model is performance, representing the processes, people and planning of customer–supplier chains in order to recognize the importance of meeting customer requirements. The model recognizes that all organizations have chains of internal customers and suppliers, therefore performance must be achieved across all levels of activity and combines planning, people and the processes. In essence, TQM is about

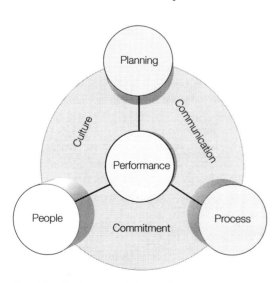

Figure 8.1 **Oakland's model of TQM**
Source: Oakland, 2003, 2004

managing people, business processes and planning to ensure the customer is satisfied at every stage of the process.

For example, in a manufacturing plant, raw materials are received into stores from suppliers, and are then fed into the first production process. Here the materials are worked on in some way and then passed on to the next department (the next internal customer) where they are worked again. At each stage value is added until the final product is sold to the external customer. Each operator in the chain is therefore both a customer and a supplier, with each having the responsibility of meeting their respective customer's requirements. Failing to do so at any stage results in inferior quality and a need to correct or rework the WIP stock or the FG. At every stage, the work process and the skills of the operator must be capable of doing the job correctly to the designed specification.

Process: quality systems

To achieve consistency in work processes, a company must be organized so that the required standards are known and understood by all employees. This requires management systems to plan, monitor and control all activities. For many organizations, this is achieved by setting out objectives through a quality 'policy' and the use of a fully documented quality system such as ISO 9000. Using such a system ensures a consistent level of quality, which, in turn, promotes customer confidence. In addition, these systems help the organization to manage internal and external operations in a cost-effective and efficient way.

Planning: tools and techniques of quality

The quality system provides a framework for recording and dealing with quality problems. However, simply asking staff to take responsibility for solving their own quality problems is usually not enough. Employees often must be trained and educated so that they can identify problems and deal with them effectively. Many organizations now train staff in basic problem-solving tools and other quality techniques, encouraging them to become proactive in quality improvement activities.

People: teams and the organization

Clear lines of authority and responsibility are important in most organizational structures. Just as important, however, is the need to ensure that departments and functions do not become so compartmentalized that barriers develop. In most modern manufacturing and service companies, work processes are complex in nature and are often beyond the control of any one individual. A team approach, therefore, offers a number of advantages.

The use of teams allows more complex problems to be solved because it brings together different skills and expertise. Interdepartmental teams can resolve issues that cross over functional boundaries and will also help reduce problems of internal politics. Teamworking can also help develop skills and knowledge and it is often more satisfying for the individuals involved – improving morale, participation and decision-making.

Commitment, culture and communication

Achieving right-first-time quality requires a dedicated, well-motivated and loyal workforce who have been educated and trained to do the job properly. This requires leadership, policy setting, careful planning and the provision of appropriate resources at every level of the company. Senior managers must demonstrate their own commitment and the 'quality message' must be communicated and understood by everyone in the organization. The development of a TQM culture usually takes many years and must be demonstrated from senior management level down through the whole organization.

Example   Walmart: setting standards

The US supermarket Walmart implemented TQM practices to improve various elements of its business operations, including continuously sourcing quality products from supply networks to deliver the best products at the lowest available prices to the consumer. By continuously working with its suppliers, Walmart ensures that its products are of a standard that meets consumer expectations and are therefore deemed of an acceptable quality. The quality requirements also ensure that Walmart's standards remain competitive and comparable with industry best practices.

Quality award and assessment frameworks

The realization that quality is a key determinant of the competitive position of a business has brought about a number of methods of recognition. Accordingly, every developed economy has its own government-sponsored award to recognize those organizations that have achieved high quality and to stimulate others to follow the same path. These frameworks are all based on the philosophy of TQM and have much in common. The high profile and publicity gained by the winners of these internationally recognized awards give organizations significant marketing opportunities. Three of the major frameworks in use today are the Deming Prize (Japan), the Malcolm Baldrige Award (USA) and the EFQM European Quality Award.

These frameworks have continued to evolve and are now becoming adopted by countries worldwide in similar forms. The primary use of the frameworks is as a self-assessment tool by which companies can critically review their own activities against a comprehensive set of criteria. Typically, an organization prepares a detailed written submission of strengths and weaknesses for all aspects of its operations and business performance. For the best companies – those which demonstrate the highest levels of achievement – the submission can be used to judge them for the award. More importantly, and for most organizations, any weaknesses they have identified can be prioritized and developed into an action plan for business improvement.

The Deming Prize, established in 1950 in honour of W. Edwards Deming, has several categories including prizes for individuals, small companies and factories. Hundreds of companies apply for the Deming Prize each year. Each applicant must submit a detailed account of quality practices and methods and from these submissions, a shortlist of companies is selected for site visits and assessment. The Malcolm Baldrige National Quality Award, named after a former US secretary of commerce, was designed to operate in a similar manner to the Deming Prize.

Table 8.4 **Companies that have received the Baldrige Award**

Year	Recipients
2009	Honeywell Federal Manufacturing & Technologies, MidwayUSA, AtlantiCare, Heartland Health and VA Cooperative Studies Program Clinical Research Pharmacy Coordinating Center
2008	Cargill Corn Milling North America, Poudre Valley Health System and Iredell-Statesville Schools
2007	PRO-TEC Coating Co., Mercy Health System, Sharp HealthCare, City of Coral Springs and U.S. Army Research, Development and Engineering (ARDEC)
2006	Premier, Inc. MESA Products Inc. and North Mississippi Medical Center
2005	Sunny Fresh Foods Inc., DynMcDermott Petroleum Operations, Park Place Lexus, Jenks Public Schools, Richland College and Bronson Methodist Hospital
2004	The Bama Companies, Texas Nameplate Company Inc., Kenneth W. Monfort College of Business and Robert Wood Johnson University Hospital Hamilton
2003	Medrad Inc., Boeing Aerospace Support, Caterpillar Financial Services Corp., Stoner Inc., Community Consolidated School District 15, Baptist Hospital Inc. and Saint Luke's Hospital of Kansas City
2002	Motorola Inc. Commercial, Government and Industrial Solutions Sector, Branch Smith Printing Division and SSM Health Care
2001	Clarke American Checks Inc., Pal's Sudden Service, Chugach School District, Pearl River School District and University of Wisconsin-Stout
2000	Dana Corp.-Spicer Driveshaft Division, KARLEE Company Inc., Operations Management International Inc. and Los Alamos National Bank
1999	STMicroelectronics Inc.-Region Americas, BI Performance Services, The Ritz-Carlton Hotel Co. and Sunny Fresh Foods
1998	Boeing Airlift and Tanker Programs, Solar Turbines Inc. and Texas Nameplate Co. Inc.
1997	3M Dental Products Division, Solectron Corp., Merrill Lynch Credit Corp. and Xerox Business Services
1996	ADAC Laboratories, Dana Commercial Credit Corp., Custom Research Inc. and Trident Precision Manufacturing Inc.
1995	Armstrong World Industries Building Products Operation and Corning Telecommunications Products Division
1994	AT&T Consumer Communications Services, GTE Directories Corp. and Wainwright Industries Inc.
1993	Eastman Chemical Co. and Ames Rubber Corp.
1992	AT&T Network Systems Group/Transmission Systems Business Unit, Texas Instruments Inc. Defence Systems & Electronics Group, AT&T Universal Card Services, The Ritz-Carlton Hotel Co. and Granite Rock Co.
1991	Solectron Corp., Zytec Corp. and Marlow Industries
1990	Cadillac Motor Car Division, IBM Rochester, Federal Express Corp. and Wallace Co. Inc.
1989	Milliken & Co. and Xerox Corp. Business Products and Systems
1988	Motorola Inc., Commercial Nuclear Fuel Division of Westinghouse Electric Corp. and Globe Metallurgical Inc.

Source: Baldrige National Quality Programme, National Institute of Standard and Technology, 2009

Baldrige awards are given in manufacturing, service, small business, education and healthcare. They have the specific aim of improving the competitiveness and performance of organizations by promoting performance excellence, recognizing achievements and publicizing their successful strategies. Promotion of successful strategies in this way guides other organizations to observe and learn from them through benchmarking (see Table 8.4).

It is the third of the awards mentioned above that we will consider in more detail – the EFQM model.

8.4   The EFQM excellence model

Following the success of the Deming Prize and the Malcolm Baldrige Award, 14 leading European organizations, supported by the European Commission, formed the Brussels-based European Foundation for Quality Management (EFQM) in 1988. By 2001, across Europe, membership of the EFQM had grown to over 850 member organizations in most sectors of commercial and not-for-profit activity. EFQM's mission is: 'To energise leaders who want to learn, share and innovate using the EFQM Excellence Model as a common framework' (www.efqm.org/en). The EFQM excellence model is shown in Figure 8.2.

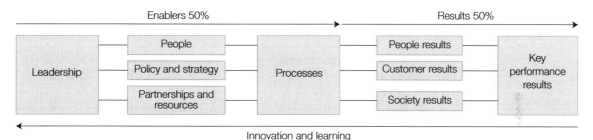

Figure 8.2 The EFQM excellence model

Source: www.efqm.org/en/

The EFQM excellence model is based on the following premise: 'Excellent results with respect to Performance, Customers, People and Society are achieved through Leadership driving Policy and Strategy, that is delivered through People, Partnerships and Resources, and Processes' (www.saeto.com/efqm.htm). Excellence is defined by the EFQM as outstanding practice in managing the organization and achieving results and is based on eight fundamental concepts (EFQM, 2010a, 2010b).

The excellence model contains nine criteria, five 'enablers', which cover what an organization does, and four 'results', which cover what an organization achieves. Results are caused by enablers and enablers are improved using feedback from results. The model can be used by all types and sizes of organization. Published guidelines are specifically written by the EFQM (www.efqm.org/en/PdfResources/EFQMcatalogue.pdf). The model offers a rigorous and structured self-assessment approach to business improvements based on hard facts. Careful assessment against each criterion allows an organization to calculate an overall score from a total possible 1,000 points. This score can then be viewed as a benchmark for comparisons with other organizations. Award-winning organizations achieve scores of around 700 points.

One of the most powerful attractions of the model is its use as a self-assessment diagnostic tool. This forms the basis for a company-wide plan of improvement activities, which can be prioritized to yield best results. Improvements can be measured and revisited year after year to observe progress. Benchmarking both internally and externally provides a powerful method of setting realistic improvement targets, and is referred to constantly within the model. Because of its importance, benchmarking will be discussed in more detail later in this chapter.

The enabler criteria

The first five criteria of the EFQM excellence model examine how an organization sets itself out to manufacture goods or provide services to customers.

Leadership

This first element looks for a visible demonstration of commitment to excellence by all managers within the organization. Managers must develop the mission, vision and be 'role model' leaders of a culture of excellence. They should define priorities, provide the resources and ensure the management system is developed, implemented and continuously improved. They should also be involved with customers and suppliers, promoting partnerships and joint improvement 'win–win' activities.

Policy and strategy

Policy and strategy for any company must be based on comprehensive and relevant information (this being the purpose of strategic analysis). It is important to understand customers' needs and to exploit, as far as possible, the strengths of suppliers. To ensure competitiveness, the organization needs to review performance and use benchmarking to compare with best practice, the competition and other best-in-class organizations.

People

The knowledge, competences and capabilities of employees must be identified, managed and developed. The organization should encourage individual and team participation in improvement activities and empower staff to take action.

Partnerships and resources

Partnerships and resources refer to all the resources employed by the company, other than the human resources covered above. These include external partnerships, financial resources, information resources, suppliers and materials, buildings, plant and equipment, technology and intellectual property. The company must demonstrate how it manages and exploits its resources to gain competitive advantage.

Processes

Each key process must be systematically designed, measured and managed to established standards (ISO 9000). Constantly striving to be more competitive requires regular reviews of processes and actual performance levels. Excellent companies talk to their customers and suppliers, and proactively involve them in the design of products and services. The use of best practice benchmarking helps to identify innovation and new technologies and leads to improvements.

The results criteria

The remaining four criteria of the EFQM excellence model examine what the organization is actually achieving, with regard to 'customer results', 'people results', 'society results' and 'key performance results'. To achieve a high score, a company must have strong positive trends for at least five years in business results and profitability. Measures must also be in place showing strong satisfaction trends from all stakeholders – customers, suppliers, employees and the wider community.

In 2010, there were five prize winners and eight finalists for the EFQM Excellence Award:

The EFQM award

- Alpenresort Schwarz – Finalist
- Bradstow School – Prize Winner in Leading with Vision, Inspiration & Integrity and a Prize Winner in Succeeding through People
- Domino-World – Finalist
- Dr. Germain Becker & Associés – Finalist
- Eskisehir Maternity and Child Illness Hospital – Prize Winner in Leading with Vision, Inspiration and Integrity
- Liverpool John Moores University – Finalist
- Olabide Ikastola – Prize Winner in Adding Value for Customers and a Prize Winner in Succeeding through People
- Osakidetza - Comarca Gipuzkoa Ekialde – Finalist
- Robert Bosch Fahrzeugelektrik Eisenach – Finalist
- Siemens Congelton – Finalist
- Stavropol State Agrarian University – Prize Winner in Nurturing Creativity & Innovation and a Prize Winner in Leading with Vision, Inspiration & Integrity
- Vamed-KMB – Prize Winner in Succeeding through People
- Worthington Cylinders – Finalist.

8.5   Six Sigma and lean sigma

Six Sigma is a relatively new concept compared to TQM as a whole. It began in 1986 when Bill Smith, a Motorola Inc. employee, introduced a statistically based method to reduce variation in electronic manufacturing processes in the company in the USA. Initially, Six Sigma was developed as an alternative to TQM; however, Six Sigma and TQM have many similarities and are compatible in varied business environments, making both equally valid. TQM has helped companies (both service and manufacturing) to improve quality, while Six Sigma has the potential to deliver statistically tested, quantitative results.

We have seen that TQM is often associated with the development, deployment and maintenance of organizational systems that are required for various business processes. It is based on a strategic approach that focuses on maintaining existing quality standards as well as making incremental quality improvements. Six Sigma, on the other hand, is more than just a process improvement programme, as it is based on concepts that focus on continuous quality improvements for achieving near perfection by restricting the number of possible defects to less than 3.4 defects per million. Thus the basic difference between Six Sigma and TQM is the approach. Six Sigma is based on DMAIC – define-measure-analyse-improve-control. Other abbreviations include DMAICT, which is DMAIC, plus transfer of best practice, and DMADV – define-measure-analyse-design-verify. Six Sigma is designed to help in making precise measurements, identifying exact problems and providing solutions that can be measured. It is driven by data, and provides quantifiable and measurable results. So, while TQM views quality as conformance to internal requirements, Six Sigma focuses on improving quality by reducing the number of defects. The end result may be the same in both concepts. Table 8.5 shows the DMAIC steps and the various tools

> **Six Sigma** is based on concepts that focus on continuous quality improvements for achieving near perfection by restricting the number of possible defects to less than 3.4 defects per million.

and techniques that can be used. Table 8.5 is sourced from iSixSigma.com, the largest community of professionals with an interest in Six Sigma. The website is worth viewing for more detail on current thinking in the field of Six Sigma.

Table 8.5 **The DMAIC steps and tools used for Six Sigma**

DMAIC Phase Steps	Tools Used
D – Define Phase: Define the project goals and customer (internal and external) deliverables.	
• Define Customers and Requirements (CTQs) • Develop Problem Statement, Goals and Benefits • Identify Champion, Process Owner and Team • Define Resources • Evaluate Key Organizational Support • Develop Project Plan and Milestones • Develop High Level Process Map	• Project Charter • Process Flowchart • SIPOC Diagram • Stakeholder Analysis • DMAIC Work Breakdown Structure • CTQ Definitions • Voice of the Customer Gathering
Define Tollgate Review	
M – Measure Phase: Measure the process to determine current performance; quantify the problem.	
• Define Defect, Opportunity, Unit and Metrics • Detailed Process Map of Appropriate Areas • Develop Data Collection Plan • Validate the Measurement System • Collect the Data • Begin Developing Y=f(x) Relationship • Determine Process Capability and Sigma Baseline	• Process Flowchart • Data Collection Plan/Example • Benchmarking • Measurement System Analysis/Gage R&R • Voice of the Customer Gathering • Process Sigma Calculation
Measure Tollgate Review	
A – Analyze Phase: Analyze and determine the root cause(s) of the defects.	
• Define Performance Objectives • Identify Value/Non-Value Added Process Steps • Identify Sources of Variation • Determine Root Cause(s) • Determine Vital Few x's, Y=f(x) Relationship	• Histogram • Pareto Chart • Time Series/Run Chart • Scatter Plot • Regression Analysis • Cause and Effect/Fishbone Diagram • 5 Whys • Process Map Review and Analysis • Statistical Analysis • Hypothesis Testing (Continuous and Discrete) • Non-Normal Data Analysis
Analyze Tollgate Review	
I – Improve Phase: Improve the process by eliminating defects.	
• Perform Design of Experiments • Develop Potential Solutions • Define Operating Tolerances of Potential System • Assess Failure Modes of Potential Solutions • Validate Potential Improvement by Pilot Studies • Correct/Re-Evaluate Potential Solution	• Brainstorming • Mistake Proofing • Design of Experiments • Pugh Matrix • House of Quality • Failure Modes and Effects Analysis (FMEA) • Simulation Software
Improve Tollgate Review	
C – Control Phase: Control future process performance.	
• Define and Validate Monitoring and Control System • Develop Standards and Procedures • Implement Statistical Process Control • Determine Process Capability • Develop Transfer Plan, Handoff to Process Owner • Verify Benefits, Cost Savings/Avoidance, Profit Growth • Close Project, Finalize Documentation • Communicate to Business, Celebrate	• Process Sigma Calculation • Control Charts (Variable and Attribute) • Cost Savings Calculations • Control Plan
Control Tollgate Review	

Source: http://www.isixsigma.com/index.php?option=com_k2&view=item&layout=item&id=1477&Itemid=343

Lean Six Sigma is an evolution of Six Sigma, where lean manufacturing/ production approaches and principles are merged with those of Six Sigma. Lean is an approach that seeks to improve flow in the value stream and eliminate waste. Six Sigma uses the DMAIC framework and statistical tools to uncover root causes to understand and reduce variation. A combination of both provides a structured improvement approach and effective tools to solve problems. This creates rapid transformational improvement at lower cost.

> **Lean** is an approach that seeks to improve flow in the value stream and eliminate waste.

Example   Six Sigma in action

Apart from being an active continuous improvement methodology in the manufacturing industry, Six Sigma has also found acceptance in the service sector. The banking industry provides an active platform for the application of Six Sigma as a continuous improvement philosophy and tool. Major financial institutions in the USA, Europe and South Asia (Llyods TSB, NatWest, GE, JPMorgan Chase, Bank of America, ICICI Bank) have adopted Six Sigma methodologies in order to improve their service quality, increase customer satisfaction, reduce expenses, increase earnings and reduce risk. For example, using Six Sigma tools, JPMorgan Chase identified several expense reduction areas and saved $500,000 per annum in the use of unnecessary SWIFT messages (Doganoksoy et al., 2000). Similarly, GE improved its call centre performance by reviewing its processes using Six Sigma methodology. The net result was that the rate of a caller reaching a live person in GE improved from 76% to 99% (Pande et al., 2000).

8.6   Quality and strategic analysis

Garvin (1987) proposes eight dimensions of quality that can provide a guiding framework for strategic analysis. These dimensions are performance, features, reliability, conformance, durability, serviceability, aesthetics and perceived quality (Table 8.6). Delivering these eight dimensions will lead to a degree of competitive advantage and enhance the strategic position of organizations.

Table 8.6 **Garvin's eight dimensions of quality**

Dimension	Description
Performance	The primary operating characteristics of a product or service must be seen to perform to users' expectations
Features	A secondary aspect to performance, as they are supplementary to the basic functioning of the product or service
Reliability	A measure of the probability of the product or service failing to work. The more durable a good is, the greater the requirement for reliability
Conformance	The degree to which characteristics meet established standards
Durability	The measure of a product's life, often a balance against value for money
Serviceability	The speed, competence and ease of repair
Aesthetics	A highly subjective measure, reflecting looks, sensory pleasure and individual preference
Perceived quality	The degree of incomplete information held by the consumer and the value attached to the good, based on what is expected or inferred rather than reality itself

8.7 Benchmarking

One of the key features within the above frameworks is the importance of benchmarking. Superior performers in most industries regularly review themselves against the competition and other best-in-class companies to remain at the top. *Fit for the Future*, a report published by the Confederation of British Industry (CBI) in 1997 examined the strengths of UK companies. The report concluded: 'The most powerful process any company can adopt and which delivers immediate, measurable and sustainable productivity improvements is the transfer of Best Practice.'

This is the key to successful benchmarking – for an organization to analyse its own performance and then compare performance in several areas against competitors. If, for example, one competitor in an industry enjoys a lower rate of waste or higher quality than others, questions can be asked as to what this company has done to bring about the superior performance. By using benchmarking in this way, best practice procedures can be emulated and performance improved in the lower performers.

Successful benchmarking usually rests on the premise that competitors in an industry are willing, to some extent, to share, collaborate or make information available on their performance and processes. The happy result of successful benchmarking is that all participants in an industry have improved quality performance, so improving customer satisfaction with the industry's products.

In recent years, the interest in benchmarking has grown. What started out as a relatively simple concept has become increasingly complicated. Benchmarking has proved to be a profitable source of income for management consultants who have developed and published many different approaches and methodologies. For any organization just beginning to benchmark, reading the literature will confirm that there are many types of benchmarking in existence. Where do they start? Which form of benchmarking is best? We will consider the different types under three broad headings, metric, diagnostic and process benchmarking. A simple way is to view them along a continuum, as shown in Figure 8.3.

From Figure 8.3, we can see that there is an increase in effort, resources and costs as we move from metric benchmarking through to full process benchmarking. At the lower end, metric benchmarking can provide an indication of relative performance and perhaps identify leading competitors, but it is unlikely to yield any real ideas on how to change. At best, it will only help to define performance gaps.

Moving up, diagnostic benchmarking requires a little more effort but in return will identify areas of strength and more detail on areas of weakness for the organization. Done correctly, it will also help to prioritize which processes should be targeted for improvement activities.

Process benchmarking requires considerably more resource, effort and time, but organizations successfully completing the process will be rewarded with many benefits of transferred best practice.

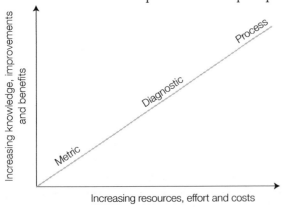

Figure 8.3 **Types of benchmarking**

Metric benchmarking

Many organizations, in both manufacturing and service-based sectors, use metric benchmarking as a means of direct comparison both internally and externally with other organizations. Metrics are performance indicators used as comparative measures. There are many published forms of metric data from which simple comparisons can be drawn, for example league tables published by government agencies or public sector organizations such as (in the UK) the NHS. Another example is the university league tables published by the *Financial Times*. In the manufacturing sector, we have the Best Factory Awards from *Works Management*/Cranfield University.

Metrics are performance indicators used as comparative measures.

Metric benchmarking is often used by companies to make inter-site comparisons using key performance indicators, such as product costs, staffing levels, resources per unit produced, waste or rework levels, stock turnover rates and so on. These can be useful, provided that each site is measured in the same way using like-for-like comparisons. Perhaps the biggest disadvantage of metric benchmarking is that even when it shows a performance gap between two companies, it does not explain how better performance can be achieved.

Example   Xerox and benchmarking

In the early 1980s, Xerox initiated the Leadership through Quality programme, aimed at reducing costs and improving quality within Xerox. When Xerox had benchmarked itself against its Japanese rivals, it found that its products were of lower quality and the lead time between product design and market was considerably higher in comparison with Japanese competitors. Accepting its lack of focus, Xerox introduced the Leadership Through Quality programme, and defined benchmarking as 'the process of measuring its products, services, and practices against its toughest competitors, identifying the gaps and establishing goals. Our goal is always to achieve superiority in quality, product reliability and cost.' Gradually, Xerox developed and successfully implemented its own benchmarking model. Xerox is now considered a world-class player in quality initiatives and its practices have redefined benchmarking standards.

Source: http://www.improvementandinnovation.com/features/project/
benchmarking-how-xerox-regained-its-competitive-edge.

Diagnostic benchmarking

PROBE (PROmoting Business Excellence) is a suite of diagnostic and best practice benchmarking tools, developed by the CBI in conjunction with industry leaders and leading academics in the early 1990s. PROBE helps businesses to understand how their performance and practices compare with world-class companies, by measuring and comparing businesses on world-class performance scales. *Made in Europe* (Hanson et al., 1994) was a large-scale study that compared hundreds of manufacturing organizations across Europe, examining the relationship between practice and performance. The research found that good practice correlated strongly with performance. PROBE has been followed by a number of similar instruments, some of which have been designed for particular industry sectors. Examples include Learning PROBE, developed for use by the further education sector, and Service PROBE, which looks at the components of world-class excellence in the services industry.

CASE STUDY   Foreshore Engineering Ltd

Foreshore Engineering Ltd makes, delivers and installs high value, energy-efficient water, heating and lighting systems for the building industry. Starting from a small base in a small town in north Yorkshire, Foreshore has grown to the point at which it has contracts all over the UK. Last year, the total turnover was £42m, with retained profit of £9.5m.

The vast majority of work comes from fitting these systems in new buildings, especially offices, shops and factories. In recent years, Foreshore has extended its operations into fitting these systems into existing premises, which can be difficult and complex, because Foreshore staff have to operate while work is going on in these premises. Foreshore therefore charges much more for installations in existing working premises than it does for working on new facilities. This area of its work, although a small part of the company's operations at present, is one it wishes to explore and develop further if at all possible.

Foreshore is at the cutting edge of what is still a young industry. By being an early mover, it has secured a strong position in this part of the building and construction industry. However, it is an attractive, growing field, and new companies are coming in all the time.

The company makes the systems to individual order for each customer. Foreshore guarantees its work for five years. The quality of the engineering is very good, and the Foreshore installation builders and engineers have a reputation for cheerfulness as well as expertise. Projects are nearly always delivered on time and to the cost and quality required. Complaints only come in once every two or three months, and when this does happen, each is assessed and put right to the satisfaction of the individual customer. All remedial work takes place by agreement, and, to date, Foreshore has lost no business as the result of customer complaints.

Foreshore is due to be inspected by the Health and Safety Executive (HSE) and the trade federation of which it is a member. It is also due to receive a major visit from a consortium of clients, which, if successful, will lead to major new contracts being awarded.

The HSE and trade federation visits duly came and went, and Foreshore received a clean bill of health from both. They found that the factory and the quality of the work was fine, all the premises were clean, working practices were excellent and staff training was fully in place and rigorously carried out. The only criticism that either had to make was on the comprehensiveness of the documentation, and the factory general manager was given the task of putting this right.

It quickly became clear that this was a crucial task that needed completing before the client consortium asked to see full evidence of the approach to quality management in the production and installation of systems, in the nature of the service delivery, including after-sales and post-installation relationships, and in the management and rectifying of complaints. The factory general manager was not sure how to proceed with this, and so turned to the trade federation for advice.

The trade federation sent in a small team of consultants. The consultants found that everything was being done, but nothing was being recorded. The documentation would not pass a quality audit, and it would not gain any British, European or ISO 9000 accreditation. If Foreshore wanted the new client consortium contracts, it would have to have a full audit and comprehensive documentation. Because of the imminent visit of the consortium, the work would have to be carried out immediately. This would be expensive, in the order of £400,000. However, all things being equal, the standards would be then awarded, which would lead to the new batch of contracts, and would be good for the long-term future of the business.

The Foreshore board of directors met to discuss the matter and, after a brief debate, engaged the consultants to do the quality audit. The consultants found that everything was indeed in order as promised, and the standards were duly awarded. The new client consortium awarded the contracts to Foreshore, and everything returned to normal.

However, events took another turn. First, the consultants wanted Foreshore to benchmark its practices and operations against others in similar lines of work; and they recommended comparison with a specialist motorcycle manufacturer with nearby premises. The consultants also introduced the concept of zero defects, with all that this entailed – no defects in the manufacturing or engineering processes. Most crucially, they stressed the need for 'quality' in customer service and the establishment of standards to which everyone could subscribe.

Having read their report, the factory manager spent the next three days quietly observing things. She found that, in practice, much of the quality side of the work was being managed on an ad hoc basis. The manufacturing and installation leaned heavily on people checking each other's work – there were no procedures. The customer service side had no rules at all – everything was done on a purely reactive basis, which she knew was fine until a crisis happened. However, she also knew that the natural environment that existed within Foreshore meant that there was every likelihood that any attempt to introduce formal procedures would be met with resistance.

Researchers from the Newcastle Business School at Northumbria University developed a scaled-down version of PROBE, called PILOT. It was a questionnaire-based survey instrument, which asked around 50 questions on practice and performance measures, suitable for both manufacturing and service sector organizations. On completion of the questionnaire, the participating organizations received feedback showing them how they compared against other organizations in the area. Like the PROBE analysis, the PILOT study found that good practice correlated strongly with business performance.

Process benchmarking

By far the most involved form of benchmarking, process benchmarking is where the most substantial benefits can be found. The focus is on any key business process that has been identified as an area for improvement.

Fundamental to the success of process benchmarking is the recognition that many organizations have functions that use generically similar business processes, regardless of sector or industry type. Thus one main advantage of process benchmarking is that businesses need not restrict themselves to observing practices in companies that are considered direct competition. Most business organizations issue invoices, collect payables (debts), appoint new people and so on and these types of 'generic' activities can be benchmarked regardless of industry.

Benchmarking activities can be widened to include partners from different sectors and this can enable completely new ways of working to be identified. This can lead to significant improvements in operating efficiency across industrial sectors.

Process benchmarking can be divided into four stages:

1   Understanding the nature and complexity of the business processes that are to be benchmarked. This requires careful process mapping and measurement of process metrics.

2   Identifying potential and willing benchmarking partners – not always a straightforward task as some corporate cultures resist 'opening up' to outside organizations.

3   Data collection and measurement. It is important to ensure that processes are compared on a like-for-like basis.

4   Implementation of change and transfer of best practice for a given process. This is not always easy because cultural, demographic or technological barriers may present unforeseen problems.

For test questions, extra case studies, audio case studies, weblinks, videolinks and more to help you understand the topics covered in this chapter, visit our companion website at www.palgrave.com/business/campbell.

VOCAB CHECKLIST FOR ESL STUDENTS

Baseline
Blacksmiths
Brainstorming
Commensurate
Compartmentalized
Conformance
Consortium
Diagnostic

Extrinsic
Flowchart
Flushness (refers to straightness of edges. See 'plumb' in 'plumb line')
Histogram
Interdepartmental
Metrics

Proliferation
Remedial
Role model
Scatter plot (see 'scatter diagram')
Tangible
Testimony
Transformational

Definitions for these terms can be found in the 'Vocab Zone' of the companion website, which provides free access to the Macmillan English Dictionary online at www.palgrave.com/business/campbell.

REVIEW QUESTIONS

1   Explain what is meant by the term 'quality' and 'total quality management'.
2   Describe the EFQM model and explain the difference between enablers and results.
3   Explain how benchmarking may help an organization improve its quality regime.

DISCUSSION TOPIC

Statistical techniques for improving quality, like Six Sigma, are a fad. What is important is people. Discuss.

HOT TOPICS – Research project areas to investigate

For your research project, why not investigate …

- … whether lean sigma can be applied to a voluntary organization.
- … what consumers in the luxury car market believe constitutes good quality.
- … how organizations measure the quality of their processes.

Recommended reading

Badri, M.A., Davis, D. and Davis, D. (1995) 'A study of measuring the critical factors of quality management', *International Journal of Quality & Reliability Management*, **12**(2): 36–53.

Black, S.A. and Porter, L.J. (1996) 'Identification of the CSFs of TQM', *Decision Sciences*, **27**(1): 1–21.

Breyfogle, F.W. III, Cupello, J.M. and Meadows, B. (2001) *Managing Six Sigma*, New York: John Wiley.

Davis, A. (2003) 'Six Sigma for small companies', *Troy*, **42**(11): 20.

Ghobadian, A. and Gallear, D. (1997) 'TQM and organisation size', *International Journal of Operations & Production Management*, **17**(2): 121–63.

Harry, M. and Schroeder, R. (2000) *Six Sigma: The Breakthrough Management Strategy Revolutionizing the World's Top Corporations*, New York: Random House.

Hoerl, R. (1998) 'Six Sigma and the future of the quality profession', *Quality Progress*, **35**(1): 35–42.

Klefsjo, B., Wiklund, H. and Edgeman, R.L. (2001) 'Six Sigma seen as a methodology for TQM', *Measuring Business Excellence*, **5**(1): 31–5.

Lee, G.L. and Oakes, I. (1995) 'The pros and cons of TQM for smaller forms in manufacturing: some experiences down the supply chain', *Total Quality Management*, **6**(4): 413–26.

McAdam, R. (2000) 'Quality models in an SME context: a critical perspective using a grounded approach', *International Journal of Quality & Reliability Management*, **17**(3): 305–23.

Yusof, S.M. and Aspinwall, E. (2000) 'TQM implementation: issues, review and case study', *International Journal of Operations & Production Management*, **20**(6): 634–55.

Chapter references

CBI (Confederation of British Industry) (1997) *Fit for the Future, How Competitive is British Manufacturing?*, London: CBI, http://webarchive.nationalarchives.gov.uk/+/http://www.dti.gov.uk/comp/competitive/wh_int1.htm.

EFQM (European Foundation for Quality Management) (2010a) *The EFQM Excellence Model*, Brussels: EFQM.

EFQM (European Foundation for Quality Management) (2010b) *The Fundamental Concepts of Excellence*, Brussels: EFQM.

Garvin, D.A. (1987) 'Competing on the eight dimensions of quality', *Harvard Business Review*, November–December: 108–9.

Hanson, P., Voss, C., Blackmon, K. and Oak, B. (1994) *Made in Europe: A Four Nations Best Practice Study*, London: IBM UK/London Business School.

Imai, M. (1986) *Kaizen: The Key to Japan's Competitive Success*, New York: McGraw-Hill.

Oakland, J.S. (1993) *Total Quality Management: The Route to Improving Performance* (2nd edn), Oxford: Butterworth-Heinemann.

Oakland, J.S. (2003) *TQM: Text with Cases* (3rd edn), Oxford: Butterworth-Heinemann.

Oakland, J.S. (2004) *Oakland on Quality Management*, Oxford: Butterworth-Heinemann.

Pande, P.S., Neuman, R.P. and Cavanagh, R.R. (2000) *The Six Sigma Way*, New York: McGraw-Hill.

CHAPTER 9

ETHICS AND CSR IN INTERNATIONAL BUSINESS

OUTLINE OF THE CHAPTER

Introduction

Managing global business activities: what are the ethical challenges?

◻ Ethical capacity and the company
◻ Ethical choices from the start
◻ Ethical challenges as the business grows

How has thinking on corporate purpose changed?

Business–society relations: concepts and theories

◻ Corporate social responsibility (CSR)
◻ Corporate social performance
◻ Corporate citizenship
◻ Stakeholder management theory

Social contract theories

Political CSR: does democratic theory offer new insights?

Applying ethical theories in international business

◻ Ethics and law: mutually reinforcing
◻ Ethical theories in the business context

Conclusions

ETHICAL THEMES IN THIS CHAPTER

◻ Moral rules and cultural divergence
◻ Businesses as part of society

THE AIMS OF THIS CHAPTER ARE TO

◻ Identify ethical challenges in global business
◻ Appreciate the role of business in society
◻ Relate CSR principles to international business in differing societies
◻ Apply ethical theories in international business

H&M: CAN THE CHAMPION OF CHEAP FASHION ALSO BE ETHICAL?

Hennes & Mauritz, better known by its brand, H&M, is a fashion retailer founded in Sweden which has grown to become a global leader in the 'fast fashion' sector. The rise of Spain's Inditex (owner of Zara) in this sector has now seen H&M drop to second place globally. Fast fashion has been driven by the mastery of global supply chains by these large companies. The time required to produce a garment, from the design phase through to delivery to outlets, has been reduced to only a few weeks in some cases. Sourcing raw materials in volume and production in low-cost environments are key to these companies' success. Inditex sources much production in Europe and North Africa. H&M has relied largely on Asian suppliers, which are more distant from European markets, but claims to be as fast as Inditex (Milne, 2013b). However, H&M prides itself on much more than fast fashion. It has sought to establish itself as a champion of sustainability in a sector which would seem to contradict the very values associated with sustainability.

Photo 9.1 *H&M stores are a familiar feature of shopping centres, but the ethical challenges of 'fast fashion' remain unresolved. (© iStock.com/JenGrantham)*

These values include ethical sourcing, concerns for health and safety, concerns for environmental protection and human rights. The textile industry has notoriously relied on cheap labour in poor countries such as Bangladesh, where legal regulation of working conditions is weak. In Bangladesh, unsafe conditions were dramatically brought to the public's attention by the collapse of the Rana Plaza which took the lives of nearly 1,200 people in 2013. As the largest customer of the Bangladesh garment factories, H&M attracted much media attention. Its garments were not produced in the Rana Plaza building, as its code of conduct prohibits doing business with manufacturers in residential buildings. Nonetheless, H&M has been quick to sign up to the accord on fire and safety which has been one of the initiatives launched in the wake of the disaster. It is also rethinking its supply chain strategy in light of its sustainability goals.

H&M has produced CSR reports since 2002, all of which highlight the difficulties of dealing with manufacturers in low-wage countries where it is difficult to monitor conditions. From 2009, the report has been titled the 'sustainability report', possibly suggesting a more environmental focus. The 2012 sustainability report lists seven commitments (H&M, 2013a). Serving customers and working with partner firms in manufacturing are the first two. The third is 'be ethical'. The next three are environmental: climate change policies, recycling, and using natural resources responsibly. The last one is to 'strengthen communities'.

H&M has been at the forefront in its sustainability policies. It is the world's biggest user of organic cotton in manufacturing, and aims to increase its use of organic cotton, as well as to promote more sustainable practices in conventional cotton production. But its huge and increasing demand for cotton seems in contradiction with sustainability goals. A cotton garment could conceivably last for many years. But underlying the company's strategy is the fact that customers view fashion items as having a short lifespan. One of H&M's responses is a garment collecting scheme, introduced in 2012, which encourages customers to return old clothes to the stores for recycling. In European stores, customers bringing old clothes are given a voucher for 15% discount off new purchases. The scheme thus relies on incentives which encourage further purchases. The old clothes are recycled, but, as sceptics point out, textile recycling is very limited (Balch, 2013).

Under its ethical policies it highlights transparency, integrity, honesty and human rights. In fact, under its second commitment, on relations with manufacturers, it highlights many ethical issues, such as overtime and wages. It has stressed human rights in earlier reports, highlighting these same issues. In the 2012 report, these processes are subjected to a rating system, from 'started', to 'more to do', to 'on track'. Higher wages, reduction in overtime and health improvements are all rated in the middle category, 'more to do'. These issues have been in the company's Code of Conduct for suppliers for many years, and it is something of an admission that little progress seems to have been made. In the 2012 report, it concedes, overtime 'remains a core issue' (H&M, 2013a: 43). The nature of fast fashion requires rapid responses and filling orders quickly. Ethical principles are difficult to implement in practice, given the existence of hundreds of different suppliers. For 2012, H&M took the further step of making public the list of suppliers in the report. H&M also takes a stand against corruption, noting that corrupt 'facilitation payments' for shipments are common in the sector. A prohibition on such payments was included in its Code of Conduct in 2012.

The head of sustainability at H&M stresses that 'we can make a difference to hundreds of thousands of people working in our supply chain' (H&M, 2013b). She goes on to say that there are structural issues associated with the supply chain which would require an industry response. Many western brand owners, both luxury and mass-market, use the same manufacturing companies. She says, 'the truth is that the price of a garment does not tell us much about how it is produced' (H&M, 2013b). H&M's CEO confirms this observation, saying that they see medium to luxury brands in the same factories, but these charge 10, 20, or even 100 times more than H&M (Milne, 2013a). H&M itself has a number of brands, including new brands such as COS (Collection of Style) aimed at the more upmarket customer.

In common with other Swedish companies, H&M is a family-dominated business. Its current CEO, Karl-Johan Persson, is the third generation of his family, his grandfather having founded the firm in 1947. H&M's IPO was in 1974, on the Swedish stock exchange, where it is the country's largest listed company. There are two classes of shares, the A shares carrying ten times the voting strength of the B shares. The Persson family own 38% of the shares, but control nearly 70% of the vote. Although the company's business is fast fashion, which has a short-term perspective, its CEO takes a long-term perspective on the family business.

Figure 1 *H&M's expansion*

Number of stores

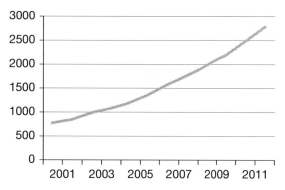

Source of data: H&M (2013) *Annual Report 2012*, p. 40 at www.about.hm.com (18/09/14).

The company has expanded aggressively in the past decade, increasing the number of stores by 10–15% each year (see figure), even following the financial crisis of 2008. The number of stores increased by 304 in 2012, and ten countries have been added in the past two years. There are now 2,800 stores in 48 countries. The first H&M store to open in the southern hemisphere was in Chile in 2013, and the CEO foresees expansion in Latin America. He is also thinking about production in Latin America or possibly Africa. Although this rethink is not necessarily linked with the disaster in Bangladesh, he is aware of the challenges. The company has invested in improving worker conditions in Bangladesh and has supported rises in wages. But it cannot guarantee labour conditions which conform to its stated policies. Its head of sustainability says of 'guaranteeing' labour conditions, 'Of course we cannot when we are such a huge company operating in very challenging conditions' (H&M, 2013b). She goes on, 'Remember that H&M does not own any factories itself. We are to some extent dependent on the suppliers – it is impossible to be in full control' (H&M, 2013b). These admissions acknowledge the bigger issue, which is the business model itself, which has been called 'the elephant in the fitting room – a business model predicated on producing millions of units and of a fashion cycle that favours 30–50 trend-driven fashion seasons a year' (Siegle, 2012). H&M's branded production amounts to over 500 million garments a year, and it produces none of them itself. The CEO invites consumers to ask themselves the following when shopping: 'Is this a decent company that acts in a responsible way?' (Milne, 2013a).

Sources: H&M (2013a) *Conscious Actions Sustainability Report 2012*, at www.about.hm.com; H&M (2013b) *Interview with Helena Helmersson, Head of Sustainability*, at www.about.hm.com; Milne, R. (2013a) 'A defender of fast fashion', *Financial Times*, 20 May; Milne, R. (2013b) 'H&M rethinks sourcing policy', *Financial Times*, 20 May; Siegle, L. (2012) 'Is H&M the new home of ethical fashion?', *The Observer*, 7 April; Balch, O. (2013) 'H&M: can fast fashion and sustainability ever really mix?', *The Guardian*, 3 May, at www.theguardian.com (18/09/14).

DISCUSSION QUESTIONS

▫ **What ethical issues stand out in the case study?**

   ▫ **The 'elephant in the fitting room' is the business model of fast fashion. To what extent has H&M overcome the ethical challenges in fast fashion?**

      ▫ **Look at the question posed by the CEO at the end of the case study. Would you buy clothes from H&M? Why?**

INTRODUCTION

In this chapter, ethical concepts and theories are applied in a variety of international business settings. Modern discourse on business ethics focuses particularly on the relationship between business and society. Large MNEs typically operate in numerous societies. They do more than merely 'exist', however: they are active forces in economic life and often active forces in governance and the shaping of legislation. While these are potentially forces for the public good, companies can also have negative impacts in societies, perpetuating poor working conditions and environmental degradation. What is more, they often take legal steps to avoid regulatory hurdles and minimize liabilities such as tax. Globalization has been the driver of much of this global scanning. Corporate profits have benefited, but critics among consumer, environmental and employee groups have raised ethical criticisms.

These criticisms have led to widespread rethinking of ethics in business. Numerous recent theorists have addressed these issues of business–society relations, bringing in the role of governments and regulation. In this chapter, we look at recent theories of corporate social responsibility (CSR), corporate citizenship and stakeholder management, with a view to applying them in the current world of globalized supply chains. We also take into account the rise of emerging economies with state-guided industries and a proliferation of state-controlled companies. Ethics might seem to be overshadowed in the rapid developments of the global economy. However, we find the contrary is true. Ordinary people are more and more concerned with basic issues like integrity of corporate leaders, decent work practices, humane working conditions and ethical sourcing.

MANAGING GLOBAL BUSINESS ACTIVITIES: WHAT ARE THE ETHICAL CHALLENGES?

Ethics is about consciously making distinctions between right and wrong and following them through in practice. Ethical behaviour rests on applying values that have a universality which transcends the numerous cultural environments in which an international business might be involved. This is a broad view of the sphere of ethics, encompassing businesses as well as individuals. When managers are asked about their ethics, it is not uncommon to point to the staff's code of ethical conduct, and how effectively wrongdoers within the firm are held to account for activities such as harassing other staff or falsifying expenses. Although matters such as staff honesty and transparent advertising are important in the overall picture, they are only part of that picture.

ETHICAL CAPACITY AND THE COMPANY

While it is generally accepted that a natural person has moral capacity, moral capacity of a company is often contested (Wartick and Cochran, 1985). The company is sometimes said to be merely an association which is 'amoral', capable of neither right nor wrong. It is made up of real people, however. A natural person has a conscience and will, but, it is argued, a company, which is a separate artificial entity, does not. This view that companies are some-how above standards of right and wrong has gained ground in conjunction with the view of the company as solely an economic entity which acts in pursuit of the self-interest of its owners. Advocates of this view say the company exists for economic purposes only, and cannot legitimately be judged on ethical or social criteria. They do accept, however, that companies are subject to law, and can be faced with penalties for legal wrongdoing. There are large bodies of corporate law in most countries, which recognize the company as a distinct legal entity, for example, for tax and regulatory purposes. But there is also a grow-ing amount of evidence that the company is not an ethical and social 'black box' separate from those who run it.

The company in law is an artificial person, or 'juridical' person, which has a separate exis-tence from the people who set it up, its directors and shareholders (see Chapter 5). The company has perpetual existence, which carries on despite changes in owners and managers. The company has no independent will: it acts only in the ways which real people dictate. Because of limited liability, they are not generally liable for its debts, but if fraud is committed in the company's name, they can become personally liable. Company directors are often accused of wrongs committed by the company, and face the consequences, even though, in some cases, they personally have not been involved. As we have seen in Chapter 5, where there is a serious wrong such as insider dealing, the company incurs a fine, and the guilty directors can go to jail. But recall the discrepancy in the case where the company admitted crimes of insider dealing, while its leading trader claimed innocence.

When moral wrongs are committed by the company, consumers are quick to blame the executives. And in practice, many directors accept responsibility. This is largely because of potential damage to corporate reputation, of course, which can impact on profits if consumers feel so strongly that they stop buying from them. Economic goals themselves are thus not as unambiguous as they might seem to those who rely on assumptions of rational self-interest driving the company.

ETHICAL CHOICES FROM THE START

Ethical challenges affect all aspects of the business: how it makes products, how it organ-izes people and how it respects the environment. An entrepreneur with a business idea

Figure 9.1 *Ethical choices start with the birth of the business*

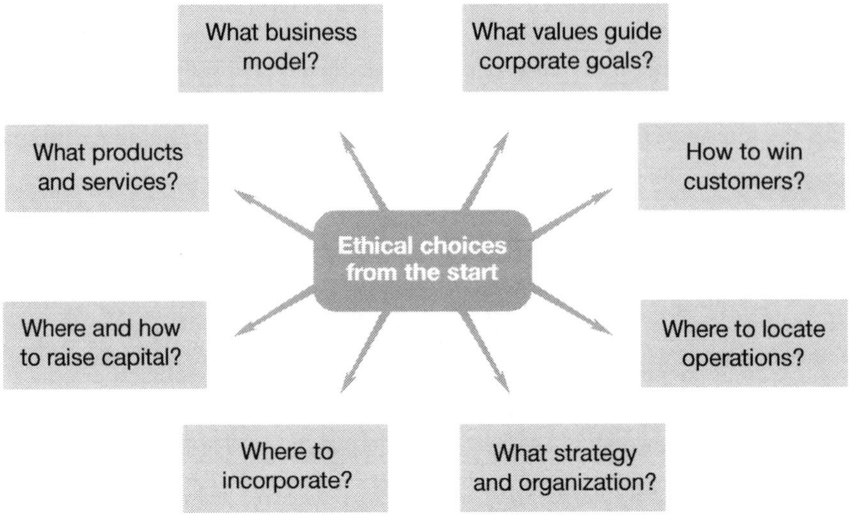

faces numerous choices in getting the enterprise up and running. These choices are laden with ethical implications. Indeed, ethical challenges arise even before the business is founded. Entrepreneurs must address a range of questions in which some of the alternatives are superior on ethical grounds than others. These ethical choices are shown in Figure 9.1.

Perhaps the most influential of the questions posed in Figure 9.1 is the nature of the business model, as answers to other questions flow from it. Many new businesses originate in the highly competitive high-tech sector, relying on innovative ideas to launch either products or services. The company in this sector is likely to envisage a core set of key employees as the creative heart of the organization, and rely on outsourced manufacturing for products such as high-tech devices. But a business model based on outsourced manufacturing in advantageous locations such as Asia raises ethical questions over working conditions and human rights. A closely related question which must be addressed is core values. What matters most to the founders? Great, innovative products which delight customers in all markets? Most technology entrepreneurs would probably identify with this goal, and most people would consider it worthy. After all, the products are good because they are bringing real benefits to users, improving people's daily lives. But this goal, ostensibly laudable in principle, is more problematic when applied in the real global competitive environment. Smartphones and other high-tech devices are almost all manufactured in low-cost, outsourced manufacturing environments. Brand owners who do not manufacture their own products are good examples of globalization in practice. Producing great

Making money for owners is at the heart of the capitalist business.

products is a means of generating wealth for the insiders in the company. Making money for owners is at the heart of the capitalist business. This in itself does not make it unethical, but how far is too far for entrepreneurs to go in seeking to maximize profits?

Global choices of location come into play for every aspect of the business. Where to register the company is one, as laws on disclosure, financial reporting, taxation and governance come into the equation. It used to be assumed that corporate founders would register their business as a company in the country where they founded it, or in the individual state in the US. But this has ceased to be the case. Countries now present themselves as advantageous locations for companies, offering minimal regulation, light taxes and legal protection of owners' controlling rights. The British government states that it is 'committed to creating the most competitive tax regime in the G20' (Schmidt, 2013). The G20 is a loose grouping of advanced and emerging countries, which meets to air issues of common concern, but has no legal authority over governments (see Note 1). In the US, the state of Delaware has become the favoured jurisdiction for registering companies. Similarly, when the founders think of listing the company, they can choose a stock exchange which is similarly advantageous. As was discussed in Chapter 5, the company need not be active in either the country of registration or the country of listing. But, as Figure 9.1 suggests, these decisions in fact present ethical challenges. In ethical terms, it seems wrong for a company to carry on business activities in a country, but register itself offshore and shift profits offshore in order to reduce tax burdens. Companies can register subsidiaries in tax havens for this purpose, and also use charitable foundations for ownership purposes due to their advantageous tax positions. The charity, of course, is founded on a worthy cause, but, as we have seen in Chapter 3, charitable forms can be used as an umbrella to cover a range of other activities which serve self-interested purposes of individuals.

PAUSE TO CONSIDER...

If you were launching a company, would you do either of the following, and why?

a. Register the company in a Caribbean tax haven
b. Outsource manufacturing to a low-cost Asian country

ETHICAL CHALLENGES AS THE BUSINESS GROWS

A start-up is likely to focus on a few core products or services at the outset, and keep decision-making concentrated on the founders and their associates. It is likely to be looking at targeting multiple markets as the firm grows. As Figure 9.2 shows, in a global environment, opportunities are greater than ever.

Global corporate strategy constantly reviews location advantages and disadvantages as they change over time. We have seen in the first part of this book how low-cost manufacturing environments find their comparative advantages difficult to sustain. There are inevitable pressures on factory owners to improve conditions and wages of workers, which send up costs. And government incentives which might have helped in the early stages of setting up operations eventually run out. Other locations with lower wages are sought. New suppliers also come on the scene. It is not long before a company starts to think about how it can extend success in one product range to other products or services which are complementary, especially if it is building a strong brand. It might also diversify into other businesses as opportunities arise.

Organizationally, the MNE enjoys the flexibility to set up subsidiaries and invest in affiliate companies, which help to spread both opportunities and also dilute risks. But new businesses present new risks, and also raise ethical challenges. Much financial thought goes into a company's decision to establish subsidiaries or branch offices in a new location. A subsidiary is a separately registered company, subject to national law where it is registered, whereas in many countries a branch office is not subject to the same regulation. It also follows that the subsidiary established in an offshore location offers advantages for receiving profits and

A nondescript building in Wilmington, Delaware is the registered address of 278,000 companies.

Figure 9.2 *Encountering ethical challenges as the business grows*

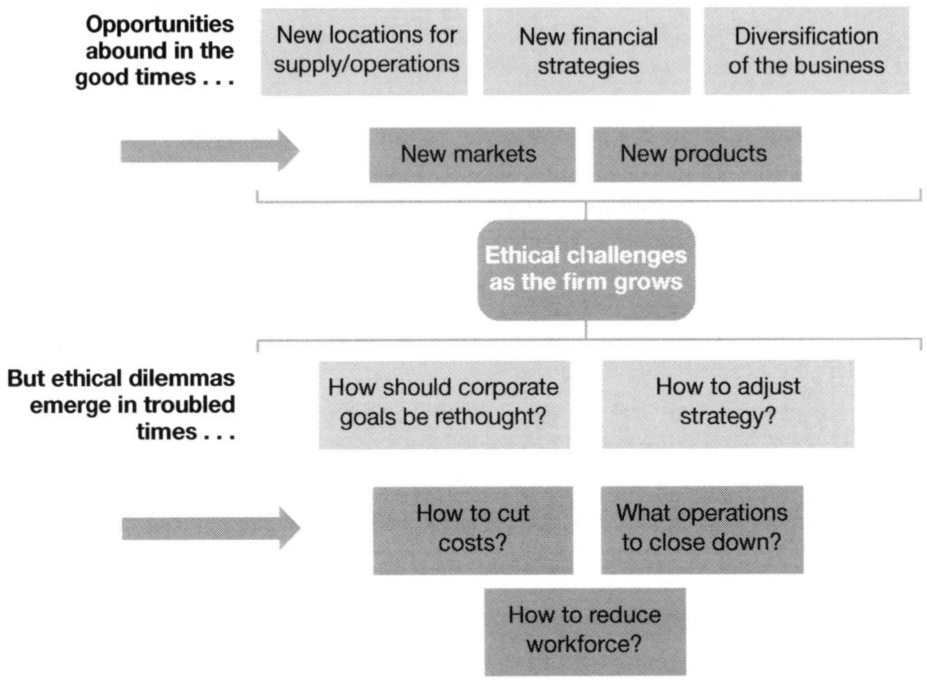

Opportunities abound in the good times . . .

New locations for supply/operations

New financial strategies

Diversification of the business

New markets

New products

Ethical challenges as the firm grows

But ethical dilemmas emerge in troubled times . . .

How should corporate goals be rethought?

How to adjust strategy?

How to cut costs?

What operations to close down?

How to reduce workforce?

royalties, as we have seen in Chapter 5. A nondescript building in Wilmington, Delaware is the registered address of 278,000 companies. Such subsidiaries exist on paper, but might have little real existence and hardly any employees. The function they serve is nonetheless valuable, potentially 'saving' millions in tax. Shifting from one manufacturing centre to another to cut costs invites accusations that the firm pays little heed to ethical standards. While workers in an outsourced factory are not employed by the brand owner, consumers are nowadays likely to see the brand owner as at least partly responsible for their conditions, as we discuss later in this chapter.

Just as expansion presents challenges, so does the necessity to deal with downturns and shocks to the business, as shown in Figure 9.2. Companies which run into difficulties financially or find their products have been overtaken by rivals in the marketplace face challenges in turning around performance. But as cost-cutting is involved, decisions must be made about where to trim costs, including employees and even whole units. No firm likes to lay off staff, and employment laws offer some protection to workers in most countries. The ethical firm will respond to a crisis with transparency and even-handedness, helping workers to find employment in other sections of the organization. Indeed, this is a legal requirement in some countries. Such a firm views employees as stakeholders and is also likely to have a sense of social responsibility. But many firms profess to take social responsibility seriously and nonetheless proceed with downsizing on purely economic considerations. This gives the impression that managers consider CSR desirable 'if we can afford it'. Viewed as a cost, CSR gives way to 'bottom line' considerations which appear in accounts.

Many of the troubles that arise are difficult to foresee and plan for. These include natural disasters and government action. But some spectacular corporate failures have resulted from managerial negligence, over-risky financial strategies or misconduct within the company. Banks and other financial services companies highlighted in Chapter 5 are examples. There are others, including energy trader, Enron, which collapsed in 2001. As became well known in the aftermath of the Enron scandal, the company had a CSR policy and code of ethical conduct which looked impeccable on paper (Beecher-Monas, 2003). But in practice, these turned out to be worthless. A superficially ethical approach which has little bearing in reality can undermine general public confidence in corporate communications. When corporate scandals erupt, consumers are now accustomed to firms putting out statements that they take law and ethics very seriously, and that what happened is an aberration. These firms assure the public that they simply need to tighten their systems so that there is no repetition. But consumers are justifiably sceptical. Nike assured consumers along these lines in the 1990s, when they were accused of tolerating sweatshop labour practices, but there were further scandals. BP, which had a record of safety lapses, similarly assured the world that there would be no repeats after a serious refinery fire in 2005, but the Macondo oil spill in the Gulf of Mexico followed in 2010. Is the capitalist enterprise essentially one of profit maximization, in which ethical considerations are an add-on?

HOW HAS THINKING ON CORPORATE PURPOSE CHANGED?

We found in Chapter 5 that companies such as Google are forthright and unapologetic in stating that they are doing nothing wrong in shifting profits to low-tax jurisdictions. Indeed, they assert that they are taking legal obligations seriously, reminding critics that they owe an obligation to shareholders to maximize profits. Google is a public company, having listed in 2004. It exemplifies the shareholder primacy model, reflecting the view that the capitalist company exists for maximizing returns to shareholders as owners. This is also called the economic model of the company because of its primary aim to make money. The shareholder focus itself involves multiple interests, some in conflict with each other, as we will discuss in the next chapter on corporate governance. Hence, the 'economic model' is perhaps a more accurate way of identifying this type of company, serving to contrast its profit-maximizing purpose with CSR perspectives. The rise of the economic model to a position of supremacy is a fairly recent development, dating from the 1970s. Before then, the mix of capitalist enterprise and social purposes was a subject of lively debate which has been rather overshadowed in today's finance-driven business environment. Here, we revive the arguments about corporate purpose afresh, with a view to seeing how recent theory on CSR and stakeholders fits into a continuing debate.

Many decades ago, it was common for companies, when asked what purposes they serve, to reply with a list of goals which revealed corporate values (Stout, 2012). Although producing great products would be included, also included were providing employment, improving people's lives, and contributing to the community. In the post-war period of rapid growth in the US, the founder of the retailer, Sears, listed four parties in the business in order of importance: customers, employees, community and stockholders (Clarkson, 1995). He said that if the needs of the first three are looked after, then profits will flow to stockholders. The 1920s and 30s in the US was an era of vibrant academic debate on the nature of the company in society. Up to then, companies had been mainly private companies, owned and controlled like personal property. By the 1920s, American companies had grown large and had become public corporations with numerous small shareholders who played no role in running the company. These corporate giants controlled large amounts of wealth, which led to a view that the existence of many small shareholders turned these companies into social institutions with responsibilities to the public (Bratton, 2001). With the stock market crash of 1929 and the ensuing Great Depression, government intervention on grounds of public welfare became accepted, and corporations were seen as part of this effort (Bratton, 2001).

A famous debate took place in the 1930s, between a leading corporate law specialist, Adolph Berle, who championed shareholder primacy, and Merrick Dodd, a corporate law professor who held that the corporation is 'an economic institution which has a social service as well as profit-making function' (Stout, 2012: 17). Social legislation in the form of the New Deal dates from this period. It included social security, housing regulation, recognition of trade unions, and labour standards. Regulatory frameworks such as the Securities and Exchange Commission date from this period. So too do government subsidies of agriculture, designed to support farming livelihoods (see Chapter 6). Although these programmes were considered 'liberal' in the American context and were opposed by supporters of the Republican Party, many endured and continue to exist to this day. However, in mainstream corporate thinking, the trend was in the opposite direction.

From the 1970s, largely under the influence of the Chicago School of neoclassical economics, led by Milton Friedman, the ideas of shareholder primacy and profit maximization became the predominant view of the purpose of the company.

Friedman believed that making money is the company's only legitimate goal.

Friedman believed that making money is the company's only legitimate goal, subject to basic legal and ethical constraints imposed by society. When the company spends money on social purposes, it is, in effect, acting illegitimately, as it takes away wealth which is due to shareholders (Wartick and Cochran, 1985). This economic paradigm gained a grip on thinking in academic scholarship as well as in business practice. Its academic influence extended from economics to law and management. The manager, according to this orthodoxy, should follow market indicators, referring back to utilitarian assumptions and also libertarian views of economic freedom (Ostas, 2001). Faith in markets was central to this model, and share price became a convenient measure of corporate value, allowing comparative performance to be assessed between companies and over time. The theory chimes with classical economic theory, going back to the foundations of capitalism. As we have seen in Chapter 2, the pursuit of rational self-interest has a theoretical simplicity and objectivity. The neoclassical economists of the Chicago School went further, however, in defence of profit-maximizing behaviour. Not only was profit maximization legitimate, they asserted that it was imposed by law (Stout, 2012). In response, lawyers in both the US and UK stress that this view of the company's obligation is wrong in law. In both the US and UK, legal duties are owed to the company itself, not to individual shareholders or to shareholders as a whole (Kay, 2013). But the view of legal obligations to shareholders has been accepted uncritically in both academic and business circles nonetheless. So assured were adherents of the shareholder-oriented model that theirs was the only valid model of the public corporation, that it was seen as universally applicable (Stout, 2012).

However, other interpretations of corporate purpose, though overshadowed, had not disappeared. Evidence abounded of corporations' activities in social and political life in the US, suggesting that companies at an empirical level engage in active roles in society. Even in the 1970s, there was considerable legislative activity in the US in areas of equal opportunities, health and safety, environmental protection and consumer product safety. In all these areas, companies are involved in applying the law, thus becoming part of the structure of social life. One could say that these activities are consistent with the economic model, which accepts that companies have legal obligations. But they are also active in lobbying (see Chapter 3), suggesting a more active role in shaping public policy. Their activities are mainly directed at reducing regulatory burdens, but, whatever their motives, they are playing social roles. Any company which has employees and physical operations exists in a social and ethical context, whatever the country. The development of a coherent body of theory on social purpose and ethical business practices has grown up over the last several decades, recognizing this fuller picture of the business in society.

The neoclassical approach to corporate purpose has been undermined by a succession of market failures, the largest of which was the financial crash of 2008, which call into question its assumptions about markets operating efficiently (see Chapters 2 and 5). It has been challenged from outside its heartlands by the evolution of different approaches to the corporation in countries where market reforms are taking place in the absence of foundations in individualist cultures or capitalist economic development. One of the older of these is Japan, which has a long history of recognizing social responsibility as an essential aspect of corporate culture. More recently, there are post-communist countries, such as Russia, the states of the former Soviet Union, and states in Central and Eastern Europe. In China, market reforms are taking place in the context of continuing domination of the Communist Party. Capitalist enterprises abound in all these countries, and many are listed on stock exchanges. However, despite legal forms which look similar, these companies have differing views on the role of the company in society. State-owned enterprises, also listed on stock exchanges, are explicitly associated with social and political goals, as well as economic activities, with a focus on guided economic development (see Chapters 2 and 3). The idea of the company as an independent economic entity grew up in liberal market economies, giving rise to a perceived dichotomy between the company on the one hand, and government intervention on the other. This rather polarized way of thinking was characteristic of neoclassical economic theory. It is much less relevant in economies where the state is perceived as guiding development and is seen as a good thing in that role. But even in liberal economies, it has become evident that 'business and society are interwoven, rather than distinct entities' (Wood, 1991: 695).

PAUSE TO CONSIDER...

Although the Berle–Dodd debate on shareholder primacy vs social purpose took place in the 1930s, the topic is highly relevant today. What points would be made on each side in a modern re-run of their famous debate?

BUSINESS–SOCIETY RELATIONS: CONCEPTS AND THEORIES

Interactions between business and society have been the focus of theories in a number of academic areas which attempt to move beyond the economic model. As noted already, lawyers have been active. Some have looked at the concepts in legal and economic contexts (Ostas, 2001). Management theories have explored CSR as a concept and also how it can be applied in practice, through corporate social performance (CSP) (Wood, 1991). Economists have contributed to questioning the economic orthodoxy in terms of stakeholder interests (Preston and Sapienza, 1990). In this section, we look at three of these theories.

CORPORATE SOCIAL RESPONSIBILITY (CSR)

Corporate social responsibility (CSR) as a concept rests on the idea that the company has a broader range of responsibilities in society than merely economic obligations. These responsibilities 'rest on an ethical understanding of the organization's responsibility for the impact of its business activities' (Maon et al., 2009). The range of responsibilities has been set out by Carroll in a model of CSR which comprises economic, legal, ethical and philanthropic responsibilities. Carroll's pyramid model, shown in Figure 9.3, suggests an order of priority among the four components of CSR. His model has served to lay the conceptual groundwork of CSR, and has become a basis on which later theories have been built.

Carroll begins with economic responsibilities, including generating profits, maintaining a strong competitive position and maintaining a high level of efficiency. Without economic success, the company will falter, but Carroll notes the transformation of 'profit motive' into 'profit maximization'. Set against this dominant paradigm was a growing body of literature which highlighted the importance of the company in the social environment. His analysis of legal and ethical responsibilities is more nuanced than appears in the figure itself, which suggests entirely separate categories. Both 'embody ethical norms', he points out, and represent expectations of those in society (Carroll, 1991: 41). Legal responsibilities, including a broad duty to obey the law, rest on expectations of obedience. The phenomenon of firms obeying the letter of the law, but managing to get round the legislators' intent has always been a challenge for law-makers, and is highlighted in a more recent article co-authored by Carroll, which points out the opportunistic attitude of some companies (Schwartz and Carroll, 2003). Recently, tax avoidance has attracted much negative

Figure 9.3 *Carroll's pyramid of CSR*

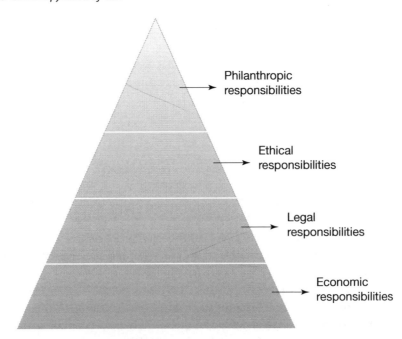

Source: adapted from Carroll, A.B. (1991) 'The Pyramid of Corporate Social Responsibility: Toward the Moral Management of Organizational Stakeholders', *Business Horizons*, 34: 39–48, at p. 42.

media attention. Carroll stresses that it is important for a company to be a law-abiding corporate citizen. In Carroll's CSR typology, corporate citizenship relates to three of the sets of responsibilities: legal, ethical and philanthropic. Carroll has also contributed a theory of corporate citizenship, which rests on the same four sets of responsibilities as his CSR pyramid, suggesting that he sees these concepts as interchangeable (Carroll, 1998). Corporate citizenship, however, implies that the company is a member of society in a way analogous to a human being, which is rather more precise than simply a social role, as will be discussed below.

Carroll sees ethical responsibilities in a number of different perspectives. Environmental concerns, civil rights and consumer protection are highlighted as areas where ethical concerns are voiced, and followed up by legal enactment. There is thus a dynamic interaction between law and ethical principles. Businesses are expected to meet 'newly emerging values and norms' (Carroll, 1991: 41). He also distinguishes between moral values of groups in society and the ethical principles of moral philosophy. Recall the opening case study of Chapter 4, on the death penalty in the US. The death penalty is legal in numerous individual states, but some companies are refusing on ethical grounds to supply the drugs used in killing people. The US Supreme Court has taken a view that the law reflects changing ethical norms in society, rather than transcendent ethical principles. Carroll says that businesspeople are constantly being pushed to higher ethical standards than required by law.

Similarly, companies are fulfilling expectations of society when they give to charities and take part in charitable activities. Philanthropic responsibilities, the final element of the pyramid, represent discretionary spending by the company on items like cultural goods, which improve the quality of life in communities. These activities, too, are said to be those of the good corporate citizen. Carroll says that contributions to charities are not an ethical obligation. Companies often contribute money, facilities and time to charities, but if they do not, they are not regarded as unethical organizations. He notes a growing trend among companies to equate corporate citizenship with charitable giving. This narrow interpretation, he says, is not a socially responsible approach. The three other elements of CSR are more important than philanthropy, which is merely the 'icing on the cake' (Carroll, 1991: 42). In Carroll's later re-working of his CSR theory, he omits philanthropy as a separate level, highlighting the three main 'domains' of CSR (Schwartz and Carroll, 2003). His later view is that philanthropy is probably now an aspect of ethical responsibilities, as it is expected by society, rather than merely discretionary. Nonetheless, it is helpful to retain philanthropy as a separate category, as it differs in essence from other aspects of ethical responsibilities, for the reasons given by Carroll in his original pyramid model. Society might expect companies to give to charities, but responses to expectations are not the same thing as acting out of ethical duties.

The three other elements of CSR (economic, legal and ethical) are more important than philanthropy, which is merely the 'icing on the cake'.

Carroll applies the pyramid model in terms of stakeholders, arguing that stakeholders are the 'social' in CSR. Stakeholders are often seen in terms of economic claims on the company, but Carroll broadens their relevance to include legally and ethically legitimate claims, which in some cases can seem to give rise to conflicts. A difficulty which other theorists have addressed is how to apply CSR concepts in practice, in the many situations highlighted at the start of this chapter as ethical challenges. This is especially true of the MNE which operates in different societies.

Transnational CSR becomes complicated in that societies in which an MNE operates are likely to have differing expectations of CSR and differing ethical concerns (Artaud-Day, 2005). Conflicts between them can arise. Cultural and social differences, as well as differing legal requirements, impact on the ways in which societies view CSR. In some developing countries, it is often thought that economic concerns come first, and CSR can wait until the company is established financially. The MNE is tempted to think that CSR policies should be addressed only to western markets, where consumers are perceived to be more sensitive to the issues. However, as MNEs are now seeing stronger growth in emerging markets than in more established ones, it is arguable that a rethinking of transnational CSR is needed. Theories of political CSR, discussed later, are part of this rethinking.

> Many companies consider CSR to be focused on philanthropic activities. How would Carroll argue against this position?

CORPORATE SOCIAL PERFORMANCE

While the CSR conceptual framework highlights corporate responsibilities, some theorists have developed these principles into applied theories of corporate social performance (CSP). The CSP approach involves social responses in practice, bringing in all the ways in which a firm goes about meeting challenges for business in society (Wartick and Cochran, 1985). Critics of CSR have tended to argue that the principles are vague, and there is little indication of how to apply them in practice. But CSP theory is best seen as complementing the CSR framework, not replacing it (Wood, 1991: 703). Exploring the ways in which corporate involvement in society takes place is the main focus of CSP theorists. Social responsiveness is one of the processes which CSP seeks to address. Whereas corporate responsibility suggests normative principles, social responsiveness suggests acting in a context of social norms which present themselves in particular situations. Social responsiveness is thus linked closely to stakeholder management (discussed below). It takes place in a social context in which moral issues arise, but its focus is on social responses rather than ethical actions. A firm could conceivably be socially responsive but acting unethically. It has been argued that this is a limitation in CSP theory (Scherer and Palazzo, 2007). Critical analysts of CSP argue that the theory is more instrumental than normative, focusing as it does on outcomes in a context of economic goals, rather than on normative principles associated with CSR (Scherer and Palazzo, 2007).

Social responsiveness serves to highlight a process of engagement with social issues. Wartick and Cochran give an example of a firm which prioritizes the safety of its products but is suffering from quality problems, resulting in its products having to be recalled. Each time its product is found unsafe, it responds by recalling it. After ten recalls, one could still say the firm has been socially responsive, but not socially responsible (Wartick and Cochran, 1985: 763). It responded to immediate concerns, but failed to address the wider issues of CSR strategy. The two concepts are both necessary. Responsibility plays a macro role, and responsiveness a micro role. CSP adds an 'action' dimension to complement the normative content of CSR. Wood provides a comprehensive definition of CSP. Corporate social performance, she says, can be defined as 'a business organization's configuration of principles of social responsibility, processes of social responsiveness, and policies, programs, and observable outcomes as they relate the firm's societal relationships' (Wood, 1991: 693).

In her definition, CSR principles remain the first element. Wood sees three facets to social responsiveness: environmental assessment, stakeholder management and issues management. Managing the three elements involves having processes in place, for which methods of analysis and assessment have been developed. Scanning techniques are used for environmental assessment, while there are frameworks for assessing stakeholder salience (Mitchell et al., 1997). Issues management, which would seem to have more of a policy orientation, has also been the subject of monitoring and assessment techniques. These have focused on external and internal relations of the company. External issues include political strategies and public affairs. As companies become more involved in political discourse and interactions with governments, these become more important and also more susceptible to scrutiny by stakeholders. Internal processes include the design and use of corporate codes of ethics. Whether formal codes of conduct contribute to better CSP is one of the issues addressed. These methods of assessment give indications of outward processes associated with CSP, so that empirical assessments of social responsiveness can be made. One of the outcomes has been an increase in the inclusion of these elements in company reporting. Companies increasingly include in annual reports their social and environmental perform-ance measures, in addition to financial disclosures. The three elements make up triple bottom line reporting. Indeed, in some countries, social and environmental reporting are now legally required.

CORPORATE CITIZENSHIP

Corporate citizenship rests on the analogy that the company is a member of society in a way analogous to the individual citizen. As we have seen, good corporate citizenship features in Carroll's CSR model. Many companies have latched onto the concept as related to philanthropy only, and hold themselves out as good corporate citizens in communities. They draw attention to charitable activities such as improving local environmental ameni-ties. This shallow approach to corporate citizenship seems to have become popular among businesses, but academic scholarship has attempted to define corporate citizenship as a deeper theoretical approach (Matten and Crane, 2005). Given Carroll's linking it with CSR, how helpful is corporate citizenship in its own right?

The international business is involved in different ways in numerous societies. It seems to be stretching common sense to say that a company is a corporate citizen in all of them. Citizenship in relation to human beings is an administrative category, linking a person with a particular sovereign state, which is the person's nationality. Only rarely is a person a citizen of multiple countries. In most societies, the distinction between citizen and non-citizen is a sensitive one. Non-citizen residents, such as immigrants, are likely to have fewer civic rights and welfare entitlements. They are also likely to suffer from discrimina-tion. As is often pointed out by advocacy groups, immigrants have human rights recog-nized in international law even though they do not have citizenship rights in the countries where they reside. The citizen has political rights recognized most fully in democracies. The citizen can vote in elections and stand for office, but normally the non-citizen resident in a country cannot. It is usually said that the citizen of a country must pay taxes and obey the law of that country, but paying taxes and obeying the law applies to any residents of a country, citizens or not. How do these points apply to the company? The company's nationality is the country where it is registered. The MNE operates in many societies, and plays an economic and social role in them, sometimes a highly important role, but this does not make it a citizen in ways similar to a human being. It must abide by the law in any society where it has operations. So must any organization in society, from a church to a sports club.

It has been suggested that the company's citizenship lies in the social services it performs in society, which have been on the rise in many countries (Matten and Crane, 2005). Both for-profit companies and non-profit organizations carry out many public services. Companies also often commit themselves to welfare services in conjunction with their employees or customers in a country. This can be seen in a context of CSR, recognizing social as well as economic responsibilities. For example, Novartis, the Swiss pharmaceutical company, runs a health education programme in one of China's poorest regions, the far-western rural Xinjiang province, where the ethnic Uighur population, with its distinctive culture and Islamic religion, is concentrated. Novartis is using CSR 'to build a brand in a region that has gone from zero to almost universal health insurance coverage in recent years' (Waldmeir, 2013). However, poverty, poor health and weak educational attainment are challenges recognized by the local government. The programme, the Health Express project, which is run as a public–private partnership (PPP) between the government and Novartis, aims to educate school children in the basics of hygiene, such as washing hands. It is hoped that they will persuade their parents to take up these basic hygiene habits, which will lead to general improvement in health. Novartis see this programme as a CSR project. It is run on a zero-profit basis, and ultimately the company hopes to gain a positive awareness of the brand among the population. This is a long-term goal for Novartis in China's growing healthcare market.

Novartis is using CSR 'to build a brand in a region that has gone from zero to almost universal health insurance coverage in recent years.'

The Novartis Health Express project can be differentiated from the PPP and outsourcing of public services that is taking place in many countries. Novartis offers its health visitor services as an adjunct to its business, whereas for the companies which specialize in providing social services, this is their main business. Some governments have sought as a matter of policy to privatize or 'outsource' public services. Companies typically take over services in health, education and prisons, formerly carried out by government agencies. The companies which operate in these sectors do so for profit. Their business models are based on contracting with governments to offer services, stepping into quasi-governance roles rather than citizenship roles. Real citizens are on the receiving end, and when there is a breakdown in services, people tend to blame the government as much as the company in charge of the services on the ground. These companies have been criticized for lack of transparency and weak accountability in relations with government bodies (see the closing case study).

An issue which arises in connection with corporate citizenship is how it operates in different societies, including authoritarian regimes. Some authors have seen corporate citizenship as similar to the participation of individual citizens in a democracy (Moon et al., 2005). This limits the application of corporate citizenship to countries with democratic political systems. All countries have citizens, not just democratic ones. How does a company go about being a good corporate citizen in China, for example? In the context of China's one-party rule, the good Chinese citizen would comply totally with what the party leadership dictates. Companies such as Yahoo, which co-operate with Chinese government censorship of political dissent on the internet, are accused by people outside China of flouting ethical principles. But any company which does business in China faces legal obligations. It might disagree with them on ethical grounds. Internet companies have long seen themselves as empowering individuals in the freedom of a borderless cyber environment. They face particular ethical challenges when governments impose internet controls or use surveillance mechanisms to gather private data on individuals. Although reluctant, they must comply with government requirements.

An important element in democratic politics is civil society, which covers the many organizations which people voluntarily join and through which democratic participation and political debate can thrive (see Chapter 3). A principle of democracy is political equality – every person's voice should be heard. The richness of civil society organizations is an indication of pluralism in political life. Countries where rulers suppress political dissent set back democratic participation, but what about ostensibly democratic countries where corporate money plays a major role in politics? Corporate actors with their deep pockets can shape political debate and dominate election campaign advertising in some countries such as the US. They also cultivate links with civil society organizations. An organization called the European Privacy Association, which was set up in Brussels, looks on the surface like a grassroots group wishing to participate in the EU's privacy policy debate. However, it emerged in 2013 that the group is financed mainly by US technology companies. This tactic, known as 'astroturfing', is familiar in Washington's lobbying circles, but new in Brussels. One Member of the European Parliament says, 'They have brought Washington-style campaigning infused with a lot of Silicon Valley money' (Fontenella-Khan, 2013). After its financing was revealed, the organization registered itself in EU's voluntary register of lobbyists.

'They have brought Washington-style campaigning infused with a lot of Silicon Valley money.'

The idea of the company as analogous to the individual citizen received legal endorsement from the US Supreme Court in 2010, when it was held that the corporation enjoys the constitutional right of free speech in the same way that a natural person does. The *Citizens United* judgment, mentioned in Chapter 3, paved the way for unlimited secret donations to political causes. This judgment seemed to run counter to legal precedent, which had held that too much corporate money would risk undermining individual citizens' faith in the electoral system.

The majority decision in *Citizens United* was strongly criticized in a dissenting opinion by Mr Justice Stevens (Supreme Court of the US, 2010). He reiterates that the company is not like a human being in terms of citizenship. It cannot vote in elections or hold office. The company may be foreign controlled, and is treated in law in almost every respect as being a separate artificial entity, not a human being. He stresses the economic role of companies in society, but expresses concern about their growing political role in the US. His concerns are echoed by surveys of US voters. A Demos poll, shown in Figure 9.4, shows that over 80% of registered voters felt corporations have too much political power, leading to corruption and the jeopardizing of political equality (Kennedy, 2012).

PAUSE TO CONSIDER...

Think about a civil society organization which you have had contact with. It could be a sports club, a religious group, a trade union, or a single-issue group such as a society against animal cruelty. What role, if any, has business played in the group?

Figure 9.4 Corporations' influence on democratic processes in the US

Respondents were asked, 'Do corporations and corporate CEOs have too much political power and influence?'

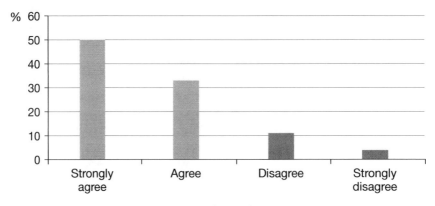

Source of data: Demos Analytics Poll, 2012, at www.demos.org (18/09/14).

STAKEHOLDER MANAGEMENT THEORY

Responsibilities of companies to stakeholders feature strongly in management theories as well as CSR theories. Freeman is one of the early theorists of stakeholder management whose work has become highly influential. He defines the stakeholder as 'any group or individual who can affect or is affected by the achievement of the organization's objectives' (Freeman, 1984: 46). Stakeholders, he says, are 'those groups which make a difference' (Freeman, 1984: 42). Freeman justifies this broad definition by saying that the stakeholder is an 'umbrella' concept in both business strategy and corporate social responsiveness. The strategist must deal with the people who affect the firm's business directly, but to be effective in the long term, the business must look to those groups it affects or can potentially affect. This distinction gives us a clue to the different uses of the concept, in both descriptive contexts and normative contexts.

Stakeholders are those groups which make a difference.

Freeman makes a distinction between primary and secondary stakeholders which has been followed by other theorists. Primary stakeholders are those who are directly involved in the business, and whose interests are essential to its success (see Figure 9.5). They include shareholders, employees, suppliers and customers. These groups have different roles. Among them, shareholders stand out as being distinctive. In a company, they are legally the owners, but, with the separation of ownership and management, they play little role in running the business (see Chapter 8). Employees are central, but their status can be ambiguous, especially in supply chains and networked organizations, where employees can move from one organization to another. Many companies have relatively small workforces employed full-time, but many more marginal workers, who are part-time workers, agency workers or workers on fixed-term projects.

Theorists highlight criteria which apply to these diverse stakeholders, which help to identify them and assess their impacts. Two of these criteria are legitimacy and power. The stakeholders listed all have legitimate interests, and they are in positions to exert pressure.

Figure 9.5 *Stakeholder management*

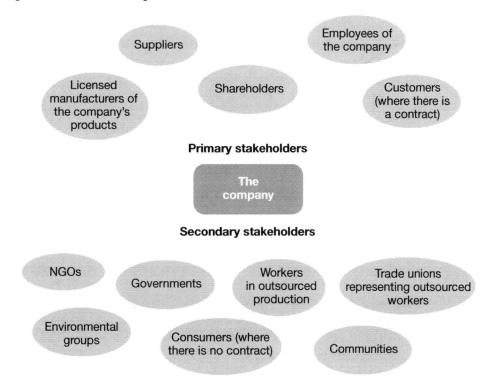

For example, if customers are dissatisfied with a firm's products and stop buying them, this directly affects corporate performance. A third criterion is urgency (Mitchell et al., 1997) which refers to time sensitivity. A claim that is urgent can take precedence over other legitimate claims. Identifying, evaluating and managing their interests in relation to the firm's goals are central to stakeholder management. Stakeholder theory thus fulfils a descriptive function, in that it describes how managers deal with these groups. Clarkson describes the corporation itself as a system of primary stakeholder groups (Clarkson, 1995: 107).

Secondary stakeholders fall within the broad umbrella of stakeholders described by Freeman, but their interests are not so vital to the survival of the company. As he noted, the company's activities affect these stakeholders over the long term, but the interactions are not as direct. The media and special interest groups would fall into this category, according to Clarkson. So too would NGOs. Although Clarkson considers public stakeholders such as governments and communities to be primary stakeholders, for most companies in market economies, they would be secondary stakeholders. For an internet service provider, for example, the extent of public investment in high-speed internet infrastructure is important, but this does not make the government a primary stakeholder. On the

Taking these stakeholder interests into account involves an ethical perspective rather than merely descriptive criteria of urgency and power.

other hand, for a company which specializes in outsourced public services, such as Serco, the government is a primary stakeholder, as it contracts with governments as part of its business (see the closing case study). Secondary stakeholders tend to represent community interests, which give rise to issues of social responsibility. Environmental concerns should be taken into account by the company, as these are legitimate stakeholder issues, but there could well be few powerful stakeholders speaking for environmental concerns. They might include community groups and NGOs, but these are not primary stakeholders. Taking these stakeholder interests into account involves an ethical perspective rather than merely descriptive criteria of urgency and power. Stakeholder management in respect of these stakeholders thus becomes more normative than descriptive.

Conflicts can arise. Customers value cheap clothes manufactured in low-cost locations. Brand owners and retailers seek out manufacturing centres such as Bangladesh, where the government has sought to attract these companies (see opening case study). On a stakeholder analysis of a retailer such as Primark, primary stakeholders are customers who buy their clothes and licensed manufacturers who make the clothes. Both are contractually tied to the company. Workers in the factories are not contractually linked to the brand owner, and would thus seem to be secondary stakeholders, as are the trade unions which press for safer working conditions. Even more remote are subcontractors who acquire work from licensed manufacturers, a practice which makes it even more difficult for brand owners to keep track of factory conditions (see Figure 2.3). Some brand owners consider the manufacturers of their products to be mere suppliers, and have codes of conduct for suppliers which cover factory conditions. But there is a difference between a supplier of a component and a supplier of a finished product which bears the company's brand. Both are suppliers in a broad sense, but the second one is more closely linked to the brand. Gap refers to its manufacturers as 'vendors', and has a code of conduct for outsourced production which is called a 'Code of Vendor Conduct' (at www.gap.com). The code is about conditions in the factories where Gap's brands are made, including the issue of child labour. There is a conflict between the interests of primary stakeholders, which are to keep costs down, and the stakeholder interests of those who work in the factories.

Normative stakeholder theory views stakeholders as having moral claims. It has been argued that each stakeholder group can be thought of in terms of Kant's categorical imperative, that is, having a right to be treated as an end and not as a means to an end (Donaldson and Preston, 1995). This normative approach reflects a focus on the philosophical foundations of ethical theories and also the rights-based social contract theorists (discussed in Chapters 1 and 3). We now turn to these business ethics theorists, beginning with social contract theories.

For each of the following stakeholders, assess whether it is a primary or secondary stakeholder, and to what extent it exerts moral claims on the company:

o A patient in a hospital run by Hospitals-4-you, a for-profit company.
o Wildlife in a river next to a carpet factory in China owned by Sun Carpets, a Taiwanese-owned company which manufactures carpets under licence for Carpets-R-Us, a London-listed company. The factory uses chemicals which occasionally escape into the river.

SOCIAL CONTRACT THEORIES

Carroll refers to ethical environments in communities, as well as theories of moral philosophy, as sources of ethical principles. The tension between cultural relativism and universal ethical theories has been discussed in Chapter 1. The tensions become particularly apparent in international business. The cultural relativist would argue that practices such as militaristic disciplinary regimes in factories are acceptable because this is the way factories

'The Foxconn structure is very autocratic and can be, I think to some people, somewhat demeaning.'

in the country routinely operate. In other countries, these practices are seen as contrary to values of human dignity. Hon Hai, the Taiwanese owner of Foxconn, which operates factories in China, has found that its militaristic regime does not go down well with workers elsewhere, including the US, Eastern Europe, and Latin America. A senior Foxconn manager in the US has said, 'they really wanted to employ/deploy the management strategy that they had in China and that just didn't work very well here … The Foxconn structure is very autocratic and can be, I think to some people, somewhat demeaning' (Mishkin and Pearson, 2013). Foxconn has recognized the need to understand and adapt to differing cultures. This is a management response rather than a principled stance on adopting higher ethical standards. In China, where the vast bulk of Foxconn's outsourced manufacturing takes place, CSR has been seen as a western import, applying employment and labour standards demanded by western brand owners (Wang and Juslin, 2009). It is only in the last decade that Chinese companies have come to embrace social responsibilities more positively, often prompted by governmental pressures to improve working conditions. In some cases, these moves have stemmed from worker unrest and strikes, suggesting that local employment conditions are influential.

Responding to worker dissatisfaction is a management challenge arising from the importance of employees as stakeholders. A strike or riot indicates a breakdown in relations between management and workers. Workers' expectations change over time. While migrant workers put up with poor conditions and humiliating treatment in the early years of the manufacturing boom, new recruits nowadays do not share the same attitudes. Cultural changes taking place in China indicate a growing desire for a better quality of life, including one's working life. Companies can respond in a short-term way, doing the minimum required by changing laws. But they could take a longer-term view, asking themselves deeper questions about their role in society. Foxconn now operates in several different cultural environments, and seems to be responding in each of them in ways that simply deal with the immediate local issues.

The social and moral norms of communities are recognized in social contract theory, which is based on a contractual view of the company in society. The idea of the social contract is a familiar one in political theory. We found in Chapter 3 that social contract theorists such as Locke and Rousseau took up the idea of a whole community consenting to government, in an 'original contract'. Donaldson and Dunfee, theorists of business ethics, hold that there are two levels of social contract which operate in the business environment. At a local level, people consent to microsocial contracts reflecting local moral norms, which equates to 'moral free space' (Donaldson and Dunfee, 1994: 260). Informed consent is a crucial element, giving the microsocial contract its authenticity, and it is important that there is a right of exit. They do note the difficulty, however, where jobs are scarce and people take jobs which involve poor working conditions. These workers stay on because they need the money, so that any right of exit is more theoretical than real. The extent of their consent could be questioned in these circumstances. Above this level there is consent to a macrosocial contract, which represents all rational contractors. The macrosocial contract is seen as an implicit contract similar to that envisaged by earlier theorists.

While the microsocial contract rests on cultural relativism, the second contract rests on a transcendent view of ethical principles, which the authors call hypernorms. Hypernorms, they state, 'are principles so fundamental to human existence that they serve as a guide in

SPOTLIGHT ON ETHICAL BUSINESS

The UN Global Compact and sustainability *Chris Harrop*

Chris Harrop

*Chair of United Nations
Global Compact (UNGC)
Network UK, and Director
at Marshalls plc*

Chris Harrop is Group Marketing Director and the Director of Sustainability at Marshalls plc, a leading supplier of hard landscaping products. In his roles at Marshalls, he has been instrumental in promoting sustainability in the company's strategy and operations. Chris is also chairman of the UN Global Compact UK Network, and a non-executive director at the Ethical Trading Initiative. He holds a BA Hons Business Studies, an MBA, and several professional qualifications. He is a chartered director of the Institute of Directors and a chartered marketer of the Chartered Institute of Marketing.

Visit **www.palgrave.com/companion/morrison-business-ethics** to watch Chris talking about the UN Global Compact in general and the activities of the Global Compact's UK network in particular. Chris discusses the key areas of the Global Compact: human rights, labour rights, the environment and anti-corruption. He emphasizes the links between the four areas, and the challenges raised by extended global supply chains. Although the challenges are daunting, notably in contexts of resource constraints, he stresses the potential benefits to businesses – and societies – of a focus on sustainability.

Before watching this video, take time to look again at related sections in the chapter and elsewhere in the book. Look at the section on 'Comparing CSR and legal frameworks' in Chapter 9, where there is a discussion of the UN Guiding Principles for Businesses, which Chris mentions. The four key areas of the Global Compact are featured in Figure 9.6. In Chapter 10, there is a detailed discussion of sustainability. Look particularly at the first three sections. The Millennium Development Goals (MDGs) are featured in Figure 10.2.

When you have watched the video, think about the following questions:

1 For a company which relies on sourcing through a global supply chain, how can participating in the Global Compact help it to raise ethical standards?

2 Recession has posed challenges for companies. Some might say that they should just focus on the bottom line and leave CSR until later. How can a re-focus on sustainability and responsibility help a company in formulating a post-recession strategy?

3 Chris distinguishes between a 'do-no-harm' approach and a 'do-good' approach. From an ethical perspective, how is the do-good approach preferable?

evaluating lower level moral norms' (Donaldson and Dunfee, 1994: 265). Hypernorms help to bridge the gap in the so-called 'naturalistic fallacy', which is deriving 'what ought to be' from 'what is'. The two authors wish to base obligations on consent in ways similar to the earlier contract theorists, but they wish also to develop a normative approach to business ethics. Hypernorms represent a convergence of principles from religious, cultural and philosophical sources. They share a view of human dignity and rights which transcend specific beliefs and values. For the business, these act as a guide. Microsocial contracts

Figure 9.6 The UN Global Compact

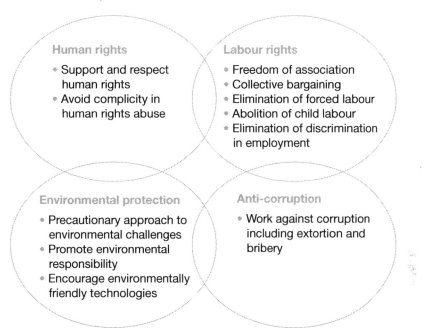

Human rights
- Support and respect human rights
- Avoid complicity in human rights abuse

Labour rights
- Freedom of association
- Collective bargaining
- Elimination of forced labour
- Abolition of child labour
- Elimination of discrimination in employment

Environmental protection
- Precautionary approach to environmental challenges
- Promote environmental responsibility
- Encourage environmentally friendly technologies

Anti-corruption
- Work against corruption including extortion and bribery

Source: United Nations (2013) 'The Ten Principles', the *UN Global Compact*, at www.unglobalcompact.org (18/09/14).

should be compatible with hypernorms. A difficulty is the practical one of how to apply these broad principles in practice. Some companies seek to adopt a universal code of conduct. This is the approach of the UN Global Compact. It reflects the idea that there are universally agreed principles in areas of human rights, labour rights, environmental protection and anti-corruption, shown in Figure 9.6.

The principles listed in these four broad areas are derived from international law and conventions. For labour standards, they are contained in the ILO's Declaration of Fundamental Principles (1998). Environmental principles are in the Rio Declaration (1992). Anti-corruption principles are in the UN Convention against Corruption (2003), and the human rights principles are in the UN Declaration of Human Rights (UNDHR). The UNDHR is discussed in Chapter 9. The company which signs up to the Global Compact accepts the application of these principles in all its operations, whatever the location. The standards, however, are not legally enforceable. Legal commitments in each area are the responsibilities of governments. Law in many places falls short of these standards. For the company, therefore, this commitment is to higher ethical standards.

Integrated social contracts theory, as Donaldson and Dunfee's theory is known, offers a normative approach to business ethics which focuses on global ethics, while recognizing the role played by local community norms in business relations. The idea of contracting based on rights and expectations has thus moved from the political sphere envisaged by earlier theorists to wider social groupings. It has also moved from geographically-defined entities such as communities and states to relational ties which are unbounded by geography. Companies recognize fundamental rights and duties among stakeholders in locations scattered across the globe.

POLITICAL CSR: DOES DEMOCRATIC THEORY OFFER NEW INSIGHTS?

Critics of integrated social contract theory argue that there are no universally recognized hypernorms, only standards which differ between cultures and countries. Similarly, echoing the positivist position, they argue that law-making and enforcement are essentially national, as there is no global legislature. Hence, both moral and legal authority seem to be lacking at global level. Is it still possible to derive a normative basis for CSR which takes a transnational approach and avoids a presumption of universal norms? Some theorists feel that the answer lies in the views of deliberative democracy held by Jürgen Habermas. Scherer and Palazzo put forward a theory of CSR that envisages the company as a political actor in a globalized society (Scherer and Palazzo, 2007). They point out that globalization is eroding the roles of traditional national governments, while companies are taking on wider roles in society formerly carried out by governments. These roles were highlighted in the section above on corporate citizenship. In this context, companies are becoming part of a wider participative process, also involving civil society and governments.

This deliberative concept of CSR sounds similar to stakeholder dialogue, but its advocates point out that it goes beyond stakeholder considerations, based as they are mainly on interests of particular groups. The key to this new concept of CSR lies in the theory of Habermas, for whom the deliberative democratic process itself constitutes ethical discourse and confers legitimacy. Democratic procedure is not merely an expression of political will, but a wider deliberative process (Habermas, 2001: 110). Habermas criticizes traditional views of liberal democracy, which tend to focus on institutions such as elections and take a limited view of citizens' roles. His view of deliberative democracy derives its legitimacy from the involvement of all groups, so that the corporation becomes a player in this new democratic interaction. A sceptic might ask, however, what assurance is there that the corporation will not continue to behave as a mainly economic actor in exerting its influence through these processes?

Habermas's thinking has evolved over a long period, and in early works he was rather more pessimistic about democracy than he has been in his later works. In early works, he observed the power of dominant industrial élites that put particular interests above those of the public good (Staats, 2004). His later work sees corporations as embedded in the democratic process, but it could be argued that companies still see themselves as economic actors, and wield corporate power which outweighs civil society voices (Staats, 2004). As we have noted, companies have become adept at utilizing organizations ostensibly grounded in civil society to exert influence over agenda setting in public debate on issues which affect them. As Habermas has himself observed, national cultures and states remain strongly linked to democracy (Habermas, 1999). However, most of the world's people live in countries where economic and political élites are dominant, even where there are democratic constitutions. And there is little trust in politicians to focus on the public good rather than self-interest (see Chapter 3). A contribution of political CSR is that it stresses the importance of normative legitimacy in business behaviour, but this process-based normative framework looks rather idealistic. Scherer and Palazzo, it could be argued, underestimate the evolving consensus on global standards and international law that this book has highlighted (see also Chapters 4 and 9). These standards reflect ethical principles which transcend cultural differences, with legal support in international law. They perhaps represent a sounder way forward for changing business behaviour in practice.

APPLYING ETHICAL THEORIES IN INTERNATIONAL BUSINESS

Hypernorms reflect ethical principles which transcend cultural differences. This way of looking at the foundations of ethics has a long history, dating back to the leading philosophers introduced early in this book. This approach highlights a challenge of applying ethical principles in practice: they seem vague and non-specific, and it is difficult to apply them in practice. On the other hand, if principles, such as those contained in laws, are highly specific, then actors are inclined to take a rule-governed approach to them, applying particular laws but not necessarily staying true to the principles. A tension between rule-governed behaviour and principle-governed behaviour can result. In this section, we look first at how law and ethics reinforce each other. We then apply the main ethical theories to the challenges facing international business.

ETHICS AND LAW: MUTUALLY REINFORCING

The prospect of a personal gain of $10 million, we saw in Chapter 5, is likely to tempt financial services professionals to commit an act of insider dealing, which they know to be a crime. Insider dealing is widespread, difficult to prove, and there is a low likelihood of being caught. Setting these factors against the possible gain, it looks to many like a risk worth taking. The person who thinks and acts this way has little sense of morality and integrity, and is deterred from wrongful acts mainly by the thought of the policeman round the corner. Many businesses have similar attitudes. They see the obligation to abide by the law in principle, but skate on the edge of legality and sometimes go to great lengths in setting up schemes to circumvent the law. They claim to abide by the letter of the law, but they do not adhere to the spirit of the law. Cadbury, the confectionery company taken over by Kraft Foods in 2010, was such a company. It had a long tradition of ethical and philanthropic values, but, it later emerged, had been artificially setting up aggressive tax avoidance structures for years before the takeover (Ford et al., 2013). Cadbury, along with many other companies, took the view that profit maximization was the only measure of corporate performance, and any means was acceptable as long as it did not involve breaches of formal law. The law is viewed as a hurdle to be overcome or circumvented, and, as long as the company seems to be successful in avoiding legal and regulatory infringements, it can assert that it has done nothing wrong. We found in Chapter 5 that such practices have become common among MNEs.

The more socially-nuanced version of this view holds that ethics in business consists of abiding by standards imposed by society, often in the form of governments and regulators. But this, too, comes down to a legalistic approach which skirts round the ethical issues. Business is seen as a kind of game, and the business plays by the rules of the game – an outlook made famous by Friedman (Boatright, 2000). This attitude overlooks the fact that the rules are not imposed from outside, but derive from interactions which take place in society, among businesses, governments and multiple stakeholders. Businesses play active roles in shaping the laws and, importantly, shaping the values which inform the laws. In the area of data protection and privacy, for example, technology companies are aggressive in making their preferences for future legislation known to law-makers in the US and the EU. The large technology companies, including Google, Microsoft, Facebook, Yahoo, Apple and eBay, spent an estimated seven million euros in 2012 in lobbying EU law-makers, and this is thought to be an underestimate (Fontenella-Khan, 2013). The privacy officer of one of these companies says, 'You would expect any tech company to actively participate in the discussion over the rules that will shape the future of our industry' (Fontenella-Khan, 2013). Their activities are much more developed in Washington, where they were estimated to have spent over $35 million in lobbying the US federal government. These are companies which, as in the Cadbury example above, adopt elaborate tax avoidance schemes. They thus hold ambivalent views of the law. They acknowledge their input when they press their own corporate interests to legislators, but when those interests involve legal contortions to avoid tax, they portray the legislators as too interventionist. Legal interference is thus justified if it benefits the company, but not if it imposes obligations which add to costs. This approach is not based on ethical considerations or ideas of social responsibility, but in business terms it has proved highly profitable. These technology giants are now powerful global corporations. But globalization, coupled with the internet, has also enhanced the power of individuals and societal groups (Boatright, 2000). These individuals and groups, including consumers, employees and ordinary citizens, increasingly draw attention to ethical issues in globalized business and demand greater transparency in governance – which includes corporate players as well as governmental ones.

In reality, MNEs are continually engaged in social and legal interactions in multiple locations and at international level. As we have seen in Carroll's theory, a CSR approach views legal and ethical responsibilities as a continuum, the law often reinforcing ethical values. Companies are confronted with ethical and social issues which are often intertwined, as we found when looking at ethical challenges in the early sections of this chapter. Moreover, ethical decision-making and behaviour involves both the attitudes of the decision-makers and the decisions which flow from them. To return to the financial services professional who is tempted to pass on insider information for a gain of $10 million, a decision not to go ahead with it does not necessarily reflect a morally right choice, but just a decision that it is not worth the risk.

ETHICAL THEORIES IN THE BUSINESS CONTEXT

Four major theoretical strands stand out in business ethics: the utilitarian school of thought, the deontological theorists such as Kant, rights-based theories and Aristotle's virtue ethics. These theories were introduced in Chapter 1. They are shown in Figure 9.7. Here, we revisit these theories in order to apply them in business and society. Applying these theories to international business today might seem far-fetched, as these theorists were concerned mainly about the individual in society and the role of governments. We noted in Chapter 1 that theorists were not purely 'ivory tower' philosophers. Most were sensitive to social issues of their time, and were influenced by events happening around them, often criticizing governments. With the exception of Rawls, they could not have imagined the growing power of business over people's lives, not to mention the extent of globalized businesses. But this is the reality which current ethical theorists must address. Issues of the individual in society are still relevant, even though the circumstances are very different from those envisaged by earlier theorists. Similarly, the concepts remain valid, and can help us to understand the ethical challenges of changing circumstances. We look at each type of theory in turn.

Figure 9.7 The right act and the good person

	The Right Act	The Good Person
Consequentialist (utilitarians)	Material benefits outweigh costs	Seeks to maximize self-interested benefits
Categorical imperative (Kant)	Fulfils moral duty to treat others as ends and not means	Fulfils a higher moral purpose
Rights-based (Locke, Rawls)	Recognizes natural/human rights	Upholds moral responsibility for social justice
Virtue ethics (Aristotle)	Knowingly chosen for its pure virtue	Develops virtuous character

Figure 9.7 shows the main ethical theories arising in business ethics. The utilitarians' theories are the most closely linked to business activities, as they are associated with the emergence of the capitalist enterprise. The self-interested individual is the focus, usually linked to the egoism of Hobbes' state of nature (see Chapter 1). But whereas Hobbes envisaged an authoritarian state as the solution, utilitarians looked to the opposite solution, urging the maximum of individual freedom and minimum of government interference. They saw the market as resolving conflicts, along the lines of Smith's 'invisible hand'. The utilitarians' consequentialist ethics flows from their assumptions about human nature. Actions are considered good to the extent that they maximize pleasure and minimize pain. People are assumed always to make rational calculations and choices which result in maximizing happiness for themselves. However, people act for various reasons, not just rational calculations, and they are also capable of altruistic behaviour. One person's happiness might come at the expense of another person's pain. For critics, even those such as J.S. Mill, who was part of this tradition, the ethical shortcomings of the theory were apparent in the absence of any sense of moral duty and the failure to recognize in human nature an ethical capacity towards others in society.

The second theory in Figure 9.7 provides an ethical framework in the way the utilitarians could not. Kant sees moral development of the individual as the highest form of existence. This development equates to a sense of freedom in recognizing a higher law. This transcendent quality of morality places Kant's theory in the deontological school of thought. From an ethical perspective, it benefits from its universality. The categorical imperative, to treat all human beings as ends rather than as means, recognizes an innate human dignity and applies to people everywhere. Kant recognizes that all people desire happiness, but that this in itself does not make them good. Only obedience to a higher moral duty leads to a good life, in contrast to a life of material well-being only. This moral development culminates in the kingdom of ends which Kant envisages in the state.

The categorical imperative is generally accepted as an ethical principle which is relevant to business ethics. Its relevance can be seen in situations where global companies are engaged in activities such as extraction and outsourced manufacturing in countries with weak rule of law and poor governance. Abiding by the law in these locations might mean little, serving to give an appearance of right behaviour to business activities which are ethically wrong. In these cases, employees and inhabitants in target countries are seen as instrumental. Workers matter only as production operatives, not real people. Pressures from consumers, journalists and NGOs bring poor conditions into the public domain, highlighting the failures to abide by principles of human dignity. As we noted at the outset of this section, applying broadly-worded ethical principles in specific situations is not something managers and decision-makers are trained to do. They would prefer to have a set of specific rules or laws to apply, in which case they can rely on a 'compliance' officer to do the job. Ethical issues are nonetheless real, even in the absence of a specific rule. The call for transparency which is now being heard from users and consumers of corporate goods and services is an indication that people in general have an idea of the difference between right and wrong in specific circumstances, even when companies seem not to.

We turn next to theories which offer a principled view of ethics, but somewhat outside the deontological approach. These are rights-based theories which adopt a view of human dignity as their starting point. This is similar to Kant's categorical imperative, but it takes a different view of social ethics. Kant's views of the moral state are seen by many as conflicting with the value of individual freedom. The utilitarians stressed negative freedom to too great an extent, but Kant's views of positive freedom tend to underestimate the need for individual freedom of action. Rights-based theories lay stress on rights of individuals in societies and social justice. They often begin with the idea of a social contract which represents an agreement among people to recognize the natural rights of each other and the need for social co-operation. The just society is one in which people respect the inherent worth and goals of other people. Rawls' idea of justice as fairness implies equality of opportunity. In a grossly unequal society, the poor and least advantaged people have little freedom and little scope for self-fulfilment. Rawls values individualism and the idea of freedom in the negative sense, as implying space to achieve our own goals, but tempers these values with a concern for others. He invokes what he calls his Aristotelian principle, saying that each person enjoys the realization of moral capacity over time. Despite this nod towards Aristotle, Rawls' theory focuses on rights and duties towards others in society, rather than on the development of the moral capacity of the individual person.

In a grossly unequal society, the poor and least advantaged people have little freedom and little scope for self-fulfilment.

From a Rawlsian perspective, inequality in societies globally is an ethical concern, in both developed and emerging economies. Despite poverty reduction, inequality has grown in China (OECD, 2012). In the US, the very rich have become richer while the bulk of the population has seen falling living standards. Protests by Walmart workers and fast-food employees over their 'starvation wages' swept through a number of cities in 2013, giving some indication of the impacts of what Rawls would see as social injustice (see Chapter 9). While the political dimension was Rawls' focus, the politics of inequality encompasses the growing power of corporate interests, which have gained enormous influence in political decision-making. Today's Rawlsian would agree with Mr Justice Stevens that the influx of corporate money 'undermines the integrity of elected institutions' (Supreme Court of the US, 2010). The risks to political equality in the US have also increased with the judgment by the US Supreme Court to abolish crucial elements of the Voting Rights Act 1965, which was intended to eliminate racial discrimination in voting arrangements (Supreme Court of the US, 2013).

Today's Rawlsian would agree with Mr Justice Stevens that the influx of corporate money 'undermines the integrity of elected institutions.'

As we found in Chapter 3, politics is about power relations, whether within a country or internationally. Business, too, involves power relations, now played out on a global stage and routinely involving political interactions in both local and international spheres. The capitalist enterprise has triumphed: communist political systems embrace capitalism, and state-owned companies worship profit maximization. But in emerging economies, like advanced ones, consumers and residents have seized the idea of having rights against companies as well as governments. They feel they have *rights* to safe food, safe consumer products, a clean environment and high standards of healthcare. They criticize greedy politicians, financiers and industrial tycoons whose power and money help to channel scarce resources into private coffers rather than public goods. They call for socially responsible businesses which pay taxes and offer decent employment, but they also call for integrity and honesty in the people who run them. These might seem old-fashioned values, but they are perhaps due for a renewal in corporate executive suites. Recall Barclays Bank, featured in the closing case study of Chapter 5, whose new CEO said the company needed a change of culture, shredding the legacy of the recent past (Lawrence, 2013).

Aristotle recognized the importance of personal character and integrity in his virtue ethics (see Chapter 1). Virtue for Aristotle is an internalized value. Acts matter, but the motive is crucial. The person must choose a way of acting knowingly because it is virtuous, not for any personal gain (Whetstone, 2001). And the virtuous act is part of a bigger picture of character development over a person's whole life (Nussbaum, 1999). Theorists of business ethics who focus on virtue ethics tend to highlight the personal and individual approach. The emphasis on the actor's character rather than the rule can be applied in management of people (Bertland, 2009). The virtuous manager promotes the capabilities of employees, allowing them to develop as human beings, rather than focusing on rights and duties. The same approach could be applied to other stakeholders, viewing interactions as encouraging moral development, rather than simply dealing with material interests, as stakeholder relations are often depicted. Virtue ethics as focused on the individual, however, was only one aspect of Aristotle's theory. He saw virtue in a social and political context, which is essential to the moral fulfilment of the individual. Aristotle's conception of the Greek city state, as noted in Chapter 1, was more akin to our notion of 'society'. He would not have had in mind the business corporation which modern business ethics focuses on. Indeed, Aristotle criticized business activities which pursue materialistic goals and rest on greed (Boatright, 1995). The modern corporation, based on capitalist values, is not conducive to the good life in the way that the civic values of Aristotle would have been.

Modern theorists of virtue ethics tend to highlight Aristotle's personal ethics at the micro level while disregarding his political views. This overlooks an integral element of this theory, but it need not undermine the relevance of virtue ethics as part of an overall approach to business ethics. Virtue ethics' focus on character of the person, while not providing guidance for specific actions nor relating to organizations of the type we are familiar with, nonetheless provides an essential insight into ethics: the 'doing' matters outwardly, but so does the 'being' of the person.

Recall the example of the financial professional tempted by $10 million for passing on insider information. Insider dealing is a criminal offence as well as a moral wrong. How would the following philosophers view the person who refrains for fear of being caught as opposed to the person who refrains because of a sense of moral duty?

a. Kant

b. Aristotle

CONCLUSIONS

One of the commitments listed by H&M in the opening case study of this chapter was to 'be ethical'. As we have seen, however, laudable principles are difficult to translate into practice, and situations which present themselves are usually more complex than first meets the eye. Challenges abound at every turn in international business, and many of these stem from the social dimension of business activities. The socially desirable decision can often conflict with economic goals. H&M chose to sign up to the safety accord in Bangladesh because it was the right thing to do, but the company is also aware that future accidents could damage its reputation. Businesses must now weigh up not just economic responsibilities, but also social and ethical impacts. There is emerging a changing perception of the company, from one which is focused on economic goals, to one in which economic goals are intertwined with social and ethical goals, as envisaged by CSR theorists. Indeed, it is becoming clearer that the company intent on pursuing competitive advantage is best advised to take a CSR approach to strategy as the most sustainable economically over the long term.

The social dimension of business tends to be analysed in terms of stakeholders, a broad category which includes just about any interest or claim that a company could face. These interests cover economic impacts as well as social and environmental claims. They have a moral aspect too, in that right behaviour is behaviour which reflects social values. In international business, the commitment to be ethical is not capable of being achieved in absolute terms. Ethical behaviour, as we have seen, is not just about actions, but intentions and attitudes. Managing stakeholder interests involves weighing up differing claims, some of which conflict with each other. Ethical theories show us that interests are not simply material interests of some groups over others. Moral choices matter in the social context of every business. A just and fair society is as much in the interests of business enterprises as it is in the interests of ordinary people.

NOTE

1 G20 members are Australia, Argentina, Brazil, Canada, China, European Union, France, Germany, Japan, India, Indonesia, Italy, Mexico, Russia, Saudi Arabia, South Africa, South Korea, Turkey, United Kingdom, and the United States.

REFERENCES

Artaud-Day, M. (2005) 'Transnational corporate social responsibility: A tri-dimensional approach to international CSR research', *Business Ethics Quarterly*, 15(1): 1–22.

Beecher-Monas, E. (2003) 'Corporate governance in the wake of Enron: an examination of the Audit Committee solution to corporate fraud', *Administrative Law Review*, 55(2): 357–94.

Bertland, A. (2009) 'Virtue ethics in business and the capabilities approach', *Journal of Business Ethics*, 84(1): 25–32.

Boatright, J. (1995) 'Aristotle meets Wall Street: the case for virtue ethics in business', *Business Ethics Quarterly*, 5(2): 353–9.

Boatright, J. (2000) 'Globalization and the ethics of business', *Business Ethics Quarterly*, 10(1): 1–6.

Bratton, W. (2001) 'Berle and Means reconsidered at the century's turn', *Journal of Corporation Law*, 26: 737–70.

Carroll, A.B. (1991) 'The pyramid of corporate social responsibility: toward the moral management of organizational stakeholders', *Business Horizons*, 34: 39–48.

Carroll, A.B. (1998) 'The four faces of corporate citizenship', *Business & Society Review*, 100(1): 1–7.

Clarkson, M. (1995) 'A stakeholder framework for analysing and evaluating corporate social performance', *Academy of Management Review*, 20(1): 92–117, at 106.

Donaldson, T. and Dunfee, T. (1994) 'Toward a unified conception of business ethics theory: integrative social contracts theory', *Academy of Management Review*, 19(2): 252–84.

Donaldson, T. and Preston, L. (1995) 'The stakeholder theory of the corporation: concepts, evidence, and implications', *Academy of Management Review*, 20(1): 65–92.

Fontenella-Khan, J. (2013) 'Astroturfing takes root', *Financial Times*, 27 June.

Ford, J., Gainsbury, S. and Houlder, V. (2013) 'The great tax fudge', *Financial Times*, 21 June.

Freeman, R.E. (1984) *Strategic Management: A Stakeholder Approach* (Boston, MA: Pitman).

Habermas, J. (1999) 'The European nation-dtate and the pressures of globalization', tr. G.M. Goshgarian, *New Left Review*, Vol. 235: 46–59.

Habermas, J. (2001) *The Postnational Constellation* (Cambridge: Polity Press).

Kay, J. (2013) 'Directors have a duty beyond just enriching shareholders', *Financial Times*, 5 June.

Kennedy, L. (2012) 'Citizens *actually* united', *Demos brief*, October, at www.demos.org (18/09/14).

Lawrence, F. (2013) 'Barclays secret tax avoidance factory that made £1bn a year profit disbanded', *The Guardian*, 11 February, at www.theguardian.com (18/09/14).

Maon, F., Lingreen, A. and Swaen, V. (2009) 'Designing and implementing corporate social responsibility: an integrative framework grounded in theory and practice', *Journal of Business Ethics*, 87(1): 71–89.

Matten, D. and Crane, A. (2005) 'Corporate citizenship: toward an extended theoretical conceptualization', *Academy of Management Review*, 30(1): 166–79.

Mishkin, S. and Pearson, S. (2013) 'Foxconn challenged as global reach grows', *Financial Times*, 3 January.

Mitchell, R.K., Agle, B.R. and Wood, D. (1997) 'Toward a theory of stakeholder identification and

salience: defining the principle of who and what really counts', *Academy of Management Review*, 11(4): 853–86.

Moon, J., Crane, A. and Matten, D. (2005) 'Can corporations be citizens? Corporate citizenship as a metaphor for business participation in society', *Business Ethics Quarterly*, 15(3): 429–53.

Nussbaum, M. (1999) 'Virtue ethics: a misleading category?', *Journal of Ethics*, 3(3): 163–201.

OECD (2012) China in Focus: Lessons and Challenges, at www.oecd.org (18/09/14).

Ostas, D. (2001) 'Deconstructing corporate social responsibility: insights from legal and economic theory', *American Business Law Journal*, 38(2): 261–300.

Preston, L. and Sapienza, H. (1990) 'Stakeholder management and corporate performance', *Journal of Behavioral Economics*, 19(4): 362–75.

Scherer, A.G. and Palazzo, G. (2007) 'Toward a political conception of corporate responsibility – business and society seen from a Habermasian perspective', *Academy of Management Review*, 32(4): 1096–120.

Schmidt, E. (2013) 'Why we need to simplify our corporate tax system', *Financial Times*, 17 June.

Schwartz, M.S. and Carroll, A.B. (2003) 'Corporate social responsibility: a three-domain approach', *Business Ethics Quarterly*, 13(4): 503–30.

Staats, J.L. (2004) 'Habermas and democratic theory: the threat to democracy of unchecked corporate power', *Political Research Quarterly*, 57(4): 585–94.

Stout, L. (2012) *The Shareholder Value Myth* (San Francisco: Berrett-Koehler).

Supreme Court of the US (2010) Citizens United v. Federal Electoral Commission, Number 08-205.

Supreme Court of the US (2013) Shelby County, Alabama v. Holder, Number 12-96.

United Nations (2013), 'The Ten Principles', *The United Nations Global Compact*, at www.unglobalcompact.org (18/09/14).

Waldmeir, P. (2013) 'Novartis builds for future by educating China's rural poor', *Financial Times*, 18 June.

Wang, L. and Juslin, H. (2009) 'The impact of Chinese culture on corporate social responsibility: the harmony approach', *Journal of Business Ethics*, 88(3): 433–51.

Wartick, S. and Cochran, P. (1985) 'The evolution of the corporate social performance model', *Academy of Management Review*, 10(4): 758–69.

Whetsone, J.T. (2001) 'How virtue fits with business ethics', *Journal of Business Ethics*, 33(2): 101–14.

Wood, D. (1991) 'Corporate social performance revisited', *Academy of Management Review*, 16(4): 691–718.

REVIEW QUESTIONS

1 What is the 'economic model' of the company? In what ways has this model become dented in recent years?

2 Explain Carroll's pyramid model of CSR. How are legal and ethical responsibilities interrelated?

3 What are the strengths and weaknesses of corporate social performance (CSP) as a complementary theory to CSR?

4 To what extent is the concept of corporate citizenship helpful in analysing the position of a company in society?

5 What are the differences between primary and secondary stakeholders? Which are more important in stakeholder management: economic interests or moral claims?

6 In what ways does the theory of integrated social contracts take in both cultural differences and international ethical standards?

7 What are the four areas covered by the UN Global Compact? Why is it considered a benchmark even though it is not legally binding?

8 How does the normative approach of political CSR aim to improve on both normative CSR theories and stakeholder theories of management? What criticisms can be made of political CSR?

9 In applying ethical theories to business, which matters most: the right act of the good actor? Explain.

10 Which of these ethical theorists are most relevant to business ethics: the utilitarians, Kant, Rawls or Aristotle?

SERCO AND THE PRIVATIZATION OF PUBLIC SERVICES

CLOSING CASE STUDY

Serco is a large international company, listed on the London Stock Exchange and employing 120,000 people in 30 countries. In the UK, it employs 53,000 people and is active in a wide range of services used by millions of people. Yet many people would probably not be familiar with the name or know much about it. This is largely because its services are not offered under its own brand, but as public services which it operates on behalf of government agencies. Although the company logo appears on signs at establishments which it runs, members of the public are not necessarily aware that a service such as a healthcare is being provided by a for-profit outsourcing company. However, the outsourcing of public services has grown around the world and has become big business. Serco's UK contracts are worth an estimated £750 million. Serco and G4S, its main rival, are among the few companies big enough to take on large government contracts.

Photo 9.2 *The running of prisons like this by private-sector companies for profit has given rise to criticisms. (© iStock.com/ compassandcamera)*

Serco is the largest provider of services in the UK. It is active in delivering public services in numerous sectors, including security, healthcare, prisons, education, trains, immigration removal centres, the national nuclear laboratory, and the management of the UK's ballistic missile early warning system. It even runs hire bicycles, known as 'Boris bikes' in London. Its activities in other countries include an immigration detention centre run on behalf of the Australian government. As outsourcing has grown, so have Serco's profits, which were up 27% in 2012. Its revenues were up 41% in 2012 (Serco, 2012).

Serco's growth and diversity of services could well cause some alarm. How can it possibly have expertise in all these specialized areas? And how can it take on so many new contracts so quickly? Serco benefits from the fact that governments which are hard pressed to control public spending are keen to outsource services in order to save money. Typically, there are only one or two bidders and little competition. These contracts create 'quasi-monopoly private providers' (Harris, 2013), and the duration of the contracts can be several years. The contracts specify levels of performance of the services, but companies are invariably stretched to provide a high level of service and also generate profits. The bulk of employees of Serco UK are former civil servants, and the company is legally bound to offer them the same employment terms as their former public employers. But it is common for the new private-sector employer to reduce the number of staff, as happened when Serco took over community health services in Suffolk from the National Health Service (NHS). The company aimed to reduce bureaucracy, utilize technology to a greater extent and deliver services more efficiently. New staff were hired to implement changed systems, but they were hired on less good pay and conditions than those transferred from the public sector (Harris, 2013). It might be asked why the new approach involving greater technology could not have been introduced under the NHS. Private providers face pressures to cut costs while also generating profits. Although Serco asserts its commitment to first-class public services, many failings and criticisms have come to light, suggesting difficulties in balancing tight budgets against standards people expect in public services.

Thameside Prison, a new prison run by Serco, is rated one of the three worst in Britain, and a cause of 'serious concern' by the Ministry of Justice (Travis, 2013). The Prisons Inspectorate found that a large number of prisoners were locked up for longer hours than should have been the case. However, the Ministry of Justice was content that Serco was working hard to deliver the contract.

The company has also had contracts for the electronic tagging of offenders who are subject to curfew orders. Both Serco and G4S have been accused of serious overcharging under their contracts for electronic tagging. The companies were alleged to be charging for tagging a number of offenders who had died, had been placed back in custody, or had left the country (Morris, 2013). This overcharging, which could amount to many millions of pounds, has possibly been taking place over several years, in which case staff at the Ministry of Justice might have been able to question the overcharging. A fraud investigation into the two companies was announced by the Minister of Justice in 2013, leading to falls in the share prices of both companies. Serco had bid for more tagging contracts, and but withdrew from the bidding process on the announcement that it was being investigated.

A concern which arises often in relation to privatized public services is that of accountability of the companies for poor performance. The contracts with the government are subject to 'commercial confidentiality', which means that their terms are shrouded in secrecy. Although a government agency is subject to a request for information from public under the Freedom of Information legislation, this does not apply to the private-sector companies which carry out government services.

Parliament's Public Accounts Committee has taken an interest in the performance of public services by outsourcing companies. In one of its reports, it found failings in out-of-hours medical services in Cornwall. Serco had a five-year contract worth £32 million with the primary care trust. The report by the Public Accounts Committee found it had lied about its performance and altered data on 252 occasions (Public Accounts Committee, 2013). By falsifying data, it was effectively overstating its performance. Serco blamed two members of its staff for the wrongdoings, and said they had left the company, but the terms of their departure were subject to a confidentiality agreement and could not be revealed. The two staff were not paid bonuses, but the contract manager was paid a performance-related bonus. Serco itself had received performance-related bonuses in 2012, but offered to repay them.

Serco also runs detention centres for immigrants. It runs two removal centres in the UK (Colnbrook and

Yarl's Wood) and the Christmas Island detention centre, run on behalf of the Australian government. Its treatment of people in these centres has been criticized on human rights grounds. The conditions in which people are confined have been compared to prison conditions, although the people being detained are not criminals. A report on Yarl's Wood by the UK Children's Commissioner in 2009 showed poor treatment of children, especially those with healthcare needs (Dugan, 2009). The Commissioner called for the end of detention of children, and the coalition government has agreed in principle with this goal, but as of 2013, children were still being detained in facilities which hold those awaiting deportation (Gower, 2013).

Serco describes its business model as incorporating its four governing principles (Serco, 2012). The first is to be entrepreneurial; the second is to enable 'our people' to excel. The third is to deliver on its promises, stating, 'we only promise what we can deliver' (Serco, 2012: 13). The fourth is to build trust and respect, stating that the company never compromises on safety and always operates in an ethical manner. The company does not have a policy described as CSR, nor does it see its role in terms of corporate citizenship. Serco does have web content on 'corporate responsibility', which includes sections on 'our people', health and safety, the environment and the community (at www.serco.com). The section on the community is entirely about philanthropic activities. It

states a commitment to invest 1% of pre-tax profits to give back to society, and describes other charitable activities.

The announcement of the investigation into possible fraud in electronic tagging was potentially highly damaging for the company. The CEO resigned late in 2013, in the hope that the company's reputation could be restored. Having received compensation of £2.5 million, including bonuses, in 2012, he left with a combined package worth over £6.5 million: a payout of £2.6 million, a pension pot of £2 million and share options worth £2 million at the time of his departure.

Sources: Lawrence, F. (2013) 'Private contractor fiddled data when reporting to the NHS, says watchdog', *The Guardian*, 7 March; Harris, J. (2013) 'Serco: the company that is running Britain', *The Guardian*, 29 July; Public Accounts Committee (2013) *The Provision of Out-of-Hours GP Service in Cornwall*, Parliament, at www.publications.parliament.uk; Dugan, E. (2009) 'Inside Yarl's Wood: Britain's shame over child detainees', *The Independent*, 26 April; Travis, A. (2013) 'Two private prisons among worst three jails, inspectors find', *The Guardian*, 25 July; Gower, M. (2013) *Ending Child Immigration Detention: Commons Library Standard Note*, 2 January, at www.parliament.uk; Morris, N. (2013) 'G4S and Serco face £50 million fraud inquiry', *The Independent*, 12 July; Serco (2012) *Annual Report 2012*, at www.serco.com; Treanor, J. and Syal, R. (2013) 'Serco CEO quits before investigation into electronic tagging charges', *The Guardian*, 25 October, at www.theguardian.com (18/09/14).

- Some of the failings and poor performance in public services highlighted in this case study suggest failings by both the outsourcing company and the government oversight. Highlight examples.

- What are the pros and cons of outsourcing public services to private-sector companies?

- How would you assess Serco in terms of corporate social performance in the societies where it has become crucial in delivering public services?

Contextualizing human resource management

Jawad Syed and Dk Nur'Izzati Pg Omar

10

After reading this chapter, you should be able to:

- ☐ Understand the importance of local context and its implications for HRM
- ☐ Identify the external contexts that affect the policies and actions involved in HRM
- ☐ Learn how to design context-appropriate HRM
- ☐ Understand the pros and cons of a crosscultural transfer of HRM practices
- ☐ Identify future directions for contextualizing HRM

Introduction

Contextualizing HRM in a global village

Contextual influences on HRM

Critical discussion and analysis

Conclusion

For discussion and revision

Further reading

Case study: HRM in Brunei's public sector

References

Introduction

Human resource management (HRM) as a management concept originated in the 1950s in North America with the seminal works of Drucker (1954) and McGregor (1957), and has subsequently been adopted and widely used across the world. HRM is defined as the managing of people within employer–employee relationships. This usually involves maximizing employees' performance (Harris, 2002), and human resources need to be effectively utilized in order to obtain maximum productivity and performance. By the 1980s, the concept of HRM had gained wider international recognition, particularly in English-speaking countries (Sparrow and Hiltrop, 1994).

The theories and practices of HRM have since made inroads into continents other than North America and Europe, such as their adoption and integration into Asia and Africa (see, for example, Bennington and Habir, 2003; McCourt and Foon, 2007). However, despite more than two decades of academic research and practice, the HRM literature has been only partly successful in offering a universal solution for the complexities of managing people that can transcend national, institutional, cultural and economic divides. Özbilgin's (2004) survey of academic scholarship and journals in the field of international HRM points towards a limited geographical coverage by the 'mainstream' scholarship in HRM, which remains dominated by North American and Western European theorization and empirical studies. In other words, HRM is not culturally neutral. The limited geographical reach of HRM is also highlighted by other authors, such as Baruch (2001) and Clark et al. (2000), who have argued for an ethical duty on the part of HRM scholars and journals to widen their geographical spread. Critical Thinking 10.1 highlights the parochial nature of HRM resulting from its geographical and theoretical limitations.

Although HRM is today an international phenomenon, the nature and scope of its links with local institutions, labour laws, corporate strategies and indus-trial relations vary greatly across national borders (Özbilgin, 2004). Despite the fact that the mainstream HRM theories, which were overwhelmingly formulated in management schools in North America (see, for example, Beer et al., 1985; Schuler and Jackson, 1987) and the UK (Storey, 1992) in the 1980s, quickly found their way to other developed countries (Maurice et al., 1986; Tung, 1993) and later to developing countries (Budhwar and Debrah, 2001), few models of HRM found in the mainstream literature derive from outside the English-speaking world. This is despite an increasing consensus that mainstream human resources theories and practices are inadequate in addressing the human resource issues facing international and multinational companies (Clark et al., 2000). As a result, and also because of a growing pursuit of effective ways of managing human resources in crosscultural contexts (Taylor et al., 1996), it is important to develop a contextualized understanding and operationalization of HRM. The interest of scholars and practitioners in this topic is expected to grow further due to the relevance of issues such as crossnational and comparative HRM, expatriate management and diversity management (Caligiuri, 1999).

This chapter begins with a literature review on the adoption and implemen-tation of HRM and the contextual forces that influence it. We also consider certain latent tensions between globalization and HRM. The case study at the end of the chapter presents an empirical study of HRM practices in Brunei Darussalam, describing the influence of the macroenvironmental context on the design and implementation of HRM strategies, policies and practices in government sector organizations in Brunei.

Critical Thinking 10.1
Parochialism in the HRM literature

In the 'mainstream' English-language texts on HRM, there are hardly any references to resources in other languages (Özbilgin, 2004). Exceptions to this rule are some European languages, for example French-, German- and Spanish-language publications, which are also only very occasionally cited in English-language texts. The inclusion of materials not written in English is hardly encouraged and is often left to the linguistic competence of individual authors. As a consequence, the mainstream writing in the field of HRM remains influenced and dominated by the English-speaking world.

Adler (1991) refutes any claims of universal reach and offers the notion of 'parochialism' in management writing. Clark et al. (1999) identify two forms of parochialism in the international HRM texts: (1) that a sole reliance on English-language sources poses a major challenge; and (2) that the texts often fail to acknowledge the methodological complexities of studying crossnational and international management issues. The limiting impact of the English language appears to be the most insidious as it simply demarcates our knowledge of and imagination related to HRM practice to those geographies where the English language is spoken.

Similarly, the difficulty of formulating overarching conceptual frameworks, theoretical models and critical approaches is a recurring theme in the international HRM literature. Large-scale empirical studies in this field are rare, and such studies come with long descriptions of the limitations of their method and analysis. However, due to their rarity, great significance is attributed to the studies that are available, and their findings are often overstated, misinterpreted or used out of context. For example, although Hofstede's work in the 1960s and 70s challenged the assumption that the theoretical frameworks developed in the USA would be universally applicable (Schneider, 2001), Hofstede's IBM studies were later quoted as a clear indicator of the convergence and divergence of management practices, without much questioning of the nature of his study.

Questions
1 What are the implications of the dominance of English-language literature for theories and practices in HRM?
2 How can scholars and practitioners of HRM benefit from the literature on HRM that has been published in languages other than English?

Source: Adapted from Özbilgin (2004)

Contextualizing HRM in a global village

Global integration has driven dramatic changes in the economic and institutional contexts of HRM. Globalization refers to the shift to a more integrated and interdependent world economy (Hill, 2009). It focuses on the maximization of profits and, as an economic driver, has had a significant effect on the way in which human resources are managed. Globalization has also changed the image of a company. Companies have become multinational, each one seeking to attain the competitive advantage, and the human resources of a company may just be the key to that. For this reason, HRM policies are changing in order to better respond to different cultural and institutional contexts.

Context is multilayered, multidimensional and interwoven (Collin, 2007), and different contexts may have dynamic and divergent influences on the organization of work within their sphere of influence. Globalization has steadily and gradually created a world in which:

> barriers to cross-border trade and investment are declining; material culture is starting to look similar the world over; and national economies are merging into an interdependent, integrated global economic system. (Hill, 2009: 4)

During current times, when the world economy and businesses are shaped and structured by the process of globalization, it is imperative to understand and contextualize the policies and practices of HRM.

Although it is no longer possible to divide the world economy into separate, distinct national economies isolated from foreign markets and influences, it would be wrong to ignore the fact that employment relationships in almost all countries remain largely shaped by national systems of employment legislation and the cultural contexts in which they are operationalized. Critical Thinking 10.2 highlights the case of varying perspectives on working hours in the European Union (EU).

Although factors such as culture, history and language underlie much of the variation in management practices, the practice of HRM is, more than that of any other business function, closely linked to national culture (Gaugler, 1988). Culture can mean many different things for people with different backgrounds. Culture, according to Tylor (1924: 1), is 'that complex whole which includes knowledge, belief, art, morals, law, custom, and any other capabilities and habits acquired by man as a member of society'. Within employment contexts, there is ample evidence that people's behaviours are affected by specific national cultures. Hofstede (1991) suggests that the significance of national culture is that most inhabitants of a country share the same mental program. Based on that, other researchers have sought to discover to what extent individuals' national culture influences their way of working and thinking, and to identify how people in different countries may have a collective programming, that is, a predisposition to behave in a certain way (Stredwick, 2005).

Although globalization is pervasive, it is not without serious criticism. Critics argue that globalization has demoted national governments as regulators of the free market system (Chomsky, 1999). Among other things, globalization may at times create inequality and environmental challenges. In 1996, the United Nations reported that the assets of the world's 368 billionaires exceeded the combined incomes of 45 per cent of the planet's population (Faux and Mishel, 2001). The Kyoto Protocol in 1997 and subsequent agreements at the Copenhagen climate summit in 2009 have highlighted issues (the need to reduce emissions of carbon dioxide and greenhouse gases) that directly affect the behaviour of organizations and countries. Organizations will lobby their governments to prevent the ratification of such treaties and lessen other external pressures that may affect their economic interests. For example, in 2002, Canada potentially faced unemployment losses through plant closures and costs in the manufacturing sector relating to curbing their emissions (Chase, 2002). When firms seek foreign investment or outsourcing to take advantage of economies of scale, lay-offs of workers in the home country may drain the economy through welfare benefits, and the demand for cheaper services in the host country of globalizing firms may entail making adjustments in the local labour markets.

Globalization has created dynamic alternatives for multinational firms. Corporations can outsource production and services to more economically viable locations, allowing multinational enterprises to drive down costs and increase their efficiency. For example, several clothing giants in the UK and the USA now outsource much of their manufacturing to South Asia, where production costs are much lower. And the displacement of workers caused by transferring resources away from Europe to Asia is not occurring just in the clothing industry. Many telecommunication firms too are transferring their back-office operations to India and other countries where costs are cheaper. This adversely affects the labour market in home countries that may face unemployment of the manual working classes.

In recent years, it has become increasingly evident that the global economic crisis that began in 2008 may leave many nations in recession. Many firms have reacted to this by making thousands of workers redundant, especially in sectors where the recession has hit hardest, for example financial services and the construction industry in 2009. This approach places pressure on organizations in terms of issues outside of their control, at times forcing them to relocate or restructure their operations. In these circumstances, it is essential to consider how HRM can be contextualized in its design and implementation.

Critical Thinking 10.2
Geographical variation in philosophy
Scholars and scientists list a large number of variations between countries and point towards a 'wide diversity in philosophies of people management' (Price, 1997: 122). When comparing one country with another, certain tasks that need to be completed within a line of work are given different priorities and are completed in a different way (Price, 1997). An example of this is the EU voting for a decree stating that its Member States should introduce legislation to decrease the number of working hours for employees. Every country then had to set a chosen number of hours, and it was apparent that the number of working hours thought suitable was different between different countries: the UK believed that 48 hours was reasonable, whereas France decided 35 hours was enough (Stredwick, 2005).

Questions
1 Why is it important to consider a country's sociocultural context when designing HRM?
2 What factors affect the number of working hours per week in a country?

Contextual influences on HRM

This section highlights different contextual forces that may influence HRM – we will start with a discussion of sociocultural context. Hofstede (1980) identified five dimensions of culture, and culture serves as an umbrella for all other contexts: legal, political, economic and technological contexts are all influenced by the role culture plays in a society. Noe et al. (2008) state that culture shapes people's respect and obedience for laws and regulations, hence affecting a country's legal and political system. And the way in which human capital and technology are valued by a particular society influences the economy of that country. Various HRM practices, such as recruitment and selection, training and development, compensation systems, performance appraisal and the employment relationship, are affected by the macrocontextual factors that this section will cover (Table 10.1).

Table 10.1 An organization's macroenvironment

Legal and political factors	Economic factors
National legislation (current and future)	Home economy
International legislation	Trends in the economy
Regulatory bodies and processes	Overseas economies
Government policies	General taxation
Government term and change	Taxation specific to the product/service
Trading policies	Seasonality issues
Funding, grants and initiatives	Market/trade cycles
Home market pressure groups	Specific industry factors
International pressure groups	Distribution trends
Ecological/environmental issues	Customer/end-user drivers
Wars and conflicts	Interest/exchange rates
	International trade and monetary issues
Sociocultural factors	**Technological factors**
Lifestyle trends	Information and communications
Demographics (age, gender, literacy)	Development of competing technology
Language	Associated/dependent technologies
Ethnicity/race	Replacement technology/solutions
Religion/sect	Maturity of technology
Ethical issues	Manufacturing maturity and capacity
Social policy	Research funding
Technology	Technology legislation
Media views	Innovation potential
Consumer attitudes and opinions	Intellectual property issues
Company image	Global communications
Fashion, brand, role models	
Major events and influences	

Table 10.1 suggests that the strategies and practices of human resources ought to be examined in a broader context, and that social, legal, economic, political and technological influences all have a different impact when putting HRM into a context. For example, the global economic crisis and the near collapse of the banking system in 2008 are powerful contextual events that affect both national economies and organizations. Macrocontextual analysis will lay the groundwork for an investigation of the extent to which and how local cultural and institutional contexts affect HRM (Figure 10.1).

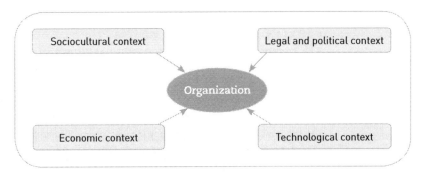

Figure 10.1 Key factors of the macroenvironment.

Sociocultural context

Several elements in the sociocultural context have consequences for the design and efficacy of HRM. Culture dynamics and population demographics affect many aspects of the business environment. Rousseau (1990) argues that culture is a set of common values, beliefs, expectations and understandings that are obtained through socialization; it is learnt and shared by the members of the community (Noe et al., 2008). Culture can be defined as a system of values and norms that are shared among a group of people (Hill, 2009). It is dynamic and changes over time, for example when a nation becomes more affluent.

According to Tayeb (2005), HRM is a 'soft' aspect of an organization. Hence it is more influenced by culture than are financial and technical matters, which are considered to be the 'hard' aspects of an organization. Culture has a significant role in attracting, motivating and retaining individuals in organizations. Other key areas that are usually influenced by culture are training, performance management and compensation.

Table 10.2 Hofstede's cultural dimensions

Individualism	The degree to which individuals are integrated into groups
Power distance	The extent to which the less powerful members of organizations and institutions accept and expect that power is distributed unequally
Uncertainty avoidance	A society's tolerance for uncertainty and ambiguity
Masculinity	The distribution of emotional roles between the genders
Long-term orientation	Long-term-oriented societies foster pragmatic virtues oriented towards future rewards, in particular saving, persistence and adapting to changing circumstances. Short-term-oriented societies foster virtues related to the past and present, such as national pride, respect for tradition, preservation of 'face' and fulfilment of social obligations

Source: Adapted from http://www.geerthofstede.nl/culture/dimensions-of-national-cultures.aspx (accessed July 2011)

Hofstede's (1984) five dimensions of culture can influence management practices and the culture of organizations. The five categories are outlined in Table 10.2 and are also discussed below.

Individualism versus collectivism

This dimension describes the strength of the relationship between individuals in a society, that is, the degree to which people act as individuals rather than as members of a group, or the extent to which the individuals are integrated into groups. In individualist cultures such as the USA, the UK and The Netherlands, people are expected to look after their own interests and the interests of their immediate families. South-East Asian countries are more collectivist – they look after the interests of the larger community. Collectivist cultures tend to owe total loyalty to their group.

Low versus high power distance

This cultural dimension concerns hierarchical power relationships and refers to the unequal distribution of power. It describes the degree of inequality among people that is considered to be normal in different countries. For example, Denmark and Israel have a small power distance, whereas India and the Philippines have a larger one. Another obvious example is the way people are addressed. In a business context, Mexican and Japanese people always address each other using titles, for example Señor Smith or Smith-San, but in the USA, first names are preferred. The reason for this is to minimize power distance.

Low versus high uncertainty avoidance

This dimension deals with the fact that the future is not perfectly predictable. For example, in Singapore and Jamaica, cultures of weak uncertainty avoidance, individuals are socialized to accept uncertainty and take each day as it comes. However, Greek and Portuguese culture socializes people to seek security through technology, law and religion.

Masculinity versus femininity

This dimension indicates the extent to which the dominant values in a society tend to relate to assertiveness and a greater interest in things than in people and quality of life. A 'masculine' culture is one in which dominance and assertiveness are valued, as is evident in the USA, Japan and Venezuela, for example. A 'feminine' culture, as can be found in The Netherlands and Sweden, promotes values that have been traditionally regarded as feminine, leaning more towards quality of life and relationships in society. Hofstede (1984) notes that most South-East Asian countries fall the between the masculine and feminine poles.

Long-term versus short-term orientation

Long-term orientation focuses on the future and holds values in the present that will not necessarily provide an immediate benefit; examples of countries adopting this approach are Japan and China. The USA, Russia and West Africa have a short-term orientation, being oriented towards the past and present, and promoting respect for tradition and the fulfilment of social obligations.

It is, however, important to acknowledge the criticism raised by some authors who view Hofstede's conceptualization of culture as static and essential. For example, Ailon (2008) and McSweeney (2002) caution against an uncritical reading of Hofstede's cultural dimensions, particularly because of their allegedly ethnocentric interpretations, which may lead to stereotyping.

Other scholars have identified additional dimensions of culture, including its informal, material or dynamic orientation (Adler, 1991; Ronen, 1994). They have compared HRM across countries and observed that cultural values and orientations are determinants of the differences found between them (see, for example, Arvey et al., 1991; Brewster and Tyson, 1991; Triandis et al., 1994; Brewster, 2007). However, culture may not explain all the differences in HRM found across countries (Lincoln, 1993; Jackson and Schuler, 1995) – such differences may also be an outcome of variations in economic and political conditions (see, for example, Carroll et al., 1988), laws and social policies (see, for example, Florkowski and Nath, 1993), industrial relations systems (Strauss, 1982) and labour market conditions (see, for example, Levy-Leboyer, 1994).

Legal and political context

The legal and political context is represented by national laws and sociopolitical policies and norms. Given that culture is a codification of right and wrong that exists in a country's laws, political systems and laws often reflect what constitute the legitimate behaviour and norm of a particular country (Tayeb, 2005; Noe et al., 2008). These contexts have the power to shape the nature of the employment relationship and the way in which HRM practices and policies are enacted (Bratton and Gold, 2007). Jackson and Schuler (1995) claim that almost all aspects of HRM are influenced by political and legal regulations, and Noe et al. (2008) have identified training, compensation, hiring and lay-offs as some of the HRM practices most commonly affected by this context.

The UK, the USA and most European countries, for example, place a strong emphasis on eliminating discrimination in the workplace; hence, equal employment regulations are put into effect. To focus on one example, in the UK the Sex Discrimination Act 1975, the Disability Discrimination Act 1995, the Race Relations Act 1976, the Employment Equality (Age) Regulations 2006, the Employment Equality (Religion or Beliefs) Regulations 2003 and the Equality Act (Sexual Orientation) Regulations 2007 are the laws that are included under the heading of Equality Employment Regulations. These regulations play a major role in developing HRM policies in relation to recruitment and dismissal procedures (Noe et al., 2008). Not only that, but pay and compensation can also be affected, with the setting of minimum wages for employees and a determination of the extent to which unions have the legal right to negotiate with the management.

The role of the state and its political system is crucial in determining the nature of employment relations in a country. Tayeb (2005) points out that workers in Germany have a legal right to 'co-determination', in which their participation in management is ensured; therefore, any HRM matter must abide by such laws (Noe et al., 2008). The Brunei case study at the end of this chapter provides another example of how the state impacts on employment relations. Furthermore, the European Economic Community can also affect the political-legal system relating to HRM because it provides workers' fundamental social rights. These rights include freedom to be fairly compensated, freedom of association and collective bargaining, and equal treatment for men and women.

Legal influences affecting HRM practices can take the form of how local regulations affect the labour market (see Critical Thinking 10.3). Different countries will impose regulations on minimum wages and working hours as well as the involvement of trade unions, as has been seen in most Western developed economies. In the UK, government legislation has gradually worn down the power of trade unions and given rise to managerial flexibility and decentralized employment regulation. Although it is employers who control the design of HRM practice at an organizational level, managers need to be aware or informed of external developments in the legal context.

Politically related external conflicts may have acute implications for firms operating in a particular country, and managers need to be aware of political manoeuvrings relevant to their interests. The state does not, however, have a monopoly of control over the conduct of business – firms too can lobby and influence state policies to meet their needs (Needle, 2004). This was the case with the USA's mohair farmers, who were paid numerous cash payments from the Federal budget (Wheelan, 2003). The mohair agricultural subsidy has now disappeared, but it highlights the importance and power of organized institutions.

External pressures in the global political environment may directly affect how business and employee relationship are conducted. The collapse of the Communist system in 1989 in East Europe and Central Asia paved the way for new market economies based on the Western capitalist market system. Employment regulation and managerial responsibility were taken away from government and replaced by the power of institutions and organizations.

Critical Thinking 10.3
Employment relations in India

Labour unrest haunts auto sector in Tamil Nadu
Madhu Bharati, May 4, 2010 (Chennai)

In recent decades, the Indian State of Tamil Nadu has been attracting enormous investment into automobile and accessories manufacturing. However, investors and manufacturers have of late become quite worried about repeated labour unrest, which is also impeding future investment in the state.

Hyundai, the second largest car maker in the country, is facing a similar situation. In May 2010, Hyundai employees threatened a sit-in strike after the company refused to reinstate 35 employees who had been dismissed for alleged misconduct. According to a news report, the company was not able to meet the agreed deadline to reinstate the dismissed workers. The company has been making frantic efforts for a possible settlement with the dismissed employees, offering them certain financial compensation as a part of the settlement.

If the strike announced in May 2010 does go ahead, it will be the third strike at Hyundai over the past year. Previously, in April 2009, employees went on strike for 18 days after the company laid off 65 workers. Then again, in July 2009, employees went on strike protesting at a wage agreement that had allegedly been signed by a minority union (or pocket union).

However, Hyundai is not the only company suffering as a result of labour unrest. In May 2009, workers at MRF struck work for several months, demanding recognition of their union. In September 2009, a senior official at Pricol was killed in workers' unrest in the auto-ancillary hub of Coimbatore, which resulted in a work closure lasting more than a month.

According to Abdul Majeed, an auto sector leader at PWC, labour laws are to be blamed: 'Our labour laws need an amendment. No one wins when it comes to dealing with labour. There has to be a give and take to some level amongst everyone. But our labour laws are the biggest of problems.'

The existing labour laws in India require large companies to seek prior permission from state governments before laying off workers or hiring workers on contract. These laws have been blamed by managers for encouraging workers to go on frequent strikes. With India positioning itself as the hub of small car production, such labour unrest may not send the right message to international investors.

Questions

1 In the light of this example, is it correct to blame laws for encouraging workers to strike?
2 Is it always possible to reconcile the ethical and business implications of labour laws?

Source: Adapted from NDTV Profit, May 4 2010

Economic context

Although the economic context of a country is hardly predictable and stable, it is most likely to have long-term consequences for HRM (Tayeb, 2005). The attitudes and values that are embedded in every individual are formed by culture (Noe et al., 2008), hence the claim of human capital theory that a culture that encourages continuous learning is most likely to contribute to the success of the economy. Jackson and Schuler (1995) argue that skills, experience and knowledge are of significant value for the economy, and enhancing them can make individuals more productive and more adaptable to changing economic conditions.

The need to improve human capabilities relates back to whether the economic system supplies sufficient incentives for developing human capital. For example, Tayeb (2005) found that socialist economies offer a free education system, which provides an opportunity for human capital to be developed, thus enabling employees to obtain greater monetary rewards based on their competencies. This is evident in the USA, where levels of human capital are reflected in the differences in individuals' salaries, higher skilled employees, for example, earning better compensation than lower skill ones (Noe et al., 2008). In fact, it has been discovered that for each additional year of schooling, individuals' wages increase by about 10–16 per cent (Noe et al., 2008). Conversely, the opportunity to enhance human capital is smaller in capitalist systems due to the high costs of training employees; hence, human resource development is lower in capitalist countries (Tayeb, 2005).

Tayeb (2005) highlights the role of market conditions in determining employees' rights in capitalist countries that have 'centre right' policies. According to Flamholtz and Lacey (1981), investments in human capital are usually made in anticipation of future returns; besides improving employees' competencies, the costs also include factors such as motivating, monitoring and retaining these employees in order to benefit from their gains in productivity (Jackson and Schuler, 1995). Chapter 11 in this book offers a detailed discussion of HRM in contemporary transnational businesses.

Of course, different forms of political capitalism, for example in terms of their socialist or free-market orientation, will have different effects on the way in which HRM is practised domestically as well as internationally. Even the most global of companies may be deeply rooted in the national business systems of their country of origin. For example, Edwards (2004), Hu (1992) and Ruigrok and van Tulder (1995) have argued that, on several dimensions, multinational corporations exhibit national characteristics.

There are various ways in which HRM can increase organizations' human capital, for instance offering attractive compensation and benefits packages to individuals, what Jackson and Schuler (1995) claim is 'buying' human capital, which is apparent in recruitment and selection processes. Creating equal opportunities in training and development can also help to 'make' human capital in an organization; at times of tight labour supply, this method is usually adopted. Training and developing existing employees' capabilities, as well as enhancing their wages, benefits and working conditions, can help in retaining them, especially when there is a scarce supply of human capital in the economy.

At times of economic boom and similarly in times of recession, the supply and demand of labour forces may vary in relation to a country's unemployment level. When the economy is booming and the level of unemployment is low, employees have much greater power and influence over their working conditions, pay and other employment rights (Tayeb, 2005). Having said that, managers in return gain more prerogatives during recessions and periods of high unemployment by controlling employees' working conditions and compensation, thus weakening the power and influence of both workers and trade unions. Jackson and Schuler (1995) note that it is common in such periods for absenteeism and turnover rates to fall because competition for jobs is more intense and employees' poor performance may result in retrenchment. It has been identified that, in the USA, excess demand typically relates to low unemployment, whereas high unemployment is reported to be associated with excess supply (Jackson and Schuler, 1995).

Technological context

Technology has evolved along with globalization, which is often associated with advances in communication and information technology. The way people throughout the world communicate, exchange information and learn about their world has changed as computer usage has become more prevalent in almost every part of the globe, further enhanced by the increase in the number of information technology-literate individuals (Burton et al., 2003). The influence of technology is also apparent in HRM (Critical Thinking 10.4), especially with the transformation of traditional HRM to IT-based HRM, or what is known as e-HRM (Bondarouk and Ruel, 2009), as a result of the growing sophistication of IT.

e-HRM, for example, deals with the implementation of HRM strategies, policies and practices through the full use of web-based technologies. Bondarouk et al. (2009) believe that e-HRM can reduce the cost of traditional methods of processing and administration of paperwork, as well as speeding up transaction processing, reducing information errors and improving the tracking and control of human resources actions. However, the effectiveness of e-HRM may depend upon the types and levels of knowledge that are required by the system and the extent to which tasks and people are interdependent (Jackson and Schuler, 1995).

When face-to-face HRM services become obsolete, higher levels of motivation and commitment are required (Othman and Teh, 2003). This is because employees are expected to work independently with little supervision, so the supervisor's role is greatly reduced as control over employees' work behaviour can no longer be exerted through direct observation. According to Bondarouk and Ruel (2009), e-HRM eliminates the 'human resources middleman' who is initially responsible for dealing with human resources matters.

Besides ensuring independent work through the introduction of e-HRM, IT also enables organizational learning to help employees improve their capability, adaptation, knowledge and understanding (Othman and Teh, 2003) because the use of teams is practised, which helps the transfer of learning from the individual to the organization. Othman and Teh claim that, with the growing usage of IT, people are expected to think critically, be able to solve problems, communicate and work in teams, creatively and proactively, as well as bring diverse and newer perspectives to their work. This requires a change in organizational structures and processes, for example selection processes, training, performance appraisals and rewards. Put simply, this means that the way employee performance is monitored has to rely on data interpretation and on assessing outputs.

There are, however, some critiques of the usage of IT in organizations. Based on findings from Othman and Teh (2003), the workforce is deskilled and controlled by managers through the use of IT. There is less chance for employees to develop their intellectual skills when their role has already been weakened by IT. Additionally, while most management invests heavily in acquiring technology, insufficient resources tend to be allocated to managing the organizational change process; thus HRM issues are neglected, and technology usage fails to meet expectations.

Critical Thinking 10.4
Technological context and HRM

The correlation between new technology and work can be identified in many different forms. Academics have, however, pinpointed three specific areas in which HRM practices are directly affected (Millward and Stevens, 1986):

- *Advanced technology change:* new plant machinery and equipment that has incorporated microprocessor technology.
- *Conventional technological change:* machinery and equipment not aided by microprocessor technology.
- *Organizational change:* substantial changes in work organizations not involving new plant, machinery or equipment (Bratton and Gold, 2007).

Across many workplaces, microprocessor technology plays an active role: in 1998, 87 per cent of manufacturing workplaces in the UK used microprocessor-based technology, a large jump from 44 per cent in 1984 (Bratton and Gold, 2007). This reflects how great an influence the technological context may have on designing HRM. Entire organizations are administered based on their information system. In addition, manufacturing process concepts are part of the technological context that are

able to directly impact upon organizations. Similarly, performance enhancement and organizational restructuring have vigorously shaped business processes in order to gain a competitive advantage.

Total quality management (TQM) focuses on maximizing profits by increasing service and product quality and decreasing costs (Hill, 2005). TQM and other quality management innovations such as Six Sigma are ground-breaking institutional approaches to improving organizations and are an example of how the technological context has influenced the design of HRM. However, quality management may also pose a problem for managers and organizations: although the system welcomes key aspects of quality – between suppliers and customers – it demands mutual commitment from every party involved in the organization and requires rigorous implementation and corporate governance, which may cause a hegemonic conflict between top and mid-level management and the workforce whom they direct.

Questions
1 Do technological advances always have positive implications for employees in organizations?
2 What role can HRM play in coping with changes in the technological context of an organization?

Critical discussion and analysis

HRM is constantly being reshaped by new economic, sociocultural and political realities. Changes in the levels of unemployment, structural transformation (for example, privatization and deindustrialization) and social trends (an ageing population) will all shift the balance of power in individual and collective contract negotiations.

Furthermore, increasing globalization and advances in information and communication technologies are fast transforming the world into a global village in which management practices cannot remain isolated from external influences. As demonstrated in this chapter, we will be ill-advised to believe that globalization will cause organizations to become isolated or aloof from the society in which they operate. Conversely, local contexts will remain a key influence on the way in which human resources are treated and managed.

It is, however, a fact that some types of HRM system may be used effectively across countries that are culturally quite dissimilar (Wickens, 1987; MacDuffie and Krafcik, 1992), and that organizational and industry characteristics remain key determinants of managerial practices and employee behaviours (Hofstede, 1991). Our understanding of the role of national culture in HRM could also benefit from investigations examining how multinational corporations develop HRM systems that are simultaneously consistent with multiple and distinct local cultures and yet internally consistent in the context of a single organization (cf. Heenan and Perlmutter, 1979; Tung, 1993; Jackson and Schuler, 1995).

From an academic perspective, certain specialized fields, for example industrial-organizational psychology and social work psychology, may be very useful in advancing our understanding of HRM in context. In this age of unprecedented internationalization as well as sociocultural specificity, the dearth of comparative publications in HRM is both surprising and alarming (Özbilgin, 2004). Several shifts in approach may be required: from treating organizational settings as sources of error variance to attending as closely as possible to individual characteristics; from focusing on individuals to treating social systems as the target for study; from focusing on single practices or policies to adopting a holistic approach to conceptualizing HRM systems; from research conducted in single organizations at one point in time to research comparing multiple organizations across time, space and culture; and from a search for the 'one best way' to a search for the many possible ways to design and maintain effective HRM systems (Jackson and Schuler, 1995) .

Conclusion

In conclusion, it is imperative that local contextual factors are considered when designing and operationalizing HRM policies. Although HRM and organizations are currently evolving due to the evolving nature of globalization, culture continues to have a vital effect on people and organizations. As Stredwick notes 'indeed to the observer in one country, the workplace practices in another might seem downright absurd ... any attempt to impose the ways and methods that he or she knows best in that other national context might be doomed to failure' (2005: 442).

The chapter has demonstrated that the field of HRM will have limited value if it does not adequately take into account cultural and institutional contexts. Global policies may seem an easy solution, but the issue of the expatriate workers, diversity and institutional and cultural variances must not be neglected. As Sparrow and Hiltrop (1994) suggest, care must be taken to escape the trap of ignoring significant differences between national cultures.

In this chapter, we have identified a number of elements in the macrolevel environment, that is, the sociocultural, legal, political, economic and technological contexts, that affect HRM in different ways. Economy is an important context that influences the design and outcomes of HRM; the financial crisis occurring at the time of writing this book has affected employment environment across many nations, and this is in turn affecting the behaviour of local labour markets. Similarly, cultural values, such as age and gender traditions and stereotypes, are significant social contexts relevant to HRM.

Managers also need to be aware of legal contexts that have the potential to affect employment relations. Local culture and other external pressures will influence the design of HRM, but institutions can, in their turn, influence the contexts affecting them – political leveraging and lobbying has, for example, been conducted by corporations against agreements that have had the potential to affect employment behaviour, such as the Kyoto agreement.

External contexts can also be linked to the pursuit for competitive advantage, as is usually emphasized in organizations in industrialized Western economies linking HRM strategy to competitive advantage. Towards that end, HRM practitioners will need to analyse and respond to external contextual issues and deal with them in a coherent and strategic manner.

❓ For discussion and revision

1 How do macrocontextual factors affect the design and operationalization of the following HRM functions:

* Recruitment and selection
* Training
* Performance management
* Reward management
* Career management.

2 Make a study of HRM policies and practices in a specific company. Identify the various ways in which the HRM policies and practices in that company are affected by its sociocultural, political, legal and economic contexts.

3 What are various tensions between the globalization and contextualization of HRM? What are implications of such tensions for the future of HRM?

4 Identify at least one resource in a language other than English which deals with issues related to HRM. Feel free to seek help from a friend who speaks a language other than English. What can you learn from this resource?

5 How does the dominance of US and UK literature in the field of HRM affect the contextualization of HRM?

6 According to Hofstede (1991), organizational and industry characteristics may be more important than national cultures as determinants of managerial practices and employee behaviours. Discuss.

Further reading

Books

Dowling, P. J., Festing, M. and Engle, A. D. (2008) *International Human Resource Management. Managing People in a Multinational Context* (5th edn). London: Thomson Publishing.

Price, A. (2007) *Human Resource Management in a Business Context* (3rd edn). London: Thomson Learning.

Quinn, J. B., Mintzberg, H. and James, R. M. (eds) (1988) *The Strategy Process: Concepts, Context, and Cases*. Englewood Cliffs, NJ: Prentice Hall International.

Journals

Budhwar, P. and Khatri, P. (2001) HRM in context: the applicability of HRM models in India. *International Journal of Cross Cultural Management*, 1(3): 333–56.

Jackson, S. E. and Schuler, R. S. (1995) Understanding human resource management in the context of organizations and their environment. *Annual Review of Psychology*, 46: 237–64.

Kamoche, K. (2002) Introduction: human resource management in Africa. *International Journal of Human Resource Management*, 13(7): 993–7.

Khatri, N. (1999) Emerging issues in strategic HRM in Singapore. *International Journal of Manpower*, 20(8): 516–29.

Schmidt, V. (1993) An end to French economic exceptionalism? The transformation of business under Mitterand. *California Management Review*, (Fall), 75–98.

Selmer, J. and Leon C. D. (2001) Pinoy-style HRM: human resource management in Philippines. *Asia Pacific Business Review*, 8(1): 127–44.

Wan, D. (2003) Human resource management in Singapore: changes and continuities. *Asia Pacific Business Review*, 9(4): 129–46.

Other resources

Institut Perkhidmatan Awam (2008) About IPA. Available from: http://ipa.gov.bn/ipaonline/ipa_information/ipa_history.aspx [accessed 31 December 2009].

Laman Rasmi Jabatan Pekhidmatan Awam (n.d.) Hal Ehwal JPA. Available from: http://jpa.gov.bn/hal_ehwal/index.htm [accessed 31 December 2009].

Case Study HRM in Brunei's public sector

Brunei is a monarchical government that is governed by Sultan Haji Hassanal Bolkiah Mu'izzaddin Waddaulah, who has executive authority and is assisted and advised by five constitutional bodies. The concept of 'Malay Islamic Monarchy' (MIB) is often thought of as a 'national philosophy', incorporating both the official Malay language, culture and customs and the importance of Islam as a religion and a set of guiding values.

Brunei, situated in South-East Asia, has an estimated population of 390,000, of whom 67 per cent are Malay and 15 per cent are Chinese, the remaining 18 per cent comprising indigenous groups, expatriates and immigrants. About 54 per cent of the overall population is made up of the 20–54-year age group, which is the economically productive group. The main source of income for Brunei is the oil and gas industry, followed by the private and government sectors. The public sector is the main employer for the majority of citizens and residents of Brunei (Brunei Economic Development Board, n.d.).

Owing to Brunei's distinct political system, it has different employment structures from those of other South-East Asian countries. Brunei is ruled by a strict essence of conformity and consensus that does not allow organization or individuals to challenge the government and its policies. Brunei's public sector may be seen as a 'model employer' (Beattie and Osborne, 2008), in the sense that the public sector sets an example to the private sector in terms of the fair treatment of employees and providing good conditions of service – this includes high levels of job security, better leave entitlement and generous pensions (Black and Upchurch, 1999). In this case study, we seek to explore how HRM policies and practices in the public sector are shaped by contextual influences in Brunei.

In the public sector, the *General Order and State Circulars* shape HRM practices. The General Order dates back to 1962; its content covers many key elements of HRM, for example appointments, promotions, benefit entitlement, work etiquette and discipline, although certain current issues related to HRM may not be present in the booklet. State Circulars cover more current HRM issues not addressed in the General Order, including those which have just arisen. All government bodies are sent Circulars whenever any new issues arise. Circulars often call upon the command of the Sultan of Brunei, who holds the absolute power in the way Brunei should be managed.

All civil servants are required to have a detailed knowledge of – and abide by – both the General Order and State Circulars in order to carry out their jobs and to progress in their careers. Every officer, supervisor or clerk who is aspiring towards promotion or a rise in salary will have to sit a written examination based on the content of both these sets of government policies.

A recent innovation within HRM in the Brunei public sector is the *Government Employee Management System* (GEMS), which is currently being trialled. This is a web-based system that enables efficient data input and greater transparency, which allows a better management of HRM practices such as recruitment and selection, compensation and benefits, as well as human resources administration. In addition, this will reduce paper usage and help Brunei to become more 'green'. Human resources administrators, government employees and the public are the three main stakeholders that GEMS is focusing on.

GEMS allows human resources administrators to manage job advertisements, and update and approve allowance and benefit applications. Government employees can apply for allowances and benefits online, retrieve useful information such as the latest policies that have been introduced, check their balance of leave entitlement and participate in surveys and forums where they can express their suggestions for how to improve the civil service. The public, on the other hand, can check job vacancies online, submit job applications and track their progress (Government Employee Management System, 2010).

Interviews conducted with a number of mangers and non-managerial staff in three departments within the Brunei public sector have provided an insight into how the local context has an impact on the design and implementation of HRM practices.

Socioculture

Many interviewees felt that Brunei's close-knit socioculture was an important factor in HRM practices. In particular, family relationships have a significant impact on workplace relations with supervisors and colleagues alike. As one interviewee stated:

> Working in the public sector, we are expected to respect our supervisors and officers. Supervisors and officers, regardless of their age, are like a father or leader to us; we share an informal relationship and talk to them in person if we have any issues or problems. A very family-like relationship is what motivates me, in particular, because it gives me a feeling of belonging and

10

security. Although we have an informal relationship, it does not mean that we respect our superiors any less.

Previous research in other countries has highlighted that close-knit relationships often result in subjective and informal recruitment and selection processes (see, for example, Myloni et al.'s [2004] research in Greece). The majority of the employees interviewed for this case study claimed that family connections do not influence the way people are employed. This is evident in the following except:

> Yes we have a very close relationship in our culture, but I must say that it has no direct influence on the way we recruit and select applicants. Because everyone goes through the same procedure, that is, a written exam and then interviews for short-listed applicants. Furthermore, there are guidelines and procedures that need to be followed when recruiting people. Also, there is a group of committee members who decides on the final result'; this is based on consensus agreement. There is no room for favouritism. ... Personally, when the one who is newly recruited happens to be the son/daughter of an authority figure in the public sector, it is because he/she is qualified for the position, he/she might have already been trained with the kind of traits and skills that we are looking for. That is not nepotism.

However, the above account contradicts statements made by at least three other participants, who felt that 'nepotism' is still the essence of recruitment and selection, particularly in the government sector. Overall, the interviews suggest that close-knit social relationships in Brunei society have an impact on employment relationship in the workplace. However, the impact is moderated in HRM practices, particularly in recruitment and selection, because governmental regulations still affect HRM policies.

Law and politics

The national philosophy of MIB has an important influence on the way HRM works in the public sector. One interviewee noted that:

> Malay culture teaches us to be respectful and courteous to others. Islam instils honesty, trust, loyalty and good faith in oneself. Monarchic government means that His Majesty the Sultan holds the ultimate power in decision-making; no one is allowed to go against His Majesty's command. So, basically MIB influences us, in terms of the way we bring ourselves, the way we

perform our work as a loyal subject of His Majesty. Every aspect of government affairs revolves around the concept of MIB.

The political influence of the state has in other studies been shown to either strengthen or undermine the role of HRM (Tayeb, 2005): a more cooperative government will have a better chance of adopting HRM efficiently, and vice versa. When asked whether monarchical government hinders employee participation in decision-making, one interviewee stated that:

> Any grievances, complaints or suggestions that are made by employees are attended to by respective supervisors or officers. Obviously in a monarchical government like Brunei, His Majesty holds the absolute powers in major decisions. But other than that, we do value employees' suggestions and points of view. We always take their opinions into consideration. In my position as an officer, I make sure that my door is always open for them to come in and express any problem or suggestion that they may have. We ensure that we include them into any problem-solving and decision-making, because it is important that they feel included.

When asked about how the General Order and State Circulars are dealt with by public sector workers, managers underlined the critical importance of these, not only for their own careers, but also to provide a basis for all government servants for what should and should not be done while working in the public sector. As one interviewee noted:

> Every circular is by command of His Majesty The Sultan; we are obliged to obey them. Officers are directed to encourage and make employees aware of existing circulars.

Non-managerial staff, however, tended to take a less rigorous approach and were sometimes unfamiliar with the content of these documents. Regulations were still poorly enforced regardless of the availability of the General Order and State Circulars.

With regards to the content of the General Order, benefits entitlements and working hours are usually included and practised in workplace policies. Participants generally felt that the policies adopted by the government are flexible and family-friendly. For example, one married female participant stated that:

> Yes it is very family-friendly. One of the most obvious aspect is the working hours in the government sector. In the regulation book, General Order, it states that one should work maximum 8 hours from 7.45 am to 4.30 pm, but

there is some flexibility when it comes to family responsibility, such as sending or picking up children to/from school. Also, in terms of leave entitlement, a married woman can take unpaid leave to follow her husband who was sent to work abroad and her job is still available when she comes back.

Economics

Research suggests that, for individuals to be more productive and adaptable to changing economic conditions, experience and knowledge have to be significantly valued (Jackson and Schuler, 1995). In the Brunei public sector, this valuation of education and human capital seems to have been achieved. When asked whether different economic situations influenced the need for educated or experienced workforce, one manager noted that:

> In the government sector education plays a very important role because we believe fresh graduates have new ideas, which would ultimately benefit the organization over a person with experience who might not have anything new to bring to the organization.

From an economic perspective, Brunei is currently facing an excess supply of labour in the job market. An officer thus explained this:

> This is a very challenging issue Brunei is facing. The demand for jobs is overwhelmingly high but the supply of jobs to accommodate the demand is rather low. This is because a new post will only be available when someone retires, resigns, there is end of contract of an employee or a budget is allocated to create new posts.

This is consistent with Jackson and Schuler's observation that a country is likely to experience high unemployment in times of oversupply of its labour force. Brunei is currently experiencing this problem, and thus many students are sponsored to study abroad to temporarily alleviate the number of workers currently seeking jobs. The problem with an oversupply of labour is that very few vacant positions are usually available in the government sector. For example, in response to a recent advertisement (at the time of this research) for a clerical position, 1,000 applications were received for only four vacancies.

Technology

Technology is a new element in the government sector in Brunei. The Sultan has allocated billions of dollars for IT to be used effectively. In particular, the introduction of GEMS, described above, is indic-

ative of a new approach to technology in HRM practice. Public sector workers have mixed reactions to this new system. One manager noted that:

> It's very convenient because there's less paperwork and sharing of documents will be easier as it is computerised. Leave applications, benefits entitlement, car and house loans, all are accessible any time and anywhere.

Another, less positively, argued that:

> We currently have an online method of inputting data called SIMPA; it is in Malay and it is very straightforward. But it is only for data entry and nothing else. Well, GEMS from what I have tried is a bit too complex for me because there are so may folders to click on and most importantly, it is in English. To be honest, I am not good in English language, so I don't know how I will be able to get used to the changes.

Officers in general tend to agree with the technological changes that the government intends to implement, whereas the staff are slightly hesitant about the changes. For example, a training officer stated that:

> Every human resources development representative of each government department is given courses to train their respective employees on the usage of this new system. Emphasis is given to clerical positions as they are the ones who handle most paperwork.

From the interview data, one obvious challenge facing HRM in Brunei relates to how well individuals can adjust themselves to technological changes. Moving away from the traditional face-to-face HRM services may cause some difficulty and stress for some employees. Training, on the other hand, may assist staff and officers to adapt effectively to such changes.

Conclusion

This study of HRM in Brunei makes clear that the macroenvironmental context has a huge impact on the way HRM polices are designed and implemented. Culture serves as the overarching umbrella for all the other contexts, such as the legal and political system, the economy and adaptation to technology. In the main, HRM in Brunei revolves around the MIB ideology, which signifies the extent to which Western-originated HRM practices are customized and applied in the country. Human capital is given great importance and has high value in the job market; incentives are, therefore, given to improve human capital. However, the monarchical government of Brunei limits the ability for freedom of speech, freedom of associations and collective bargaining.

A hierarchical relationship is present in the government sector, but power distance is not a key concern, as is evident from the interview data. These show that Brunei does have a hierarchical relationship as claimed by Hofstede (1984) but that the power distance is not very great and is often a sign of respect for authority and for one's superiors. The relationship shared between officers and subordinates positively affects employees' participation rates in problem-solving and decision-making. However, close-knit relationships seem not to excessively influence the recruitment and selection process, which is regulated by state laws and procedures.

From a legal and political context perspective, the MIB ideology seems to have a visible impact on HRM. It enhances the initiatives of various departments in ensuring that everyone gets 100 hours of training and development. It also prohibits employees from setting up or joining trade unions, instead encouraging a more peaceful and harmonious negotiation with officers and supervisors. The General Order and State Circulars are still weakly enforced, although superiors tried to stress their importance. In addition, MIB and state laws help to create a family-friendly policy that is flexible for working parents and employees with dependants.

From an economic context perspective, human capital, education, knowledge and skills are encouraged through continuous learning for all employees and officers. The benefits offered by the public sector create the perception of its being the most stable and secure workplace, and hence provide an advantage when recruiting and retaining human capital. Oversupply of the workforce is a prominent issue in Brunei. This affects HRM processes in making sure that the public sector recruits the right people for the right jobs.

Technology seems to be an upcoming aspect in the government sector. Not much information could be gleaned, except for the perceptions of older workers that there is a shift towards an online-based system of HRM. Some older workers find it difficult to adjust to this, but they are still able to do so slowly. Also, when officers and staff were asked whether this would increase convenience, most participants answered positively, saying that IT is helping to speed up their work and lessen their workload.

It can be concluded that local culture and politics (MIB) have a much greater impact on the implementation of HRM in Brunei. We recommend that further research be conducted on a larger scale to explore the contextualization of HRM in Brunei and other national contexts. Preferably, academia–industry partnership-based research in these government departments might allow for a deeper understanding of the topic.

Questions

1 How do culture and politics affect the design and implementation of HRM in Brunei?

2 Culture serves as the overarching umbrella for all the other contexts, such as the legal and political system, the economy and adaptation to technology. Critically discuss this.

3 How can HRM enable individual employees to adjust themselves to technological changes in their organizations?

4 How does HRM in Brunei different from HRM in a Western country?

References

Adler, N. J. (1991) *International Dimensions of Organizational Behavior*. Boston, MA: PWS-KENT Publishing.

Ailon, G. (2008) Mirror, mirror on the wall: culture's consequences in a value test of its own design. *Academy of Management Review*, 33(4): 885–904.

Arvey, R. D., Bhagat, R. S. and Salas, E. (1991) Cross-cultural and cross-national issues in personnel and human resources management: where do we go from here? *Personnel and Human Resource Management*, 9: 367–407.

Baruch, Y. (2001) Global or North American top management journals? *Journal of Cross-cultural Management*, 1(1): 131–47.

Beattie, R. S. and Osborne, S. P. (2008) *Human Resource Management in the Public Sector*. London: Routledge.

Beer, M., Lawrance, P. R., Mills, D. Q. and Walton, R. E. (1985) *Human Resource Management*. New York: Free Press.

Bennington, L. and Habir, A. D. (2003) Human resource management in Indonesia. *Human Resource Management Review*, 13(3): 373–92.

Black, J. and Upchurch, M. (1999) Public sector employment. In Hollinshead, G., Nicholls, P. and Tailby, S. (eds) *Employee Relations*. London: Financial Times Management.

Bondarouk, T. V. and Ruel, H. J. M. (2009) Electronic human resource management: challenges in the digital era. *International Journal of Human Resource Management*, 20(3): 505–14.

Bondarouk, T., Ruel, H. and Heijden B. V. D. (2009) e-HRM effectiveness in a public sector organization: a multi-stakeholder perspective. *International Journal of Human Resource Management*, 20(3): 578–90.

Bratton, J. and Gold, J. (2007) *Human Resource Management: Theory and Practice* (4th edn). New York: Palgrave Macmillan.

Brewster, C. (2007) Comparative HRM: European views and perspectives. *International Journal of Human Resource Management*, 18(5): 769–87.

Brewster, C. and Tyson, S. (eds) (1991) *International Comparisons in Human Resource Management*. London: Pitman.

Brunei Economic Development Board (n.d.) Introducing Brunei. [Online]. Available from: http://www.bedb.com.bn/ [Accessed 9 November 2009].

Budhwar, P. S. and Debrah, Y. A. (2001) *Human Resource Management in Developing Countries*. London: Routledge.

Burton, J. P., Butler, J. E. and Mowday, R. T. (2003) Lions, tigers and alley cats: HRM's role in Asian business development. *Human Resource Management Review*, 13(3): 487–98.

Caligiuri, P. M. (1999) The ranking of scholarly journals in international human resource management. *International Journal of Human Resource Management*, 10(3): 515–19.

Carroll, G. R., Delacroix, J. and Goodstein, J. (1988) The political environments of organizations: an ecological view. *Research in Organizational Behavior*, 10: 359–92.

Chase, S., 2002. Ratifying Kyoto. *Globe and Mail*, 27 February, p. B6.

Chomsky, N. (1999). *Profit over People: Neoliberalism and the Global Order*. New York: Seven Stories Press.

Clark, T., Gospel, H. and Montgomery, J. (1999) Running on the spot? A review of twenty years of research on the management of human resources in comparative and international perspective. *International Journal of Human Resource Management*, 10(3): 520–44.

Clark, T., Grant, D. and Heijltjes, M. (2000) Researching comparative and international human resource management. *International Studies of Management and Organization*, 29(4): 6–17.

Collin, A. (2007) Contextualising HRM: developing critical thinking. In Beardwell, J. and Claydon, T. (eds) *Human Resource Management: A Contemporary Approach*. Harlow: FT Prentice Hall, pp. 83–116.

Drucker, P. (1954) *The Practice of Management*. New York: Harper & Row.

Edwards, T. (2004) The transfer of employment practices across borders in multinational companies. In Harzing, A.-W. and Ruysseveldt, J. V. (eds) *International Human Resource Management*. London: Sage, pp. 389–410.

Faux, J. & Mishel, L. (2001) Inequality and the global economy. In Hutton, W. and Giddens, A. (eds.) *On the Edge: Living with Capitalism*. London: Vintage Books.

Flamholtz, E. G. and Lacey, J. M. (1981) Personnel management, human capital theory, and human resource accounting. Cited in Jackson, S. E. and Schuler, R. S. (1995) Understanding human resource management in the context of organizations and their environments. *Annual Review of Psychology*, 46: 237–64.

Florkowski, G. W. and Nath, R. (1993) MNC responses to the legal environment of international human resource management. *International Journal of Human Resource Management*, 4: 305–24.

Gaugler, E. (1988) HR management: an international comparison. *Personnel*, (August): 24–30.

Government Employee Management System (2010) About GEMS: GEMS Background. [Online]. Available from: http://www.jpa.gov.bn/gems/EN/About_GEMS/background.htm [Accessed 10 January 2010].

Harris, L. (2002) The future for the HRM function in local government: everything has changed – but has anything changed? *Strategic Change*, 11(7): 369–78.

Heenan, D. A. and Perlmutter, H. V. (1979) *Multinational Organization Development*. Reading, MA: Pearson Addison Wesley.

Hill, T. (2005) *Operations Management*. Basingstoke: Palgrave Macmillan.

Hill, C. (2009) *International Business: Competing in the Global Marketplace* (7th edn). New York: McGraw-Hill.

Hofstede, G. (1980) *Culture's Consequences: International Differences in Work Related Values*. Beverly Hills: Sage.

Hofstede, G. (1984) Cultural dimension in management and planning. *Asia Pacific Journal of Management*, 1(2): 81–99.

Hofstede, G. (1991) *Cultures and Organizations*. London: McGraw-Hill.

Hu, Y.-S. (1992) Global or stateless corporations are national firms with international operations. *California Management Review*, (Winter): 107–26.

Jackson, S. E. and Schuler, R. S. (1995) Understanding human resource management in the context of organizations and their environments. *Annual Review of Psychology*, 46: 237–64.

Levy-Leboyer, C. (1994) Selection and assessment in Europe. In Triandis, H. C., Dunnette, M. D. and Hough, L. M. (eds) *Handbook of Industrial and Organizational Psychology* (2nd edn, Vol. 4). Palo Alto, CA: Consulting Psychology Press, pp. 173–90.

Lincoln, J. R. (1993) Work organization in Japan and the United States. In Kogut, B. (ed.) *Country Competitiveness: Technology and the Organizing of Work*. Oxford: Oxford University Press, pp. 93–124.

McCourt, W. and Foon L. M. (2007) Malaysia as model: policy transferability in an Asian country. *Public Management Review*, 9(2): 211–29.

MacDuffie, J. P. and Krafcik, J. (1992) Integrating technology and human resources for high performance manufacturing. In Kochan, T. and Useem, M. (eds) *Transforming Organizations*. New York: Oxford University Press, pp. 210–26.

McGregor, D. (1957) *The Human Side of Enterprise. Fifth Anniversary Convocation of the MIT School of Industrial Management.* Cambridge, MA: MIT Press.

McSweeney, B. (2002) Hofstede's model of national cultural differences and their consequences: a triumph of faith – a failure of analysis. *Human Relations*, 55(1): 89–118.

Maurice, M., Sellier, F. and Silvestre, J.-J. (1986) *Bases of Industrial Power*. Cambridge, MA: MIT Press.

Millward, N. and Stevens, M. (1986) *British Workplace Industrial Relations 1980–1984*. Aldershot: Gower.

Myloni, B., Harzing, A. K. and Mirza, H. (2004) Host country specific factors and the transfer of human resource management practices in multinational companies. *International Journal of Manpower*, 25(6): 518–34.

Needle, D. (2004) *Business in Context* (4th edn). London: Thomson.

Noe, R. A., Hollenbeck, J. R., Gerhart, B. and Wright, P. M. (2008) *Human Resource Management: Gaining a Competitive Advantage* (6th edn). New York: McGraw Hill.

Othman, R. and The, C. (2003) On developing the informated work place: HRM issues in Malaysia. *Human Resource Management Review*, 13: 393–406.

Özbilgin, M. (2004) Inertia of the international human resource management text in a changing world: an examination of the editorial board membership of the top 21 IHRM journals. *Personnel Review*, 33(2): 205–21.

Price, A. (1997) *Human Resource Management in a Business Context*. London: International Thomson Business Press.

Ronen, S. (1994) An underlying structure of motivational need taxonomies: a cross-cultural confirmation. In Triandis, H. C., Dunnette, M. D. and Hough, L. M. (eds) *Handbook of Industrial and Organizational Psychology* (2nd edn, Vol. 4). Palo Alto, CA: Consulting Psychology Press, pp. 241–70.

Rousseau, D. M. (1990). Assessing organizational culture: the case for multiple methods. In Schneider, B. (ed.), *Organizational Climate and Culture*. San Francisco: Jossey-Bass, pp. 153–92.

Ruigrok, W. and van Tulder, R. (1995) *The Logic of International Restructuring*. London: Routledge.

Schneider, S. (2001) Introduction to the international human resource management special issue. *Journal of World Business*, 36(4): 341.

Schuler, R. S. and Jackson, S. E. (1987) Linking competitive strategies with human resource management practices. *Academy of Management Review*, 1(3): 207–19.

Sparrow, P. R. and Hiltrop, J.-M. (1994) *European Human Resource Management in Transition*. London: Prentice Hall.

Storey, J. (1992) *Developments in the Management of Human Resources: An Analytical Review*. Oxford: Blackwell.

Strauss, G. (1982) Workers participation in management: an international perspective. *Research in Organizational Behavior*, 4: 173–265.

Stredwick, J. (2005) *An Introduction to Human Resource Management* (2nd edn). London: Elsevier.

Tayeb, M. H. (2005) *International Human Resource Management: A Multinational Company Perspective*. New York: Oxford University Press.

Taylor, S., Beechler, S. and Napier, N. (1996) Toward an integrated model for strategic international human resource management. *Academy of Management Review*, 21(4): 959–71.

Triandis, H. C., Dunnette, M. D. and Hough, L. M. (eds) (1994) *Handbook of Industrial and Organizational Psychology* (2nd edn, Vol. 4). Palo Alto, CA: Consulting Psychology Press.

Tung, R. L. (1993) Managing cross-national and intra-national diversity. *Human Resource Management Journal*, 23(4): 461–77.

Tylor, E. B. (1924). *Primitive Culture* (7th edn, Vols 1 and 2). New York: Brentano's.

Wheelan, C. (2003) *Naked Economics: Undressing the Dismal Science*. New York: W. W. Norton.

Wickens, P. (1987) *The Road to Nissan*. London: Macmillan.

Human resource management in contemporary transnational companies

Tineke Cappellen, Patrizia Zanoni and Maddy Janssens

11

After reading this chapter, you should be able to:

☐ Understand the implications of globalization for today's workers

☐ Explain how human resource management can facilitate integration and differentiation within transnational organizations

☐ Discuss the role of global professionals within organizations

☐ Critically reflect on the new forms that power relations take in contemporary transnational organizations

Introduction

The global context

Overview of classical theories and key concepts

The contentious nature of HRM in transnational companies

Critical analysis and discussion

Conclusion

For discussion and revision

Further reading

Case study: View Corporation

References

Introduction

In today's economy, the majority of national companies are converting into international companies, entering new markets and creating value-adding activities in geographies outside their home country (Galbraith, 2000). They have grown from an international towards a multinational, then a global and finally a transnational mentality (see, for example, Ghoshal and Nohria, 1993; Bartlett et al., 2004). In the transnational form, which is the highest level of international development (Galbraith, 2000), subsidiaries are no longer independent national subunits (a multinational form), and global authority is no longer centralized in the company's native headquarters (a global form). Rather, the transnational scope moves beyond the global one, aiming for a combination of homogenized global products characterized by high quality and low cost along with local responsiveness that reasserts national preferences (Bartlett et al., 2004). Subsidiaries take leading and contributory roles to generate value-adding advantages, creating a power structure that is distributed throughout the firm.

Due to this increasing transnational character of their activities within a global economy (Bartlett et al., 2004), companies are today changing their approach to employees' mobility and cross-border transfers. Traditionally, they relied mainly on expatriate assignments, whereby employees were sent from headquarters to foreign branches for a period spanning 2 years or more. Today, companies instead make use of a range of alternative forms of international work, such as short-term assignments, commuter assignments, international business travel and virtual assignments (Collings et al., 2007). Alongside these assignments, which are short term and directed towards specific purposes, globalization has given rise to 'global professionals' who coordinate functional domains on a global scale (Bartlett and Ghoshal, 1992).

In this chapter, we will discuss the latest evolution in human resource management (HRM) in transnational organizations and the emergence of the global professional as a new profile within these organizations. The structure of the chapter is as follows. In the first section, we will discuss the global context within which transnational companies and global professionals need to work. Afterwards, we present an overview of classical theories and key concepts relevant to transnational companies and their employees. In the third section, we will discuss the implications of the transnational form of international development for several HRM issues within contemporary companies. For each section presented in this chapter, we will first discuss the 'mainstream' approaches and then reflect on them by drawing on more critical literature. Finally, the chapter ends by discussing the benefits of studying HRM from a critical perspective and making recommendations in terms of organizations, managers and employees.

The global context

According to Govindarajan and Gupta (2001), the global context refers to the interdependence of countries, industries and companies as reflected in an increasing cross-border flow of three things: goods and services, capital, and know-how. As such, it reflects a dynamic complexity in which the dimensions of multiplicity, interdependence and ambiguity interact to multiply each other's effects (Lane et al., 2006):

- First, *multiplicity* reflects the different models for organizing and conducting business that should enable organizations to function in an environment characterized by more (number) and different (nature) players.
- Second, *interdependence* points to the cross-border flows and exchanges that remove the isolated status of organizations through interdependent arrangements such as outsourcing, alliances and network arrangements.
- Finally, *ambiguity* refers to the vast amount of information available, which is unclear because of the multiple meanings, incorrect attributions, erroneous interpretations and conflicting interests that hinder effective guidance of the organization's actions.

Overview of classical theories and key concepts

Transnational organizations in a global economy

The activities of multinational corporations (MNCs) have been increasingly global in scope, reflecting the growing interdependence of countries, industries and companies (Box 11.1) (Govindarajan and Gupta, 2001). In the earliest stages of internationalization, foreign operations used to be distant outposts of the parent company fully controlled by headquarters, whose main task was to sell the company's products in foreign markets. Nowadays, organizations are increasingly organized along a transnational structure that enables them to deal with simultaneous demands for global efficiency and worldwide innovation on the one hand, and national responsiveness on the other (Bartlett and Ghoshal, 1989; Galbraith, 2000).

Organizations rely on a strong global management to ensure communication and coordination between the units across geographical, cultural and functional boundaries (Galbraith, 2000). In this way, they can identify customers across the world, realize cost-minimizing economies of scale and scope, and exchange information, products and people (Bartlett and Ghoshal, 1989, 2000; Ghoshal and Nohria, 1993). However, they also need a strong national subsidiary management that understands and can meet the changing needs of local customers, as well as dealing with the pressures (that is, employment and tax legislation, health standards, and so on) that host governments and regulatory agencies put upon them (Rosenzweig and Singh, 1991). As a result of this evolution, key activities and resources are today disseminated across different locations, turning subsidiaries into sources of a given product or expertise that can enhance value globally (Bartlett and Ghoshal, 2000). Accordingly, transnational organizations are structured as integrated networks of distributed and interdependent resources and capabilities.

> **Box 11.1** Characteristics of a transnational firm
>
> **Organization structure**
> ☐ Subsidiaries take leading and contributing roles in generating advantages
> ☐ There is a distributed power structure
> ☐ An integrated and interdependent network is present
>
> **Management process**
> ☐ Headquarters does not evidently play a dominant role
> ☐ There is an awareness of location-specific advantages and lead markets outside the home country
> ☐ The firm seeks to achieve both global efficiency and local responsiveness
> ☐ There is a large flow of products, people and information between the subsidiaries

This transnational, networked structure of the organization has generally been interpreted as an evolution towards less hierarchical relations between headquarters and subsidiaries, with power being less centralized and more evenly distributed (Galbraith, 2000). More critically oriented scholars have, however, challenged this view. Some have argued that subsidiaries in 'developing countries' continue to be cheap production centres owing to their lower labour costs, reproducing a classical international division of labour to the advantage of the West (Banerjee and Linstead, 2001; Mir et al., 2006).

Others, drawing on post-colonial theory, have rather argued that, under globalization, inequality is reproduced in a more subtle way through new types of control (Westwood, 2004). Whereas power was previously directed towards changing the behaviour of the colonized peoples, to serve the colonizer's interests, more subtle types of control today aim to change identity and the very sense of self (Prasad, 1997). It is a subjugation process that passes primarily through the symbolic and the cultural dimensions of relationships, rather than being solely one of military, political and economic domination. Drawing on Bhabha's notion of 'mimicry' (1994), Frenkel has recently argued that those who are colonized are expected and encouraged to imitate the colonizer, yet such imitation can never be perfect, excluding colonized individuals from becoming 'an essential and legitimate part of the colonizing society' (2008: 927).

Owing to unequal relations at the macro level, the subsidiaries and the company's headquarters can never be equivalent parties within transnational organizations. Yet others have shown how knowledge originating in non-Western countries continues to lack legitimacy in the eyes of the West (Wong-MingJi and Mir, 1997; Özbilgin, 2004; Frenkel, 2008), affecting the unequal exchange of practices and technologies throughout organizations (Frenkel, 2008; Leonardi, 2008; Mir et al., 2008).

Mini Case Study 11.1
The changing management process at Farmers' Future

Farmers' Future is a non-governmental organization (NGO) with roots in the Christian civil society movement of a Western European country. Their mission is to promote sustainable agriculture and a better future for farmers all over the world. Farmers' Future carries out two main types of activity: awareness-raising and education in the home country, and rural development programmes abroad. To achieve its goals, the organization raises funds from private and public donors and collaborates with rural organizations in developing countries. Seven regional offices led by expatriates support development programmes in Africa, Asia and Latin America that involve 152 local rural partners, one third of which are farmers' organizations.

Farmers' Future emerged over a decade ago from the merger between four NGOs operating in agriculture. At that time, public donors were asking for more professional management of NGOs and cooperation with local parties that focused on capacity-building to enhance market functioning while the grassroots transnational movement for sustainable agriculture was emerging. Facing the distinct approaches and expertise of the merging organizations, the rising institutional pressures and their increasingly important transnational advocacy role, the staff at Farmers' Future needed to build a new shared understanding of the organization's activities, structure and working practices.

Attempting to address donors' new demands, the headquarters identified a new strategic approach for the activities of Farmers' Future abroad. The focus shifted from agricultural production to capacity-building aimed at overcoming structural problems in all phases of the product chain, including enhancing farmers' access to markets. The organization also reorganized into two units covering local education and advocacy, and programmes abroad, respectively. Finally, a new, more professional financial reporting system was created and implemented in the organization.

Although the headquarters frequently discussed the changes with the regional officers, the new strategy, structure and practices clearly reflected external pressures on the headquarters. These external pressures were, however, felt much less in the overseas offices. As a result, new systems and procedures were increasingly perceived as being an imposition from headquarters. Pressures on regional representatives to reformulate their programmes to meet the new strategy met with much resistance as they were used to managing their programmes autonomously. The regional representatives were increasingly becoming executors of headquarters' global programme, but they were receiving little extra support to do this and remained fully accountable for the success or failure of their programme.

Questions
1 How does a transnational company differ from companies that operate under a more ethnocentric orientation?
2 What types of management structures and processes are essential for becoming a transnational firm?

Global professionals as key actors

Transnational organizations rely for their functioning on global professionals (Peiperl and Jonsen, 2007), managers who ensure that people and activities are coordinated and integrated into a worldwide value-added network contributing to the success of the organization as a whole (Martinez and Jarillo, 1989; Bartlett and Ghoshal, 1992; Galbraith, 2000). Unlike expatriate managers, who transferred knowledge and values from the headquarters to subsidiaries (Edström and Galbraith, 1977; Adler and Bartholomew, 1992), global professionals need to understand the complexities of working in an interdependent and complex global network (Box 11.2) (Adler and Bartholomew, 1992; Kedia and Mukherji, 1999). Their task is to recognize opportunities and risks across national and functional boundaries (Pucik and Saba, 1998) and to decide when it is opportune to be locally responsive and when to emphasize global integration (Adler and Bartholomew, 1992).

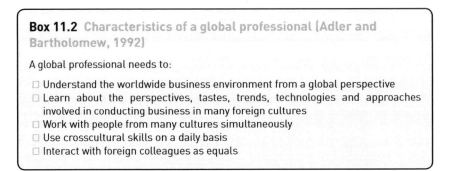

Box 11.2 Characteristics of a global professional [Adler and Bartholomew, 1992]

A global professional needs to:

☐ Understand the worldwide business environment from a global perspective
☐ Learn about the perspectives, tastes, trends, technologies and approaches involved in conducting business in many foreign cultures
☐ Work with people from many cultures simultaneously
☐ Use crosscultural skills on a daily basis
☐ Interact with foreign colleagues as equals

Because of working with multicultural teams, workforce diversity is a major challenge facing global professionals (see Chapter 4 on 'Diversity Management'). Conceptual literature indicates that they are expected to learn about the perspectives and approaches to conducting business that many foreign cultures use, be flexible and open-minded towards a multitude of cultures, and have a broad cultural perspective and appreciation for cultural diversity (Adler and Bartholomew, 1992; Pucik and Saba, 1998). However, recent empirical research questions this ability to gain an in-depth knowledge on a multitude of cultural contexts (Janssens and Cappellen, 2008).

More important than their cognitive ability, authors agree, is that global professionals are expected to overcome an ethnocentric mindset and develop an openness to other perspectives, selectively incorporating foreign values and practices into the global operations (Box 11.3) (Adler and Bartholomew, 1992; Janssens and Cappellen, 2008). These types of competency differ significantly from the ones of expatriate managers who, working within a particular foreign culture for a predetermined period of time, need to become knowledgeable in that specific culture (Adler and Bartholomew, 1992; Pucik and Saba, 1998). The working style of global professionals is also necessarily more collaborative. This is due, first, to the interdependence between team members, and second, to the lack of clearly defined hierarchies of structural and/or cultural dominance and subordination that once defined interactions between expatriates and their foreign colleagues (Adler and Bartholomew, 1992; Pucik and Saba, 1998).

Box 11.3 The global mindset

Global professionals need a global perspective that consists of a global mindset supported by appropriate skills and knowledge (Kedia and Mukherji, 1999). Not only do they need to be competent to operate across borders, but competent global professionals are also forced to adapt to the demands of significantly greater

▷

▷
> complexity. These may include a heightened need for cultural understanding, a greater need for a broad knowledge that spans functions and nations, wider and more frequent boundary-spanning, more stakeholders, a more challenging and expanded list of competing tensions, heightened ambiguity and more challenging ethical dilemmas (Bird and Osland, 2006).
>
> A global mindset is the ability to develop and interpret criteria for personal and business performance that are independent of the assumptions of a single country, culture or context, and to implement those criteria appropriately in different countries, cultures and contexts (Kedia and Mukherji, 1999). It reflects an openness to and an awareness of diversity across cultures and markets, with a propensity and ability to integrate this diversity.

Expatriates based in the host country could exert control over subsidiaries through a mixture of direct and indirect mechanisms (Edström and Galbraith, 1977; Jaeger, 1983; Shenkar et al., 2008). The direct mechanisms stand for formalized norms imposing a certain type of behaviour on individuals fulfilling established criteria (that is, position in the hierarchy). The indirect mechanisms represent the ideological control that shapes employees' sense of the self in a way that fits with and is productive in terms of managerially defined objectives (Alvesson and Willmott, 2002). Global professionals, who are not steadily present in the host country and coordinate teams dislocated across the world, necessarily rely more on ideological forms of control. Locally embedded managers have a greater degree of discretion over how to implement ideas, yet the two work together to construct professional identities that achieve commitment and compliance. This shift reflects a more general trend within organizations from direct to indirect modes of control, yet in culturally diverse organizations the intercultural dimension is key to this process (Peltonen, 2006; Zanoni and Janssens, 2007).

Mini Case Study 11.2
The quest for a global mindset

One of the main challenges for people working in a transnational organization is to have a global mindset. Alice, a worldwide sales and marketing manager of a utility company, explains this challenge as follows:

> The most difficult thing is to create a worldwide team, you know. And making people understand that by doing something local, they help the world. That's the first point. Second point, by doing something local, they may have an impact in another part of the world, because our customers are global as well. Because, for example, I know Kakogawa in Japan; he is investing in Dubai for a big project, and the decision-maker will be in Japan. And if the sales guy

doesn't meet the decision-maker in Japan, we will never get the order in Dubai. But how do you convince the sales guy in Japan that he has to spend time on a project in which he will never see an order, because the order will come in Dubai?

So Alice wants to convince her local sales manager in Japan to talk to a Japanese company in order to generate an order in Dubai.

Questions
1 What is the main problem that Alice is encountering?
2 What are some solutions for this problem? How would you go about convincing the local sales manager?

The contentious nature of HRM in transnational companies

The transnational nature of organizations brings with it a shift in the goals and approach of HRM. In order to contribute to the success of the company, HRM is expected to attract, develop and deploy talented employees who can work together effectively despite differences in their culture, language and location. Organizations today are still discovering the complexities of managing and organizing work in this new context (Lane et al., 2006; Boussebaa, 2009).

On the one hand, as transnational organizations are characterized by a range of employees with heterogeneous cultural, cognitive and emotional orientations, they need to have a set of explicit or implicit corporate values and shared beliefs that facilitate interpersonal collaboration and integration across the different parts of the organization (Bartlett et al., 2004). Yet, at the same time, management practices arising from the corporate level must be adopted to fit local cultural and legally mandated expectations (Paik and Sohn, 2004). Studies show that HRM is the function within organizations with the strongest tendency to diversify its practices to fit the local environment (Rosenzweig, 1994), as these are often mandated by local regulation or shaped by strong local conventions. It is therefore important for the central human resources department to adopt an appropriate 'parenting style' towards the diverse local human resources units. Techniques that are more formalized and centralized are used to provide consistent practice, to reduce uncertainty and to underpin the legitimacy of the corporate decision-making process (Ghoshal and Bartlett, 1990).

Critical perspectives view corporate values and global practices not just as facilitators of collaboration and integration, but rather as powerful culture-specific tools that emanate largely from the mother company to exert control over employees across the organization (Peltonen, 2006). At the same time, some authors have observed that culture is strategically used to justify not applying headquarters' employment conditions throughout MNCs but to allow less favourable conditions in the subsidiaries (Adler, 2002; Shimoni and Bergmann, 2006; Frenkel, 2008).

International employee resourcing

Today, organizations compete on the effectiveness and competence of their human talent pool around the world (Caligiuri and Tarique, 2006). As a result, one of the main challenges is to identify and develop talent to function effectively within a transnational organization. Careful selection practices are essential for global leaders (Osland et al., 2006). In contrast to expatriates, who are home-country nationals, transnational organizations no longer select talent exclusively from within their home country. Operating as a network across the globe, transnational organizations make use of their worldwide presence to select employees from a worldwide pool of human resources.

Given the fact that specific values and motivations are necessary to develop global leadership skills (Cappellen and Janssens, 2008), Caligiuri (2006) suggests selecting individuals on that basis. According to Spencer and Spencer (1993), this is the most cost-effective approach because motive and trait competencies cannot be taught. They also argue that people's values and motivations distinguish superior performers from good performers and are therefore a suitable way of selecting employees.

In a similar vein, a cultural intelligence (CQ) approach could be used to select superior performers for positions as global professionals (Janssens and Cappellen, 2008). Following Spencer and Spencer's reasoning (1993), this is especially true as CQ goes beyond other forms of intelligence, including not only cognitive, but also behavioural and motivational abilities, to deal with cultural contexts (Ang et al., 2007). As such, CQ may serve as a selection instrument, specifically selecting candidates based on their skills and values/motivations to work effectively in culturally diverse settings. In a similar vein, Kyriakidou (see Chapter 8 on 'Recruitment and Selection') refers to a renewed interest in personality testing as part of effective personnel selection. Technical knowledge and skills, which are complementary to motive and trait competencies, can be acquired in organizational training sessions. Therefore, they do not necessarily need to be part of the process to resource international staff.

International management development

Whereas the management development literature on expatriation focused on individuals' adjustment, performance and repatriation (Mendenhall et al., 1987; Thomas, 1998; Lazarova and Caligiuri, 2001), the more recent literature increasingly focuses on globally mobile professionals viewed as strategic human resources (Peltonen, 2006) with competencies considered to be crucial to the success of these organizations (Makela and Suutari, 2009). But unlike the situation for expatriates, recent research has indicated a lack of human resources support for alternative types of international work, because these individuals do not need to be relocated with their families (Mayerhofer et al., 2004; Collings et al., 2007). With the burden then placed on employees themselves, global professionals increasingly rely on self-management, building their career competency profile by focusing on their personal identification with work (Cappellen and Janssens, 2008). Instead of referencing their careers to the organization, these competencies enable them to reference their career to the global economy and thereby fulfil their career aspirations to work across borders and cross borders to work (Cappellen and Janssens, 2010a). This does not, however, imply that global professionals are job-hoppers; rather, they take agency over their own career even within the context of a single employer (Cappellen and Janssens, 2010b).

So far, the careers of global professionals have not been studied from critical perspectives. Peltonen (2006: 531) argues that a strategic human resources approach:

> makes it more difficult to think about and theorize expatriates as individuals-in-context, especially to understand how internationally mobile employees' work and career processes are affected and affect the wider circuits of power and control in international businesses.

However, running the organizational and individual perspectives of global professionals in counterpoint might offer a fruitful path that would better reflect the complexity of power dynamics in international management, abandoning the assumption that the interests of organizations and their global professionals are in agreement.

Developing crosscultural understanding

In an increasingly global business environment, employees must interact effectively with colleagues and customers from different cultural backgrounds. For expatriate managers, organizations have developed specific language and culture training programmes directed at working in one specific culture (Forster, 2000). Empirical research on global professionals indicates that they themselves question their ability to acquire in-depth cultural knowledge because of the multitude of cultural contexts they have to deal with and the cursory nature of their contact with them (Janssens and Cappellen, 2008). Rather than focusing on knowledge, they stress the importance of cultural awareness in intercultural communication, acknowledging the participants' differing perspectives and searching for compromises that will integrate these differences.

According to Friedman and Berthoin Antal (2005), the ability to recognize and use cultural differences as a resource for learning and to design action in specific contexts is the core intercultural competence today. Instead of learning the specific cultural values and norms of a single culture, as expatriates do, global professionals may benefit from approaching every intercultural situation as a unique and distinct one. This requires an awareness of their own cultural frame of reference, and an understanding of how this affects their thinking and behaviour. If the professional can then apply this to their counterpart in intercultural communications, reality can be negotiated, leading towards a jointly designed best way of generating ideas, decisions and actions (Friedman and Berthoin Antal, 2005).

Mini Case Study 11.3
Worldwide coordination and its mechanisms of control

Inherent in global professionals' core task of worldwide coordination is the need to be responsible for work that is remotely implemented. Steve, a worldwide quality manager at a water company, recounts how he experiences this challenge:

You are obliged to work in a very different way. If you need to get something done across borders, you need to send an e-mail, but in case he doesn't answer this e-mail, you can guess. Or he didn't bother, or he is overloaded, doesn't understand it, something which happens quite often, or he feels there is no need to answer, so you need to do it quite differently. You need to start calling him, and then he can still say yes, but in the end, you have to guess whether or not he has done it. So you need to check, whereas when it is in your own surroundings, you can see it.

So actually, you need to learn how to let them feel your presence, with all those people, from top to

11

bottom, and in the end to occupy yourself with the right issues in quite a different way. Each time you do something, you need to get these people to go along, buy in, saying explicitly where it is you want to go, checking whether they have understood. It sounds very simple and sometimes quite stupid, but … And then in the end, you need to check whether they have implemented it in the right way.

Questions
1 Can you help Steve to facilitate his work with people who are dislocated across the world?
2 How would you resolve Steve's problems to check whether your own team members have implemented the work in a correct way? Can you think of two additional strategies?
3 Reflect on the nature of your control strategies. Do you use direct or indirect mechanisms of control? Do you rely on more ideological forms of control?

Critical scholars of international management are unanimously supportive of conceptualizations of culture as being continuously constructed and reconstructed through interactions between individuals in specific contexts (Frenkel, 2008). In this sense, their perspectives are closer to those of the global professional, whose competencies are based on recognizing culture as a dynamic and relational process, than to the traditional expatriate, who was trained to acquire a specific culture, understood as a fixed set of values and rules, in order to be able to enact 'culturally appropriate' behaviour in the host country (Forster, 2000). Yet, differently from the mainstream literature on global professionals, critical scholars examine the power dynamics underlying such interactions, highlighting the participants' diverging interests (Ybema and Byun, 2009). Along these lines, Shenkar and colleagues (2008) have recently proposed replacing the metaphor of 'cultural distance', largely dominant in the international management literature, with the one of 'cultural friction', to better reflect the power dimension of intercultural relations.

Also focusing on power dynamics in intercultural interactions, Janssens et al. (2006) have examined how female managers can actively shape relations in a way that is more favourable to them. Here, culture is seen as one of the power-laden identity discourses affecting intercultural interactions, rather than as something monolithic and 'given'. Individuals, as agents, do not necessarily need to conform to culture but can rather draw from the alternative discourses available to them – in this case gender and hierarchy – to actively shape intercultural interactions, thus enhancing their professional success.

Mini Case Study 11.4
The search for effective crosscultural training
CULTRAINING is an organization in Belgium that has created a new training concept for those who want to interact more consciously and effectively with other cultures. In order to acquire knowledge, insight and inspiration for a specific cultural context, the organization organizes trips to new economies such as China, India, Indonesia, Turkey and the United Arab Emirates that are currently being explored by Belgian MNCs as business locations. Participating in these training exercises, people should become acquainted

▷

with the culture in terms of living and working in each of these contexts. For foreigners working in Belgium, CULTRAINING organizes exploration sessions that introduce them to the Belgian cultural context.

The organization offers a multifaceted training programme, including formal and informal encounters, introductions to the history of the country and its business context, visits to tourist highlights and remarkable projects, gastronomic experiences and entertainment. Because of its local embeddedness, the organization promises to guide participants outside the beaten paths.

Besides a cultural training programme, participation in these training episodes also provides access to valuable local contacts and networks. Through intense exchange, a theoretical framework and debriefing, individuals should be enabled to develop a strong connection with the country or region they have visited. People who have participated in such training have indicated that they not only learnt how others lived and worked, but were also enabled to reflect on their own cultural framework and learn to value other alternatives. In sum, the organization aims to create and/or heighten cultural sensitivity, which in turn teaches people to communicate and conduct business more effectively in a context of cultural diversity.

Questions

1 What challenges do companies face in managing the complexities of working with global professionals?
2 How can human resources activities support the creation of a global mindset?

Ethical considerations in transnational organizations

Traditionally, the focus of corporate governance has been on financial performance, reporting to and protecting shareholders (De Cieri and Dowling, 2006). Organizations are, however, increasingly expected to behave ethically, be transparent and be responsive to the needs of society in general and employees and customers in particular. They need to find ways of including environmental, social and governance considerations in their management systems (DeCieri and Dowling, 2006) and human practices (see Chapter 5 on 'Human Resource Management and Ethics'). As a result of large-scale business failure to meet societal expectations – as, for example, with energy company Enron's financial dealings, or the case of chemical company Union Carbide in Bhopal – ethics has in recent years become the object of much debate among business scholars and practitioners (Carroll and Buchholtz, 2009).

Transnational organizations face a particularly large challenge in terms of identifying and enforcing ethical standards in multiple contexts. Although some basic values – such as honesty, integrity and the protection of society – are found in all cultures, appropriate behaviour to conform with those values differs strongly in different societal contexts characterized by different cultures, styles and institutions (Schneider and Barsoux, 2003). International business therefore has to deal with global ethical pluralism (DeGeorge, 1993): it needs to consider not only a variety of ethical norms and standards (ethical pluralism), but also cultural ones (globalization), making it a difficult exercise to find out what is shared and what is culture-specific. International business scholars have argued that only in this way can a level playing field be created where the rules of the game can be negotiated and clearly spelled out (Schneider and Barsoux, 2003). As global citizens, global professionals need to be aware of the heterogeneity of ethical norms in the multiple cultural contexts they encounter; in this way, they will be able to build a shared consensus on what is expected and acceptable behaviour across them. As a result, the organization will be able to deal with ethical dilemmas and operate in an ethically responsible way when conducting its international business.

Overall, critical scholars are much more sceptical about the possibility that businesses can genuinely embrace social and environmental concerns. In radical critical thought, the very reason for the existence of companies, which is the maximization of profit, is in itself unethical because it derives from the exploitation of human and environmental resources (Marx, 1976; Adler, 2009). Accordingly, a focus on ethical norms and behaviour is, from a critical perspective, misplaced as it shifts attention away from the structural problem of capitalism as an economic system to the moral dimension of the organization's and the individual's behaviour (Jones et al., 2005; Banerjee, 2008).

The contradictions inherent in business ethics are particularly visible in transnational organizations as the power inequalities between these companies and the locally embedded actors with which they deal, such as employees and states, are particularly large. These local entities are generally in a relatively weak position to enforce what is best for local employees or the country as a whole. In a recent book on business ethics, Jones and colleagues (2005) straightforwardly identified 'global capital' as the denial of ethics. Arguably, the transnational structure of contemporary organizations is in itself a strategy to find contexts with more advantageous institutional conditions for the company, such as a cheaper labour force, as well as weaker trade unions and lower levels of legislative protection for consumers and the environment.

Although the increasingly global circulation of information has facilitated international campaigns publicly condemning the most extreme forms of exploitation of labour and natural resources – such as Nike's employment standards in Asia and Nestlé's unethical marketing practices for baby formula food in Africa – critics argue that these few cases are only the tip of the iceberg of a widespread 'dark' business reality on which the wealth of Western corporations and consumers is based. Although such campaigns can raise awareness in (Western) consumers, they might also have unintended negative effects as they do not address the structural problems in developing countries. For instance, Khan and colleagues (1997) have shown how a well-meant international campaign to ban child labour in the production of soccer balls in Pakistan in fact negatively affected the living conditions of women and children. This case suggests that ethical issues might be so inherently complex that it is hard to envisage what the 'ethical' behaviour of individuals and organizations might be.

Critical analysis and discussion

Studying HRM in transnational organizations from a critical perspective allows future managers to gain a better understanding of the multiple perspectives of the different actors involved. This should be one taking into consideration not only their 'cultural difference', but also structural inequalities that exist at the multiple levels of interpersonal relations, teams, the organization and different countries. Interpreting transnational phenomena by taking into account differences in both culture and power (and the relationship between the two) will in turn enable future managers to better assess situations, diagnose problems and find appropriate solutions.

Conclusion

This chapter has discussed the contentious nature of globalization and its implications for the organization and its employees. It has shown how contradicting forces of global integration and local responsiveness need to be balanced in transnational organizations, and how global professionals are deployed in order to coordinate functional domains on a worldwide basis. Taking a critical perspective, this chapter has also questioned the proclaimed power relations in these transnational organizations, discussing how new and more subtle types of control are being executed. The critical literature, however, does agree with recent research arguing that global professionals should negotiate reality in each crosscultural interaction rather than aiming for in-depth cultural knowledge. Albeit for different reasons, both types of literature in the end conclude that culture is continuously constructed in every interaction between people from different contexts.

For global professionals, the multicultural nature of their work strongly suggests the need for a 'culture-general' knowledge (Hofstede, 2001). This type of knowledge is based on people's awareness of their own mental make-up and the fact that this (may) differ from that of other cultures. Global professionals should start their work with a mindfulness of their own cultural background and how this influences them to approach issues in a certain way.

According to Thomas (2006), mindfulness is a linking process between knowledge and behavioural ability in which people are aware of their own assumptions, ideas and emotions, and their selective perception, attribution and categorization. It implies an enhanced attention to the particular current experience or present reality and its context, while creating new mental maps of other people's personalities and cultural backgrounds as a basis for immediate action (Thomas and Inkson, 2004). Being mindful, global professionals will be able to approach a situation with an open mind, focusing their attention on personal and context-specific details (Thomas, 2006). In this way, they can open themselves up to divergent cultural influences and experiences (Koehn and Rosenau, 2002) and negotiate reality (Friedman and Berthoin Antal, 2005).

Organizations can help global professionals to become mindful by training them to have an active awareness of their own cultural framework and how this may influence their perceptions and behaviours. At a later stage, training interventions may focus on an exploration of underlying assumptions in other cultures and their use as a basis for learning new ways of seeing and doing things in an effective way in a different cultural context.

This chapter has also shown that, up until now, organizations have had no equivalent in terms of repatriation programmes for expatriates. As such, global professionals are left with the burden of being responsible for their own management development. Being aware of this lack of support might challenge organizations to use personal development plans that guide the careers of global professionals throughout the organization. By discussing and revising these plans jointly on a regular basis, organizations can support the further development of global managers by providing them with viable career opportunities for the future.

❓ For discussion and revision

Questions

1 Can you think of three localizing and three globalizing forces in business today?

2 Can you think of other functions within transnational companies besides human resources that might show a strong tendency to diversify in line with local conventions?

3 Would you prefer to work as a global professional or as an expatriate manager? Why?

4 What do you think of the argument that specific culture knowledge (for example, on eating and greeting rituals) promotes stereotypical thinking?

5 How does the notion of the global professional match the nature of the transnational organization?

6 Identify the main challenges for organizations working with global professionals?

7 How has globalization changed the nature of intercultural competencies?

Exercises

1 You are a crosscultural training advisor. Your client is a transnational organization that has employed you to train its employees in crosscultural communication. Divide your class into two groups:

- The first group of training advisors will design a training programme for a home-country employee who will be sent to Japan as an expatriate, managing the corporation's subsidiary in Tokyo.
- The second group of training advisors will design a training programme for a host-country employee (coming from one of the corporation's subsidiary countries) who has been promoted to a position as a global professional within the corporation. Working as a global professional, she will have to deal with the following countries: the USA, Mexico, Brazil, South Africa, Morocco, Egypt, the United Arab Emirates, Italy, Germany, France, China, Russia, Japan, Australia and the Philippines.

Compare the two training programmes in class. What are the main similarities and differences? Why?

2   Discuss ideological, more subtle types of control that can be executed within transnational organizations. Develop a role-play to present in class that illustrates these types of control.

Further reading

Books

De Cieri, H. and Dowling, P. J. (2006) Strategic international human resource management in multinational enterprises: developments and directions. In Stahl, G. K. and Björkman, I. (eds) *Handbook of Research in International Human Resource Management*. Cheltenham: Edward Elgar, pp. 15–35.

Janssens, M. and Cappellen, T. (2008) Contextualizing cultural intelligence: the case of global managers. In Ang, S. and Van Dyne, L. (eds) *Handbook of Cultural Intelligence. Theory, Measurement and Applications*. Armonk, NY: M. E. Sharpe, pp. 356–71.

Journals

Adler, N. J. and Bartholomew, S. (1992) Managing globally competent people. *Academy of Management Executive*, 6: 52–65.

Collings, D. G., Scullion, H. and Morley, M. J. (2007) Changing patterns of global staffing in the multinational enterprise: challenges to the conventional expatriate assignment and emerging alternatives. *Journal of World Business*, 42: 198–213.

Case Study View Corporation

View Corporation started as a Belgian television manufacturer in the mid-1930s. Even back then, the company had international connections, as it imported parts from the USA for its televisions. By the end of the 20th century, it had acquired several other companies and established a number of foreign subsidiaries, becoming a truly global company.

Today, View is a global technology company active in more than 90 countries and employing 3,300 people worldwide. It designs and develops visualization solutions for a variety of selected professional markets such as media and entertainment, security and monitoring, medical imaging, presentation, and simulation and avionics. View's headquarters are located in Brussels, yet the company has branches for sales and marketing, customer support, research and development and manufacturing in Europe, America and the Asia-Pacific region.

View Corporation is structured along its professional markets into five divisions. Each of these divisions has functional units in operations, research and development, marketing and sales, finance, and human resources. At the group level, similar functional units across the divisions collaborate, ensuring an integration of policies and practices and the creation of economies of scale and scope. Being a truly transnational organization, the company has a policy of capitalizing on location-specific advantages. For instance, the medical imaging division recently acquired a company in northern Italy with specific expertise in hospital display technology. View decided to make the unit a centre of excellence within the company rather than transferring the expertise to Belgium.

Although the company traditionally relied on expatriates to manage its foreign subsidiaries, expatriate assignments are now rather rare. They are only used for specific purposes such as carrying out an acquisition or in response to an employee's explicit request to move. The company is exploring new ways of working across borders, such as commuter assignments.

After the acquisition of a company in Edinburgh (UK), the president of the medical imaging division suggested that one of his vice-presidents move there. He told them it was an important acquisition, costing View some €35 million, so it would be important to have someone on site. Based on his loyalty towards View, Pete decided that he would go, given the fact that the other vice-president had small children, whereas his son was already 16 years old. But instead of relocating to Edinburgh, he commuted. The company rented an apartment there, enabling him to leave his wife and son every Sunday evening to go to Edinburgh, and come back home every Friday evening, taking the last flight home.

Although this meant that Pete's family did not have to relocate, he experienced this commuter assignment very negatively:

> My family didn't go along, and that damaged our relationship. And it was very lonely. Why? Because at night, you're sitting there alone. In general, you're working longer hours, often until 9 pm, and then you go to your apartment, but to do what? You're sitting there, on your own, nothing to do. You are also away from your company. I was very surprised about that. Physically, you're not present, you're no longer in the action, and you really have to make an effort to make sure you can stay in the action, because they forget you really fast.

After this negative experience, Pete decided never to commute again. However, he liked working in an international business environment, so he continued his work as a global professional. At View, global professionals make sure that coordination is ensured and knowledge is transferred. This can be done in a number of ways, combining trips with telephone and video-conferencing, and Pete uses this approach: 'I got a phone call today from India, yesterday I had a videoconference with Switzerland, and last week I was in the US, where I had to deal with some Japanese problems.' View uses global management positions to ensure a flexible presence across the globe, without the costs associated with relocating workers and their families. Even in early stages of their career, from their junior or middle management position at headquarters onwards, View's employees are already being given responsibility for worldwide coordination.

Although global professionals in View frequently use the communication facilities described above, travelling remains necessary. Throughout the years, Pete has travelled a lot:

> You cannot believe where I have been. I save all my flight tickets, it's a large pile, I save them in my attic, and when I retire, I'm going to input all that into a spreadsheet, to see how many miles I've travelled. To give you an idea: I have about a million frequent flyer miles with American Airlines, eight hundred thousand with Air France, about one and a half million miles with Sabena and six hundred thousand with Lufthansa. Apart from Africa and South America, I have visited all states of the USA, Australia, China, you name it.

Travelling is important as it remains the only way to establish a sound relationship with colleagues around the world. For Pete, these local visits are the only opportunity to have face-to-face contact, getting to know his local counterparts, 'Because as a foreigner, I cannot understand all of them. They tell me something and they think I understand. It's not about language, it's about the way one looks at life.' According to Pete, getting to know this way of life through face-to-face contact facilitates future telephone and video-conferences because it allows him to better understand others' perspectives.

To support their employees who are working internationally, View organizes cultural training sessions. Recently, a training course on the cultural differences between Belgium and China was delivered by a university professor. As a global professional at View, Pete considers the world his working space, yet he questions a person's need and ability to acquire in-depth knowledge of all the cultural contexts he and his colleagues come across:

I always had a very strong interest in meeting people and different cultural contexts, because I believe that you need to open yourself to these experiences. So you need to use chopsticks in China to eat, and have burgers with a large dollop of mustard in the States, while drinking large beers. For me, that's getting the feeling of a culture. How should I say? With an American, you have to run along and say yeah, great, wow, and with Germans, you have to yell along, raising your voice in a discussion. In Japan, you have to stroll along, be quiet and at ease, while the Chinese, you have to laugh and play fun with them. And somehow, that's my ... I don't think about that and I try not to figure out these cultures, cause I think that's not useful. For example, in the States, you have to go once to a baseball game; you cannot understand why it's such an event. How these things are ... you can't imagine. But I don't make the effort. There are colleagues here who try to unravel these cultures ... I don't take the time. Just go with the flow, join them in talking, yelling and so on ... and you'll be accepted as a business partner.

Questions

1 Although Pete likes to work in an international context, he clearly experiences some frustration in the way in which View Corporation manages its international work. What kind of advice would you give the organization to improve this?
2 How do you evaluate View's training policy? Why?
3 What are the specific needs of global professionals in terms of crosscultural interaction?
4 Reflect on Pete's strategy for working effectively with his colleagues across the world.

Critical analysis of the case study

This case study above portrays the perspective of a global professional working at the headquarters of a transnational organization. Such individual experience highlights the difficulties of combining a career as a global professional with the private sphere, the pressure managers feel to take up jobs, and the need to find effective ways of dealing with the heterogeneous cultural contexts they constantly encounter. In other words, it shows the 'human' dimension (including the human cost) of a career as a global professional.

Such an individual perspective from a global professional based in a company's headquarters does not, however, allow us to unveil the structural privilege that this employee actually enjoys within the broader context of the transnational organization. Unequal power relations are much more likely to emerge from voices at the periphery of organizations and in subordinate positions, because those employees are more likely to experience disadvantage and marginalization, reflecting the underlying power relations.

References

Adler, N. (2002) *International Dimensions of Organizational Behavior*. Cincinnati, OH: South-Western.

Adler, N. J. and Bartholomew, S. (1992) Managing globally competent people. *Academy of Management Executive*, 6: 52–65.

Adler, P. S. (2009) Marx and organization studies today. In Adler, P. S. (ed.) *Oxford Handbook of Sociology and Organization Studies: Classical Foundations*. New York: Oxford University Press, pp. 62–91.

Alvesson, M. and Willmott, H. (2002) Identity regulation as organizational control: producing the appropriate individual. *Journal of Management Studies*, 39: 619–44.

Ang, S., Van Dyne, L., Koh, C., Ng, K., Templer, K. J., Tay, C. and Chandrasekar, N. A. (2007) Cultural intelligence: its measurement and effects on cultural judgment and decision making, cultural adaptation, and task performance. *Management and Organization Review*, 3(3): 335–71.

Banerjee, S. B. (2008) Corporate social responsibility: the good, the bad and the ugly. *Critical Sociology*, 34(1): 51–79.

Banerjee, S. B. and Linstead, S. (2001) Globalization, multiculturalism and other fictions: colonialism for the new millennium? *Organization*, 8(4): 683–722.

Bartlett, C. A. and Ghoshal, S. (1989) *Managing Across Borders: The Transnational Solution*. Boston: Harvard Business School Press.

Bartlett, C. A. and Ghoshal, S. (1992) What is a global manager? *Harvard Business Review*, 70: 124–32.

Bartlett, C. A. and Ghoshal, S. (2000) *Transnational Management: Text, Cases and Readings* (3rd edn). Irwin: McGraw-Hill.

Bartlett, C. A., Ghoshal, S. and Birkinshaw, J. (2004) *Transnational Management: Text, Cases and Readings* (4th edn). Irwin: McGraw-Hill.

Bhabha, H. K. (1994) Of mimicry and man: the ambivalence of colonial discourse. In Bhabha, H. K. (ed.) *The Location of Culture*. London: Routledge, pp. 85–92.

Bird, A. and Osland, J. (2006) Global competencies: an introduction. In Lane, H. W., Maznevski, M. L., Mendenhall, M. E. and McNett, J. (eds) *Handbook of Global Management. A Guide to Managing Complexity*. Malden, MA: Blackwell Publishing, pp. 57–80.

Boussebaa, M. (2009) Struggling to organize across national borders: the case of global resource management in professional service firms. *Human Relations*, 62: 829–50.

Caligiuri, P. (2006) Developing global leaders. *Human Resource Management Review*, 16(2): 219–28.

Caligiuri, P. and Tarique, I. (2006) International assignee selection and cross-cultural training and development. In Stahl, G. K. and Björkman, I. (eds) *Handbook of Research in International Human Resource Management*. Cheltenham: Edward Elgar, pp. 302–22.

Cappellen, T. and Janssens, M. (2008) Global managers' career competencies. *Career Development International*, 13(6): 514–37.

Cappellen, T. and Janssens, M. (2010a) The career reality of global managers: an examination of career triggers. *International Journal of Human Resource Management*, 21: 1884–919.

Cappellen, T. and Janssens, M. (2010b) Enacting global careers: organizational career scripts and the global economy as co-existing career referents. *Journal of Organizational Behavior*, 31: 687–706.

Carroll, A. B. and Buchholtz, A. K. (2009) *Business and Society: Ethics and Stakeholder Management*. Cincinnati, OH: Cengage Learning.

Collings, D. G., Scullion, H. and Morley, M. J. (2007) Changing patterns of global staffing in the multinational enterprise: challenges to the conventional expatriate assignment and emerging alternatives. *Journal of World Business*, 42: 198–213.

De Cieri, H. and Dowling, P. J. (2006) Strategic international human resource management in multinational enterprises: developments and directions. In Stahl, G. K. and Björkman, I. (eds) *Handbook of Research in International Human Resource Management*. Cheltenham: Edward Elgar, pp. 15–35.

DeGeorge, R. T. (1993) *Competing with Integrity in International Business*. New York: Oxford University Press.

Edström, A. and Galbraith, J. R. (1977) Transfer of managers as a coordination and control strategy in multinational organizations. *Administrative Science Quarterly*, 22: 248–63.

Forster, N. (2000) The myth of the 'international manager'. *International Journal of Human Resource Management*, 11(1): 126–42.

Frenkel, M. (2008) The multicultural corporation as a third space: rethinking international management discourse on knowledge transfer through Homi Bhabha. *Academy of Management Review*, 33(4): 924–42.

Friedman, V. J. and Berthoin Antal, A. (2005) Negotiating reality: a theory of action approach to intercultural competence. *Management Learning*, 36(1): 69–86.

Galbraith, J. R. (2000) *Designing the Global Corporation*. San Francisco: Jossey-Bass.

Ghoshal, S. and Bartlett, C. (1990) The multinational corporation as an interorganizational network. *Academy of Management Review*, 15: 603–25.

Ghoshal, S. and Nohria, N. (1993) Horses for courses: organizational forms for multinational corporations, *Sloan Management Review*, 34(2): 23–35.

Govindarajan, V. and Gupta, A. K. (2001) *The Quest for Global Dominance. Transforming Global Presence into Global Competitive Advantage*. San Francisco: Jossey-Bass.

Hofstede, G. (2001) *Culture's Consequences. Comparing Values, Behaviors, Institutions, and Organizations Across Nations*. Thousand Oaks: Sage Publications.

Jaeger, A. M. (1983) The transfer of organizational culture overseas: an approach to control in the multinational corporation. *Journal of International Business Studies*, 14(2): 91–113.

Janssens, M. and Cappellen, T. (2008) Contextualizing cultural intelligence: the case of global managers. In Ang, S. and Van Dyne, L. (eds) *Handbook of Cultural Intelligence. Theory, Measurement, and Applications*. Armonk, New York: M. E. Sharpe, pp. 356–74.

Janssens, M., Cappellen, T. and Zanoni, P. (2006) Successful female expatriates as agents: positioning oneself through gender, hierarchy and culture. *Journal of World Business*, 41(2): 133–48.

Jones, C., Parker, M. and ten Bos, R. (2005) *For Business Ethics*. Oxon: Routledge.

Kedia, B. L. and Mukherji, A. (1999) Global managers: developing a mindset for global competitiveness. *Journal of World Business*, 34(3): 230–51.

Khan, F. R., Munir, K. A. and Willmott, H. (1997) A dark side of institutional entrepreneurship: soccer balls, child labour and postcolonial impoverishment. *Organization Studies*, 28(7): 1055–77.

Koehn, P. H. and Rosenau, J. N. (2002) Transnational competence in an emergent epoch. *International Studies Perspectives*, 3(2): 105–27.

Lane, H. W., Maznevski, M. L. and Mendenhall, M. E. (2006) Globalization: Hercules meets Buddha. In Lane, H. W., Maznevski, M. L., Mendenhall, M. E. and McNett, J. (eds) *Handbook of Global Management: A Guide to*

Managing Complexity. Malden, MA: Blackwell Publishing, pp. 3–25.

Lazarova, M. and Caligiuri, P. (2001) Retaining repatriates: the role of organizational support practices. *Journal of World Business*, 36(4): 389–401.

Leonardi, P. M. (2008) Indeterminacy and the discourse of inevitability in international technology management. *Academy of Management Review*, 33(4): 975–84.

Makela, K. and Suutari, V. (2009) Global careers: a social capital paradox. *International Journal of Human Resource Management*, 20: 992–1008.

Martinez, J. I. and Jarillo, J. C. (1989) The evolution of research on coordination mechanisms in multinational corporations. *Journal of International Business Studies*, 20: 489–514.

Marx, K. (1976) *Capital*, Vol. I. London: Penguin Classics.

Mayerhofer, H., Hartmann, L. C., Michelitsch-Riedl, G. and Kollinger, I. (2004) Flexpatriate assignments: a neglected issue in global staffing. *International Journal of Human Resource Management*, 15: 1371–89.

Mendenhall, M., Dubar, E. and Oddou, G. (1987) Expatriate selection, training and career-pathing: a review and critique. *Human Resource Management*, 26(3): 331–45.

Mir, R., Mir, A. and Wong, D. J. (2006) Diversity. The cultural logic of global capital? In Konrad, A. M., Prasad, P. and Pringle, J. K. (eds) *Handbook of Workplace Diversity*. Thousands Oaks, CA: Sage, pp. 167–88.

Mir, R., Banerjee, S. B. and Mir, A. (2008) Hegemony and its discontents: a critical analysis of organizational knowledge transfer. *Critical Perspectives on International Business*, 4(2/3): 203–27.

Osland, J. S., Bird, A., Mendenhall, M. and Osland, A. (2006) Developing global leadership capabilities and global mindset: a review. In Stahl, G. K. and Björkman, I. (eds) *Handbook of Research in International Human Resource Management*. Cheltenham: Edward Elgar, pp. 197–222.

Özbilgin, M. (2004) 'International' human resource management: academic parochialism in editorial boards of the 'top' 22 journals on international human resource management. *Personnel Review*, 33(2): 205–21.

Paik, Y. and Sohn, J. D. (2004) Expatriate managers and MNC's ability to control international subsidiaries: the case of Japanese MNC's. *Journal of World Business*, 39(1): 61–72.

Peiperl, M. and Jonsen, K. (2007) Global careers. In Gunz, H. and Peiperl, M. (eds) *Handbook of Career Studies*. Los Angeles: Sage, pp. 350–72.

Peltonen, T. (2006) Critical theoretical perspectives on international human resource management. In Stahl, G. K. and Bjorkman, I. (eds) *Handbook of Research in International Human Resource Management*. Cheltenham: Edward Elgar, pp. 523–35.

Pucik, V. and Saba, T. (1998) Selecting and developing the global versus the expatriate manager: a review of the state-of-the-art. *Human Resource Planning*, 21: 40–53.

Prasad, A. (1997) The colonizing consciousness and representations of the other: a postcolonial critique of the discourse of oil. In Prasad, P., Mills, A. J., Elmes, M. and Prasad, A. (eds) *Managing the Organizational Melting Pot: Dilemmas of Workplace Diversity*. Thousand Oaks, CA: Sage, pp. 285–311.

Rosenzweig, P. M. (1994) Management practices in U.S. affiliates of foreign-owned firms: are 'they' just like 'us'? *Thunderbird International Business Review*, 36(4): 393–410.

Rosenzweig, P. M. and Singh, J. V. (1991) Organizational environments and the multinational enterprise. *Academy of Management Review*, 16(2): 340–61.

Schneider, S. C. and Barsoux, J.-L. (2003) *Managing Across Cultures* (2nd edn). Harlow: Prentice Hall.

Shenkar, O., Luo, Y. and Yeheskel, O. (2008) From 'distance' to 'friction': substituting metaphors and redirecting intercultural research. *Academy of Management Review*, 33(4): 905–23.

Shimoni, B. and Bergmann, H. (2006) Managing in a changing world: from multiculturalism to hybridization – the production of hybrid management cultures in Israel, Thailand, and Mexico. *Academy of Management Perspectives*, 20(3): 76–89.

Spencer, L. M. and Spencer, S. M. (1993) *Competence at Work. Models for Superior Performance*. New York: John Wiley.

Thomas, D. (1998) The expatriate experience: a critical review and synthesis. *Advances in International Comparative Management*, 12: 237–73.

Thomas, D. C. (2006) Domain and development of cultural intelligence. The importance of mindfulness. *Group and Organization Management*, 31(1): 78–99.

Thomas, D. C. and Inkson, K. (2004) *Cultural Intelligence. People Skills for Global Business*. San Francisco: Berrett-Koehler.

Westwood, R. (2004) Towards a postcolonial research paradigm in international business and comparative management. In Welch, C. (ed.) *Handbook of Qualitative Research Methods for International Business*. Cheltenham: Edward Elgar, pp. 56–83.

Wong-MingJi, D. and Mir, A. H. (1997) How international is international management? Provincialism, parochialism and the problematic of global diversity. In Prasad, P., Mills, A., Elmes, M. and Prasad, A. (eds) *Managing the Organizational Melting Pot: Dilemmas of Workplace Diversity*. Thousand Oaks, CA: Sage, pp. 340–66.

Ybema, S. and Byun, H. (2009) Cultivating cultural differences in asymmetric power relations. *International Journal of Cross-Cultural Management*, 9(3): 339–58.

Zanoni, P. and Janssens, M. (2007) Minority employees engaging with (diversity) management: an analysis of control, agency, and micro-emancipation. *Journal of Management Studies*, 44(8): 1371–97.

chapter **12**
MARKETING

chapter outline

▷ **Introduction**
▷ **Marketing in the organizational context**
  Levels of marketing
  Global marketing strategies
▷ **International market expansion**
  Why seek new markets?
  Expansion strategies
  Market selection
  Segmentation and targeting
  Market entry strategies
▷ **Products and branding**
  Global and local dimensions
  Product and brand strategies
▷ **Reaching consumers**
  Marketing mix
▷ **Marketing and ethics**
▷ **Conclusions**

learning objectives

▷ **To identify the role of marketing strategy within corporate goals and operations**
▷ **To assess appropriate market entry strategies and target markets in a variety of organizational and environmental contexts**
▷ **To appreciate the role of product markets and brands in the marketing mix for differing markets and environments**
▷ **To integrate elements of the marketing mix, including communications, pricing and distribution strategy, in international markets**
▷ **To develop awareness of ethical issues in marketing**

Introduction

Amid much fanfare, the world's cheapest car, the Tata Nano, was launched in Delhi in 2007 by legendary Indian entrepreneur, Ratan Tata. Priced at one lakh, which is Rs100,000 (about €1,700), it is about half the price of India's current cheapest car, and promises to bring car ownership within the reach of millions of Indian families, who, until now, could only afford motorcycles. Not all at the launch were enthralled by this prospect. A boom in motoring promises further congestion to India's already clogged roads and will also raise pollution levels which are already high. Tata shrugs off these concerns, as do other manufacturers who are developing their own models of the 'people's car'. Bajaj Auto, the motorbike manufacturer, is teaming up with Renault to produce a small car only slightly above the symbolic one lakh in price. But manufacturers know that any celebration of car culture in emerging markets must be seen in perspective, as environmental issues race up the motoring agenda globally. Responding to changes in today's mature markets and anticipating trends in emerging markets pose challenges and opportunities for marketing strategists, which are the focus of this chapter.

The Tata Nano is featured on the Tata Motor's website, http://tatanano.inservices.tatamotors.com.

WEB CHECK

Businesses stand or fall on the basis of the value they offer customers. The domestic company which concentrates on its home consumers builds up considerable knowledge of their needs, but must start again in international markets. International strategy involves analysing a range of potential markets to decide which products will be suitable for which markets and how best to market them. Although the potential rewards of widening markets are attractive, there are risks for firms entering markets where they have little knowledge or experience. Designing, pricing and targeting the right product for the right market has become highly competitive. Hence, the role of marketing in the organization has become critical to corporate success.

This chapter begins with an overview of marketing in the organization, assessing the customer focus which has emerged as international competitive pressures have grown. We look next at how firms choose markets for particular products. When target markets are decided, marketing strategy can be devised, including products, prices, communications and distribution. The design of the marketing mix varies according to the distinctive characteristics of each market. Customers have traditionally been viewed in transactional terms, simply as buyers. Consumers are now seen in relational terms, implying that the role of marketing is a continuing one, which builds links between customers and the company's products and brands. The notion of the consumer in society places the marketing function in cultural and social contexts. The ethical dimension of marketing, which is discussed in the last section, stems from this broader view of the role of marketing and takes a critical perspective on marketing goals and practices.

Marketing in the organizational context

Marketing as a business function has traditionally focused on the analysis of markets and provision of products targeted at particular markets. This view of marketing derives from its background in sales management, in which product planning, pricing, promotion and distribution are the relevant subfunctions (Webster, 1992). These elements are still central, but marketing is now seen more in terms of customer relations than in transactional terms. This shift reflects an evolving view of the MNE in its environment, which was highlighted in the last chapter. The large, monolithic organization, exemplified by Ford of the US, was efficient in producing standardized products for mass markets. Ford produced the first mass-market car, the Model T, which was the Tata Nano of its day, affordable by millions of ordinary Americans. But it proved incapable of adapting to consumers' wishes for greater choice. General Motors, through its network of subsidiaries, was able to offer a wider range of models, colours and features, heralding a new approach to organizational structure and also a new outlook on meeting consumer needs.

Levels of marketing

Within the MNE, marketing can be conceived at three different levels: corporate culture, competitive strategy and marketing strategy. These are shown in Figure 12.1. First, at the highest level, in the context of its *corporate culture*, the company must decide what its mission and goals are. The firm which places satisfying customer needs at the centre of its vision adopts the marketing concept. Kotler et al. (2002: 19) define the marketing concept as:

Marketing concept: An organizational focus on identifying the needs of consumers and satisfying those needs.

> the marketing management philosophy which holds that achieving organizational goals depends on determining the needs and wants of target markets and delivering the desired satisfactions more effectively and efficiently than competitors do.

The goal of satisfying customers contrasts with the 'selling concept', which focuses on products which the firm sells. This distinction is not new. It was articulated most eloquently in an article by Theodore Levitt, entitled 'Marketing myopia', published in 1960. Levitt observed that the problem faced by US railways at the time, which were losing business to other modes of transport such as roads, was that managers saw themselves in the railway business when they should have seen themselves in the transport business. They were product rather than customer oriented. He said:

> Selling is preoccupied with the seller's need to convert the product into cash, marketing with the idea of satisfying the needs of the customer by

means of the product and the whole cluster of things associated with creating, delivering, and, finally, consuming it. (Levitt, [1960] 2004: 143)

As Figure 12.1 indicates, the firm must ask itself first what customer needs it can best satisfy and who its customers are. The firm contemplating its international presence must decide which markets to enter or exit. In the large MNE which has numerous subsidiaries, marketing at this highest level focuses on the firm's overall goals. As noted in the last chapter, a shared vision is an important link among units in a multidivisional firm, in which subsidiaries may pursue a variety of different businesses.

Figure 12.1 Levels of marketing

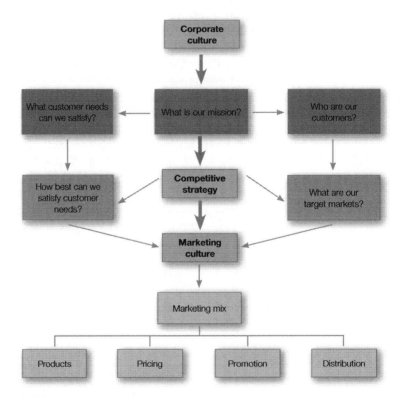

Second, a firm must decide on its *competitive strategy* in its targeted markets. Strategy may be determined at the corporate level, but in decentralized structures, managers within subsidiaries have delegated responsibility to design strategies within the firm's corporate goals. They carry out analysis of markets and devise specific strategies for market segments, targeting and positioning of the firm's products. In a customer-oriented company, decisions at this level are critical to the firm's success. Market research adds to managers' detailed knowledge of local environments. In addition, managers are likely to be involved in local networks, such as links with advertisers. These links may form a source of competitive advantage over rivals.

Third, the firm needs a *marketing strategy* to reach consumers effectively and efficiently with its products and messages. The marketing function thus implements strategic goals at the operational level. The company's strategy is implemented through the 'marketing mix': products, pricing, promotion and distribution. This level might be called the 'functional strategy', reflecting the specialist nature of the activities of marketing managers. Even at this level, however, relationships are important, as these activities are key to building the successful brand, which reflects a relationship between the company and its customers.

In a small company, the three levels of marketing may not be clearly delineated in practice, and the same people take most of the key decisions at all levels. As companies become larger and more complex organizations, variations become apparent. In a large, highly centralized company, marketing at all levels may be concentrated in the centre. Coca-Cola was traditionally such a company, even down to determining advertising for all markets. In more decentralized MNEs, while marketing at the highest level is centralized, local subsidiaries are likely to have latitude to take decisions on marketing strategy for their particular markets. In fact, centralized decision-making has been scaled back in many companies, such as Coca-Cola, in favour of more scope for local decision-making.

Global marketing strategies

In his analysis of competitive advantage, Michael Porter distinguishes three types of generic competitive strategy. These are differentiation, price and focus (see Chapter 7). These are broad strategic perspectives, describing the way firms compete globally. Similarly, in terms of marketing, there are generic strategies: the global, multidomestic and regional, shown in Figure 12.2.

TO RECAP...

Levels of marketing
The focus on satisfying consumer needs is evident in different levels of strategy and practice. At the highest level are broad organizational goals. These shape the firm's competitive strategy, which in turn influences the marketing strategies for particular products.

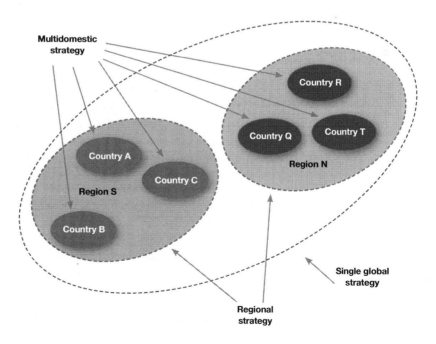

Figure 12.2 Generic marketing strategies

1 *The global strategy*: The single global marketing strategy is an extreme approach, assuming that consumers everywhere either have similar tastes or that tastes are converging. It follows that communications and adver-

tising can be standardized and applied globally. While this approach may still be appropriate in specific industries, it no longer resonates in consumer markets. Global strategy, however, may be advantageous where it has a particular focus, such as the product or the brand. A company may focus on a global product category, such as detergents. It co-ordinates strategy across markets within the product category, but is able to adapt the product, branding and advertising to local markets. Global product divisions have become popular among large companies in consumer markets. Similarly, a global branding strategy maintains the global brand and logo across markets, while allowing for adaptations of products in particular markets. The company thus benefits from consumers' recognition of its brands in increasingly global media such as the internet and satellite television.

2 *The multidomestic strategy*: The decentralized organization, while retaining strategic decisions on products and broad strategic principles in the head office, delegates to country subsidiaries decisions on marketing strategies to suit local markets. In consumer markets such as food, this type of strategy has been traditional (see the example of Unilever, featured in CS7.1). This strategy is appropriate for multinational companies with subsidiaries which have considerable authority to determine their own strategies.

3 *Regional and multiregional strategies*: The regional strategy is a middle way between global and multidomestic strategies. This strategy groups together the countries in a particular region, such as Europe, Asia or North America. The rationale behind the regional strategy is that there are similarities between the countries in the region. A regional strategy for distribution can lead to efficiencies, but markets may differ within regions in terms of products. Some regions comprise 20 or more diverse countries, so although this conceptual approach has appeal, in practice, country differences need to be taken into account. A standardized product across a whole region is perhaps more realistic than the global product for all markets, but is still problematic.

Even the most centralized global organizations now accept that the one-size-fits-all approach is not as responsive to consumer needs as the more adaptive multidomestic and regional strategies. Can the firm achieve the best of both worlds? It is possible to develop a global marketing strategy at the highest level while devolving marketing strategies to local decision-makers (see Figure 12.3). The company's global marketing strategy represents the broad principles which guide its strategy across its differing markets (Jeannet and Hennessey, 1998: 285). For example, it may choose to focus on global product categories, but does not attempt to standardize all elements of its marketing. Strategies at an operational level may differ from one to another, but the company sees these differences as having a logic within its broader picture. In this way, the three levels of marketing become integrated.

TO RECAP...
Global marketing strategies
Marketing strategies range from the single global strategy for a standardized product to regional and multidomestic strategies which are adapted to different markets. The global marketing strategy may benefit from both a global perspective and adaptations for local markets, thus integrating global and local strategic considerations.

The return of global strategy?
For global companies, the pendulum seemed to swing away from global strategy towards localization. Do you feel the pendulum is now swinging back towards global strategy, and why?

PAUSE TO REFLECT

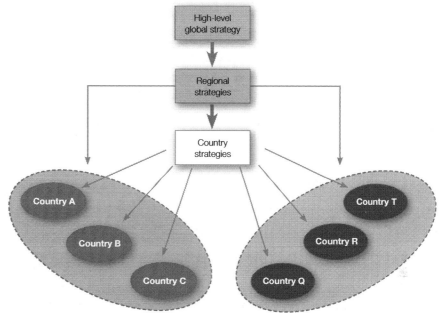

Figure 12.3 Global marketing strategy

International market expansion

In this section, we look at why and how firms seek customers for their products and services in foreign environments. The decision to enter new markets represents a strategic shift, with resource implications. Companies may decide to enter foreign markets for a variety of reasons, a common one being simply that this is what competitors are doing. Deciding which markets to enter and how to position the company's products requires extensive knowledge of the environment, as well as awareness of the risks it might present.

Why seek new markets?

Firms may take an 'opportunistic' approach to the internationalization, or they may take a more deliberate approach, planning how the new dimension will contribute towards achieving corporate goals. Seizing an opportunity which arises can prove inspired if the new market is successful, but it also represents a risk. If an impulsive decision leads to disappointment, it can be costly to exit. Of course, even companies that have put considerable research and effort into the planning can find that a particular market is not coming up to expectations. However, research and planning greatly enhance the likelihood of success.

Saturation in the home market acts as a 'push' factor towards international expansion. Firms requiring large sites may find that restrictive planning laws limit the availability of appropriate sites in home markets. To maintain its growth, the firm seeks new products and new markets, where there is more scope for growth. New markets may be countries in the same region, where the consumer markets are similar. Increasingly, firms gravitate towards the large emerging and developing economies, with their buoyant economies and greater potential for growth than the mature economies of Western Europe and America. These new markets thus exert 'pull' in attracting outside firms. As key global firms in a sector enter China and India, rivals feel they must also enter these markets, for fear of losing out. Home Depot's reluctance to enter the Chinese market when B&Q was gaining first-mover advantages was a cause of shareholder concern (see CS4.2). The company did enter China through the acquisition of an existing chain of stores, but it is playing 'catch-up'.

Expansion strategies

Expansion strategies depend on the company, its products and potential markets. A company may initially seek to build a regional strategy based on its home region. For example, European companies typically expand in the EU, benefiting from familiarity with markets and the single currency in the eurozone. The regional strategy is appropriate where customer needs are similar across the region. For Spanish companies, a logical expansion strategy has been to move into Latin American countries. This is a regional strategy, which also benefits from a common language and cultural affinity.

Many companies in consumer industries have expanded from their home region to other markets where consumer societies are similarly evolving. Hence American companies have expanded from North America to Australia, New Zealand and Western Europe. These are all countries where the business environment is stable and predictable, and where consumer markets are highly developed. Because of cultural distance, Asian markets have been seen as more challenging. A number of high-profile exits from Japan, including Carrefour of France and Boots of the UK, are indicators of the difficulties. However, the rise of China and other Asian developing countries constitutes a new spur to expand into Asia.

Focusing on developing countries or emerging markets is an appealing prospect to many companies, as they are growing quickly and consumers are eager to acquire a range of consumer goods and services. However, these countries tend to be uncertain business environments. They also differ widely in social, economic and cultural background. Government policies, while tending to become more liberalized, are unpredictable. Changes of government policy may signal a reverse towards greater restrictions on foreign companies. India is an example of mixed signals towards investors, although the size of the Indian market remains an attraction for foreign companies.

Market selection

The company which enters international markets must assess the potential of differing countries as possible markets. The screening process involves three levels of analysis: the macro-level analysis of the national environment; analysis of the consumer market in general; and micro-level analysis of factors affecting the specific product. These are depicted in Figure 12.4. We look at each in turn.

Figure 12.4 Analysis of country markets

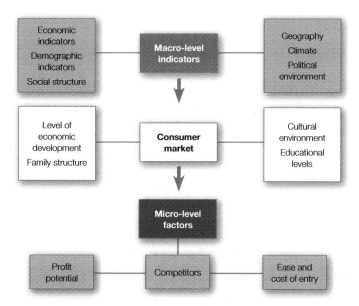

Macro-level analysis of the national environment

Assessment at the macro-level looks at geographic features, economic indicators, demographic data, social and economic structure, and the political environment. The size of the country, its geography and climate may influence the types of product that are suitable (or unsuitable), and the ease or difficulty of transporting them. Relevant economic data include GDP, GDP per capita and economic growth rates. This information is readily available from published sources, and helps to eliminate countries which are not suitable. It is not necessarily an indication of which countries *are* suitable, however. It is usually thought that if GDP per capita is below $10,000, there is too little potential for a luxury product. There may be a large and growing market among the middle classes, as in India, although GDP per capita is only $700. Demographic data show the age distribution of the population and the extent to which it is rural or urban. The world's developed economies have ageing populations. A large population of retired people may constitute a lucrative market for many products and services, such as small cars and package holidays. A country which is rapidly becoming urbanized also presents opportunities. However, as CF12.1 on China shows, unevenness of economic development can affect companies counting on prosperity spreading to rural areas.

The social and economic structure of the country indicates what types of employment are prevalent, what opportunities exist for social mobility and what role family networks play in the society. These aspects of the social structure also impact on the political environment. Political factors include levels of political instability and legal protection afforded to property, including intellectual property (such as brands). Governments may be particularly wary of foreign entrants which threaten local suppliers and jobs.

Consumer market in general

The consumer market in a country consists of the aggregate of needs and desires of consumers in the context of their buying behaviour and preferences. Consumers everywhere have certain essential needs to be satisfied, beyond which they seek to acquire non-essentials which make life more meaningful and pleasant. However, there are huge variations in priorities and tastes, even at the levels of basic needs. A firm considering a country as a potential market will need to know whether people will have the money to buy its products, and whether they will perceive the product as one they need.

The structure of consumption differs from country to country. In poorer countries, food, fuel and housing may account for the lion's share of an average consumer's disposable income. As countries develop economically and incomes grow, people are able to afford more goods to improve their quality of life. The level of economic development of a country is a broad indicator of a growing market for consumer products and services, such as appliances, cars, banking, fast-food meals and media products. However, consumers in countries at similar levels of development do not universally embrace all these products. Moreover, their choice of products depends on numerous social and cultural factors, including levels of education, religion and family priorities. Decision-making in family purchasing differs from country to country. In many countries, women are dominant in purchasing for the household. Market research indicates that for technology and entertainment spending, children play a role in decision-making (Carter, 2004). This seems not just to be 'pester power', but genuine involvement, representing a subtle democratization of family life.

The distinctive characteristics of a country's consumer market reflect people's expectations, as well as concerns, about their personal prosperity, as the example of Russia shows. Following the collapse of communism, the unbridled rise of capitalism in the early 1990s, although bringing riches to the very wealthy, brought deterioration in living standards for ordinary Russians. Since the advent of the new millennium, Russia has enjoyed a consumer boom. Russia's economic growth is boosting incomes of its upper middle class, but lower middle-class consumers, such as public sector workers, have prospered less. Among foreign MNEs, Metro, a German supermarket group, has established a wholesale business and three hypermarkets in Russia. IKEA, the Swedish furniture and interior design company, has gradually built up its Russian presence, confident of growth potential.

Micro-level analysis of product markets

Factors considered in a micro-level analysis include the ease of entry and its costs, the extent of competitors' presence, and the profit potential. Entering a new market through exporting is less costly than FDI. Retailers need a physical presence in the foreign market. This is less costly for a small format such as a boutique or fast-food outlet than for a large format such as a hypermarket. As the large retailing operation is a costly and complex investment, MNEs often choose the joint venture route. An anal-

plate 12.1 Shopping malls, now springing up in emerging markets, have become synonymous with modern consumer society.

TO RECAP...
Analysing market potential
Macro-level indicators are a starting point for analysing the market potential of a country. This profile is complemented by more detailed analysis of the consumer market in the country, which focuses on patterns of consumption. If this analysis shows market potential, the possibilities for specific product categories targeted at specific segments can then be explored.

ysis of competitors will show the degree of concentration and the extent to which foreign investors are active. If there are several competitors, all domestic, the foreign investor may gain competitive advantage through differentiation or possibly price, due to economies of scale which local competitors lack.

If there are already foreign firms in the market, it is likely that all are expecting it to grow in future. In this case, the firm has possibly missed an opportunity to capture market share early on. Once competitors are established, the new firm will find it difficult to seize market share from established rivals. Tesco found this to be the case when it entered Taiwan some years after Carrefour. It found the competitive environment difficult, especially with the continued popularity of local supermarkets. It exited the country in 2006, swapping its stores in Taiwan for Carrefour's stores in the Czech Republic and Slovakia, where Tesco has been the more successful.

Assessing markets
Which aspects of a country's macro-level environment and consumer market are most important for each of the following products:
● fast-food outlets ● banking services
● mobile phones?

PAUSE TO REFLECT

COUNTRY FOCUS 12.1 – CHINA

China's consumer boom takes off, but are all on board?

As Asia's fastest growing economy and home to 1.3 billion people, China has become a leading exporter to consumer markets the world over. Now, its domestic consumer market is becoming a focus of attention, providing opportunities for both local and foreign companies. Economic growth in the 9–10% range since 1994 has propelled China to seventh position in world retail markets. Increasing affluence is pulling more people into the middle class. In 2005, there were 42 million middle-class households in China enjoying annual incomes in excess of Rmb25,000 ($3,200). The number is expected to rise to 200 million by 2015. Of particular interest to retailers is the growing upper middle class, earning in the Rmb40,000–100,000 range. Middle-class consumers are concentrated in urban areas, as Figure 1 shows. Their spending power has pushed retail sales to increases of 13% annually for the past decade. Potential rewards for retailers are inviting, but they face significant challenges and uncertainties over future growth.

Foreign retailers aspiring to enter China learn early on that any preconception of China as a single market is misconceived. Disparities in income, regional differences in tastes and the sheer distances involved have all impacted on corporate strategies. Economic development has rested on industrialization, which is concentrated in the coastal areas with their growing urban populations. Cities are growing in both size and prosperity, while rural areas are still mainly poor. The urban population has risen to 40% of the total, from only 17% in 1975, and is expected to reach 50% by 2015. Average wages of urban residents doubled between 2000 and 2005. Urban residents accounted for 67% of Chinese retail sales in 2005. These increasingly affluent consumers are therefore the main target of retail-

Figure 1 Spending power of China's urban consumers

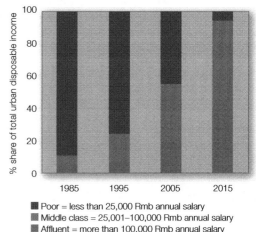

■ Poor = less than 25,000 Rmb annual salary
■ Middle class = 25,001–100,000 Rmb annual salary
■ Affluent = more than 100,000 Rmb annual salary

Source: Financial Times, 11 December 2006

ers in all sectors, from cars and luxury goods at the top of the scale down to clothing and food at the lower end. Hypermarket retailers now consider China a 'must' market, largely because of its potential growth. They are also encouraged by the government's lifting of the ban on foreign ownership of retailers at the end of 2004.

Among Western entrants into China's hypermarket sector are Carrefour, Wal-Mart and Tesco. There are also large Asian groups, including Vanguard, China's largest hypermarket retailer, which is based in Hong Kong and has 1,000 stores on the mainland. Carrefour is the largest and longest established Western retailer in China. Having entered China with a joint venture partner, it is now operating independently, with 90 stores in 23 cities. Despite 17 years in the country, Carrefour had a market share of only 0.6% in 2005, and its Chinese operations account for less than 3% of the group's overall sales. Carrefour cites difficulties in distribution networks, as distribution is almost all localized, inefficient and costly. Carrefour executives reason: 'In China, you do not have a national logistics systems, it is all very dislocated, so a company has to adapt to working with the local economy' (Dyer and Rigby, 2006). Wal-Mart has taken a strategic decision to invest in its own nationwide distribution network, a costly and ambitious move which, it hopes, will bring greater efficiencies in the long term. On the other hand, poor infrastructure and differing local conditions could thwart a nationwide strategy. Retailers are hoping that urbanization and rising wealth in rural areas will bring future growth, but these prospects are uncertain.

Despite rapid growth and industrialization, the bulk of China's population is still rural, amounting to 745 million people. World Bank researchers estimate that over 500 million live on less than $2 a day, a measure of 'moderate poverty' (Chen and Ravaillon, 2007). An important aspect of China's liberalization was the shift from communal farms to 'household responsibility' between 1977 and 1979, which gave farmers incentives to farm individual plots. While these reforms boosted productivity, the lack of legal property rights to their land, it later emerged, made farmers vulnerable to the appropriation of the land they farm by public sector projects and commercial developments. This has left many farming households landless and without adequate compensation. The government recognizes that rural development is now a priority, in order to maintain social stability and satisfy aspirations for a better quality of life for all socioeconomic groups. The natural propensity of Chinese people has been to save rather than spend, a tendency reinforced by worries over paying for health, housing, education and other needs. These concerns are more in evidence in poorer rural areas than in cities, where growing affluence is creating a boom in consumption. However, retailers have found that Chinese consumers are discriminating shoppers, and that cultural influences remain important.

To win market share, retailers have had to trim margins. They compete not only against other hypermarkets, but against a wealth of more traditional types of retailing such as markets. Organized retailing, through chains of stores with distribution networks, is much less developed than in Western environments, as Figure 2 shows. It is perhaps surprising, therefore, that there are over 120 hypermarkets in Shanghai, some districts having four or more. The competition creates even greater price pressures. While customers like foreign brands, they show little loyalty if prices are lower elsewhere. In Shanghai, which has reached saturation, some of these retailers are likely to withdraw, as capacity adjusts to demand. In addition, the government could compel future entrants to survey whether demand exists before approving new projects.

As they expand beyond the cities of Shanghai, Beijing and

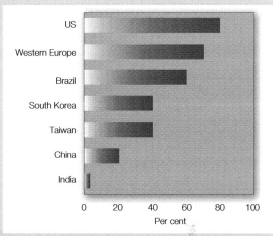

Figure 2 Penetration of organized retail

Per cent (axis: 0, 20, 40, 60, 80, 100)

US, Western Europe, Brazil, South Korea, Taiwan, China, India

Source: Financial Times, 28 November 2006

Guangzhou, retailers are finding marked differences in tastes among consumers. Fruit and vegetables, sauces and meats are matters of local preferences. Soy sauces are favoured in the north, chilli sauces in central China and oyster sauces in the south. One preference all Chinese customers share is for very fresh food, stemming in part from experiences in previous eras when food safety standards were low. In many cases, they are reluctant to buy products which have not originated in the local district. An experienced consultant says: 'You have to get the fresh [food] right, otherwise the Chinese will not respect you' (Rigby and Dyer, 2007). This priority challenges hypermarket retailers, whose strengths are global distribution networks and economies of scale. Keeping existing customers satisfied and expanding outwards from the cities will test their adaptability in this changing market.

Questions

◆ Assess China as a potential market in terms of the three levels of analysis presented in the previous section: macro-level factors, consumer markets, and micro-level product markets.

◆ How does China's rich–poor divide impact on the growth in consumer markets?

◆ Why have hypermarket retailers flocked to China?

Sources: Lau, J., 'China market leaders are the ones to watch', *Financial Times,* 5 April 2006; McGregor, R., 'Unstoppable but unsustainable', *Financial Times,* 12 December 2006; Dyer, G. and Rigby, E., 'Wal-Mart on song in China as bid is launched', *Financial Times,* 18 October 2006; Johnson, J. and Birchall, J., '"Mom and pop" stores braced for challenge', *Financial Times,* 28 November 2006; Ward, A., 'Home Depot opens the door to a growing market', *Financial Times,* 11 December 2006; Rigby, E., 'Big chains stake out their turf in China', *Financial Times,* 13 February 2007; Sachs, J. (2005) *The End of Poverty* (London: Penguin); UNDP (2006) *Human Development Report* (Basingstoke: Palgrave Macmillan); Chen, S. and Ravallion, M. (2007) 'Absolute poverty measures for the developing world', World Bank Policy Research Paper WPS4211, www.wds.worldbank.org.

WEB CHECK

For information about China, see the World Bank's website at www.worldbank.org, and click on *China* in the country list.

Developing and emerging markets
What factors should firms prioritize when contemplating expansion into these exciting new markets? What are their disadvantages in comparison with developed countries?

PAUSE TO REFLECT

Segmentation and targeting

Even in a market with good growth potential, a firm cannot realistically hope to win over all potential consumers. It may have a single undifferentiated strategy for a standardized product, aiming to reach the maximum number of consumers. Low-cost airlines are one of the few examples of this type of strategy. However, as the discussion of consumer markets above highlighted, consumers differ in their buying power, lifestyles, location and priorities. Target marketing is aimed at particular consumers who the firm judges are most likely to purchase particular products. Targeting involves dividing consumers into different segments according to their needs and other characteristics. Particular products and appropriate ways of reaching consumers will differ from segment to segment.

For international marketing, segmentation based on differing national markets is common. However, marketers also focus on socioeconomic groups and demographic factors, which target segments across national boundaries. We consider each in turn. A *national market* is a geographic and administrative entity, whose consumers share cultural characteristics. National culture focuses on language and a shared sense of identity (see discussion in Chapter 4). It is particularly relevant in the markets for products where these elements come into play, such as food and media. Magazines, therefore, have national markets, although the same titles may have different language editions. Products such as branded food and beverages are culturally sensitive, and producers market products for national tastes. Shared national culture is also important for immigrants, who form subcultures in their new countries, as SX12.1 highlights.

Socioeconomic grouping is the second basis of market segmentation. These segments transcend national boundaries. Consumer affluence and buying behaviour may nonetheless differ from country to country. Televisions are desired by consumers everywhere, but differing levels of affluence influence the models and marketing strategy in each country. High-income groups are similar in their consumer preferences, whatever country they are in, as lifestyle is in large part a matter of income. Middle-class consumers live in similar types of accommodation and seek to furnish their houses in similar ways, wherever they live. This has been the guiding philosophy of IKEA. Luxury cars, fine jewellery and expensive holiday destinations appeal to the rich everywhere. But the firm which focuses exclusively on luxury markets risks falling sales in periods of economic downturn. Many companies, such as car manufacturers, offer a range of brands for differing income groups. Renault's Logan subsidiary produces a cheap and cheerful small car, mainly in Romania, for developing and emerging

Target marketing: Marketing aimed at satisfying the needs of a particular group of consumers.

Segmentation: Division of a consumer market into groups of similar consumers who share some key characteristics, such as socioeconomic grouping, cultural identity or demographic similarity.

markets, but has been surprised that it is selling well in established European markets. As highlighted in the opening vignette, the car market is growing swiftly in India, leading Renault to adjust its strategy by forging a joint venture with Bajaj Auto to produce an even cheaper car, rivalling the Tata Nano. India is now seen as a growing market and a manufacturing centre.

The third basis of segmentation is *demographics*. Demographic segmentation includes a number of variables, the most popular being age and gender. Young consumers in their late teens and twenties are a favourite segment of marketers. They are assumed to be free spenders on the latest products, fashion items and entertainment, whatever country they are in. Mobile phone companies target this group in particular, as do drinks companies (see CS3.1 on Heineken). In mobile phones and music players, companies target teenagers in the 13–18 age range. LG Electronics is an example, seeing this segment as setting trends which others will follow (Fifield, 2004). Given the ageing populations of most developed economies, well-off pensioners are a significant segment. These consumers are a traditional target of holiday companies selling cruises and other package holidays, but there are many other products and services which these consumers seek, such as accommodation adapted to their needs and home services. Gender is another traditional basis of demographic segmentation. Products targeted at women include clothing, magazines and cosmetics. However, in all these areas, marketers are also targeting men with products designed for their needs. Men's grooming products are a growing market, making Procter & Gamble's acquisition of the well-known brand Gillette a significant strategic move (discussed in CS12.1).

The company contemplating international markets must measure the segment attractiveness against its own business strengths before deciding which countries and which segments to target. A segment may be attractive if it is projected to grow strongly, but if it does not fit with the company's long-term goals or strengths, it will probably struggle to be competitive and capture market share. The firm may choose to target several market segments, tailoring its products and marketing mix for each. This represents a **differentiated marketing** strategy, often adopted by large MNEs. Their reasoning is that strong offerings in a number of segments will contribute to its overall strength in its product category.

By contrast, some businesses have specialized strengths, for which the relevant market is rather narrowly defined. This is known as the **niche market**. The niche market consists of a subgroup of consumers with particular specialized needs. Often the smaller company finds opportunities in niche markets which larger companies overlook. Organic products, highlighted in Chapter 13, are an example. There may well be few competitors in the niche market. Large companies may offer products in niche markets in addition to their more mainstream offerings, but their main target markets are those in which they enjoy economies of scale. Niche markets may also be specific to cultural characteristics. LG Electronics has designed its 'Qiblah' phones, which indicate the direction of Mecca for Muslim consumers. These phones are targeted at Middle East consumers. Spanish-language broadcasting in the US has formerly been considered a niche market, but, as SX12.1 shows, this market is becoming mainstream.

See LG's website at www.lge.com.

WEB CHECK

Differentiated marketing: Adapting products and marketing mix for differing target markets.

Niche market: Subgroup of consumers with specific specialized needs.

TO RECAP...
Segmentation in international markets
Segmenting according to countries is a traditional approach. Socioeconomic and demographic segments straddle national boundaries, implying more globalized strategies, although national cultural factors remain influential in much marketing decision-making.

STRATEGIC CROSSROADS

12.1
Excitement mounts as Hispanic media take to a wider stage

The Hispanic market in the US has become one of the most sought-after by media companies. The growing numbers of Hispanic consumers, as well as their youthfulness, make them an attractive market for media companies and advertisers. The Hispanic population of the US consists of Spanish-speaking people who have emigrated from Latin America, mainly Mexico, in search of employment and higher living standards than their home countries offer. Their median age is 26.7 years, placing them in the middle of the 18–34 age group, advertisers' favourite age band. While it had been expected that the numbers of Spanish speakers would decline as immigrants became assimilated, their numbers are actually growing. This is good news for media companies, which have seen their mass audiences fragmented by options such as cable television and the internet. In 2006, the US media industry expanded by 5.4% overall, but the Hispanic segment expanded by nearly double that rate, at 10.4%. Rising Hispanic audiences, whose spending power is expected to grow to $670 billion in personal income by 2020, are attracting excited attention.

The leading Spanish-language media company in the US is Univision, which owns three television networks and 69 radio stations. Founded in 1992 in Los Angeles, an 11% stake was held by Televisa, the Mexican company which is the world's largest Spanish-language media group. Televisa specializes in the 'telenovela', a melodrama format akin to the soap opera, which originated in Cuba's cigar factories, where Dickens and Balzac, both masters of emotion-laden melodramas, were read aloud to workers. The company became market leaders in creating television dramas, along with their glamorous stars, with the same efficiency of the formula-driven former Hollywood studios or Bollywood producers from India. Latin American-produced telenovelas command audiences of 2 billion, mainly in Latin America, but extending to 100 countries around the world. Univision eventually persuaded advertisers to consider its networks in the mainstream of their annual spending plans, rather than a niche. In areas with large concentrations of Hispanics, such as Los Angeles, Miami and Chicago, Univision regularly achieves larger audiences than the top English-language networks, including ABC, CBS and Fox. In 2006, Nielsen, the media research company, began measuring

Univision's audiences alongside other US networks. Occasionally, its primetime ratings have beaten its larger rivals for 18–34-year-old viewers, an achievement which has sent the company's shares upwards and attracted takeover interest.

As market leader, Univision has faced competition. NBC Universal, owned by GE, bought Telemundo, a Miami-based production company, for $2.7 billion in 2002. Telemundo tackled Univision head-on with its own telenovela, *Tierra de Pasiones*. Its content is home produced, in contrast to the imported programmes of Univision. Telemundo argues that relevance to issues closer to the interests and concerns of its audiences will give it an advantage. Telemundo went so far as to establish a telenovela centre in association with a local university, to build local skills in writing the dramas, from which a pool of telenovela writers would emerge. Telemundo is also transferring material from *Tierra de Pasiones* to its websites, with accompanying advertising. Owning its content gives it flexibility and a competitive edge in the growing digital market. Telemundo also aspires to global audiences, and claims a presence in 142 markets. In 2006, it made more than $20 million selling its telenovelas to broadcasters in foreign markets such as Spain and Argentina.

Telemundo's most recent success has been in seemingly unlikely markets in Asia, including South Korea, China, Malaysia and Indonesia. Although these markets have traditionally been resistant to foreign media content, the romantic melodramas have struck a chord with viewers. The president of Telemundo International says: 'These are countries that share a lot of the same cultural values and realities. If it works in Latin America, it works in Asia' (Chaffin, 2008).

Questions
◆ Assess the reasons behind Univision's growth.
◆ How are the strategies of media firms in Spanish-language output evolving in terms of wider markets?

Sources: Chaffin, J., 'Manic for the Hispanic market', *Financial Times*, 27 June 2006; Chaffin, J., 'Hispanics warm to telenovelas with an American twist', *Financial Times*, 25 May 2006; Van Duyn, A., 'Spanish TV drama's final scene may yet need further rewrite', *Financial Times*, 28 June 2006; Chaffin, J., 'US television recognises its need to brush up on Spanish', *Financial Times*, 9 February 2006; Chaffin, J. 'Mascara melodrama eyes up Asia for the payoff kiss', *Financial Times*, 8 February 2008.

WEB CHECK
Telemundo's website is http://tv.telemundo.yahoo.com.
Univision's website is www.univision.net.

Shifting targets?
To what extent do you feel segmentation based on demographic characteristics, such as age and gender, is becoming more significant than segmentation based on national cultural differences?

PAUSE TO REFLECT

Market entry strategies

In Chapter 7, broad internationalization strategies were examined from the organizational perspective, focusing on production decisions. Here we look at entry strategies from the perspective of firms wishing to win customers in foreign markets. Market entry options, which are shown in Figure 12.5, vary with the type of product or service. For manufactured goods, companies usually consider export as a first option. Export may be indirect, through intermediaries based in the firm's home country, or direct, through intermediaries in the foreign market. Initially, a firm is likely to use agents and foreign distributors. However, as agents and distributors deal with many clients, the firm may choose to set up its own sales subsidiary in the foreign market, bypassing the intermediaries. The sales office becomes the distributor for the firm's products, holding stock, selling to buyers and engaging in marketing activities designed by the company. As it is a type of FDI, it involves a greater commitment to the location. It affords the company greater control and a better platform from which to build its new market than exporting through intermediaries.

Figure 12.5 Market entry strategies

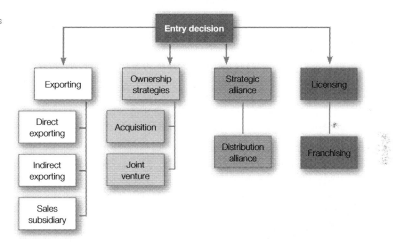

In many product categories, the firm may find production in the foreign market reduces costs. While foreign production may take the form of a greenfield operation (discussed in Chapters 2 and 7), manufacture under licence is a favoured alternative, involving less capital investment and greater flexibility. The licence is awarded by a company (the licensor) to a local producer (the licensee), giving the licensee permission to manufacture goods covered by patent or trademark, provided the terms of the licensing agreement are met. The licensee pays a royalty to the licensor, usually a percentage of sales volumes. Pharmaceutical companies use licensing agreements extensively. Food companies also use this system, as these rather low-value products are expensive to export. However, there are risks in licensing, stemming from dependence on the local partner. The quality control of the local producer may be questionable, and it may not possess the marketing skills to build market share in competition with astute rivals.

Franchising also involves licensing, but in this case, the franchisor company negotiates for an entire operation to be carried out under its name and marketing programme in the foreign location. Fast-food outlets such as McDonald's and KFC are examples. However, as highlighted in SX1.1, McDonald's has relied on managed restaurants rather than franchising in many foreign locations, a policy which is now evolving.

The advantage of ownership of assets in the foreign market is that of ultimate control over the products and marketing. Under a joint venture arrangement, the foreign entrant and a local company take equity stakes in a new company which enters the market. The hypermarkets have favoured this method of entry, dictated by legal constraints on ownership in some cases such as China, discussed in CF12.1. In developing and transitional economies, the joint venture benefits from the knowledge of the local partner and the management skills of the foreign partner. Wal-Mart has chosen an Indian firm, Bharti Enterprises, for its market debut in India. In Japan, Wal-Mart chose to purchase a stake in a Japanese retailer, Seiyu, as a low-key entry strategy. This strategy has been unsuccessful so far, as Seiyu has struggled to make profits. In the UK, Wal-Mart entered through acquisition of an existing business, ASDA, in 1999. Acquisition gives the acquirer an immediate market share, making this option attractive for companies impatient with the approach of building up a presence from scratch. ASDA has not been rebranded as Wal-Mart, but the ASDA logo now states: 'part of the Wal-Mart family'.

Strategic alliances have proved popular in some sectors. Distribution alliances link manufacturers and brand owners with companies having distribution networks already in place. For the manufacturer, the advantages are that it can reach consumers quickly, without the meticulous groundwork needed to build its own distribution network. These alliances can be equity-based joint ventures or simply contractual arrangements. General Mills, a US company which makes breakfast cereals, entered a joint venture with Nestlé, forming Cereal Partners Worldwide (CPW), a company owned equally by both partners. General Mills benefited from Nestlé's worldwide distribution network, while Nestlé benefited from General Mills' product lines, which compete against Kellogg's, the market leader. CPW is based in Switzerland and manufactures for markets outside the US and Canada.

Market entry analysis is outlined in Figure 12.6. Each possible market entry strategy has associated costs, which must be balanced against expected gains from sales. Environmental factors in the new market come into play. Political uncertainty is particularly relevant if the company has acquired ownership of assets in the foreign market, which may be jeopardized by changes in government or policies, as CF12.2 on South Africa highlights. Currency risk may affect the expected profits. The company must also consider what timescale it is contemplating for yielding the desired returns. While patience is rewarded in many markets, in others, the situation may deteriorate, often due to external factors. If the strategy fails to achieve the firm's objectives, market exit can be costly, and the company faces the unenviable task of deciding how long to wait before abandoning its strategy, with inevitable damage to its reputation.

Cereal Partners' website is www.cerealpartners.co.uk. ASDA's website is www.asda.co.uk.

WEB CHECK

TO RECAP...

Market entry alternatives
Exporting, either directly or indirectly, is a traditional market entry strategy. For large firms, acquiring an existing business or entering a joint venture with a local partner involve ownership stakes. Licensing a foreign producer is a means of market entry which does not involve ownership of foreign assets. Strategic alliances are helpful in particular functional areas such as distribution. Decision-making must take into account costs, market potential and environmental factors.

Figure 12.6 Market entry analysis

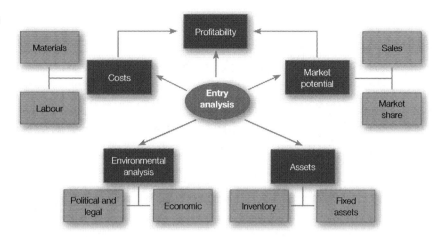

COUNTRY FOCUS 12.2 – SOUTH AFRICA

Buoyant South Africa on a wave of optimism

South Africa has become sub-Saharan Africa's most prosperous economy, its GDP four times that of neighbouring countries. Since the collapse of apartheid in 1994, democracy and economic development have bred growing optimism. Economic growth in the 3–6% range (shown in Figure 1), although not stunning in comparison to the fast-growing emerging markets, is a cause for optimism, following decades of disappointment. It has taken 25 years for real GDP per capita to recover to 1981 levels. Current GDP per head of over $6,000 ($15,000 at PPP) places South Africa in the group of middle-income countries. The economy is gradually shifting from mining and other heavy industries, on which it has traditionally depended, to service

sectors such as business process outsourcing (BPO) and tourism, which are growing globally. Figure 2 shows the break-down of 2006 GDP growth for each sector.

Government priorities have been providing social welfare programmes and increasing participation of black South Africans in economic prosperity. A growing middle class is spending on consumer goods such as cars and new houses, and shopping at new shopping malls which are springing up all over the country, not just in the large cities. Low interest rates mean affordable mortgages and car payments, leaving consumers more money to spend on other goods.

South African consumers' spending spree has been welcome

Figure 1 South Africa's economic growth, 1984-2008

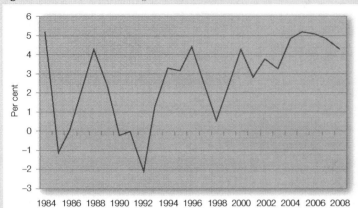

Note: Estimates for 2007 and 2008

Source: IMF (2007) World Economic Outlook, October, www.imf.org

news to banks and retailers. Barclays, the UK bank, exited South Africa in 1987, due to pressures from anti-apartheid protests. In 2005, it returned with vigour, acquiring a 56% stake in South Africa's largest retail bank, Absa. This acquisition became the single largest foreign investment in South Africa since 1994. Barclays hopes ultimately to generate 10% of its total earnings from Absa, boosting its earnings from outside the UK to one-third the total. The attractions were Absa's 7.7 million retail customers, with further potential for mortgages, credit cards and commercial property finance. With its expertise in credit cards, Barclays was especially keen to enter this market, which has ample growth potential, as only 10% of South Africans had credit cards in 2005. Absa's loans and advances rose 26% in the first year of Barclays control, and retail customers rose to 8.4 million, boding well for future growth. However, analysts have questioned the long-term viability of the South African investment. The consumer boom is offering business opportunities, but longer term prospects depend on continued economic growth, which could be affected by political risk.

Although consumption has forged ahead, South Africa's export industries have suffered from currency volatility. The currency, the rand, has doubled in US dollar terms since 2001, causing headaches for exporters, particularly manufacturers, who are important to GDP growth (see Figure 2). South Africa is in a less favourable position than the fast-growing emerging markets, such as China, which have relied on export-oriented manufacturing, although growth in high value-added services is encouraging. The strong rand has helped consumers to buy flat-screen televisions and other imported goods, but exporters have less to cheer about. Unemployment is high, at 26%, and the rate is closer to 36% if discouraged workers who have stopped looking for work are included. The economy would need to grow at over 6% annually to create enough jobs. At present, despite government training programmes, the lack of skills is holding back foreign investment as well as local businesses.

South Africa is still beset by the wide gap in incomes and quality of life between the better off classes and the 22 million very poor inhabitants, who comprise nearly half the total population. Of these, less than half have access to primary education, and some 5.5 million are suffering from HIV/Aids. Growing tax revenues are funding programmes to deal with health and deprivation, but hopes of halving poverty and unemployment by 2014 seem optimistic. The lack of skilled workers has deterred investors, but as suitably skilled candidates enter employment, prospects for bringing more citizens into salaried employment are improving.

Services are providing new jobs and growth potential. In BPO, South Africa has attracted investors such as Lufthansa, Virgin Mobile, IBM and Carphone Warehouse. South Africa offers them cost savings of about 30% compared to their home economies, as well as other benefits. The time zone, a relatively neutral accent and greater cultural affinity with northern European countries have helped to attract call-centre operations. Back-office operations are also taking off, including finance and IT. On the negative side, the costs of telecommunications are high, owing to the slowness of reforms in dismantling the state-owned monopoly provider. The numbers of candidates for BPO jobs are rising as education improves among black students. These new recruits are likely to stay in jobs longer than those in countries such as India, which has a greater supply of qualified workers. While South Africa is never likely to compete with India's high-volume BPO operations in cost savings, it is targeting niche markets in areas such as conflict resolution and HRM, in which it can build expertise.

Tourism is another growth sector which, while not offering prospects of high volumes, attracts upmarket tourists looking for stunning scenery and wildlife. Tourism's contribution to the economy has doubled since the transition to democracy in 1994. Overseas visitors number about 2 million a year, which

Figure 2 Composition of South Africa's GDP growth in 2006

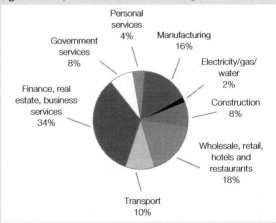

Source: Statistics South Africa, www.statssa.gov.za

should be boosted by the football World Cup in 2010. Service standards, transport and infrastructure are improving. Tourism authorities are also hoping to broaden the country's appeal, attracting younger clients who seek alternatives to beach holidays and safaris. However, they are aware that these popular types of holiday are available more cheaply in other locations, and that broadening appeal could deter the more affluent visitors. Several factors could dampen growth in tourism. Weak international air access, shortages of skilled staff and high levels of violent crime are among them.

South Africa has become a successful emerging economy, which stands out among its poorer neighbours. However, its economic landscape is one of contrasts, in which some areas are developed while others are much less developed. The bestselling product at Edcon, one of the country's largest retailers, is not flat-screen TVs or the like, but light bulbs, which have risen in demand as electricity gradually reaches into poorer communities. The less good news is that power cuts are a common phenomenon across the country, as the power generation network struggles to keep up with demand. Maintaining power to industrial and commercial customers, as well as household consumers, is one of the many challenges facing South Africa.

Questions

◆ In 2005, some criticized Barclays for its acquisition of Absa as being too risky an investment. Assess the pros and cons of the decision. Does the bank now seem to have got it right?

◆ Assess the entry decision-making process for a company from the EU considering South Africa as a possible location for its call centre.

◆ Construct a SWOT analysis of a South African company offering upmarket packages for foreign tourists.

Sources: Reed, J., 'Good times put system under strain', *Financial Times*, 6 June 2006; White, D., 'Black middle class helps fuel a spending spree', *Financial Times*, 6 June 2006; White, D., 'In defiance of gravity', *Financial Times*, 24 May 2005; Reed, J., 'Scouting for more happy customers', *Financial Times*, 6 June 2006; Reed, J., 'Swept up in a mood of optimism', *Financial Times*, 24 May 2005; Barber, L. and Russell, A., 'Softly, softly: Mbeki seeks ways to limit chaos to the north and tensions within', *Financial Times*, 3 April 2007; IMF (2006) Country report for South Africa, www.imf.org/external; Statistics South Africa (2006), www.statssa.gov.za.; Russell, A., 'A long journey', *Financial Times*, 27 June 2007; Hawkins, T., 'Out of the doldrums', *Financial Times*, 5 June 2007.

WEB CHECK

See information about South Africa by going to the World Bank's website at www.worldbank.org, and clicking on *South Africa* in the country list.

plate 12.2 The affluence of Cape Town, South Africa, seen in the modern buildings shown here, reflects the country's economic growth.

Emerging market entry
Which entry strategies are best suited to developing and emerging markets, and why? Give examples in manufactured products and in retailing.

PAUSE TO REFLECT

Products and branding

Product: Goods (tangible), services (intangible), or a combination of the two, which a firm offers to potential customers in exchange for payment, usually money.

Products and brands may have a local, national, regional or global focus. Within a product area, a company can adapt product features and marketing to national or local markets. It may also aim to build global brands, complemented by local brands or niche brands for products targeted at local markets or particular segments. Decisions on products and brands are central to marketing strategy.

Products are probably the most crucial ingredient of success in any market. The product may be a good, which is a tangible product that the consumer can physically touch, or a service, which is intangible. We tend to think of companies as specializing in one or the other, but the marketing concept, which focuses on consumer satisfaction, implies that service to the customer is an aspect of providing goods. While the traditional focus of Ford was simply to produce and sell cars, in the 1960s, GM realized that offering after-sales service was a way of winning over customers. Goods and services are therefore linked in the experience of the consumer. In some cases, there is a direct link. For example Apple's iPod music player and iTunes music downloading complement each other.

Every product has attributes which distinguish it from others in the same broad product category. These attributes or features may be crucial in appealing to certain market segments. Dyson's vacuum cleaner designed for the Japanese market is smaller and lighter than those offered in other markets, to make it suitable for small apartments (see SX2.2 on Dyson). In fact, these qualities have made it popular in other markets as well. Apart from physical attributes, the product may have intangible attributes, such as its recognition in society as a status symbol. An Indian marketing executive says of his desire to trade his motorbike for a new Tata Nano: 'A car says you are in a good position, a good career' (Johnson, 2008a).

The **brand** has a legal dimension and an image-creating dimension. Legally, it is a trademark or logo which distinguishes the product from similar products by other producers. When the trademark is registered, the owner has ownership rights in the form of intellectual property, which authorizes the taking of legal action against other firms which use the trademark without permission. Unfortunately, in many parts of the world, brand names and logos, although protected in theory, are weakly enforced, allowing counterfeiters to produce falsely labelled goods in large quantities. These are inevitably cheaper than the proper branded product and are usually of poor quality. Brand owners wage a constant battle against these practices, which they feel could affect legitimate sales in some markets.

Global and local dimensions

Local products and brands are the mainstay of companies which concentrate on home markets. Foreign entrants may struggle to build market share where there is strong consumer attachment to local offerings. On the other hand, if the MNE has a strong global brand, it may convey a notion of quality and prestige which will attract consumers. They will probably have to pay a premium price for the global brand, but they feel the brand is a guarantee of quality, while local products could well have inconsistent quality. In many countries, the global brand is aspirational. A Costa Rican consumer says: 'Local brands show what we are; global brands show what we want to be' (Holt et al., 2004). In areas such as pharmaceuticals, the global brand is a guarantee of safety in countries where many medicines produced by local

Brand: Trademark or logo distinguishing an organization's products from those of rivals, which is an important asset capable of legal protection.

TO RECAP...
Products and brands
In addition to providing the right product for target markets, companies aim to attract consumers by branding through trademarks.

manufacturers are unsafe and ineffective, in addition to being produced in breach of patents.

A few global brands, such as Microsoft, Coca-Cola and McDonald's, have become iconic. These brands consistently feature in global brand rankings. The top 10 from two of these ranking systems are presented in Figure 12.7. Both systems calculate financial value on the basis of brand strength in terms of consumer demand and expectations for future growth. Microsoft and Coca-Cola regularly jostle for first place. Google's swift rise to the top of the Millward Brown rankings indicates the growing power of the internet. Google is still strongly identified with the idealism of its founders, which shapes its brand image.

The brand's image-creating dimension is a source of its appeal to customers. The brand evokes a number of images in the minds of consumers, which relate to the company's reputation and values, as well as the consumer's own lifestyle, social status and values. Indeed, the consumer's aspirations to a particular lifestyle or status are perhaps more relevant: the consumer's self-image is enhanced by the brand. The company which is able to build a strong brand in the eyes of consumers builds a relationship with them which generates brand loyalty. The concept of 'brand equity' is the added value that the brand brings to the product and its owner. For this reason, brands may be worth considerable sums of money as assets in their own right. The share that brands contribute to a firm's overall value is estimated to have risen from 50% in 1980 to 70% in 2007 (Gapper, 2007).

The global brand built on quality acts as a guarantee to consumers regarding its products (Steenkamp et al., 2003). If the brand owner allows quality to suffer, the strong brand may protect it for a time but, eventually, consumers will desert the brand. Consumers also expect brand owners to maintain high standards in areas such as corporate social responsibility (Holt et al., 2004). Reporting on their CSR throughout their global operations has become common among global companies. Issues such as relations with stakeholders in local communities, employee conditions and the provision of services such as health and education for employees in developing countries are aspects of CSR, discussed further in Chapter 14.

Figure 12.7 Rankings of global brands for 2007

Sources: Interbrand, *Interbrand Best Global Brands 2007*, www.interbrand.com; Millward Brown Optimor, *Brandz Survey 2007*, www.millwardbrown.com

Millward Brown Brandz Survey				Interbrand rankings		
Brand	Brand value $millions	% change on previous year		Brand	Brand value $millions	% change on previous year
1 Google	66,434	77		1 Coca-Cola	66,324	–3
2 GE	61,880	11		2 Microsoft	58,709	3
3 Microsoft	54,951	–11		3 IBM	57,091	2
4 Coca-Cola	44,134	7		4 GE	57,569	5
5 China Mobile	41,214	5		5 Nokia	33,696	12
6 Marlboro	39,166	2		6 Toyota	32,070	15
7 Wal-Mart	36,680	–2		7 Intel	30,944	–4
8 Citi	33,706	9		8 McDonald's	29,398	7
9 IBM	33,572	–7		9 Disney	29,210	5
10 Toyota	33,427	11		10 Mercedes	23,568	5

A brand may benefit from associations with its country of origin. Perceptions of quality and prestige enhance the brand's image, becoming part of its brand equity. 'Made in Germany' suggests quality engineering and benefits Germany's motor manufacturers and industrial engineering companies. Italy is associated with fashion and quality in clothes and accessories, and is home to some of the most coveted brands, such as Armani and Prada. A number of Armani-label clothes, some in the top-end Armani Collezioni range, are now made in China. Although the company maintains that its stringent quality control standards remain the same, the 'made in China' label could possibly damage the firm's image. A number of luxury brands outsource manufacturing to China, and some, unlike Armani, carry no such label. LG Electronics of South Korea has launched an upmarket mobile phone under the Prada brand, extending the notion of Italian style to the mobile phone, perceived as a fashion accessory by many consumers.

Product and brand strategies

The fashion-conscious consumer seeking out the Prada-branded mobile phone represents one of many segments targeted by LG Electronics. A large company may have a portfolio of numerous products and brands, from which it chooses which brands and products are suited to different markets and segments. The global brand may be of such value that it can be extended to other products. Known as 'brand extension', this strategy relies on consumers' positive perceptions of the brand and the image it creates. For example, fashion retailers, such as Zara, extend their products to home furnishings, creating a lifestyle image consistent with the company's clothes. Jewellery and accessories are other common extensions of brands. These extensions are a means of persuading the consumer who is attracted to the brand to buy a range of other products which are associated with the same image and in the same price range.

The company may choose to differentiate its brands according to market segment. Linde, a German company which supplies forklift trucks to industrial users, has three forklift truck brands, Linde, STILL and OM Pimespo, each for a different type of forklift truck. Linde trucks are diesel powered, Still vehicles are powered with electric motors and OM Pimespo covers warehouse trucks. Each of these sub-brands is a separate division of the company. This multi-brand strategy may seem fragmented, but the company feels it does more business than it would if all the products were sold under one brand. The parent company has rationalized the parts, utilizing common parts where possible across the brands. Multiple brands may also designate different products depending on whether they are basic market entry products or more upmarket products. Car manufacturers offer numerous models in various price ranges for people with differing levels of income. Many are branded with the corporate brand, such as VW, but separate brands may be used in different markets. VW markets cars in emerging markets under the Skoda brand and also owns Audi, an upmarket brand.

A valuable brand may well form the cornerstone of a firm's international expansion. If the brand is not well known outside its home country, the firm will have to build its reputation from scratch. Alternatively, the company

Sub-brand: Brand created to serve a distinctive product or market segment under the umbrella of the firm's corporate brand.

may acquire a local company which has a strong brand and build market share on the strength of the local brand. This was the approach of Nestlé, when it acquired Rowntree of the UK. Brands such as KitKat were then added to the company's portfolio of brands.

Emerging and developing countries offer some of the most enticing prospects for market growth for consumer product companies. There are crucial differences between these markets and developed countries, in terms of income, segments and the range of appropriate products. MNEs have typically found that, although their offerings reach mass markets in developed countries, in developing countries, only a small proportion of the population is acquainted with global brands and can afford branded imported products (Dawar and Chattopadhyay, 2000). This segment may amount to only about 5% of the population. The company may reason that, as these economies are developing quickly, this proportion is likely to grow and tastes will converge with developed countries. These developments, however, may be slow to materialize. Furthermore, the assumption that these consumers will converge with Europeans or Americans might turn out to be wrong. Localizing products is an alternative, to attempt to build mass-market appeal in the developing country. Extensive knowledge of the consumer market is required, and the foreign MNE is up against knowledgeable local competitors. CS12.1 on P&G highlights the challenges of this strategy. Prices must be in the range which target consumers can afford. Unilever's Lifebuoy soap is popular in Africa, India and Indonesia. It is a basic product made from local ingredients and packaging, keeping the price low. Unilever has learned from its experience in these markets that all the elements of the marketing mix, including product, packaging, distribution and communication, must be driven by price considerations. Unilever's example indicates that strategies for emerging markets may translate from one to another.

One of the reasons that MNEs in developed consumer markets are now looking to emerging and developing markets for future growth is that the competitive environment has become intense in their home markets. Here, they rely on new and innovative products to boost sales and differentiate themselves from rivals. However, brand owners have encountered competition from supermarkets and speciality retailers who sell products under their 'own' label, or private brands. They include goods, such as food and clothing, as well as services, such as insurance. The UK has been at the forefront of this trend. Own brands are usually cheaper than the global brand and capture considerable market share in numerous product lines. Own brands accounted for 36% of retail sales in Britain by value in 2006, as seen in Figure 12.8. This share looks set to rise as consumers feel more confident of the quality of the own-brand products. Although Tesco was once perceived as working class, differentiating itself mainly

Private brand: Brands owned by supermarkets and other retailers, which are produced for sale in their outlets alone; also known as 'private labels' and 'own brands'.

Figure 12.8 Own-label share of consumer packaged goods spending
Source: *Financial Times*, 26 January 2006

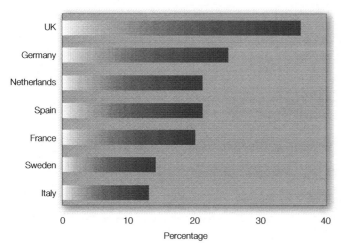

Percentage

on price, it has now shifted to an emphasis on good value, whatever the price, appealing to all segments. Like other supermarkets, it has a segmented own-brand offering, with 'value', 'standard' and 'finest'.

Companies such as Unilever and P&G spend large sums on R&D, maintaining a leading role in creating new products. Their innovative products are often copied by manufacturers producing for private brands of supermarkets and multiple retailers. P&G has taken legal action against some of these producers for IPR infringement. The global brand owners argue that the own brands can never replicate the original product exactly, but the rise of their popularity with consumers suggests that they pose a real threat (Kumar and Steenkamp, 2007). In reality, retailers are building equity in their own brands. Note that Wal-Mart is ranked in seventh place in the Millward Brown rankings in Figure 12.7.

TO RECAP...

Product and brand strategies

In theory, the global brand is a strong competitor in all markets, but in practice, MNEs tend to have a portfolio of products and brands designed for differing national markets. The global brand owner faces competition from the private brands of retailers, whose products tend to be cheaper. Local producers, with their lower costs and local knowledge, offer competition to foreign entrants.

Waning of the global brand?
Global brands have faced consumer resistance in many markets, from consumers who prefer low-cost own brands and from those who object to the economic power and practices of large global companies. To what extent do you feel that the reputation of global brands is declining? Give examples.

PAUSE TO REFLECT

Case study 12.1: Global brands and local products light up Procter & Gamble

Procter & Gamble (P&G) started out supplying candles to the Union army in the American Civil War. The company grew into a symbol of American corporate success, its brands of consumer products featuring on the shelves of supermarkets across the globe. These include Tide laundry detergent, Crest toothpaste and Pringles crisps. P&G's strength has been innovation, offering new products and improved versions of familiar products to reflect changing consumer needs. However, the 1990s saw its innovation wane under growing bureaucracy and a complacent corporate culture, which eventually affected financial performance. In 1999, a new CEO, Durk Jager was brought in to restructure the organization. A radical restructuring ensued, sweeping away the national 'fiefdoms' of country managers and bringing in global business units based on product areas. The new product divisions would work with regional and local managers on marketing and distribution. The rapid restructuring caused considerable disruption, causing further disappointment and costing Jager his job. A.G. Lafley, who replaced him in 2000, kept the new structure, a decision which seems to have been justified by impressive earnings growth, as shown in Figure 1. The inward-looking corporate culture remained a concern when he took over. Refocusing on consumer needs and innovation has become a priority.

Under Lafley's leadership, acquisitions have helped to shape strategy and operations. The acquisition of Clairol and Wella hair care brands boosted the beauty segment, which has grown rapidly and contributes significantly to earnings. The expansion of beauty and healthcare has reflected global trends. About 40% of P&G's total staff of 110,000 employees have come from acquired compa-

nies. The largest acquisition has been Gillette, bought in 2005 for $57 billion, which also owned Duracell batteries and Braun. Gillette's expertise in innovation and its global consumer relations systems were attractions for P&G, which has placed Gillette executives in key posts. Gillette also brought 22 major

Figure 1 P&G net earnings

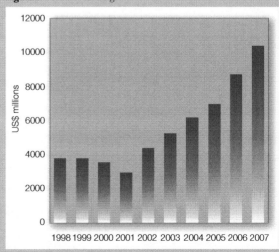

Source: P&G Annual Report 2007, www.pg.com

Figure 2 Percentages of net earnings by business unit

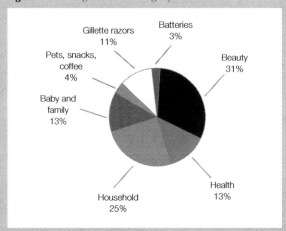

Figure 3 P&G's advertising expenditure

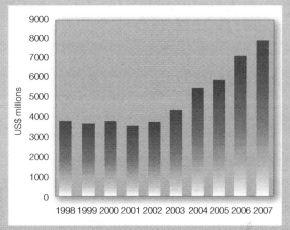

brands, generating over $1 billion in sales. As Figure 2 shows, Gillette and its battery business have contributed 14%, whereas pet health, snacks and coffee have contributed only 4%. These latter products, which include Iams, the pet food brand, have faced strong competition from supermarket own brands, such as Wal-Mart.

Some of the biggest challengers are private brands, as P&G's products are almost all supermarket lines. Lafley accepts that they have a role: 'A private label or a retailer brand cannot exist without branded comparison. Frankly, when we do our job well we are not very vulnerable at all to private labels, because our position broadly is middle of the market and up' (Grant, 22 December 2005). However, competition should be fair. P&G has taken legal action against Percara Enterprises and Cumberland Swan Holdings for infringement of trademark and unfair competition. These are cases where brands such as Head & Shoulders shampoo, Old Spice aftershave and Crest toothpaste feature on supermarket shelves alongside own brands designed to look similar to the P&G brand, thus possibly misleading the customer.

For P&G, advertising has been crucial, having been a pioneer in the use of mass media, particularly television. It prides itself on its constant pursuit of new ways of communicating with customers. As media options have multiplied, it has tried 'just about everything' in terms of methods and venues (Silverman, 2005). It has advertised at rock concerts and sports events. Television, it finds, is still efficient in many markets, but for beauty products, public relations are effective. Where the company has two brands in the same category, the markets and the media mix are different for each. The increasing complexity of marketing strategies and experimentation with new means of reaching consumers have led to increasing costs, as Figure 3 shows.

One of the major shifts in corporate strategy which coincided with the Gillette acquisition has been the targeting of emerging and developing economies. Of the world's 6 billion potential customers, P&G has traditionally targeted its consumer products at the world's most affluent 1 billion. These have been mainly in developed markets. The same products, such as Crest toothpaste,

would be exported from the US to other countries, where they would be bought by relatively small numbers of affluent consumers. The company has now decided that serving the world's other 5 billion customers would be its next challenge. These markets, such as China and India, offer higher growth prospects than developed economies. In addition, there is a 'push' factor, in that the power of retailers in its main markets has been a source of competitive pressure. Products in these new markets need to be affordable, accompanied by appropriate marketing, and still allow these lower margin products to be profitable. The chief financial officer says: 'We've had to, in large part, create a new business model inside the company' (Grant, 15 July 2005).

A basic toothpaste and a basic laundry detergent were developed following extensive research in P&G's laboratories on particular needs in developing countries. For example, products were tested in sweltering heat and humidity, to replicate summer conditions in India. Detergents were tested on clothing stains caused by curries in India and cooking oils in China. While P&G has a central laundry laboratory in the US, 40% of P&G's R&D staff are based in their home markets, liaising with networks of P&G researchers worldwide. The company's vast expertise in science and technology research gave it an edge in product development which local producers could not match. But could these basic products compete on price with local versions? This is often a difficult test for global companies. However, P&G claims not to be perturbed by the fact that the local rival detergent in China has a 40% market share. To keep costs down, the innovation standard has changed. According to the chief technology officer: 'Prior to 2000, we were always going to deliver the absolute best, then "cost save". We have changed that to "cheaper and better"' (Grant, 16 November 2005).

Reaching consumers is another challenge in developing countries, where products must be distributed in towns and villages, often in the hinterlands, where people buy shampoo and toothpaste from kiosks. P&G has developed distribution systems in rural areas. Gillette has a stronger relationship with Western retailers in the larger cities. Here, segmentation is needed, as top-tier and middle-tier consumers can afford more expensive products. The theme which links P&G's newer markets with their established ones is satisfying consumers. Lafley says: 'Just as I believe the consumer has the power in the purchase chain, I think the consumer has the power in the consumption and media and message chain. So

Questions

1 How have acquisitions strengthened P&G's brand portfolio?
2 In what ways has P&G dealt with the challenge of supermarket own brands?
3 How have global product divisions shaped P&G strategy and culture?
4 What is P&G's product strategy in developing markets?

Sources: Grant, J., 'Check the depth of the new customer's pocket', *Financial Times*, 16 November 2005; Grant, J., 'Mr Daley's mission: to reach 6bn shoppers and make money', *Financial Times*, 15 July 2005; Buckley, N., 'The calm reinventor', *Financial Times*, 30 January 2005; Foster, L, 'Optimistic P&G hails improved outlook', *Financial Times*, 1 November 2006; Grant, J., 'Procter doctor: how Lafley's prescription is revitalising a tired consumer titan', *Financial Times*, 22 December 2005; Silverman, G., 'The soap opera makes room for racing and rock concerts', *Financial Times*, 22 December 2005; Grant, J., 'P&G launches suit against private labels', *Financial Times*, 6 May 2006; Grant, J., 'P&G learns lessons as it integrates 557 billion Gillette deal', *Financial Times*, 22 December 2005; P&G Annual Reports, 2005, 2006 and 2007, www.pg.com.

she's the boss – or he's the boss. And so the world is shifting from a "push" to a "pull"' (Grant, 22 December 2005).

WEB CHECK
The P&G website is
www.pg.com.

Reaching consumers

To implement their overall competitive marketing strategy, firms use a variety of marketing tools. Having decided on its target market, the firm must reach consumers with products which satisfy their needs, appropriate communication and prices they are willing to pay. Covering all the elements at this tactical level is the term 'marketing mix'.

Marketing mix

Marketing mix: Set of co-ordinated marketing tools focusing on the four Ps (product, promotion, price and place), designed to satisfy the needs of targeted consumers.

The **marketing mix** can be defined as 'the set of controllable tactical marketing tools that the firm blends to produce the response it wants in the target market' (Kotler et al., 2002: 109). Four groups of variables are usually highlighted, known as 'the four Ps': product, promotion, price and place. Each of the Ps represents a number of facets, as Figure 12.9 shows.

Figure 12.9 The marketing mix

Product

The product element of the marketing mix refers to the totality of the offering to the consumer, including both goods and services. All the elements of the product offering should be consistent. If the brand is an upmarket one, presentation, design, quality and customer service should blend together. If product quality or design is found to be disappointing, consumers will feel even more let down if they have paid for a premium product. On the other hand, the low-cost basic product also needs to satisfy consumers, that is, it needs to function as described, or sales could be lost to a competitor, of which there are likely to many in mass-market products. The product may come with a guarantee or warranty from the manufacturer, which may extend to one or two years. The retailer may be part of a dealer network, which is linked with the manufacturer or even owned by the manufacturer, thus conveying to the customer the message that the firm prioritizes services and after-sales maintenance.

For many consumer goods, packaging is important, not simply as a functional aspect of the product, but as part of its image. High-quality packaging suggests a high-quality product to the consumer, important in markets such as Japan, where gift-giving is prominent in social relations and the appearance of the product is crucial. On the other hand, many consumer products companies, such as P&G, are reducing packaging to limit harm to the environment, often in response to consumer concerns.

Promotion

The second 'P' of the marketing mix is promotion, which covers all types of communication with target customers. Advertising is an important area of expenditure, as the case study on P&G highlighted. Personal contact and word-of-mouth recommendations are also important. In sectors such as industrial products and machinery, which are customized for business customers, or which involve a significant service element, personalized service may be crucial. However, even in mass-market consumer goods, if the salesperson is well informed, enthusiastic and able to help consumers by discussing particular needs, this helps to sell the product and also helps to build consumer loyalty.

Firms now have many different ways of reaching target markets through advertising. The traditional means have been television, radio and print media such as newspapers and magazines. Until fairly recently, the television commercial was a favourite vehicle, but dwindling television audiences and the rise of other media are causing firms to rethink their strategies. Digital media, including the internet and interactive cable and satellite services, offer more opportunities for advertising, tailoring the medium and messages for particular products and target consumers. The company website is now seen as a medium with several functions, including selling products, providing information and advertising. Website design is becoming a critical tool for marketing. The website may help to build relations with customers, inform them of interesting uses of the products, and get their permission to send them emails telling them about new products. The internet, it should be remembered, is accessed by only 16.9% of the world's population, consisting of the more affluent consumers (see Figure 2.11). Advertising media and messages designed in the context of developed Western societies are inappropriate in less affluent markets.

To reach consumers outside the home, advertising may appear in public spaces, including billboards, buildings and on the sides of vehicles such as taxis. These low-tech ways of reaching consumers are heavily used in developing countries, where high-tech media reach only a small fraction of the population. Sports-related advertising has become popular. This category

TO RECAP...

Marketing the product
The product's design and quality need to reflect expectations in its target market. The product includes its presentation, packaging and after-sales services, in addition to its functionality.

Promotion: All types of marketing communication; one of the four Ps in the marketing mix.

includes sponsorship deals with football clubs and other sports, or simply advertising at sporting events. Sports-related advertising has the added advantage of reaching a large television audience in some cases. These types of advertising require detailed planning and implementation on the ground. They are more local in their orientation than the global television campaign.

Companies have become sensitive to the need for advertising to be adapted to local environments, even when advertising a global product. Many different styles of advertising exist, and consumers react differently to different styles. The humorous message may be successful in some countries, but not in others. Celebrity endorsements may be persuasive, but the celebrity must be widely known and admired by the target consumers. For differing country markets, choosing the right magazine or newspaper, which is likely to be a local title, can be crucial to reaching the target audience. In developing countries, print media, like the internet, may reach only a small audience of relatively affluent and educated people. If the target market is broader, aiming to reach lower income consumers, billboards and other advertising in public spaces may be more appropriate. Nestlé has found that, in Brazil, local radio advertising gives better interaction with consumers than advertising on national television networks.

TO RECAP...

Changing approach to advertising

While reaching affluent consumers through new media such as the internet has opened up new possibilities for marketing interaction, where products are targeted at lower income consumers in developing countries, advertising in public spaces is more effective.

Pricing

Pricing strategy, the third of the four Ps, straddles different functions within the firm. Besides marketing, it also involves finance, sales and manufacturing operations. Pricing specialists are therefore in many parts of the organization, with differing perspectives. Ideally, they are co-ordinated from the centre, giving the firm a coherent pricing strategy across all brands and products. While central pricing policies would simplify strategy, differences in local markets imply that there needs to be scope for local decision-making on pricing to adapt to local market conditions.

The price of any product must take account of the costs to produce, the desired level of profits, and competitive pressures from substitute products in the market. The ability of the seller to determine price depends largely on the market. As noted in Chapter 6, the seller with a monopoly has maximum freedom to set prices in theory, but government regulations may impose restrictions. Microsoft is in the position of being a near-monopolist without regulatory intervention. Where there is monopolistic competition, there are many sellers with differentiated products, giving each more freedom to set prices than in an oligopolistic market, where there are only a few sellers offering similar products. In this type of market, a rise in price by one, if it is not followed by the other sellers, can lead to a shift away from the more expensive product.

The product will be priced differently depending on whether it is new or established in its market. The price will also vary according to the product or brand's position in the company's portfolio. The superior product with added features will have a premium price attached. However, if it is new to the market, a lower promotional price might entice customers. The pricing in this case depends partly on the nature of the market. If competitors with similar offerings abound, the question arises whether the new product can justify a premium price for its added-value features, or whether price will play a part in winning market share. These can be difficult decisions to take. A 'price floor' is largely determined by costs, and is the minimum price the firm can contemplate. A 'price ceiling' reflects demand for the product. In the middle is an 'optimum price', which is a function of the demand for the product, given the willingness and ability of consumers to buy it. The price must be high enough to generate a profit, but low enough to produce demand. Cost-plus pricing is a simple way of determining price, by calculating costs and adding a standard mark-up. By contrast, value-based pricing bases price on the perceived value of the product. In this case, the product is designed with a view to a target price rather than costs.

In every national market, there are factors which influence demand and the prices consumers are willing to pay. For this reason, it is unrealistic for a company to think in terms of a single global price. European consumers complain that many consumer goods, from Levi jeans to PlayStations, cost more in their home markets than they do in the US, even though production of these products is globalized for all markets. Companies respond by saying that the costs of marketing and distributing the products are higher in European markets. Keeping national markets separate, however, may be difficult, as individual consumers and businesses are able to buy the product in the cheapest location. If the buyer is a business, it may then resell it in the country where prices are high. Although these activities may have limited impact on overall markets, they can be more influential if the markets are neighbouring countries. This is especially true in eurozone countries, where the single currency allows consumers to see instantly how prices compare. For example, practising price discrimination between France and Germany is difficult.

The producers of luxury products for affluent consumers globally are less concerned that competitors will undercut their prices than the producers of mass-market products. The principles at work are those of elasticities. Elasticity of demand is a measure of consumer response in terms of demand to a change in price, as shown in this equation:

$$\text{Elasticity of demand} = \frac{\% \text{ change in quantity demanded}}{\% \text{ change in price}}$$

High elasticity of demand prevails when a small change in price produces a large change in demand, as in mass-market goods. Demand is less elastic when a large change in prices produces only a slight change in demand. Demand elasticity is greatest in markets where income levels are low. Here, the slightest change in price may cost sales, as consumers are very price sensitive. As noted above, consumers in developing countries typically have little left to spend after paying for food, fuel and accommodation. High elasticity of price prevails where price rises have a minimum impact on demand, as commonly occurs in markets where consumers are better off. Here, people have more money to spend on consumer products such as washing machines. In these markets, however, there are likely to be numerous competitors producing washing machines, causing high elasticity of demand. Thus, even in a wealthy country, a firm which raises prices significantly above those of competitors may lose sales. Companies at the premium end of the market,

Cost-plus pricing: Price based on costs plus a standard mark-up.

Value-based pricing: Price based on buyers' perceptions of value.

High elasticity of demand: Market condition in which a small rise in prices produces a significant drop in demand

High elasticity of price: Market condition in which prices can be raised with minimum adverse effect on demand for a product.

WEB CHECK

Miele's website is at www.miele.com. Note the upmarket image conveyed.

such as Miele of Germany, can justify high prices because of the superior quality of their products. Miele, whose appliances are designed to last at least 20 years, derives 30% of its sales in Germany, but is a premium brand leader in over 30 other countries. Thus, both the segment and the national environment are important in pricing strategy. McDonald's has three tiers of pricing in Europe, to cater for different budgets. Its head of European operations also recognizes national differences in economic development: 'We've got 41 countries at very different stages of development and we've got to respect that' (Wiggins, 2007).

Motorola provides an example of the effects of poor pricing strategy. Its sleak, clamshell mobile phone, the Razr, attracted consumers away from Nokia, which was compelled to rethink its strategy. Motorola's market share rose from 14% in 2003 to 22% in 2006. However, the gains came at the expense of profit margins, as the company made steep price cuts in its medium and high-end phones, while relying on increasing sales of low-end phones which had low profit margins. The effect was a loss in profitability in the handset business, which generates two-thirds of the company's revenues. The company admitted that it had got its pricing strategy wrong: 'We cannot grow at the expense of driving premium products and margins down' (Taylor, 2007). Motorola had started seeing the Razr simply as a product, allowing it to become commoditized, when it should have looked to build it as a premium brand with frequent upgrades. The CEO said: 'We need to keep the "wow" factor and enhance the customer experience' (Taylor, 2007). Motorola's experience is a lesson in the links between pricing and market strategy at the highest level.

TO RECAP...

Pricing strategy

Pricing depends on costs, level of demand and the competitive nature of the market segment. While global companies often aspire to set prices according to differing national market conditions, this policy is coming under pressure as cross-border transactions increase.

Price sensitivities

Price discrimination policies operated by global companies are becoming more widely publicized, largely thanks to the internet. Do you feel there should be greater regulatory control over the pricing of sensitive products such as medicines and essential foods, or should market considerations be allowed free rein?

PAUSE TO REFLECT

Place

Place, referring to distribution, is the fourth of the four Ps. It affects how easy or difficult it is for consumers to find products, where they can be bought and how reliable supplies are. For international operations, these can be complicated processes, involving outside firms and intermediaries, whose reliability is crucial for consistent supply. Similarly, the manufacturer may depend on a range of retailers of varying sizes and types. A **distribution channel** consists of all the organizations and stages that are involved in the product's journey to the hands of the consumer.

The traditional distribution channel consists of a number of independent organizations, including producers, wholesalers and retailers. These are shown in Figure 12.10. Each is a separate business which seeks to make profits on its own account. Contractual agreements between the parties govern each stage separately. An alternative is the vertical marketing system, in which the process is integrated by a dominant organization which owns or controls all the stages. This vertical integration reduces transaction costs. The dominant organization is often the producer or retailer. Alternatively, the producer may reach consumers through different channels designed to

Distribution channel: Interlinked stages and organizations involved in the process of bringing a product or service to the consumer or industrial user.

suit different products or segments. Some customers, such as business users, may require direct sales force. Consumer products may be distributed through retailers or by web-based sales. Dell Computers opted for internet sales only, bypassing intermediaries (see CS10.2). Its advantage has been that it can customize products for consumers, which has been particularly beneficial for business customers.

Figure 12.10 Distribution channels

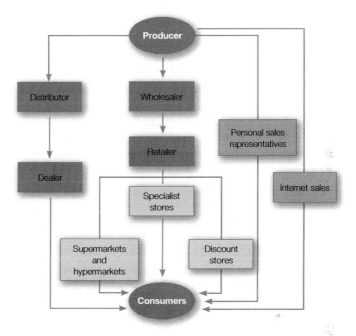

There is now enormous variety among retailers, in both size and location. The advent of the hypermarket, which sells all types of consumer product under one roof, has transformed retailing. These huge stores, of over 10,000 sq m, combine the food offerings of supermarkets with many non-food products such as clothing, appliances and electronics, often in a warehouse-type environment and at discount prices. Many conventional retailers such as supermarkets, speciality stores and department stores have struggled to compete against hypermarkets. Typically located in out-of-town malls, they attract shoppers from relatively long distances, who are happy to drive half an hour to reach them. The hypermarket usually offers services such as free parking, restaurants, travel agency, pharmacy and banking services. Hypermarkets such as Carrefour and Wal-Mart now have enormous bargaining power over producers and distributors, so achieving economies of scale. As noted earlier, hypermarkets offer their own-brand products alongside global brands. Owners of premium brands, however, sometimes feel their image suffers in the hypermarket environment, and opt for speciality shops. The choice of channel depends on the product, the brand and the target consumers.

For international marketing, channel management is crucial. Wholesalers, transport firms and other intermediaries must be co-ordinated, sometimes over long distances. Differing national environments affect how efficiently and reliably products can reach consumers. Marketing logistics concerns the co-ordinating of stages in the entire supply chain. Logistics management is discussed in Chapter 10. For the present, we highlight the marketing perspective. The aim in distribution management is to provide customers with products of the description they need, when they require them, where it is convenient for them, and with the level of service they require. Some recent trends can be highlighted. One is the growth in technology, which is transforming supply chain management. A second is the rise of specialist logistics companies which are able to offer fully integrated services. A third is the rising level of customer expectations. The car company which takes six months to deliver a car or spare parts is likely to lose business to competitors. The globalization of production has introduced global networks which offer efficiencies in production, but these benefits may be eroded unless matched by channel design and management which satisfy today's increasingly demanding consumers.

CS12.1 on P&G highlighted the growing importance of developing country markets. These environments pose challenges for distribution, as transport infrastructure is poor and consumers in rural areas may be a long way from supermarkets and other organized retail outlets. Nestlé utilizes a network of door-to-door local salespeople to deliver small packs of dairy products, biscuits and coffee to consumers in Brazil who live in poor urban areas known as 'favelas', not serviced by supermarkets. One who has been selling this way for 14 years says: 'In the *favelas*, you have to be part of the community or you just don't get in' (Wheatley and Wiggins, 2007). Nestlé has opened its 27th factory in Brazil, making products designed for low-income consumers, to be sold in neighbourhood shops and door to door.

TO RECAP...

Distribution strategy

The traditional approach to distribution, involving a series of intermediaries, is giving way to greater choice, allowing producers and manufacturers to adopt different channel strategies for different products and markets. There is a wide variety of retailing options, and direct sales through the internet or personal sales representatives offer opportunities to customize products to consumer requirements.

STRATEGIC CROSSROADS

12.2
Changing attitudes to advertising to the under-12s

In 2007, Masterfoods, which makes Mars and Snickers chocolate bars, announced it was planning to stop marketing confectionary to children younger than 12 in all its markets across the world. The move represents an advance on the company's existing policy of not advertising these products to children under 6. Masterfoods is one of the world's largest owners of global brands in food services. It is a major global advertiser, although, as a private company, little corporate financial information is disclosed. The dramatic step reflected growing concern about the links between advertising and childhood obesity. It also places other large food companies in the spotlight on their advertising policies.

There are no global rules on what constitutes acceptable advertising. There is regulation at national level by governmental agencies, but standards vary greatly from country to country, depending largely on the cultural environment. For

EU member states, the EU Commission is another tier of regulation. The Commission has expressed concern over the targeting of children. Many companies decide to take the initiative if they foresee compulsory rules coming into force in the near future. In addition, self-regulation through voluntary codes exists in many industries. Soft drinks companies which are members of the Union of European Beverages Association voluntarily altered their marketing policies in 2006, agreeing to halt advertising to children under 12. The UK has pursued a policy of encouraging food manufacturers to restrict their advertising of 'junk' foods to children. These are foods which are high in sugar, salt and fat and include soft drinks, crisps and confectionary.

Protecting children from junk food advertising raises practical issues. Halting television advertising aimed at children during the hours when they are likely to be watching is easier than preventing children from accessing the many websites which feature snack foods and confectionary. Websites typically offer games and other interactive activities. Requiring parental consent is an option, but parents might not want to stop their children's access to the games. In any case, children, like other consumers, can get round restrictions such as requirements to register their age.

Coca-Cola has long placed vending machines in schools, but has agreed voluntary restrictions following public pressure in the US. It is notable that the Masterfoods initiative is planned to apply globally. Nestlé and PepsiCo, which both make numerous snack foods popular with children, have no age limits on their advertising. Cadbury Schweppes does not target children under 8 globally. Kraft said in 2005 that it would phase out advertising junk food to children under 12 in the UK. Its marketing to children between 6 and 11 would focus on healthy foods. These large food companies have all introduced healthier products such as fruit juices and wholewheat snacks, in response to consumer concerns as well as possible legislation. McDonald's is now marketing heavily in China, where it targets mothers with small children. Having suffered from the US backlash against high-fat food, it is conscious of a similar risk in China, where childhood obesity is a growing urban problem.

Questions

◆ Why have companies re-examined their policies on advertising junk food to children?

◆ Assess the range of responses to the issues reflected by companies featured in this discussion.

◆ Do you approve the Masterfoods initiative, and why?

Sources: Ward, A., 'Coke joins battle for the brand', *Financial Times*, 21 November 2006; Dyer, G., 'Ronald helps McDonald's head off China backlash', *Financial Times*, 25 November 2006; Wiggins, J., 'Mars to pull "child" adverts', *Financial Times*, 5 February 2007; Roberts, D., Silverman, G. and Hall, B., 'Obesity fears prompt Kraft to stop targeting children with junk food ads', *Financial Times*, 13 January 2005.

WEB CHECK

See the Mars healthy eating policy at www.marshealthyliving.com. Masterfoods Europe's website is www.masterfoods-foodservice.com. Kraft provides a comprehensive website, covering brands and corporate policies, www.kraft.com.

plate 12.3 A favourite with children, but the burger is now seen as contributing to childhood obesity.

Marketing and ethics

Marketing activities impact on consumers and societies in many different ways. Businesses and consumers benefit from the huge array of products and services available worldwide. These provide day-to-day essentials such as food, and also a range of products which enhance standards of living and quality of life. However, ethical concerns are increasingly being voiced, raising firms' awareness of this dimension of their activities. Ethics concerns adherence to recognized values and principles which people in international markets generally would consider standards of right and wrong in business practices. Ethical issues include high safety standards, adherence to environmental protection principles, honesty in communications with customers and respect for the interests of employees and other stakeholders. International firms are also aware that social and cultural environments have

Figure 12.11 Overlapping spheres of ethical issues

Ethical marketing: Approach to marketing activities which prioritizes utmost fairness, safety, honesty and transparency in the interests of consumers, even in situations where the law is less stringent.

differing values. What would be considered ethical in one society, such as the paying of bribes, would not be acceptable in another. There is a growing consensus, however, on the ethical practices and values of MNEs, and on areas in which they fall beneath those standards. For example, the targeting of young people by tobacco companies would receive widespread condemnation. We will look at the broad issues of social responsibility in Chapter 14, but for now, we focus on the marketing-related aspects.

Ethical concerns in marketing are covered by law in many countries, as Figure 12.11 shows, reflecting the society's view that standards should be mandatory. Safety standards in food and other products are subject to law. Similarly, products which are potentially harmful are subject to regulation. The manufacturer or retailer (or both in the EU) will be liable for physical injury from faulty products. Products, their contents, packaging and advertising are all aspects of marketing which raise concerns in the minds of consumers and, increasingly, governments, as consumer society becomes more widespread. Advertising is increasingly regulated, to reflect social norms, as SX12.2 shows in relation to advertising to children. The sale and advertising of addictive products such as tobacco and alcoholic beverages is restricted by law. In many countries, especially in the developing world, regulation is weaker, and companies may market products more freely. As these are growing markets, opportunities abound, but MNEs which devise strategies based on targeting young consumers in developing countries might be considered to be acting unethically, even though their activities are not illegal in these markets.

The MNE's legal obligations are primarily based on national law (see Chapter 5). However, the company's broader range of stakeholders may also feel that ethical standards should influence how it generates its profits. Many consumers would now argue that abiding by legal obligations, which differ from country to country, is only one element of responsible behaviour. The firm which takes an ethical stance looks to apply high standards everywhere it operates. Large MNEs now accept that consumers expect ethical standards in marketing, not just adherence to the law. Ethical marketing focuses on issues of fairness, safety, honesty and transparency in the interests of consumers. Large global companies have become sensitive to ethical issues. Coca-Cola's flagship products, carbonated drinks, have been highlighted as contributing to obesity. Companies are also targeted over environmental issues, such as the contribution of packaging to environmental degradation (see Chapter 13).

Kotler et al. (2002: 68–73) urge that a balance should be struck between protecting consumers and allowing firms maximum freedom in their marketing activities. Businesses and consumers value freedom of enterprise and choice, but government intervention is sometimes needed in the interest of consumer protection. Areas of legislation include misleading advertising, liability for faulty or dangerous products, and regulation of high-pressure selling of products and credit deals. Such legislation features prominently in developed countries with relatively open markets. In many international markets, especially in emerging and developing countries, the institutional environment is weaker, providing limited consumer protection. On the other hand, political leaders may take a strong interventionist position in curtailing business activities and media output, especially if they feel national cultural interests are being jeopardized. In these environments, companies may face ethical dilemmas in their marketing activities. If there is little legislative protection for consumers from high-pressure selling, an ethical position would dictate that they refrain from these tactics nonetheless. Where governments routinely exert controls over content on the internet and media, a company might face the dilemma whether to proceed under the restrictions or withdraw from the market (see SX15.2).

Conclusions

◻ Marketing focuses on satisfying consumer needs with products they desire at prices they are willing to pay. While a domestic firm acquires experience of consumer needs from the outset, the firm which seeks international markets faces a more complex task of acquiring knowledge of potential markets, differing cultures and the needs of differing groups of consumers. It must also assess the strengths of existing suppliers in any potential market. Only then can country selection and entry strategy be decided upon, always bearing in mind the firm's own resources and culture. Emerging and developing countries present some of the most attractive markets in today's world, as growing incomes and changing lifestyles encompass more and more consumers. While they are attractive as markets, however, they can be uncertain business environments, in which political instability and weak legal systems may afford scant protection for contractual arrangements and property rights. Market entry through joint ventures or acquisition of a local business allows the foreign entrant to benefit from a local partner's knowledge of the cultural and business environment.

◻ The success of products and brands in differing markets depends heavily on the needs of particular groups of consumers and their perceptions of the firm – perceptions largely governed by the image of the firm's brands. Global brands were once thought to hold universal appeal, but that appeal is now rather fragmented. In many Western markets, retailers' own brands have made inroads into the market shares of global brands. In developing countries, global brands are typically associated with high quality, but it is a quality which most consumers cannot afford. MNEs seeking a wider spectrum of low-income consumers are using their innovative skills to design products specifically for these markets. Similarly, reaching consumers in developed countries through advertising and media exposure contrasts with communications in developing countries, where levels of technology are lower. In addition, the content and design of marketing messages must reflect cultural sensitivities and tastes. As companies venture deeper into new markets, ethical issues associated with products, selling methods and advertising are being voiced by consumers and other

stakeholders. Global brands have basked in high levels of brand awareness worldwide, but they are now discovering the downside of being well known, feeling the heat of consumer concerns over health, fair marketing practices and the environment.

Marketing codes of ethics
Devise a brief code of marketing ethics, consisting of the 10 principles you feel are most important in international marketing.

PAUSE TO REFLECT

Review questions

Part A: Grasping the basic concepts and knowledge

1. What are the three levels of marketing within the organization, and how do they interact to form a consistent marketing focus?
2. How does the firm's competitive strategy influence its marketing strategy?
3. Define the single global marketing strategy, and give examples of firms and products for which this strategy is suitable.
4. What are the benefits and drawbacks of a regional marketing strategy?
5. Describe 'push' and 'pull' factors in new markets.
6. How does macro-level analysis contribute to country selection for potential market entry?
7. What characteristics fall within an analysis of a country's consumer market, and why are these important in market selection?
8. Define 'segmentation'. What are the main types of segmentation in international markets?
9. Outline the main market entry strategies, and give an example of each.
10. Compare acquisition of an existing business and joint venture in terms of advantages and disadvantages from a marketing perspective.

11. What is a brand, and why have brands become crucial to companies seeking to build global markets?

12. What are the challenges facing global brands from retailers' private brands?

13. What are the benefits of having a portfolio of brands for differing segments and national markets? What are the disadvantages?

14. Describe the four 'Ps' of the marketing mix.

15. How has marketing communication changed with the growth of the internet and other media?

16. How can marketing communication be adapted for consumers in developing countries?

17. How do price elasticities affect pricing decisions in different national markets?

18. Why do firms find it difficult to operate price discrimination between different national markets?

19. What alternative distribution channels are available for a manufacturer of a consumer product such as a PC? What factors should the company consider in deciding which channel(s) to use?

Part B: Critical thinking and discussion

1. Why is China now the 'must' market for global companies? What are its drawbacks as a consumer market, and how do they differ between sectors?

2. In what ways can the global brand be described as a 'mixed blessing'? What strategies are available to promote the global brand while cultivating a localized image in consumer perceptions in different countries?

3. In what specific areas do ethical concerns impact on marketing? How does a company's stance in relation to ethical marketing influence its brand image? Give some examples.

Case study 12.2:
Restoring the shine to the golden arches

The golden arches, McDonald's iconic symbol, lost their gloss in the first years of the new millennium. Symbolic of American fast-food culture, McDonald's had grown into the world's largest fast-food chain. Weakening sales in its home market and European markets led to a rethinking of the company's mission and strategy. Numerous critics generated negative publicity, from those who criticized its poor employment conditions (encapsulated in the derogative term 'McJobs'), to those who criticized its products as unhealthy. The year 2002 was a low point, when the company announced its first quarterly loss in its 47 years. Sales growth worldwide was only 1.7%, as Figure 1 shows. Its share price was down 60% from 1999. Change rose to the top of the menu, but it was several years before sales and share price recovered.

Figure 1 Sales growth of McDonald's worldwide

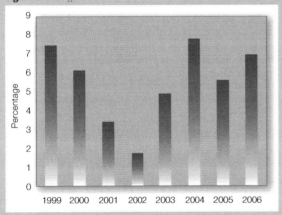

Sources: McDonald's Annual Reports, 2004, 2005 and 2006, www.mcdonalds.com

McDonald's fall from grace was a consequence of three underlying factors. First, an expansionist strategy had focused on opening as many restaurants around the world as possible, without enough attention to quality and service. Over 2,000 new restaurants were opened each year between 1995 and 2001. The business rested on a combination of franchise and company-operated outlets, which became a model for others to follow, but quality and performance became inconsistent (see SX1.1). Second, the traditional fast-food menu of burgers and fries was increasingly associated with obesity in the minds of consumers. Third, menus and restaurants had become tired looking and unattractive in comparison with the more pleasant and inviting chains such as Starbucks, which were gaining ground. The result was that the image of McDonald's as a brand became tarnished, losing 6% in value in Interbrand's 2003 rankings.

The new CEO, Jim Cantalupo, who took over in 2003, concentrated on improving the quality of customers' experience. The rate of opening new restaurants was slowed. The priority became boosting sales at existing restaurants. Under Cantalupo, salads were introduced to the menu, refurbishment programmes were initiated in restaurants, and marketing was given new zest. A new global advertising slogan, 'I'm lovin' it', devised by a German advertising agency, was rolled out. It was the first time that all McDonald's outlets had used the same slogan, appearing in either English or the local language in each of the 120 countries in which the company operates. The inclusion of menu items designed to cater for local tastes had always been a feature of McDonald's. Breaded meatball krokets featured on the Dutch menu at the company's first European restaurant in the Netherlands in 1971. The new strategy was to extend localization to locally designed restaurants. The golden arches, while still a visual identity, were less prominent in many city-centre locations. The company was set back by the widely publicized documentary film of 2004, *Super Size Me*, which featured a man who ate nothing but McDonald's food for a month, to the detriment of his health and waistline.

In 2005, supersize portions were scrapped, and more healthy foods were introduced. Salads, chicken, fish, fruit and yoghurt were on the menu. The introduction of premium roast coffee in 2006 helped to win back customers from Starbucks. At the same time, the company has kept its traditional burger meals, and added breakfast meals, which have proved popular. Both the breakfast products and the healthier products sell at premium prices. By 2007, the value of the brand had risen 6%, recovering from its 2003 decline. The stock price was $45, and the company announced the strongest results for 30 years.

McDonald's re-imaging as a healthy fast-food brand contrasts with rival Burger King, which has pursued a strategy of remaining faithful to its traditional menu, in the belief that this is where its brand strength lies. Has McDonald's diluted its brand's image with its refocusing and localization strategies? Its chief of marketing says: 'The business at McDonald's is much more about local relevance than a global archetype. Globally we think of ourselves as the custodian of the brand but it's all about relevance to local markets' (Grant, 9 February 2006). The brand was built on a strong core menu, and although promotions keep it to the fore, healthier and more local products now dominate in many locations. In Asia, the most popular item is Filet-O-Fish, not burgers. In Asian locations, however, it is competing with market stalls, food courts and convenience stores, which are very popular.

The company is localizing its operations through its innovative 'flexible operating platform', which is a modular kitchen which can cook different types of meal in the same restaurant. While this new equipment will enable kitchens to produce greater variety in products, it will also add to the complexity of the business. Extra investment and expertise are needed, and, for franchise businesses, innovations are often slow to be realized, given differing local circumstances. It was only in 2006 that McDonald's country heads for Europe and Asia were moved from the company headquarters in Oak Brook, Illinois, to be based in their regions. During the company's period of falling fortunes, its sales and image in Europe were particularly damaged. European revenues, as Figure 2 indicates, are 35% of the total, making upturn in these markets essential to recovery plans. Refurbishment and re-imaging were rolled out first in France, where sofas, TV screens and more upmarket interiors have combined with the new menus to improve the quality of the customer experience. The number of outlets worldwide, which reached 31,000 in 2002, has not changed appreciably since then. Emerging markets are being targeted for future growth, but strong local competitors, who are experienced in local tastes, are a

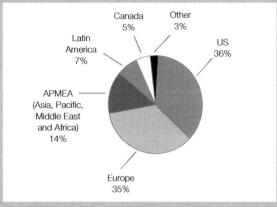

Figure 2 Share of McDonald's total revenues by geographic segment, 2005

Source: McDonald's Annual Report 2006, www.mcdonalds.com

greater threat in these markets than other Western branded market entrants.

McDonald's latest strategy, the Plan to Win, features five Ps: people, products, places, prices and promotions. With the addition of the people who are responsible for delivering its products, the focus is a marketing one. As a global brand, McDonald's is likely to see this asset as the source of its competitive advantage, although this strategy could well jar with its policy of appealing to local taste buds. Its CEO says: 'We're a local business with a local face in each country we operate in' (Grant, 9 February 2006).

Questions

1 What were the reasons for McDonald's losing its way in the new millennium?
2 Describe McDonald's strategy for transformation.
3 How has McDonald's combined localization with its global marketing strategy?
4 Assess the image of McDonald's as a brand. To what extent do you feel it has changed?

Sources: Valkin, V., 'McDonald's warns it will post first loss', *Financial Times*, 18 December 2002; Ward, A., 'The rise and rise of the golden arches', *Financial Times*, 27 January 2007; Grant, J., 'Golden Arches bridge local tastes', *Financial Times*, 9 February 2006; Grant, J., 'McDonald's smells new approach', *Financial Times*, 7 February 2006; McDonald's Annual Reports for 2004, 2005 and 2006, www.mcdonalds.com.

WEB CHECK

McDonald's is at www.mcdonalds.com.

Further research

Journal articles

Au-Yeung, A. and Henley, J. (2003) 'Internationalisation strategy: In pursuit of the China retail market', *European Business Journal*, **15**(1): 10–24.

Craig, C. and Douglas, S. (1996) 'Responding to the challenges of global markets: Change, complexity, competition and conscience', *Columbia Journal of World Business*, **31**(4): 6–18.

Pappu, R., Quester, P. and Cooksey, R. (2007) 'Country image and consumer-based brand equity relationships and implications for international marketing', *Journal of International Business Studies*, **38**(5): 726–45.

Walker, O. and Ruekert, R. (1987) 'Marketing's role in the implementation of business strategies: A critical review and conceptual framework', *Journal of Marketing*, **51**: 15–33.

Zott, C. and Amit, R. (2008) 'The fit between product market strategy and business model: Implications for firm performance', *Strategic Management Journal*, **29**(1): 1–26.

Books

Bradley, F. (2004) *International Marketing Strategy*, 5th edn, London: FT/Prentice Hall.

Kotler, P. (1997) *The Marketing of Nations*, New York: The Free Press.